T0372669

Interreligious Studies

The field of Interreligious Studies is emerging as a response to critical issues within our religiously plural world. Religious conflicts, large and small, continue to plague our society, and even people who want to get along confront challenges in navigating religious difference within families, congregations, college campuses, workplaces, communities, media, cyberspace, and the public square. This volume offers a comprehensive introduction to Interreligious Studies. After providing an overview of the history, terms, and characteristics of the field, Rachel S. Mikva explores the ethical, philosophical, and theological foundations for pluralism. She also investigates the diverse contexts and methods of interreligious encounter, with guidelines and case studies that demonstrate how interreligious understanding and solidarity can be achieved. Designed for use in undergraduate and graduate courses, the volume will also be useful to medical personnel, social workers, police officers, corporate managers, and others whose work requires multicultural competence. This volume:

- Develops the capacity to build interreligious understanding and collaboration;
- Engages readers directly in the complexity of interreligious diversity;
- Moves beyond Judaism, Christianity, and Islam, embracing the full range of spiritual lifestances and identity.

RACHEL S. MIKVA is the Herman E. Schaalman Professor of Jewish Studies and Senior Faculty Fellow of the InterReligious Institute at Chicago Theological Seminary. A leader in Interreligious Studies, she has published broadly in the field and co-chairs the American Academy of Religion's Interreligious and Interfaith Studies Program. She is the author of *Dangerous Religious Ideas: The Deep Roots of Self-Critical Faith in Judaism, Christianity, and Islam* (Beacon, 2020).

Interreligious Studies

An Introduction

RACHEL S. MIKVA

Shaftesbury Road, Cambridge CB2 8EA, United Kingdom

One Liberty Plaza, 20th Floor, New York, NY 10006, USA

477 Williamstown Road, Port Melbourne, VIC 3207, Australia

314–321, 3rd Floor, Plot 3, Splendor Forum, Jasola District Centre,
New Delhi – 110025, India

103 Penang Road, #05–06/07, Visioncrest Commercial, Singapore 238467

Cambridge University Press is part of Cambridge University Press & Assessment,
a department of the University of Cambridge.

We share the University's mission to contribute to society through the pursuit of
education, learning and research at the highest international levels of excellence.

www.cambridge.org
Information on this title: www.cambridge.org/9781108843775

DOI: 10.1017/9781108920056

First published 2023

A catalogue record for this publication is available from the British Library.

Library of Congress Cataloging-in-Publication Data
Names: Mikva, Rachel S., 1960- author.
Title: Interreligious studies : an introduction / Rachel Mikva, Chicago Theological
   Seminary.
Description: Cambridge, United Kingdom ; New York, NY : Cambridge University
   Press, 2023. | Includes bibliographical references and index.
Identifiers: LCCN 2022053398 (print) | LCCN 2022053399 (ebook) |
   ISBN 9781108843775 (hardback) | ISBN 9781108826600 (paperback) |
   ISBN 9781108920056 (epub)
Subjects: LCSH: Religions–Relations.
Classification: LCC BL410 .M55 2023 (print) | LCC BL410 (ebook) |
   DDC 201/.5–dc23/eng20230113
LC record available at https://lccn.loc.gov/2022053398
LC ebook record available at https://lccn.loc.gov/2022053399

ISBN 978-1-108-84377-5 Hardback
ISBN 978-1-108-82660-0 Paperback

Contents

v

PART III MODES OF ENGAGEMENT

Figures

Acknowledgments

I used to imagine that I ended up in this field by accident, having taken a job in Jewish Studies at what was then a primarily Protestant seminary. But that is not the case. While I was still a congregational rabbi, I was always engaged in bridge-building and inspired by individuals who could navigate diverse spaces in ways that drew people together. Interreligious Studies is replete with bridge-builders who understand the importance of spiritual lifestances among our differences. They continue to educate me and motivate my work.

Many colleagues and partners reviewed parts or all of this book to offer feedback. Others answered my random questions and engaged in substantive conversations that shaped my thinking as I was writing. I am grateful to all of them, including Russ Arnold, Reza Aslan, John Barton, Nancy Fuchs-Kreimer, Anne Hege Grung, Hans Gustafson, Brie Loskota, Kate McCarthy, Kevin Minister, Younus Mirza, Lucinda Mosher, Marianne Moyaert, Oliver Nicklin, Eboo Patel, John Pawlikowski, Jennifer Howe Peace, Ellie Pierce, Hussein Rashid, Feryal Salem, Jonathan VanAntwerpen, and Dilnaz Waraich

I am also grateful to the staff at our Learning Commons: Yasmine Abou-El-Kheir and Grace Ansani. No research would be possible without their help. And nothing comes of it without a publisher – so thank you to Beatrice Rehl and the staff at Cambridge University Press for believing in this project and making it better along the way.

Jared Beverly assisted me with research on Chapter 4 and did his usual excellent, detailed review of the manuscript to make sure it was in order (and that it made sense!). Any errors, omissions, or gobbledygook that remain are entirely my fault, of course, but I am so grateful for his insight and careful eye.

Thank you to my loving and supportive family, and to Chicago Theological Seminary for encouraging my work in Interreligious Studies. Most of all, thank you to my students, from whom I learn so much. This volume is dedicated to you.

Permissions

Segments of various chapters are adapted from the author's previous publications:

> *Dangerous Religious Ideas: The Deep Roots of Self-Critical Faith in Judaism, Christianity, and Islam* by Rachel S. Mikva (Copyright © 2020 by Rachel S. Mikva); "Six Things That Complicate Interreligious Engagement," in *Interreligious/Interfaith Studies: Defining a New Field* (Copyright © 2018 by Eboo Patel, Jennifer Howe Peace, and Noah J. Silverman). Reprinted with permission from Beacon Press, Boston, MA.
>
> "Conflict Transformation," in *The Georgetown Companion to Interreligious Studies* (Copyright © 2022 by Lucinda Mosher), serves as the foundation for Chapter 14 in this volume. Reprinted with permission from Georgetown University Press, Washington, DC.
>
> "Reflections in the Waves: What Interreligious Studies Can Learn from the Evolution of Women's Movements in the U.S.," *Journal of Ecumenical Studies* 53:4 (Fall 2018): 461–82 (Copyright © 2018 *Journal of Ecumenical Studies*). Reprinted with permission from the University of Pennsylvania Press, Philadelphia.
>
> "The Change a Difference Makes: Formation of Self in Encounter with Diversity," in *Hearing Vocation Differently: Meaning, Purpose and Identity in the Multi-Faith Academy*, ed. David S. Cunningham (Copyright © 2019 by Oxford University Press), 23–24, 27–28. Reprinted with permission from Oxford University Press, https://global.oup.com.

Several case summaries were adapted from published case studies:

- Megan Lane, "When Causes Collide: Exploring Intersectionality and the Middle East Conflict," in *Educating about Religious Diversity and Interfaith Engagement: A Handbook for Student Affairs*, ed. Kathleen M. Goodman, Mary Ellen Giess, and Eboo Patel (Sterling, VA: Stylus Publishing), 187–93. Reprinted with permission of the publisher. Copyright © 2019, Stylus Publishing, LLC.

- Elinor Pierce, "Invocation or Provocation?" and "Driven by Faith," https://pluralism.org/case-studies. Reprinted with permission of the author and director of the Pluralism Project. Copyright ©2020, President and Fellows of Harvard College and the Pluralism Project at Harvard University.
- Toby Sawyer, "Does Smudging Belong in the Workplace?" Native Case Studies, https://nativecases.evergreen.edu/collection/cases/does-smudging-belong-in-the-workplace. Reprinted with permission from the Native Cases Project.
- Karla Suomala, "Chalking Muhammad," in *Case Studies for Exploring Interfaith Cooperation: Classroom Tools* (Chicago: Interfaith Youth Core, 2013). Reprinted with permission from the publisher. Copyright © 2013, Interfaith Youth Core.

Biblical translations are adapted by the author from:

- *Tanakh: The New JPS Translation*, 2nd ed. (Philadelphia: Jewish Publication Society, 2000).
- *Holy Bible Containing the Old and New Testaments with the Apocryphal/ Deuterocanonical Books: New Revised Standard Edition with Apocrypha* (Nashville: Thomas Nelson, 1989).

Translations of Qur'anic passages rely on Abdalhaqq and Aisha Bewley, *The Noble Qur'an: A New Rendering of Its Meaning in English* (London: Ta-Ha Publishers, 1999).

PART I **Mapping the Field**

I Introducing Interreligious Studies

There has always been religious difference. Centuries of migration and conquest have made it more visible. Globalization has brought it into once-homogenous towns. Television and the Internet have broadcast it into our homes. But it has always been there, and it has had a tremendous impact on the human story.

People respond to religious difference in multiple ways. Eboo Patel, founder of Interfaith America (previously Interfaith Youth Core), describes them as bunkers, barriers, bludgeons, and bridges.[1] Adapting his schematic, I would start with blinders. People who wear blinders are generally too preoccupied with other concerns to pay much attention to religious difference, or they imagine that it does not matter, or they blithely assume that everyone sees the world as they do. Some find encounter with diversity to be uncomfortable, making them content to engage only with those who are like themselves. They may not think less of people who are different from them, but they do not take much interest. I think a lot of people wear blinders.

Those who inhabit bunkers appreciate the significance of religious difference, but they also demonstrate little interest in encountering people whose beliefs, behaviors, and mode of belonging are different from theirs. They are fully focused on their own community and preserving their own traditions. Some presume that their path is superior, but they are content to live and let live, imagining that everyone can operate in isolation.

Barriers are constructed by those who explicitly assert that their way is the right one and that those who disagree present a

---

[1] Patel, *Interfaith Leadership: A Primer* (Boston: Beacon Press, 2016), 63–65.

threat – leading the faithful astray, contaminating their beliefs, challenging their social power, or simply preventing universal realization of the capital-"T" Truth. Not everyone who believes their religion is the one true path builds barriers; many pursue fruitful relationship with religious others, established on foundations of respect. When those who are barrier-builders engage across difference, however, it is in competition; they amplify differences in ways that diminish other people.

Individuals and groups who wield bludgeons are more extreme, willing to use the weapons of law, coercion, and conquest to achieve primacy. Religious others are judged to be not just different but morally deficient. Religious hatred, oppression, and violence have unfortunately always been with us. While these elements capture a lion's share of news reports, the vast majority of humanity rejects this response to religious diversity. Global institutions have established religious freedom as an essential human right.

Patel is primarily invested in the bridge-builders, and in creating more of them – people committed to constructive relationship, collaboration, and appreciative learning; people who cultivate common ground and value our differences. Recognizing that difference is how we learn, artist/scholar Mary Anderson affirms that myriad religious perspectives "are not perverse obstacles to be feared, transmuted, hurdled over, converted, ignored, or dissolved, but invitations, prevenient signs, pointing to an infinitely rich and enigmatic ground from which genuine listening, seeing, and speaking emerge."[2]

Bridge-builders transform diversity into pluralism. Diversity is the simple fact of people from different religious, racial, ethnic, gender, geographic, and other backgrounds living or working near one another. Proximity, however, does not guarantee harmony; in fact, increased diversity left unengaged threatens social cohesion.

---

[2] Anderson, "Art and Inter-Religious Dialogue," in *The Wiley-Blackwell Companion to Inter-Religious Dialogue*, ed. Catherine Cornille (Chichester: John Wiley, 2013), 103, https://doi.org/10.1002/9781118529911.ch7.

Pluralism describes the active seeking of understanding across lines of difference.[3] Religious pluralism demonstrates respect for others' distinct religious and philosophical identities and perspectives. It stands in tension not only with religious hostility or indifference but also with the concept of a melting pot where difference dissolves by assimilating into the dominant culture and norms.

Blinders, bunkers, barriers, bludgeons, and bridges – these individual and collective choices shape human history. Religion is frequently neglected in analyses of diversity, but it remains a salient aspect of identity. The emergence of Interreligious Studies (IRS) is a response to critical issues within our religiously plural world. Religious conflicts, large and small, continue to plague our society – including violence and oppression rationalized by religious claims. The deeper challenges of navigating religious difference emerge in daily encounters among people who would like to get along and in the public square they fashion together. They unfold within families, congregations, college campuses, workplaces, communities, media, cyberspace. Ignorance, groupishness, and implicit bias undercut possibilities for connection. Among Western nations, historical Christian privilege surfaces as other lifestances strive for recognition and accommodation. Questions related to dress, calendar, public space, and prayer become issues of justice.

IRS examines all these issues, along with efforts to cultivate understanding and collaboration that are rapidly expanding throughout most of the world. It is a relatively young field, with terms and descriptions still in flux, but here is a working definition:

The field of Interreligious Studies (IRS) entails critical analysis of the dynamic encounters – historical and contemporary, intentional and unintentional, embodied and imagined, congenial and conflictual – of individuals and communities who orient around

---

[3] See The Pluralism Project (Harvard University, 2008), http://pluralism.org/what-is-pluralism.

religion differently. It investigates the complex of personal, interpersonal, institutional, and societal implications.[4]

The remainder of this chapter unpacks the emerging methods, goals, and tools for study in the field, as well as the framework for this volume. Although these details are not the most fascinating part of the book, it can be useful to have a view of the landscape before traversing it.

I.I   CHARACTERISTICS OF INTERRELIGIOUS STUDIES

Interdisciplinary. IRS is necessarily interdisciplinary, given the manifold dimensions of interreligious relations. Viewed through the lenses of Sociology, Anthropology, Psychology, Law, Political Science, History, Literature, Theology, and related fields such as Religious Studies, Cultural Studies, and Gender Studies, it yields a fuller picture of what it means when individuals and groups who orient around religion differently come to interact. While academic courses in the field are frequently lodged in Religious Studies or Theology departments, there is broad reach across the curriculum, and some schools utilize an "area studies" paradigm.

Inclusive. Scholars in the field make an effort to be inclusive. Recognizing that boundaries between religions have always been contested, negotiated, blurred, and redrawn, it is important to lift up the diversity within traditions. It is also essential to reintegrate perspectives that have been devalued or obscured in the historical study of religion, particularly Indigenous and Pagan traditions. Shifting emphasis from the "-isms" to lived religion and encounter, IRS addresses the full complexity of contemporary religious identity,

---

[4] This definition is shaped by all those who have offered one before me, especially Marianne Moyaert, "Three Approaches to Teaching Religious Diversity," in *The Georgetown Companion to Interreligious Studies*, ed. Lucinda Mosher (Washington, DC: Georgetown University Press, 2022), https://doi.org/10.2307/j.ctv27qzsb3.38; Eboo Patel, "Toward a Field of Interfaith Studies," *Liberal Education* 99, no. 4 (Fall 2013).

including individuals who are spiritual but not religious, interspiritual, humanist, atheist, or "none."

Intersectional. The field is also profoundly intersectional because people bring a range of identities and experiences into interreligious space; they do not show up as only one thing. While difference within and among lifestances is the central category of analysis in IRS, it must also reckon with ways that race, gender, sexuality, class, nationality, and other characteristics shape encounter. Sacred texts get cited to support and to challenge norms regarding sexual orientation, for example. Many religious communities have fraught racial histories; national and religious identities get interwoven. Class disparities contribute to power imbalances in interreligious space. These intersections have interpersonal and systemic consequences.

Another dimension of intersectionality, highlighted by civil rights advocate and legal scholar Kimberlé Crenshaw, is a bit harder to excavate: intersections change meaning.[5] Being a Christian in the West connotes a position of power, but the Christian minority in China is vulnerable. The significance of "woman" varies depending upon religious perspective. Meaning is thus established through social systems that determine which differences count and what they signify, shaping our experiences and our relationships with one another.

Relational. IRS emphasizes relational aspects of encounter. Thus, it is distinct from Comparative Religion, which analyzes the similarities and differences of concepts, myths, and practices among the world's religions. IRS is perhaps more akin to Comparative Theology, at least for those who engage it as a constructive practice. Their thinking is shaped in conscious response to theologies of other religions and denominations as an exercise in faith seeking understanding: "Comparative theologians seek to transcend the either/or impasse between neutral comparison and theological competition,

---

[5] Crenshaw, "Mapping the Margins: Intersectionality, Identity Politics, and Violence against Women of Color," *Stanford Law Review* 43, no. 6 (July 1991): 1241–99, https://doi.org/10.2307/1229039.

and promote instead a posture that is *both* unapologetically rooted in a particular tradition *and* open to 'deep learning across religious borders.'"[6] Yet their questions are limited to theological inquiry, and much of the work is done through study of texts rather than IRS' focus on lived encounter.

Jennifer Howe Peace, an early leader in Interreligious Studies, notes how relationality infuses every aspect of IRS:

- The object of study is relational – not about a single tradition or comparison, but about the relationships between them.
- The method of study is relational, drawing from multiple disciplines in collaborative fashion, including both critical/descriptive and confessional/prescriptive approaches.
- Its ethics are relational, attentive to power dynamics, minoritized or invisibilized perspectives, and equity – making us (and our lifestances) accountable to one another.
- Its objectives are relational, moving beyond analysis to developing skills, knowledge, and capacities for interaction that advance interreligious understanding.
- Its pedagogy is relational, with an emphasis on engagement and experiential learning. Learning with and from religious others rather than about them, IRS emphasizes intersubjectivity – recognizing our conversation partners as subjects rather than objects to be examined. They are the co-creators of our collective learning.[7]

Regarding the "method of study," there is tension between etic (outsider, objective) and emic (insider, subjective) approaches to the study of religion. In IRS, some scholars argue that even though a truly objective perspective is impossible (there is no view from nowhere), "the scholarly

[6] Barton, *Better Religion: A Primer for Interreligious Peacebuilding* (Waco: Baylor University Press, 2022),15–16. The internal quote is the subtitle of Francis X. Clooney's *Comparative Theology.*
[7] Peace, "Foundational Contributions and Next Steps: The Development of Interreligious/Interfaith Studies," in *Georgetown Companion,* 474.

and religiously neutral quality of interreligious studies is what establishes its place in the academy." It ensures that "the very terms and frameworks of interreligious interaction – such as religion, faith, pluralism, dialogue – can be interrogated and theorized."[8]

Others believe that IRS bridges the tension by fostering value-neutral learning about religious others while guiding students to understand their own positionality – without requiring them to "leave their faith at the door."[9] The transformational potential of engagement with religious difference is too substantial and too valuable to limit to etic analysis. Peace's relationality framework represents the current reality that multiple approaches are embedded in the field.

I.2   GOALS OF INTERRELIGIOUS STUDIES

Key objectives in IRS include cultivating interreligious fluency, developing tools for critical analysis, and excavating the dynamic link between theory and practice. Given this link, many courses also address formation – nurturing personal qualities that facilitate interreligious understanding and cooperation.

Interreligious Fluency. You will often hear of interreligious literacy (including in this book), highlighting the value of deep understanding of traditions and worldviews other than your own. Here I elect "fluency" for its emphasis on communication. The value of knowing about other traditions is not for the sake of assembling facts, but for developing competencies within and about interreligious encounter. Kevin Minister, a professor at Shenandoah University, writes of replacing his World Religions course with one in Interreligious Studies. Instead of the stated objective to "display familiarity with the central concepts and practices of the major religions of the world," he requires students to "demonstrate the

---

[8] Kate McCarthy, "(Inter)religious Studies: Making a Home in the Secular Academy," in *Interreligious/Interfaith Studies: Defining a New Field*, ed. Eboo Patel, Jennifer Howe Peace, and Noah J. Silverman (Boston: Beacon Press, 2018), 12.

[9] Deanne Ferree Womack, "From the History of Religions to Interfaith Studies," in *Interreligious/Interfaith Studies*, 23.

knowledge and skills necessary to navigate a religiously diverse world." He views the shift as both more relevant and more methodologically responsible.[10] Although this volume does not provide in-depth learning about religious and philosophical lifestances – still a worthy undertaking – it does advance fluency.

Tools for Critical Analysis. All of higher education strives to develop students' capacities for critical thought, of course. The ability to understand and interpret information, identify issues, assess their relevance and implications, explore their complexity (including the impact of culture and context), and synthesize multiple sources and perspectives is essential in the modern world. Self-reflection regarding the strength and limitations of your method and your argument, as well as how your positionality influences your perspective, is invaluable for personal and societal growth. Curiosity, creativity, and communication are liberating forces in human life.

The value of these requirements in the field of Interreligious Studies is evident. We do not learn unless we are inquisitive about the perspectives of people who orient around religion differently. We must be honest in facing our personal biases and be aware of our assumptions in order to listen well. As evidenced by psychosocial studies such as those of Jean Piaget, our intellectual and moral development depends on the capacity to comprehend ideas and feelings of others ("perspective-taking").[11] We must recognize similarities and differences, context and culture – with a phenomenological approach that understands people and religions on their own terms rather than through structures we impose upon them.[12] A hermeneutic of

---

[10] Minister, "Transforming Introductory Courses in Religion: From World Religions to Interreligious Studies," in *Interreligious/Interfaith Studies*, 63–64.

[11] Piaget, *The Moral Judgment of the Child* (New York: Simon & Schuster, 1965). See also Lawrence Kurdek, "Perspective Taking as the Cognitive Basis of Children's Moral Development: A Review of the Literature," *Merrill-Palmer Quarterly of Behavior and Development* 24, no. 1 (January 1978): 3–28.

[12] See Lucinda Mosher, "Beyond World Religions: Pedagogical Principles and Practices for the Encouragement of Interfaith Hospitality and Cooperation," in *Teaching for a Multifaith World*, ed. Eleazar S. Fernandez (Eugene: Pickwick Publications, 2017), 75–89.

suspicion alongside one of grace facilitates deep understanding. And, given the thick relationship of interreligious relations to politics, science, ethics, medicine, literature, philosophy, and culture, complexity is unavoidable.

Dynamic Link between Theory and Practice. The link between theory and practice is multifaceted. Like other fields with applied dimensions, IRS affirms that its research, teaching, and analysis can be deployed outside the academy to advance the public good. Patel identifies these civic values facilitated by the field and its application in the world:

- Increasing understanding and reducing prejudice;
- Strengthening social cohesion and reducing identity-based conflict;
- Bridging social capital and addressing social problems;
- Fostering continuity of identity communities and reducing isolation;
- Creating binding narratives for diverse societies.[13]

Theoretical analyses provide insight for interreligious engagement, cultivating greater self-critical awareness and sensitivity. Study of particular lifestances and the dynamics of encounter foster interreligious fluency. Courses advance skills and qualities for interfaith leadership. At the same time, we recognize that our study is dependent on lived religion and interfaith activism as "praxis labs" that constitute substantial generators of knowledge. Influence and illumination are multidirectional.

The classroom itself links theory and practice as a site of encounter. Marianne Moyaert, professor of Systematic Theology and Religious Studies at Katholieke Universiteit Leuven in Belgium, notes the importance of self-reflection about power imbalances, inequality, and privilege within course dynamics, helping students recognize their agency as they learn to be accountable to one another.[14] With an emphasis on experiential learning, students also engage religious others in their houses of worship, nonprofit work, and other sites – bringing their course learning

---

[13] Patel, *Interfaith Leadership*, 98–100.
[14] Moyaert, "Three Approaches to Teaching Religious Diversity," 356.

to inform their behaviors and utilizing their direct contacts to refine the theory. In campus contexts, there are also extensive cocurricular programs in which interreligious learning and relationship unfold. Not limited to Offices of Religious Life, applications of IRS include Student Affairs, Career Services, Dining and Residence Management, and other significant dimensions of college/university experience.

Beyond the campus, we have multiple places of meeting that test and improve theoretical understanding. Many are unintentional (see Part II), but the world of interfaith activism has been growing exponentially; it has generated organized projects of dialogue, study, spiritual encounter, social justice, advocacy, arts, and more (see Part III). IRS must both sustain its close relationship with the movement and keep a critical distance. Even though the worlds are mutually dependent and collaboratively illuminating, there needs to be some separation from the social urgency that gives the movement life and the many religious institutions that populate its projects – in order to sustain critical engagement with religious ideas and the role of religion in society. Activism's general enthusiasm for the positive potential of religion, for example, can obscure its potential for harm and occlude the necessary freedoms of atheists and others.

Formation. In the blend of theory and practice, there are norms that emerge, making the field prescriptive as well as descriptive. Normative values include respect for people of differing lifestances, valuing diversity, a tolerance for ambiguity, and commitment to peaceful, equitable coexistence. The qualities and practices fostered in IRS are discussed in detail in Chapter 9. (The chapter opens the section of the book focused on interfaith activism. Even if you are not planning to become a leader in interreligious engagement, it is worth reviewing the material for the basic formative elements.)

Formation is, in fact, coformation.[15] This claim grows from consciousness of our intersubjectivity and is informed by the teaching

---

[15] See Jennifer Howe Peace, "Coformation through Interreligious Learning," *Colloquy* 20, no. 1 (Fall 2011): 24–26.

philosophy of Brazilian educator Paulo Freire: we educate one another, in communion, in the context of living in this world.[16] Coformation unfolds in sharing personal stories as well as grappling together with the challenges and opportunities of IRS. The process asks participants to be vulnerable, to tolerate discomfort, to trust that the tensions will yield new insights and that the journey together through the wilderness will enable them to live more fully into their religious/philosophical commitments and their human potential.

Rabbi Jonathan Sacks writes, "We will need to understand that just as the natural environment depends on biodiversity, so the human environment depends on cultural diversity, because no one civilization encompasses all the spiritual, ethical, and artistic expressions of [hu]mankind."[17] The meeting place of difference is a particularly fruitful locus. Continuing the metaphor of biodiversity, consider estuaries, where freshwater and saltwater meet. They are among the most productive ecosystems in the world and provide essential buffers against destructive forces – but they are also delicate and require tending. This returns us to our bridge-builders. Bridges do not fall from the sky or rise from the ground, Patel remind us. People build them.

1.3   ABOUT THIS BOOK

Interreligious Studies: An Introduction has three sections. Part I, "Mapping the Field," provides essential background, including the emerging principles, objectives, concepts, terms, and nuances of this study (Chapters 1 and 2). Although the contemporary academic field is relatively recent, it would be a mistake to imagine that no one paid attention to religious difference before the current age – so Chapter 3 presents a selective history of interreligious study and engagement. History never exists only in the past, however; it continues to influence ideas and events. Since part of that ongoing history involves

---

[16] Freire, *Education for Critical Consciousness* (New York: Seabury Press, 1973).
[17] Sacks, *The Dignity of Difference* (London: Continuum, 2002), 62.

questions about the relative value of different religious and secular perspectives, Chapter 4 explores multiple ways in which people navigating religious difference establish ethical, philosophical, and theological grounding for their efforts – seeking parity or another framework for constructive engagement.

Part II, "Meeting Spaces," is an exploration of the multiple contexts in which we encounter religious difference on a regular basis, unpacking the challenges and opportunities. Chapter 5 discusses families and congregations, college campuses and workplaces. Chapter 6 examines the ways that media, old and new, shape our perceptions of religious others before we even meet them. Media also provide information, with a wide range of quality and purposes, and sometimes facilitate direct encounter. In Chapter 7, we investigate the public square – one of the most common and contested spaces of meeting in religiously diverse countries. Chapter 8, the final chapter of this section, is an extended discursus on antisemitism and Islamophobia – ideas about religious others unfortunately found around the globe. Examining the complex, intersectional, and interwoven dynamics of these dangerous hatreds, we reckon with their ongoing influence and explore the role of IRS in dismantling them.

Part III, "Modes of Engagement," explores work being done in the world that is specifically designed to draw together people who orient around religion differently – and the scholarship that relates to these efforts. Multiple gateways invite a broad range of individuals and groups into the interreligious world. While we cannot address all of them, we sketch some of the principles, projects, practices, problems, and possibilities of the following areas: dialogue (Chapter 10), study and spiritual encounter (Chapter 11), community-based service, organizing, and advocacy (Chapter 12), and the arts (Chapter 13). Since they all share many of the basic values and require similar personal capacities, the section begins with a general overview of practices for interreligious engagement (Chapter 9). And since conflict is an aspect of encounter, the section ends with tools for conflict transformation (Chapter 14).

Small bits of information occasionally repeat to accommodate readers who may skip around, and references to other chapters are noted so they can pursue more extensive discussion, if desired.

Most chapters include one or more case summaries, an adaptation of the case study method introduced into IRS by Harvard University's Pluralism Project. Elinor Pierce, director of the Case Study Initiative, has developed numerous two-part "decision cases" that illuminate some of the challenges in navigating religious difference. Interviewing key participants and relating events with careful detail so that the situation's complexities come into view, the first part of the case study ends just as the protagonist must make a key choice. Readers are invited to step inside the situation to discern what they would do; they then learn what unfolded when they read the second part. Not designed to judge the people involved, the purpose is to develop skills for problem solving and analysis.[18] It is an exciting tool of learner-centered pedagogy.

We do not have the capacity to include such lengthy studies in this volume, but several of the summaries included here are drawn from decision cases composed by Pierce and other scholars. Some are "library cases" that describe events drawn from news reports and related research. Two are fabrications, conflations of real people and events woven together to comprise a coherent narrative. Contexts range from American college campuses to the Nigerian film industry, from court cases to workplaces – involving people from a broad range of lifestances.

While clearly dependent on the case study method, I have identified them as case summaries to distinguish them from the more established, elaborate forms. Their function, however, is the same. They are designed for you as readers to involve yourselves in the events described, and each case has "Questions for Consideration."

---

[18] Pierce, "Toward Leadership, Listening, and Literacy: Making the 'Case' for Interreligious Studies," in *Georgetown Companion*, 408–18, https://doi.org/10.2307/j.ctv27qzsb3.44.

They invite you to contemplate how you would have responded in the situation, who the stakeholders are, what background shapes the conflict, what the ramifications may be, whether there are comparable situations in your own experience, and what we can learn about interreligious engagement from the example.

The chapters hopefully illuminate the interdisciplinary, inclusive, intersectional, and relational principles of IRS. They provide tools for critical analysis. They advance interreligious fluency with examples from multiple lifestances and contexts, practices in the interfaith movement, and ethics of engagement. Given that Parts I and II deal with "theory" and Part III deals with "practice," but they cannot be fully separated, the dynamic link between theory and practice should be evident throughout.

This book could be useful to a range of individuals, including business and religious leaders, organizers and health care professionals, lawyers and social workers who want to understand more about the impact of religious difference on their work and their world. Interfaith activists might find that it complements their efforts in the field, providing important conceptual lenses and background that enhance their effectiveness. The primary audience, however, comprises graduate and undergraduate students in IRS and related coursework. It is the textbook I want to have for my Introduction to Interreligious Studies course, and I am grateful to all my students and colleagues who have helped to shape my thinking in the field.

There are many challenges is this endeavor. Although eager to have students around the world engage the material, I cannot escape my context in the United States. It shapes not only the examples I find and the communities I meet but also the way I think about each subject and respond to its idiosyncrasies. Many of the topics in the book cannot be studied apart from their environments; Chapter 7's focus on the public square is a telling example. Its investigation of public discourse, public policy, public services, public space, and public schools is necessarily rooted in particular history, law, and culture. Context matters. While the default context is the USA,

I have tried at least to offer an expansive view from here – one that recognizes the problem of monocultural focus and learns from diverse contexts.

In addition, the book can only scratch the surface given the limitless variety of spiritual lifestances and multifarious nature of interreligious encounter. Despite my best efforts, I fall into traps of essentialization and gloss over complexities. I omit more than I can cover – not an indication of unimportance but only of finitude. All I can do is offer the tagline of a story from rabbinic tradition, in which a man comes to the second-century sage Hillel the Elder and asks to be taught the entire Torah while standing on one foot. Hillel responds, "What is hateful to you, do not do to your neighbor. That is the whole Torah; all the rest is commentary. *Zil g'mor* – go and learn it" (*b. Shabbat 31a*). My colleagues in Interreligious Studies are doing tremendous work in the field, publishing new and valuable scholarship every day. *Zil g'mor* – go and learn it.

2 Challenges in Naming and Navigating Religious Difference

Every field of study develops key terms and concepts that establish the foundation for conversation. Terms in Interreligious Studies are still in flux. That should not be surprising since the field is relatively young – and since many aspects of religion itself are still debated in the academy, including ways it has "colonized" thinking about diverse traditions. This chapter presents a range of terms and concepts, explaining how the book uses them. In the process, it illuminates some of the challenges in naming and navigating religious difference.

2.1 THE PROBLEM OF RELIGION

Interreligious Studies (IRS) inherits a number of challenges from Religious Studies. First, it is impossible to neatly identify, extract, and analyze those aspects of culture and society that are religious. People claim to support or oppose same-sex marriage on religious grounds, for example, but their convictions cannot be separated from culture and politics. Caste is not a religious concept per se, but it naturally gets folded into studies of Hinduism. Religious practices influence cultural conventions and vice versa. Consider *Día de los Muertos* observances, derived from Aztec, Catholic, and non-religious traditions; as the holiday becomes a cross-cultural phenomenon, how does its classification evolve?

How do we think about religious symbols and language that get stripped of their spiritual roots and develop new possibilities of meaning? For example, was the Sanskrit *swastika*, a graphic symbol of wellbeing or rebirth, a religious symbol in ancient Eurasian cultures? Did it cease to be one when Western countries adopted it as a symbol of good luck – or once the Nazis adopted it to represent their genocidal ideology? These liminal questions have evident interreligious dimensions.

A second problem is that the academic disciplines of Religious Studies and Theology are profoundly influenced by Western, Christian (particularly Protestant) ways of thinking; this lens determines what qualifies as religion and how it is understood. Given Christianity's universal aspirations, the modern study of religion constructed a hierarchical progression from tribal to national to universal – denigrating traditions that focus on particular communities. Particularism, however, is neither exclusivism nor parochialism; religious teachings can demonstrate concern for all of creation without expecting the whole world to adopt them. Yet drawing from Enlightenment notions that goodness, ethics, and truth must be universal, Kant argued that Christianity "from the beginning bore within it the germ and the principle of the objective unity of the true and universal religious faith."[1] This bias aligned neatly with European colonial ambitions and racial discrimination to justify denying the legitimacy of African and American Indigenous practices.

The Eurocentric and Christian universalizing worldview is often perpetuated by introductory Religious Studies courses that utilize a world religions paradigm, even though they attempt objective study that embraces the diversity of religions. Theology departments, more common in European universities, have largely moved from missiology to comparative theology in pursuit of unbiased study – but the paradigms similarly favor Christian categories of thought. Traditions may no longer be judged by the extent to which they parallel the Christian "norm," but there is still a tendency to focus on religions that are theistic and scriptural, with recognized clergy and organizational structures. Spiritual beliefs and practices are packaged in terms familiar to Christianity, so ideas like Judaism's concept

---

[1] Kant, *Religion within the Boundaries of Mere Reason and Other Writings*, trans. Allen Wood and George di Giovanni (Cambridge: Cambridge University Press, 1998), 130, https://doi.org/10.1017/CBO9780511809637.

of peoplehood get effaced because they do not match the standard model of belonging. Boundaries manufactured in the paradigm can generate or exacerbate conflict. Even the operating assumption that there is a stable genus called religion with various regional or historical species (Zoroastrianism, Daoism, etc.) can twist things to fit the mold. Hinduism, for example, is made to represent a rich assortment of cultural and spiritual traditions from Southeast Asia.

IRS approaches these problems strategically. By insisting that religious belief and practice do not fully reside within their individual traditions but instead consist of "the ubiquitous interactional, intersectional, and interpersonal facets of religious ways of being," we can "redress a history of misrepresentation of human religious experience and weaken the grasp that colonial categories have over our discipline."[2]

Historical emphasis on scripture and institutions also highlights a disparity between religion as it is described in books or prescribed by religious authorities compared to ways it is lived out in daily life. Many beliefs, behaviors, and interpretations are not found in official religion; they often do not fit what people expect religion to mean. Robert Orsi offers the example of "Lourdes" water outside a church in the Bronx; it is simply New York City tap water plumbed into a grotto with a statue of the Virgin Mary, but many people treat it as holy water. His students regularly resist treating the folk veneration as religious praxis, and he presses them to reconsider: should we think more broadly about the varieties of religious experience?[3]

These questions, raised by scholars in recent decades, appropriately problematize the study of religion – but they do not erase its utility. This book continues to treat religion as a useful category even

---

[2] Brian K. Pennington, "The Interreligious Studies Agenda: Three Dilemmas," in *The Georgetown Companion to Interreligious Studies*, ed. Lucinda Mosher (Washington, DC: Georgetown University Press, 2022), 20, https://doi.org/10.2307/j.ctv27qzsb3.5.

[3] Orsi, "Everyday Miracles: The Study of Lived Religion," in *Lived Religion in America: Toward a History of Practice*, ed. David D. Hall (Princeton: Princeton University Press, 1997), 5, https://doi.org/10.1515/9780691218281-002.

though its boundaries and interpretations – and even its meaning – are regularly contested. There are many essential terms that cannot be adequately defined; "art" and "democracy", for example, can be similarly elusive. We need to be aware, however, how our perceptions of religion are constructed and how that shapes our view of religious difference.

2.2 THE LANGUAGE OF INTERRELIGIOUS AND INTERFAITH STUDIES

In 2012, scholars gathered to discuss establishing a program unit at the American Academy of Religion, one that would support a new field to explore the dynamic encounter of people and communities who orient around religion differently. There was vigorous debate about what the group should be called, ultimately electing the somewhat cumbersome "Interreligious/Interfaith Studies."

Jennifer Howe Peace, co-chair of the unit and co-convener of the group, describes "interfaith" as the language of activism and "interreligious" as the language of the academy. Casting a broad net, she explains, "I wanted to signal with the slash mark that this was a space where scholars, activists, theorists, and practitioners alike were welcome."[4] Hans Gustafson, director of an interreligious center at the University of St. Thomas, suggests that if you could tease them apart, Interfaith Studies would be emic, confessional, prescriptive, promoting civic leadership and pluralism, allied with the interfaith movement. Interreligious Studies would be etic, critical, promoting detached knowledge generation, and distinct from the movement. Like Peace, however, he argues that the approaches are complementary rather than mutually exclusive.[5]

---

[4] Peace, "Foundational Contributions and Next Steps: The Development of Interreligious/Interfaith Studies," in *Georgetown Companion*, 473, https://doi.org/10.2307/j.ctv27qzsb3.50.

[5] Gustafson, "Introduction," in *Interreligious Studies: Dispatches from an Emerging Field*, ed. Hans Gustafson (Waco: Baylor University Press, 2020), 3.

Comparative theologian Wilfred Cantwell Smith has characterized religion as institutional and faith as personal. This distinction, however, does not work well for spiritual orientations that focus on behaviors and belonging more than beliefs. Faith is central in Christianity, and thus the term "interfaith" reflects Christian dominance in our culture; some people feel it excludes non-theistic traditions such as Buddhism or Confucianism. "Interfaith" can also be confusing since the same term is applied to families created with more than one religious tradition in its background and/or outlook. Nonetheless, the term appropriately signals that the field focuses on interaction between people of faith rather than among religions.

"Interreligious" avoids some of the traps of "interfaith" and recognizes that there are important encounters between religious communities that transcend the meeting of individuals. Yet this term has different issues – appearing to privilege institutional religion and potentially excluding those who do not identify with an established tradition. It falsely implies that there are agreed-upon definitions of fixed things called religions and we study the relationship between them. The reality is more porous, polymorphous, and provisional – a growing web of relationships within and among internally diverse spiritualities.

Anne Hege Grung at the University of Oslo suggests the term "transreligious" to signal these more fluid processes of meeting, recognizing the ways that religions have always influenced each other as well as the space in-between.[6] "Trans" is also used for individuals who themselves identify across boundaries between religions, however, and this volume elects the latter connotation. Although neither "interfaith" nor "interreligious" works perfectly, this volume uses both – but it more often elects interreligious in its broadest

---

[6] Grung, "Interreligious Dialogue: Moving Between Compartmentalization and Complexity," *Approaching Religion* 1, no. 1 (May 2011): 31, https://doi.org/10.30664/ar.67467.

sense – referencing both individual and institutional identities, etic and emic approaches, academic and activist efforts. This is a common choice in higher education, while out in the world it is more common to see the word interfaith.

Still, there is a need for more inclusive terminology. Increasingly, secular humanists, atheists, spiritual-but-not-religious individuals, and others who do not claim a religion per se are also participating in IRS and activities. In order to be accountable to people who feel marginalized by assumptions that everybody at the table identifies with a religion, some participants speak about religious and philosophical positions, or faith and non-faith traditions. The latter is problematic, however, defining individuals who do not ascribe to a specific faith tradition by what they are *not*.

Consequently, Harry Stopes-Roe introduced "life stance" (here: lifestance), a useful term that appeared already in Chapter 1 presuming that its meaning could be largely intuited. It signifies an individual or community's relationship with matters that they consider of ultimate importance. Making room for diverse convictions or concepts that shape one's worldview and the consequences for living that flow from them, the term includes religious lifestances without making them the normative orientation.[7] "Interlifestance" does not readily flow off the tongue, however, so this volume uses "interreligious" to include encounter between the full gamut of lifestances. A newer descriptor, "interpath," similarly strives to be inclusive of non-religious life-stances and you will often find the term here when discussing programs for encounter.

Another shift that can be useful for IRS is to cease viewing "secular" as an agonistic antonym for "religious." Here, we adopt the understanding of sociologist Danièle Hervieu-Léger: secularity describes the context in which religious ideas productively engage with other ways of thinking and knowing, and no institution has a

---

[7] Stopes-Roe, "Humanism as a Life Stance," *New Humanist* 103, no. 2 (October 1988): 19–21.

monopoly on meaning.[8] Rather than seeing it as a threat to religion, the secular public square serves a vital role in preserving democracy and creates broad space for spirituality in all its forms to flourish.

2.3   INTERSPIRITUALITY AND SYNCRETISM

"Lifestance" also accommodates hybrid religious identities, which have existed for millennia and have been growing in recent decades. In antiquity, many gentiles in the Greco-Roman world observed certain Jewish customs and affirmed monotheism but maintained their Hellenistic spiritual culture as well; they were called God-fearers. Chinese spirituality has historically blended Buddhist, Confucian, and Daoist teachings, with individuals combining elements in various ways; these fusions are considered natural – comprising theological convictions, practices, and patterns of belonging. Converts to Christianity during the period of European colonialism often remained committed to their Indigenous traditions. The transatlantic slave trade similarly drove religio-cultural adaptation; the Afro-Caribbean Santería and Brazilian Condomblé traditions, for instance, blended Yoruba rituals and beliefs of enslaved Africans with Catholicism. Chicana author Gloria Anzaldúa writes of such spiritual *mestizaje* (mixed ancestry) as an embodied, liberatory process, sustaining critique of oppression and renewing relation to the sacred on its own terms.[9]

Today, there are many catalysts for hybridity. Individuals may have been raised by parents with differing lifestances, or married someone of a different faith, and want to honor both. Others have lived in diverse cultures, so profoundly influenced by their relationship to the community that they carry aspects of the spiritual lifestance with them. Some are so disturbed by interreligious conflict

---

[8] Hervieu-Léger, "'What Scripture Tells Me': Spontaneity and Regulation within the Catholic Charismatic Renewal," in *Lived Religion in America*, 27, https://doi.org/10.1515/9780691218281-003.

[9] Teresa Delgadillo, *Spiritual Mestizaje: Religion, Gender, Race, and Nation in Contemporary Chicana Narrative* (Durham: Duke University Press, 2011), 1.

that they feel pressed to bridge the chasm in their own hearts, or they suffered religion-inflicted trauma and can neither fully embrace nor fully abandon their origins. Some are trying to recover their family's historical identity that was erased by missionary activity, occasionally more a project of cultural retrieval than theological concern.[10] And some have not felt quite at home in any single lifestance – at least in its institutional framework – but feel whole in the interrelation between them.

Various terms have tried to capture this orientation: multiple religious belonging, transreligious identity, polydoxy, and – the one used most often in this volume – interspirituality. Multiple religious belonging is somewhat of a misnomer, since people often adopt aspects of the identity or practice without "joining" a community; in fact, they may be prevented from doing so by institutional policies.[11]

Individualized multiplicity overlaps with syncretism, defined as "the borrowing, affirmation, or integration of concepts, symbols, or practices of one religious tradition into another by a process of selection and reconciliation."[12] In this volume, "syncretism" is used to describe communal dynamics while "interspirituality" applies to personal identity. The colonial project and slave trade mentioned above were significant syncretistic catalysts. Military conquest has historically spurred defeated populations to absorb aspects of the newly dominant culture's religion. In addition, societies in which multiple religious communities coexist stimulate multidirectional influence.

---

[10] See Monica A. Coleman, "Teaching African American Religious Pluralism," in *Critical Perspectives on Interreligious Education: Experiments in Empathy*, ed. Najeeba Syeed and Heidi Hadsell (Leiden: Brill, 2020), 15, https://doi.org/10.1163/9789004420045_003; Dalia Kandiyoti, *The Converso's Return: Conversion and Sephardi History in Contemporary Literature and Culture* (Stanford: Stanford University Press, 2020).

[11] Michael Amaladoss, *Interreligious Encounters: Opportunities and Challenges*, ed. Jonathan Y. Tan (Maryknoll: Orbis Books, 2017), chap. 12.

[12] Judith A. Berling, *The Syncretic Religion of Lin Chao-En* (New York: Columbia University Press, 1980), 9, https://doi.org/10.7312/berl94240.

Scriptural religions that identify their teachings as revealed by God tend to discount syncretistic dynamics but, whether divinely ordained or sociologically determined, Israelite religious culture clearly borrowed from Canaanite traditions, early Christianity was affected by Gnosticism as well as Judaism and Hellenism, and Islam adapted many Jewish and Christian teachings. Modern movements are often explicit about their influences: Rastafarian tradition in Jamaica, for example, blends African-Hebrew and Christian religious traditions with Caribbean freed slave practices and a pan-African social movement. Unitarian Universalism has roots in Christian Universalism and Unitarian traditions but learns from many religious and humanist lifestances and has evolved into a post-Christian denomination.

These dynamics lead to contention about the boundaries of traditions. Jews for Jesus and other Hebrew–Christian missionary movements, for instance, claim to affirm Jewish practice as well as the messianic identity and/or divinity of Jesus. The major Jewish denominations have issued statements expressing concern that these groups deceptively use sacred symbols of Jewish observance to convert Jews to Christianity and are "in radical conflict with the communal interests and destiny of the Jewish people." A few Jewish scholars, however, have suggested that such movements could be seen as part of the flourishing *intra*faith diversity of modern Judaism.[13]

Interfaith efforts are sometimes criticized as syncretistic, but this assessment is misguided. While there can be an overemphasis on cultivating common ground, the meeting of diverse lifestances is not a lowest-common-denominator religion-in-the-making. It is about fostering understanding and respect for difference, nurturing relationship, and pursuing the common good. People can come to the inter-religious table without forfeiting their truth claims or commitments –

---

[13] Compare Jewish Community Relations Council of New York, "Spiritual Deception Matters," www.jcrcny.org/wp-content/uploads/2013/07/H-CFAQs.pdf, and Dan Cohn-Sherbok, *Messianic Judaism: A Critical Anthology* (London: Bloomsbury, 2000).

and they often find that appreciative learning about other traditions deepens their relationship with their own.

It is worth noting that syncretism was not originally meant as a pejorative; Plutarch used it admiringly to discuss how communities in Crete set their differences aside to face a common enemy. Many Catholic missionaries believed that incorporating local customs (at least those that did not conflict with Christianity) would help spread the gospel. Repeatedly through history, syncretism has helped traditions adapt to new cultures and changing times. It did not become a polemical term until after the Reformation, when it was redefined as mixing things that are incompatible and hurled against sixteenth–seventeenth-century Protestant theologians who broke with Reformed orthodoxy or tried to reconcile confessional differences.[14]

Borrowing between lifestances raises concerns beyond the fear that it dilutes the purity of religious teachings; there is also the issue of appropriation. What right does one community have to take that which belongs to another? Barbara Brown Taylor calls it "spiritual shoplifting" and admits doing it frequently when she first began teaching Religion 101: "When I saw something I liked in another tradition, I helped myself."[15] Minoritized traditions often feel the injury most acutely. For example, it can be painful for Jews to learn of church seders that co-opt Jewish traditions of Passover and distort them with Christological teachings. Appropriation of Native American traditions and Buddha images often get commercialized, with profit motives that further complicate the problem.[16]

Concerns about religious and cultural appropriation are important. Christian theologian Krister Stendahl offers a compelling

---

[14] Anita Marie Leopold and Jeppe Sinding Jensen, "Introduction to Part II," in *Syncretism in Religion: A Reader* (New York: Routledge, 2014), 14–16, https://doi.org/10.4324/9781315538228.

[15] Taylor, "My Holy Envy of Other Faith Traditions," *Christian Century* (March 13, 2019), 26, https://www.christiancentury.org/article/critical-essay/my-holy-envy-other-faith-traditions.

[16] See George E. Tinker, *Spirit and Resistance: Political Theology and American Indian Liberation* (Minneapolis: Fortress Press, 2004), 55–72.

guideline when he speaks of holy envy: appreciate beautiful aspects of other traditions – precisely because they are different – and recognize that they are not yours to take.[17] Yet interspiritual identity troubles this framework a bit. If one's dynamic, multilayered sense of self does not fit tidily into a single tradition, does the intersected identity constitute appropriation? Who "owns" the traditions and who polices the boundaries?

Individuals who claim multiple religious identity (and those who identify as spiritual-but-not-religious) are sometimes accused of narcissistic "cafeteria" faith – shopping from a menu of choices to select their favorite items without committing to a community. It is censured as radical religious individualism, part of the ongoing privatization of everything that undermines institutional power and its potential for social good.[18] This book treats the phenomenon of interspirituality differently, however, trusting that individuals can creatively guide their spiritual journeys without falling into solipsistic self-centeredness. It affirms a search for identity that is not simply religiously oriented consumerism. It recognizes that the idea of strictly bounded religions is to some extent a Western academic construct, alien to numerous contexts; a lifestance may transgress boundaries laid down by religious authorities but hold together diverse elements with integrity. Multiple religious identity is part of the ongoing dynamism of religion and stands among the diversity of lifestances that the field of Interreligious Studies seeks to recognize and respect.

---

[17] Stendahl, "From God's Perspective We Are All Minorities," *Journal of Religious Pluralism* 2 (1993), www.jcrelations.net/articles/article/from-gods-perspective-we-are-all-minorities.html.

[18] See Katherine (Trina) Janiec Jones, "Reviving Shiela: Listening to the Call of Multiple Religious Belonging," in *Hearing Vocation Differently: Meaning, Purpose, and Identity in the Multi-Faith Academy*, ed. David S. Cunningham (Oxford: Oxford University Press, 2018), 43–62, https://doi.org/10.1093/oso/9780190888671 .003.0003.

2.4   DIVERSITY AND PLURALISM

As mentioned in Chapter 1, diversity is the simple fact of people from different religious, racial, ethnic, gender, geographic, and other backgrounds living or working in close proximity. When focusing on the diversity of lifestances, we may describe a multifaith or multireligious context. In this book, such terms are simply descriptive and are not used interchangeably with pluralism, which director of the Pluralism Project Diana Eck has defined as the active seeking of understanding across lines of difference.

Pluralism is more complex than it first appears. Stephen Prothero, a professor of religion at Boston University, coined the term "pretend pluralism" in response to analyses that bridge difference by imagining that it is not there or has little significance.[19] Pursuit of mutual understanding cannot be limited to our similarities. It is also clear that religion is not the only difference that matters: we must build layered practices of connection across our multiple identities of race, class, gender, sexuality, culture, nationality, age, and politics. Each requires an act of bridging, respecting the differences while forging a common life together.

Laurie Patton, president of Middlebury College, has argued for "pragmatic pluralism" as intergroup problem-solving that recognizes our need for one another with our distinctions intact. Among her examples, she called to mind a group of Jewish women who stationed themselves outside a refrigerator truck with the remains of victims from 9/11, reciting psalms as is Jewish custom before burial. Soon people of every faith and none came to join them; mourners all, they needed a collective ritual process to grieve.[20]

Religious pluralism is a normative expectation in the field of Interreligious Studies, demonstrating respect for others' distinct

---

[19] Prothero, *God is Not One: The Eight Rival Religions that Run the World – and Why Their Differences Matter* (New York: HarperOne, 2010), 5.

[20] Patton, "Toward a Pragmatic Pluralism," *Emory Magazine* (Autumn 2006), www .emory.edu/emory_magazine/autumn2006/essay_pluralism.htm.

religious and philosophical identities and perspectives. We frequently find "religious pluralism" used to describe the conviction that religious truth necessarily exists in an equally valid diversity of forms. To make more space in this work for those whose theological or philosophical commitments to do not allow for such a conclusion, however, this volume uses Eck's broader connotation. Religious pluralism does not require giving up exclusive truth claims, nor does it inevitably lead to religious relativism where knowledge, ethics, and truth are all understood to be determined by historical and cultural context. Pluralism is not simply religious tolerance, however, which suffers the multiplicity of religious practices without violence or coercion but does not indicate interest in others' lifestances or see value in the rich fabric of human spirituality.

The interpretation of religious pluralism as affirming multiple equally valid traditions derives from a theology of religions attributed to Christian theologian Alan Race in the 1980s. Numerous religious thinkers have tried to explain the existence of multiple traditions through the lens of their particular faith.[21] Lifestances without universal aspirations do not necessarily need to justify multiplicity, but the practice has taken root across many faith traditions when engaged in interreligious discourse. Race's three-fold exclusivist-inclusivist-pluralist model flows from Christian questions about salvation; it remains influential even though it has also been critiqued and many lifestances have different theological or philosophical concerns.

In the basic template, an exclusivist position maintains that one's own religious tradition represents the only way to truth, salvation, redemption, or the Divine. Pluralists affirm the sufficiency and efficacy of other lifestances and the value of multiple spiritual paths in the world. The inclusivist attitude stands somewhere in the middle, encompassing a variety of theologies and perspectives that

---

[21] See, for example, Mohammad Hassan Khalil, ed. *Between Heaven and Hell: Islam, Salvation, and the Fate of Others.* Oxford: Oxford University Press, 2013.

see beauty in multiple religious paths but claim one religion is superior and perhaps necessary to all others. In a segment on Hinduism in *The Long Search*, for example, the narrator speaks with a *pandit* (a Hindu scholar-priest) who asserts that Hinduism represents the highest stage of spiritual evolution and everyone is Hindu. Theologian Karl Rahner spoke of "anonymous Christians" – people of diverse faiths who were recipients of God's grace due to the salvific work of Jesus Christ. (The humorous version is: You might get to heaven even if you are not Christian, but there will be a cross over the gate.)

These three positions can translate to non-religious lifestances as well. Systems of philosophy or ethics may present one particular worldview as uniquely true and necessary to human fulfillment (exclusivism), or as the analytical lens through which all other systems of thought and practice can be understood (inclusivism), or as one of multiple fruitful ways to understand the human, the universe, the real (pluralism).

If we want to preserve the term pluralist to describe a bigger tent, namely all who actively work across religious difference for the common good, we need a separate term for those who also affirm the sufficiency of diverse lifestances. (Note: This does *not* connote sameness.) Process theologians have named it deep pluralism.[22] Others call it theological pluralism. The first term has been used by authors with a range of meaning, however, and the second one excludes non-religious perspectives. Thus, in this volume, I coin a new (as far as I know) term that may or may not stick: *parity pluralism*. While parity pluralism is not a normative expectation in IRS, many scholars, students, and practitioners are invested in its development; Chapter 4 explores multiple theological, ethical, and philosophical foundations as well as their critiques.

---

[22] See David Ray Griffin, ed., *Deep Religious Pluralism* (Louisville: Westminster John Knox, 2005).

2.5   INTRAFAITH DIVERSITY, REPRESENTATION, AND BOUNDARIES

There is significant diversity *within* each lifestance as well. It can be challenging to share religious identities with people who understand the practice or faith in very different ways; ongoing efforts to reach out across these boundaries are also necessary. Within Christian communities, this focus tends to be called ecumenism, while other religious groups speak of intrafaith concerns. (Ecumenical should not be used interchangeably with interfaith, since it does not include non-Christian traditions.)

Internal diversity reveals the risks of essentializing in the study of religion. Introduction to unfamiliar lifestances almost always involves broad generalizations, and every book or syllabus must exclude more than it can cover. It is impossible to capture the manifold formal expressions of a tradition, much less its lived messy multiplicity. A dominant faith may be recognized for its internal diversity, while others are reduced to singularities. If we allow ourselves to be paralyzed by this problem, however, we make learning and engagement impossible. Instead, we strive to remember that no Muslim can speak for all of Islam, no Sikh author can set the fullness of the faith before you, one Jewish community is not reflective of the rich diversity within Judaism, and so on. Adherents are encouraged to speak *from* rather than *for* their lifestances – even though we know that the perspective of those we encounter from other traditions invariably shapes how we view the lifestance in general.

Relying too much on a single story distorts our understanding, but it is only one of many challenges that IRS faces regarding visibility and representation. The common focus on Judaism, Christianity, and Islam in Europe and North America is inadequate to address today's burgeoning religious diversity – not only Eastern traditions, but also new religious movements, historically marginalized communities (e.g., Dalit, Yazidi, Romani), Pagan and Indigenous cultures that are still overlooked. Secular lifestances and the changing nature of religious identity, discussed above, complexify the work of representation even more. Also mentioned previously, religion is only one aspect of identity; race, gender, sexual orientation, class, age, and nationality powerfully shape our experiences and intersect with our lifestance in countless ways. When we add intrafaith diversity to this mix, we see that it is impossible to construct any fully representative study or program. Nonetheless, it remains vital to pursue broad inclusivity and to be sensitive to questions of representation.

The issues go beyond who is invited to the table in interreligious encounter or how one organizes the field in the academy. We return to the question of boundaries, which are often emotionally charged. Adam Seligman, the director of Communities Engaging with Difference and Religion, describes a seminar he facilitated in Bulgaria at which they screened Elizabeta Koneska's *Peace for All: St. George's Day at a Shared Multi-Religious Shrine in Macedonia*. The film showcases a site deemed holy by various Muslim and Christian sects. Many of the humanist and atheist seminar participants applauded the arrangement, viewing it as a triumph over religious parochialism. Many of the Muslim and Christian participants, on the other hand, were outraged at what they saw as a violation of boundaries: allowing foreign prayers in sacred space was sacrilege. Curiously, no one experienced the film as simply providing insight about lived religion in the Balkans; rather it was freighted with a moral agenda.[23]

Boundaries are also marked by who has a voice. Do Latter-Day Saints (Mormons) count as Christians even though many Christians reject this idea? Which form(s) of Yoruba tradition are considered authentic? Why don't the "Abrahamic" traditions include Druze, Bahá'í, Samaritan, Rastafari, and other lifestances that trace their faith to Abraham, Sarah, and Hagar? What about dissenting perspectives, such as queer people in non-affirming denominations or Buddhist monks in Myanmar who have been declared heretics by the religious court? Theology, history, ethnicity, and status all impact the make-up of interreligious space.

---

[23] Seligman, *Living with Difference: How to Build Community in a Divided World* (Berkeley: University of California Press, 2015), 136–37.

Interreligious efforts tend to resolve such queries in inclusive fashion and favor people's self-definition. Although it is a healthy instinct, it is important to remember that boundaries are not inherently hurtful; they also contribute to community cohesion. They are meeting places as well as markers of distinction – but who sets the borders? The following case introduces questions of intrafaith boundaries with interreligious implications.

Case Summary: "Sanctuary or Sacrilege?"[1]

In August 2007, two women walked into Rabbi Susan Talve's office at Central Reform Synagogue (CRC) in St. Louis with a request she had not heard before. Could they hold their Roman Catholic Womenpriests' ordination ceremony in the synagogue? No Catholic church could host it. A couple Protestant churches offered their buildings, but the women were looking for a space that felt holy to them and the synagogue sanctuary seemed just right. These candidates for ordination, Rose Marie Hudson and Elsie Hainz McGrath, hoped to fashion an inclusive faith community that would engage people who feel marginalized by the church. Moved by their desire to serve and committed to the value of women's leadership, Rabbi Talve was inclined to offer hospitality but wanted to confer with her leadership first. The staff and trustees of the synagogue approved; they knew it would strain their relationship with Catholic leaders, but they believed in CRC's historical role as a *sukkat shalom*, a shelter of peace for those who need a safe space for their bodies and spirits.

Rabbi Talve reached out to her friends in the Catholic hierarchy to let them know of the decision and to make space for them to voice their concerns. Father Vincent Heier, director of the Archdiocese Office for Ecumenical and Interreligious Affairs, maintained it was inappropriate for the synagogue to meddle in internal Catholic issues, and it would damage Jewish-Catholic relations. Sister Carla Mae Streeter, a professor at the Aquinas Institute, was troubled that Hudson and McGrath had not stopped to consider how they might compromise the Jewish community's wellbeing by instigating this conflict. As the event gained media attention, public and private criticism intensified – but the synagogue also received hundreds of letters from Catholics grateful for their actions.

There was fallout on all sides. The Jewish Community Relations Council felt compelled to issue a public statement that the synagogue was acting autonomously. Archbishop Raymond Burke, who had a reputation as a hardliner (e.g., refusing communion to supporters of reproductive rights), excommunicated Hudson, McGrath, the bishop who officiated, and some of the attendees at the ordination. He determined that the Catholic Church would not participate in any inter-religious event where CRC was a leading player – and instructed St. Cronan Church, which had partnered with the synagogue for years, to withdraw their invitation for Rabbi Talve to speak at the church. (They held the event out on the street instead.) Over time, especially after Archbishop Burke was promoted to Cardinal and called to Rome, the relationships began to heal.

Questions for Consideration

1. This case provides an example in which one religion's "gate-keeping" impacts interreligious relations. Identify all of the stakeholders, direct and indirect, and try to step into their shoes. How do you view the key issues and what would you have done, for example, if you were Rabbi Talve or a member of the synagogue? Father Heier or Archbishop Burke? A journalist covering the story? Hudson or McGrath? One of their friends? A member of St. Cronan or a Catholic in the community? A leader in the Jewish community? A leader in the local interfaith organization?
2. At one point Father Heier compared CRC's actions to a Catholic church inviting a Holocaust-denier to speak. What are the problems with that analogy, and what are more legitimate grounds for his concern?
3. No case begins or ends where the story does. What additional background and context would be useful in reflecting on this case?
4. Can you identify other examples where internal diversity in lifestances creates interreligious challenges?

[1] The case was researched and composed by Anne Feibelman (unpublished).

2.6   QUESTIONS OF POWER

The ordination case also illuminates questions of power, which come into play in multiple ways in IRS. Some relate to gender. Constructive theologian Jeannine Hill-Fletcher argues that the common "parliamentary model" of dialogue, with formal meetings of experts, disadvantages women because they have been historically excluded from hierarchies and religious elites. Anne Hege Grung demonstrates that male organizers sometimes sideline women in an effort not to offend partners who do not allow women to lead.[24] (They may, alternatively, push women front and center to "prove" the error of non-egalitarian perspectives – a different kind of power play.) Social power also shapes what happens amidst encounter; within projects that encourage self-critique, for example, disclosure can be more difficult for historically excluded groups and vulnerable minorities.

Religious demographics make Christian privilege a prominent issue in the West. In 2003, psychologist Lewis Schlosser broached this "sacred taboo" with a list of twenty-eight signs of religious privilege, including seeing people of your tradition in leadership and show business; escaping having everything you do ascribed to your religious identity; and avoiding discrimination in employment, social settings, adoption, media, and housing because of your faith.[25] This power disparity inevitably impacts the interreligious project.

Many interfaith efforts are hosted in historically Christian institutions, impacting who controls the agenda, who gets funding from foundations, who is best represented, and whose opinion carries

---

[24] Fletcher, "Women in Inter-Religious Dialogue," in *The Wiley-Blackwell Companion to Inter-Religious Dialogue*, ed. Catherine Cornille (Chichester: John Wiley & Sons, 2013), 168–83, https://doi.org/10.1002/9781118529911.ch11; Grung, "Gender and Christian–Muslim Dialogue," in *Contemporary Muslim–Christian Encounters: Developments, Diversity and Dialogues*, ed. Paul Hedges (London: Bloomsbury Academic, 2015), 67–81, http://doi.org/10.5040/9781474220293.ch-005.

[25] Schlosser, "Christian Privilege: Breaking a Sacred Taboo," *Journal of Multicultural Counseling and Development* 31 (January 2003): 44–51, https://doi.org/10.1002/j.2161-1912.2003.tb00530.x.

weight. Whether in seminary, college, or community contexts, Christian voices frequently dominate interreligious space, Christian questions shape comparative religious discourse, and Christian experience stands at the center. In non-Western contexts, these dynamics may be very different, but funding, hosting, and agenda-setting always raise issues of power. There are no completely neutral spaces in which interreligious conversation and study occur.

In American theological education, some schools have become multifaith without fully reckoning with the extent to which they are embedded in Christian history and culture. What do secular human-ists or others without a scripture do about the emphasis on sacred texts? Will a classically trained Christian practical theologian appre-ciate how pastoral/spiritual care changes in a Zen Buddhist context? Schools may adapt requirements and have multifaith faculty, but from the institutional calendar to rhythms of worship to curricular standards and cultural assumptions, Christian privilege abides.[26] Since evangelical Christians often feel marginalized in academic spheres, they may not perceive this privilege in the same way, but it is still present – woven into the fabric of society.[27]

At the same time, the field of Interreligious Studies has developed a dominant culture in which progressive religious outlooks are frequently overrepresented. Although active seeking of under-standing across lines of difference does not require *parity* pluralism, many religious conservatives have been reluctant to become involved. Some fear that the interreligious project promotes relativism, threatens purity, and weakens faith – or requires them to abandon their truth claims. Others imagine that the goal is a new syncretistic religion. Those who have engaged in interpath efforts that allayed

---

[26] See, for example, Feryal Salem, "The Challenges and Opportunities in Training Muslim Chaplaincy Students for a Burgeoning New Field," *Journal of Pastoral Theology* 32, no. 1 (January 2022): 47–54.

[27] Parts of this section and the next are adapted from Mikva, "Six Issues that Complicate Interreligious Studies and Engagement," in *Interreligious/Interfaith Studies: Defining a New Field* (Boston: Beacon, 2018), 126–28, 134.

such fears still feel that they are frequently seen as "a problem." Their convictions regarding gender roles or LGBTQIA+ people may be identified as unjust, and their theological exclusivism as offensive. Some evangelicals feel that they cannot leave their commitment to proselytize at the door, which has generally been out of bounds for interfaith engagement in Western contexts. Nonetheless, there is a growing sense of urgency in conservative quarters to be part of the solution to religious bias and conflict.[28]

While interrogations of power permeate IRS, those of us in the academy are also implicated. Researchers wield power by the questions they ask, the terms they employ, the lifestances they address, the representative voices they select, and the frameworks they use for analysis. They define, interpret, and construct knowledge. The dominant culture in Religious Studies privileges historical critical analysis of sacred texts, for instance, but few Muslim scholars view the Qur'an through this lens. If those who do then find that their perspectives are favored in interreligious scholarship, it may prompt allegations of the "native informant" – marginalized individuals drawn to support marginalizing ideologies because of cultural oppression.[29] Others will counter that such a term denigrates those who dare to articulate internally unpopular opinions, imposing a restrictive definition of the group's interest. How are these voices registered in academic discourse and community encounter?

2.7 INTERRELIGIOUS ENGAGEMENT

IRS is not isolated in the academy; it has generative interaction with work in the community to advance the promise of interreligious understanding. People naturally meet diversity in all kinds of places

---

[28] Marion H. Larson and Sara L. H. Shady, "The Possibility of Solidarity: Evangelicals and the Field of Interfaith Studies," in *Interreligious/Interfaith Studies*, 147–59.

[29] On the native informant, see Gayatri Chakravorty Spivak, *A Critique of Postcolonial Reason: Toward a History of the Vanishing Present* (Cambridge: Harvard University Press, 1999), ix, https://doi.org/10.2307/j.ctvjsf541.

(see Part II), but there are also numerous efforts designed to nurture appreciative knowledge and relationship, recognize shared values or teachings, explore and dignify difference, work together for the repair of our world, and allow for one path to illumine another without attempting conversion or persuasion. Historically, the most common form of such interaction has been interfaith dialogue. Recognizing that there are many modes for crafting interfaith encounters, some people speak of a "dialogue of life" or other framings that can include a wide range of activities (see Chapter 9). This book addresses dialogue in its more limited meaning, utilizing different terms that have become increasingly prevalent to describe the manifold methods of shaping encounter: interfaith, interpath, or interreligious *engagement*.

Interreligious Studies and engagement are impacted not only by each other but also by the world at large. Current events shape syllabi and research agendas, a largely positive phenomenon as the academy rejects an "ivory tower" posture removed from daily life. Scholarly insights regarding the continuing scourge of Islamophobia or the global rise of religious fundamentalism are needed in spaces of interreligious encounter even if they are not on the agenda. In the other direction, we see how contemporary movements such as women's empowerment, LGBTQIA+ equality, and anti-racist activism raise questions that are vital to integrate into IRS.

The influence of the public square on the academy is not value-neutral, however, and scholarship can be enmeshed in cultural conflicts in less constructive ways. The events of September 11, 2001, and the US response, for instance, spurred research on "countering violence extremism" (CVE) that was almost exclusively focused on Islam. Even courses and studies that tried to refute the association of Islam with violence ended up contributing to a good Muslim/bad Muslim paradigm (see Chapter 8). Trends like the rise of Hindu nationalism in India can skew syllabi so that non-Hindu students end up knowing little else about the traditions. With appropriate interdisciplinary rigor, however, the influence of politics, history, media, and science on IRS and engagement at least becomes visible.

In interpath engagement efforts, hot-button issues often become the proverbial "elephant in the room." If the group declines to discuss them, some will claim the encounter is inauthentic and others will stay away; they cannot agree to bracket a matter so urgent, or cannot sit down with people who do not stand with them. When groups decide to address an issue they have trouble avoiding, it often consumes all the air in the room. Participants may not have adequate information, perspective, skills, or time to deal with the complexities. Relationships that have built trust over an extended period can be more successful in traversing the minefields – but if there is no "container" for the problem, it can derail entire projects. Often, people walk smack into the elephant without meaning to.

Events need not be ripped from the headlines to have an impact. As William Faulkner wrote, "The past is never dead. It's not even past."[30] The near-genocide of Native American tribes, echoes of Crusades or *La Convivencia*, and images of the other in sacred texts are but a few of the historical developments that continue to shape interreligious perspectives and encounter. Outreach from one community to another can be fraught with background.

Case Summary: "Dear Hindu Friends"[1]

The Pontifical Council for Interreligious Dialogue and World Council of Churches (WCC) are among international Christian organizations that extend official greetings to Hindus around the world on the occasion of Diwali, a festival of lights that celebrates the victory of good over evil. (Hindus, Jains, Sikhs, and some Buddhists observe the five-day holiday, with varying associated narratives and practice.) The annual messages, posted on institutional websites and distributed

---

[30] Faulkner, *Requiem for a Nun*, Act 1, Scene 3 (1951).

through social media, constitute a sort of diplomacy. According to Marianne Moyaert, "the symbolic importance of this form of dialogue should not be underestimated: diplomatic dialogue implies the willingness of religious leaders and their institutions to leave centuries-old hostility behind them."[2]

Yet centuries of hostility occupy the background of the dialogue, including the legacy of European colonialism. Looking at the letters from 2019, the Pontifical Council sent greetings in both Hindi and English, but the WCC appears to have issued them in English alone. While the WCC message includes valued insights from Hindu texts and traditions, the Pontifical Council cites Catholic teachings almost exclusively. Each of these choices conveys a message that bears the weight of history.

Current events add to the load. The Pontifical Council's call for every religious person to be a builder of fraternity and peaceful coexistence surely had in mind – among other things – rising violence against India's small Christian minority. In 2021, hostile acts included burning Santa Claus in effigy, vandalism, and bursting in on services on Christmas Day, demanding that the congregation chant *"Jai Shree Ram"* (Victory to Lord Ram) – but the trend has been building for years. The WCC letter, lifting up the organization's thematic focus on racism and discrimination that year, could not help but conjure the religioracism that rationalized European conquest and Christian evangelism as well as ongoing conflict about caste-based discrimination.[3]

The question of audience for such declarations is also complex, (re)shaping the message with potentially competing objectives. Although addressed to the Hindu community, the letters also speak to the Christian groups they ostensibly represent. Consequently, in an introduction to the Pontifical Council letter on its website, the holiday is explained:

> Symbolically based on an ancient mythology, it represents the victory of truth over lies, of light over darkness, of life over death, and of good over evil. The actual celebration lasts three days, marking the beginning of a new year, family reconciliation, especially between brothers and sisters, and worship of God.[4]

Questions for Consideration

1. What value does "diplomatic dialogue" have for interreligious encounter, and what are its limitations? What about efforts on a smaller scale, for example reaching out to diverse members in your workplace or community on their holy days?
2. How does it complicate messaging to think about multiple audiences? Notice, for example, that the Pontifical Council's introduction to the letter mentions "God" rather than the various divinities of Hindu tradition connected to the holiday; how does it impact the message?
3. What events are unfolding in the world today that you think have an impact on Interreligious Studies and/or engagement? How is history embedded in them?

[1] See Melanie Barbato, "'Dear Hindu Friends': Official Diwali Greetings as a Medium for Diplomatic Dialogue," *Religion* 50, no. 3 (2020): 353–71, https://doi.org/10.1080/0048721X.2020.1754599.

[2] Moyaert, "Interreligious Dialogue," in *Understanding Interreligious Relations*, ed. David Cheetham, Douglas Pratt, and David Thomas (Oxford: Oxford University Press), 204.

[3] World Council of Churches, "Greetings from the WCC General Secretary on the Occasion of Diwali," October 25, 2019, www.oikoumene.org/resources/documents/greetings-from-the-wcc-general-secretary-on-the-occasion-of-diwali.

[4] "Message from the Pontifical Council for Interreligious Dialogue to Hindus for the Feast of Deepavali, 21.10.2019," https://press.vatican.va/content/salastampa/en/bollettino/pubblico/2019/10/21/191021a.html.

3   A Selective History of Interreligious Studies and Engagement

Interreligious encounter is not new, and the historical record of conflict as well as coexistence and cooperation is vital to understanding the role of religion and religious diversity in our world today.

3.1   THERE HAS ALWAYS BEEN RELIGIOUS DIFFERENCE

Sacred texts testify to the fact that there has always been religious difference. With a range of attitudes and purposes, they address some of the inter- and intrafaith diversity in their own contexts. Consider these examples:

- The Hindu text *Rigveda* discusses "the One Being the wise speak of in many ways: they call it Agni, Yama, Matarisvan" (1.164.46). Reflecting on competing Hindu traditions circa 1500 BCE, it emphasizes the limitations of speech as each name for the divine demonstrates the partial, particular nature of human understanding.[1]
- Early Buddhist texts contain accounts of non-Buddhist masters who achieve steps on the path toward enlightenment (e.g. *Majjhima Nikaya 26.22–23*), even though the Buddhist path is portrayed as the only one to go the distance.
- Hebrew Bible generally presents the polytheistic Canaanites in a negative light to discourage Israelites from following their practices, but there are exceptions. In one narrative, for example, Abraham establishes a covenant with Abimelech (Genesis 20–21); in another, Moses marries into the family of Jethro, a Midianite priest, and accepts his counsel to delegate leadership (Exodus 2–4, 18). Many of the biblical festivals are themselves adaptations of

---

[1] Anantanand Rambachan, "Are Religious Differences Only Semantic?" in *Words to Live By: Sacred Sources for Interreligious Engagement*, ed. Or Rose, Homayra Ziad, and Soren M. Hessler (Maryknoll: Orbis Books, 2018), 13–22.

Canaanite celebrations, reimagined to fit within the Bible's theological and historical perspectives.

- In the New Testament, harsh critique of the Pharisees is driven in part by a need to differentiate the Jesus movement from them – the most similar form of late Second Temple Judaism. Other passages cite Jesus encouraging his followers to transcend boundaries that divide people. (Compare, for example, Matthew 23 and 1 Corinthians 12).

- Qur'an presents multiple attitudes regarding non-Muslims. It polemicizes against Paganism, expresses both positive and negative conceptions of Christians and Jews, and also suggests that the diversity of religions is part of the Divine plan: "We have appointed a law and a practice for every one of you. Had Allah willed, He would have made you a single community, but He wanted to test you regarding what has come to you. So compete with each other in doing good. Every one of you will return to Allah and He will inform you regarding the things about which you differed" (5:48).

Negative impressions remain powerful as some scriptural images of the "Other" become archetypal in human imagination. Nonetheless, scriptural models of navigating difference peacefully can inspire respectful encounter.

People tend to live in groups with a shared identity, so particular religions become geographically predominant (and socially dominant), but they always encounter difference. Since the 2nd century CE, for example, the trans-Asian overland trade network between the Mediterranean and the Far East – now known as the Silk Road – brought Buddhists, Nestorian Christians, Jews, Manichaeans, Muslims, and others into contact, transmitting ideas as well as goods along the route. The traditions show signs of mutual influence. Manichaeism, for instance, consciously incorporated elements of Zoroastrianism, Christianity, Hinduism, Buddhism, and other faiths. Zen Buddhism is a synthesis of Daoist ideas woven into Chinese Buddhism; this "Chan" tradition became Zen as it was translated into Japanese language and culture.[2]

---

[2] Richard Foltz, *Religions of the Silk Road: Premodern Patterns of Globalization*, 2nd ed. (New York: Palgrave Macmillan, 2010); Center for Global Education, "Belief

In Africa, diverse Indigenous traditions regularly borrowed from one another. Focusing on practical rather than systematic theological concerns, the communities saw religion as a means of enhancing life. Support of multiple spirits simply augmented the requisite harmony between humanity, nature, and the realm of the divine.[3] This dynamic also shaped later encounters with Christianity and Islam, leading some Indigenous groups to adopt aspects of these conversionary religions without forfeiting their traditional spirituality – contributing to the *intra*faith diversity of today's world.

3.2   HISTORICAL PROJECTS OF INTERPATH ENGAGEMENT

We have numerous historical records of purposeful engagement between people with different lifestances, often designed as debates to interrogate truth claims. These encounters would not generally qualify as interreligious dialogue today, but they nonetheless created constructive formats for meeting religious difference and learning about other traditions. With a long history of multiple spiritual perspectives competing for adherents in East Asia, it became standard practice to prepare monks and priests with tools of logic, rhetoric, and ethics for debate. Representatives of various Hindu, Buddhist, Jain, Daoist, Confucian, and/or Shinto traditions would argue in person and in writing, collectively honing the philosophical clarity and theological nuance of their positions.[4]

Consider the story of seventh-century Chinese scholar Xuanzang. Raised with a classic Confucian education, Xuanzang was influenced by his older brother to explore Buddhist teachings. After becoming a monk, he traveled the Silk Road to India – the cradle of

Systems along the Silk Road," Asia Society, https://asiasociety.org/education/belief-systems-along-silk-road.

[3] Elizabeth Amoah, "Indigenous African Religions and Inter-Religious Relationship," International Interfaith Centre, October 22, 1998, http://iicao.org/iic-resources/lectures/african-indigenous-religions-and-inter-religious-relationship.

[4] David Peter Lawrence, "Buddhist–Hindu Dialogue," in *The Wiley-Blackwell Companion to Inter-Religious Dialogue*, ed. Catherine Cornille (Chichester: John Wiley & Sons, 2013), 187–204, https://doi.org/10.1002/9781118529911.ch12.

Buddhist civilization at the time – to clarify textual and philosophical difficulties his Chinese masters could not help him resolve. There he became expert in Mahayana Buddhist tradition and a renowned critic of Hindu and Jain teachings. An eighteen-day religious assembly was convened in Kanauj in 643, where Xuanzang allegedly vanquished 500 Brahmins, Jains, and heterodox Buddhists in spirited debate. After sixteen years away, he returned to his native China with hundreds of Sanskrit texts and spent the remainder of his life translating them into Chinese – adapting the Yogacara teachings he had learned in India to establish the Faxiang school. The *Tao Te Ching* remained an influential book for all of Chinese philosophy and religion, however, so he also translated it into Sanskrit and sent it to India.[5] These intra- and interreligious engagements are consequential, since spiritual lifestances are not formed in a vacuum. They are shaped in encounters with difference.

Another model of interreligious dialogue unfolded during the Islamic empire's Abbasid caliphate (8–13th c.), centered in Baghdad. In formal assemblies convened in the court of a prince, vizier, or caliph, and in more informal salons, diverse religious spokespersons gathered for civil debate and discussion. These *majalis* (councils) promised freedom of expression and respect for all participants. Most Muslims who took part saw the enterprise as *da'wa*, an invitation to embrace Islam as the true faith – and assurances of fair treatment in the literature did not always reflect reality. Nonetheless, the radical spirit of tolerance can be appreciated by noting the reaction of a pious tenth-century Andalusian scholar named Abu Umar. Living far from the cosmopolitan center of Baghdad, he could not abide the respectful treatment accorded to non-Muslims and their religious ideas:

> At the first session I attended I saw a *majlis* which included every kind of group: Sunni Muslims and heretics, and all kinds of infidels:

---

[5] Der Huey Lee, "Xuanzang (Hsüan-tsang) (602–664)," *Internet Encyclopedia of Philosophy*, www.iep.utm.edu/xuanzang.

Majus [Zoroastrians], materialists, atheists, Jews, and Christians. Each group had a leader who would speak on its doctrine and debate about it. Whenever a leader arrived, from whichever of the groups he was, the assembly rose up for him.

What angered him most was that they all agreed to argue based on reason, without reference to Qur'an or teachings of the Prophet Muhammad, since non-Muslims put no credence in them; Abu Umar determined never to return to the *majlis*.[6]

It is possible that such encounters with religious difference had a tangible impact, humanizing the face and faith of the other. A famous account of the Christian Patriarch Timothy's dialogue with the caliph al-Mahdi (8th c.) contains a good deal of verbal sparring, each trying to prove the superiority of his tradition. Yet the patriarch's admission that Muhammad moved his followers away from evil and taught them love of God, and that he walked in the way of the prophets, is one of the most generous assessments of Islam in medieval Christian literature.

On the other hand, structured disputations were not always so benign. In 1240, rabbis in Paris were summoned by King Louis IX to defend the Talmud against charges of blaspheming Jesus, Mary, and Christianity. It set into motion a chain of events that culminated in the seizing and burning of thousands of volumes of the Talmud. The Disputation of Barcelona in 1263 appeared to end more amicably, with Rabbi Moses ben Nahman (Nahmanides) receiving payment from King James for a job well done. Subsequent pressure by the Dominicans, however, soon forced Nahmanides to flee Spain. In fifteenth-century Tortosa, after Jews were again compelled to debate, they were subjected to increased persecution.[7]

---

[6] See Mark R. Cohen, Sydney H. Griffith, Hava Lazarus-Yafeh, and Sasson Somekh, eds., *The Majlis: Interreligious Encounters in Medieval Islam* (Weisbaden: Harrassowitz, 1999), 13–17, 62.

[7] Robert Chazan, *Barcelona and Beyond: The Disputation of 1263 and Its Aftermath* (Berkeley: University of California Press, 1992); Hyam Maccoby, ed. and trans.,

Many of these forced exchanges utilized what are now called "native informants," individuals who were formerly part of a group, deployed to testify against it. Jews who converted to Christianity had insider experience that meant they knew where to look for the most troubling material, and their abandonment of the tradition lent legitimacy to those who sought to condemn Judaism. (In the USA today, one sometimes sees Muslim native informants in the media, brought in to denounce Islam as violent or misogynist.)

Although Comparative Religion is different than Interreligious Studies (IRS) or engagement, as described in Chapter 1, the former also reflects contact with diverse ideas and persons. Medieval Muslim literature includes prototypes for scientific, systematic study of diverse religions. One of the most impressive works is a twelfth-century encyclopedia by al-Shahrastani, *The Book of Religions and Sects*. In the preface, he declares:

> I impose upon myself the obligation of presenting the views of each sect as I find them in their works without favor or prejudice, without distinguishing which are correct and which are in error, which are true and which are false; though, indeed, for minds that understand the ways of rational thought, the light of truth and the stench of falsehood will not remain hidden.[8]

While he saw the project as an effort at dispassionate study, there was still an inevitable *Tendenz* amidst the dominance of Islamic civilization. The basic definition of religion (*deen*) that al-Shahrastani offered is submission and obedience – not coincidentally, the lexical meaning of *Islam*. In his construction of self and other, all religions were interpreted and evaluated through the perspective of his own faith.

Judaism on Trial: Jewish-Christian Disputations in the Middle Ages (Plainsboro: Associated University Presses, 1982), https://doi.org/10.2307/j.ctv1rmjqp.

[8] My translation of al-Shahrastani's *Kitab al-Milal wa 'l-Nihal* from French in Daniel Gimaret and Guy Monnot, trans., *Livre des Religions et des Sectes* (Leuven: Peeters/ Unesco, 1986), 114. See also Steven Wasserstrom, "Islamicate History of Religions?," *History of Religions* 27, no. 4 (1988): 405–11, https://doi.org/10.1086/463130.

(Modern academic study of religion has substantially repeated the pattern, influenced in this instance by the dominance of Christian thought in the West.) Yet the stated goal of understanding diverse traditions as they understand themselves serves as a worthy precedent for contemporary interreligious learning.

3.3   COEXISTENCE AND CONFLICT

Religious tolerance is often a strategic choice. Minorities may promote it for self-preservation. An eighth-century stele engraved by Nestorian Christians in China, for example, celebrated an imperial proclamation with a protopluralist theology: "Right principles have no invariable name, holy men have no invariable station; instruction is established in accordance with the locality, with the object of benefiting the people at large."[9]

Yet those in power also found tolerance a useful policy. In the 6th century BCE, the Persian Empire allowed exiled peoples inherited from the Babylonians to return home and live by their ancestral law, including the Judeans who were encouraged to rebuild their ruined Temple in Jerusalem. It represented Persian strategy to keep order within their vast and diverse territory. Various medieval Christian kingdoms invited Jews to settle within their borders to establish mercantile networks; sometimes the rulers would decline to enforce Church legislation against the Jews in order to maintain stability. Even the notoriously brutal Genghis Khan (1162–1227) promoted religious freedom to advance the interests of the Mongol Empire, winning support from previously marginalized communities as he both embraced and exploited ethnic and religious difference.[10] In today's world, too, religious minorities are sometimes wooed to help secure political power. More commonly, historically and today, people promote religious tolerance in order to cultivate peaceful

---

[9] Perry Schmidt-Leukel, *Religious Pluralism and Interreligious Theology* (Maryknoll: Orbis Books, 2017), chap. 2.

[10] See Amy Chua, *Day of Empire: How Hyperpowers Rise to Global Dominance – and How They Fall* (New York: Doubleday, 2007), 88–126.

coexistence – even if some are still certain that their faith is singularly true.

It is difficult to disentangle the dynamics of religious difference from other forces at work. In the fourth century, for instance, the ruler of a Chinese province (Qin) sent a monk named Sundo to expound Buddhist teachings in the Korean peninsula. He hoped that cultural familiarity between the peoples might support an alliance against the hostile Manchurian tribes. His troops' recent defeat of the Former Yan state, which had regularly besieged one of Korea's "Three Kingdoms," made the mission a welcome gesture, and existing shamanist traditions were easily reconciled with the new teachings. Eventually Buddhism was embraced by all the Korean royal houses and became the official state religion, in part to unite the peninsula politically. Its teachings of rebirth based on karma also helped justify the privileged position of the establishment. While Buddhism largely coexisted with shamanism, Taoism, and Confucianism, its institutions reaped substantial economic benefits and the monks (many coming from the aristocracy) held considerable power at court. By the fourteenth century, resentment against corruption and abuse of power fostered a neo-Confucian revolt against Buddhist privileges.[11] It is not the only episode in the history of coexistence and conflict in which military, ethnic, economic, and political considerations seem more consequential than spiritual ones.

Certain periods are lifted up as models of coexistence, but the historical reality was more complex. *La Convivencia* in the Iberian peninsula under Muslim rule (711–1492) is one example. The term

---

[11] Jinwung Kim. *A History of Korea: From "Land of the Morning Calm" to States in Conflict* (Bloomington: Indiana University Press, 2012), 32–83; Robert Evans Buswell, Jr., "Buddhism in Korea," in *The Religious Traditions of Asia: Religion, History, and Culture*, ed. Joseph M. Kitagawa (Abingdon: Routledge, 2002), 347–53, https://doi.org/10.4324/9781315029641; A. Charles Muller, "The Buddhist–Confucian Conflict in the Early Chosŏn and Kihwa's Syncretic Response: The *Hyŏn chŏng non*," presented at the Annual Meeting of the American Academy of Religion, Chicago, November 20, 1994.

means "living together" and, although *dhimmi* status for Jews and Christians entailed legal disadvantages, they were also protected populations and there was robust cultural exchange between the "Peoples of the Book" that enabled the diverse communities to thrive. At the same time, it was a period of substantial rivalry.[12] The success of non-Muslim minorities spurred more hostile voices to protest and violence. Appointment of a Jew as vizier in Grenada, for example, prompted a poetical rant by Abu Ishaq in 1066, who complained that Muslims must now obey "the vilest ape among these miscreants." Inciting a mob who stormed the royal palace, assassinated the vizier, and massacred thousands of Jews in Grenada, he wrote:

> Hasten to slaughter him as an offering, sacrifice him for he is a fat ram.
> And do not spare his people, for they have amassed every precious thing . . .
> Do not consider it a breach of faith to kill them –
> The breach of faith would be to let them carry on.[13]

Although economic and political ambitions fueled the protracted military conflict between Christian and Muslim empires in the Middle Ages, sides were drawn by religious identity. Pope Urban II issued a call to arms at Clermont (1095), reportedly addressing the Catholic Franks as a "race beloved and chosen by God." He exhorted them to fight against the Muslim troops, characterized as a cursed people: "They have led away a part of the captives into their own country, and a part have they have killed by cruel tortures. They have either destroyed the churches of God or appropriated them for the rites of their own religion." The pope identified the Crusade to

---

[12] Compare María Rosa Menocal, *The Ornament of the World: How Muslims, Jews and Christians Created a Culture of Tolerance in Medieval Spain* (New York: Back Bay Books, 2002), and Darío Fernández-Morera, *The Myth of the Andalusian Paradise: Muslims, Christians and Jews under Islamic Rule in Medieval Spain* (Wilmington: Intercollegiate Studies Institute, 2016).

[13] Translation from Bernard Lewis, *Islam in History: Ideas, People, and Events in the Middle East* (New York: Open Court, 2013), 159–61.

conquer Jerusalem as a holy war, commanded by Christ, capable of remitting sins and guaranteeing salvation.[14]

After the fall of Seville to Christian troops in 1267, Muslim poet Al-Rundi lamented, "The tap of the white ablution fount weeps in despair" as their dwellings became inhabited by unbelievers and their mosques converted into churches. Like the Crusader call to arms, he used religious otherness to convey moral turpitude, portraying opposing troops as defilers of women and murderers of innocent children.[15] This extended geopolitical and cultural conflict still weighs heavily upon the world, framing an adversarial analysis: one side portrays Islam as an inherently violent faith irreconcilable with Western values, and the other casts the West as a reincarnation of the Crusaders, with the rise of secularism decried as *jahiliyya* (the period of religious "ignorance" in pre-Islamic Arabia).

Even during the Middle Ages, however, there were individuals who understood their faith as the foundation for bridging difference. Mystics perceived a divine unity that transcended particularity. Persian poet-theologian-jurist Jalal ad-Din Muhammad Rumi (1207–73) claims in one poem that the knower of God can reach a desert plain that is "beyond Islam and unbelief (*kufr*)." Drowning in the ocean of God's being, intellectual constructions of religion seem irrelevant and the only response is to surrender prostrate in prayer.[16] The great Andalusian Sufi ibn Arabi (1165–1240) writes:

My heart has become capable of every form:
it is a pasture for gazelles, and a convent for Christian monks,
And a temple for idols and the pilgrim's Ka'ba
and the tables of the Torah and the book of the Qur'an.

---

[14] Paul Halsall, "Urban II (1088–1099): Speech at Council of Clermont, 1095, Five Versions of the Speech," Internet Medieval Sourcebook, December 2017, https://sourcebooks.fordham.edu/source/urban2-5vers.asp#robert.

[15] James T. Monroe, ed. and trans., *Hispano-Arabic Poetry* (Berkeley: University of California Press, 1974), 332–36.

[16] Rumi, *The Quatrains of Rumi*, trans. Ibrahim Gamard and Rawan Farhadi (New York: Sufi Dari Books, 2008), Quatrain 395.

I follow the religion of Love:

whatever way Love's camels take, that is my religion and my faith.[17]

Such illustrations should not suggest a real erasure of their Muslim identity or a teaching of equivalency. Ibn Arabi compares earlier traditions to the light of distant stars and Islam to the light of the sun: "When the sun appears, the lights of the stars are hidden, and their lights are included in the light of the sun."[18] Yet the transcendence and empathy that emerge from these writings point beyond a clash of civilizations.

This quality is also central to Nicholas of Cusa's (1401–64) vision after the fall of Constantinople to the Ottomans in 1453. He imagines that a council of all faiths met in heaven and declared *una religio in rituum varietate*, a single religion manifested in different rites. While surely motivated by the vulnerability of Christendom after the collapse of the Byzantine Empire, his work still demonstrates a vital capacity for self-critical faith:

> The King of heaven and earth stated that the sad news of the groans of the oppressed had been brought to him from this world's realm: because of religion many take up arms against each other and by their power either force men to renounce their long-practiced tradition or inflict death on them. There were many bearers of these lamentations from all the earth.[19]

3.4   COLONIALISM AND ITS LEGACY

Sadly, individual sensitivity to suffering did not prevent religion from being deployed as a tool of empire. It was only forty years later that Pope Alexander VI issued *Inter caetera*, with its doctrine of discovery to legitimate Catholic claims to lands occupied by non-Christians.

---

[17] Ibn al-'Arabī, *The Tarjuman al-Ashwaq*, trans. Reynold Nicholson (London: Royal Asiatic Society, 1911), XI.

[18] Cited in William Chittick, *Imaginal Worlds: Ibn al-'Arabi and the Problem of Religious Diversity* (Albany: State University of New York Press, 1994), 125.

[19] James Biechler and H. Lawrence Bond, eds. and trans., *Nicholas of Cusa on Interreligious Harmony: Text, Concordance and Translation of* De Pace Fidei (Lewiston: Edward Mellen, 1991), 1.2.

Christianity is tightly bound up with the history of Western colonialism. Aspirations to convert the "heathen" and a sense of entitlement as God's elect aligned with the colonial project's desire for dominance and material gain. Conquistadors in Mexico, for example, were eager to plunder the gold and riches of the land, and they saw the evangelical mission as essential to the extension of Spain's power. Gerónimo de Mendieta, a sixteenth-century Franciscan commissioned to write a "History of the Indian Church," believed that Spain was chosen to convert the "last" Pagans and usher in the kingdom of God. Cortés was his Moses, liberating the Native Americans from demonic powers and winning more souls for Christ than Luther had taken from the Catholic Church.[20]

Because missionaries spent a good deal of time with Indigenous populations, they became among the most learned Westerners regarding local customs and often developed sympathetic appreciation for other religions. A twentieth-century British missionary named Constance Padwick, for instance, spent decades collecting devotional pamphlets from around the Muslim world and wrote *Muslim Devotions: A Study of Prayer Manuals in Common Use* (1961). In a tribute published shortly after her death, the project was described as "a gesture of imagination inspired by one faith towards the inner genius of another ... The one world is revealed in the seeking of the other, and the 'worlds' in that verdict are interchangeable. For it is in knowing that we are known."[21]

Some missionaries forcefully challenged white settler misconduct and opposed slavery of Indigenous peoples.[22] Nonetheless, physical aggression was frequently justified as protecting missionaries

---

[20] John Leddy Phelan, *The Millennial Kingdom of the Franciscans in the New World: A Study of the Writings of Gerónimo de Mendieta (1525–1604)* (Berkeley: University of California Press, 1970), 13.

[21] Kenneth Cragg, "Constance E. Padwick, 1886–1968," *The Muslim World* 59, no. 1 (January 1969), 35, doi.org/10.1111/j.1478-1913.1969.tb00471.x.

[22] Alan Lester, "Humanitarians and White Settlers in the Nineteenth Century," in *Missions and Empire*, ed. Norman Etherington (Oxford: Oxford University Press, 2005), 64–84, https://doi.org/10.1093/acprof:oso/9780199253487.003.0004.

even when there were clear political objectives, and Christian evangelism was central to the "civilizing" project. In Asia, Africa, and the Americas, superior European military power suggested to many of the colonizers and the colonized that the victors' religion was also superior. The world convulses still from the subsequent transformation and decimation of subject populations and cultures.

At times, colonialism's impact on the religious landscape was inadvertent. Consider the rise of Wahhabi Islam. Ibn Abd al-Wahhab challenged the Ottoman Empire's claim to represent Sunni tradition and argued that their policy of religious tolerance allowed heresy to flourish; the zeal of his followers was harnessed by Ibn Saud to legitimate territorial expansion in the Arabian Peninsula. Ottoman forces kept the rebellion contained until the demise of the empire after World War I. Britain had backed Ibn Saud against the Ottomans and enabled him to establish Saudi Arabia under the banner of restrictive Wahhabi Islam. Its spreading global influence fueled by petro-dollars was not an anticipated outcome.

The European model of the nation-state also left its mark. Imposed on colonial territories, it bred significant violence. In the Indian subcontinent, British partition between a Hindu-majority India and Muslim-majority Pakistan (1947) intensified conflict and displaced populations. It also ignored long-standing tribal identities that took precedence over religious ones, as evidenced by the Bangladesh War of Independence from Pakistan in 1971. Partition similarly ignored the substantial number of Sikhs living in the northwest on both sides of the dividing line, contributing to the rise of Sikh radicals and India's suppression of the movement in Operation Blue Star in the 1980s – which led to Indira Gandhi's assassination by her Sikh bodyguards and subsequent anti-Sikh riots. The shockwaves of partition are felt still today.

Western colonialism was buttressed by another modern development – a phenomenon in the academy that the influential scholar Tomoko Masuzawa calls "the invention of world religions." Imagining religion as a defined entity that can be extracted from other

aspects of society, academic study normalized Western ways of knowing and set up non-Christian lifestances as "other."[23] The history of
religions was tendentiously scripted as a hierarchical progression,
privileging Christianity and consigning colonized cultures to the
realm of the primitive. Academic projects like Max Müller's *Sacred
Books of the East* (1879–1910) introduced English-speaking readers to
the richness of Hindu and other textual traditions, but also reinforced
the exoticism of "Oriental" culture. While he found beauty in the
teachings, Müller could not shed the presumption of Christian superiority; he believed that accurate knowledge would assist in the missionary enterprise, just as generals need to know "the enemy's
country."[24] It has taken scholars a long time and rigorous self-critique
to deconstruct Orientalist approaches to Religious Studies and
Comparative Theology – an ongoing project since knowledge is inevitably linked to the exercise of power (see Chapters 2, 8).

3.5   THE CASE OF THE UNITED STATES

In the United States, the colonial project led to near-genocide of the
native peoples and denial of the legitimacy of their lifestances. The
Indian Removal Act, violation of multiple treaties with native populations, and withholding of US citizenship until 1924 illuminate the
long history of discrimination. Well-known, too, are the boarding and
day schools that tried to eradicate native language, culture, food,
names, values, and spirituality – replacing them with white,
Christian culture and religion. Although Roger Williams (1603–83)
recognized from the beginning the perils in championing a Christian
nation chosen by God to rule the earth and stood up for Indigenous
rights, he was banished as a heretic. John Gast's famous painting,

---

[23] Masuzawa, *The Invention of World Religions: Or, How European Universalism
Was Preserved in the Language of Pluralism* (Chicago: University of Chicago
Press, 2005).

[24] See Arie L. Molendijk, *Friedrich Max Müller and the Sacred Books of the East*
(Oxford: Oxford University Press, 2016), 152, https://doi.org/10.1093/acprof:oso/
9780198784234.001.0001.

FIGURE I John Gast, "American Progress" (1872)
Autry Museum, Los Angeles; 92.126.1

American Progress (1872), depicts prevailing attitudes in the building of the nation: the very white figure of Columbia is bringing light to the frontier – the realm of Indians and wild animals still cloaked in darkness (Figure 1). With education in her arms and technology in her wake, this metaphor for America presents national expansion as a civilizing enterprise.

Indigenous religion is expressed and embodied differently from Western conceptions, something the law has been slow to recognize. Justice William Brennan glimpsed a piece of it when he wrote in *Lyng v. Northwest Indian Cemetery Protective Association* (1988), "Native American faith is inextricably bound to the use of land. The site-specific nature of Indian religious practice derives from the Native American perception that land is itself a sacred, living being." Unfortunately, he wrote these words in dissent against the majority opinion. Even today, decades after the American Indian Religious

Freedom Act (1978) passed to protect native "access to sites, use and possession of sacred objects, and the freedom to worship through ceremonials and traditional rites," these rights are regularly violated. From the reduced size of the Bears Ears National Monument to the Dakota Access Pipeline that threatens sacred waterways, ancient burial grounds, and important cultural sites near the Standing Rock Reservation, the spiritual claims of Native Americans are undervalued.

The bias reflects not only a limited perspective on what constitutes religion but also the racialization of religious difference – a phenomenon that shows up repeatedly in American history. In 1682, Virginia passed a law justifying the enslavement of individuals "whose parentage and native country are not Christian at the time of their first purchase." Over two hundred years later, Senator Sargent spoke against the immigration of Chinese laborers; he wanted missionaries to travel to China instead, to "wash their robes and make them white in the blood of the Lamb."[25] Since naturalized US citizenship was long limited to "free white persons," there are various court cases that assessed whether certain Asian and Middle Eastern individuals were eligible. In most instances where the answer was yes, the petitioner was Christian. In *US v. Cartozian* (1925), the court maintained that skin color does not provide an adequate guide for whiteness, so it decided to rely "largely on religion (and assimilation) in its determination." In cases like these, religion stood in for race as a performance of whiteness, with the presumption that Christian culture equaled white culture.

Yet the United States imagines itself a beacon of religious freedom and interfaith cooperation. Americans proudly point to the First Amendment's protection from government establishment of or interference in the free exercise of religion. (It restricted only federal law,

---

[25] See Jeannine Hill Fletcher, "The Promising Practice of Antiracist Approaches to Interfaith Studies," in *Interreligious/Interfaith Studies: Defining a New Field*, ed. Eboo Patel, Jennifer Howe Peace, and Noah J. Silverman (Boston: Beacon Press, 2018), 137–42.

not state law, until after the Civil War.) As the Bill of Rights was moving through the states for ratification, President George Washington wrote to the Jewish congregation in Newport, Rhode Island, "The citizens of the United States of America have a right to applaud themselves for having given to mankind examples of an enlarged and liberal policy ... All possess alike liberty of conscience and immunities of citizenship." He argued that toleration is not the "indulgence of one class of people" but the exercise of "inherent natural rights." In protecting those rights, Washington asserted that the US government would give "to bigotry no sanction, to persecution no assistance."[26]

Benjamin Franklin reportedly donated to every house of worship in Philadelphia as a demonstration of his commitment to religious freedom, and he raised money for a public hall where preachers of any religious persuasion could speak.[27] Although the founding fathers would not have imagined the thriving religious diversity of the United States today, it is a result of their labors and many who followed. Religious coexistence and cooperation are aspirations, and American progress toward these goals has always required effort. Many European nations are similarly engaged in ongoing endeavors to establish more robust religious freedom and equity, built on intellectual traditions of tolerance embedded in the Enlightenment at the dawn of the modern age.

Part of the struggle is that the breadth and meaning of religious freedom is contested. Does majority rule establish democracy, or must minority rights be protected? Should immigrants assimilate as much as possible or protect their religio-cultural particularity? Is difference necessarily divisive, or can it strengthen the social fabric? E. Allen Richardson has described these competing views for the religio-cultural landscape of America as the melting pot versus "The

---

[26] "George Washington's Letter to the Hebrew Congregation of Newport," https://tourosynagogue.org/history/george-washington-letter/washington-seixas-letters.

[27] Eboo Patel, *Out of Many Faiths: Religious Diversity and the American Promise* (Princeton: Princeton University Press, 2018), 5.

New Colossus." The former presents a crucible in which difference is melted away, refined to reflect "American" identity – namely white, European, Christian culture. The latter cites the title of Emma Lazarus' poem etched at the base of the Statue of Liberty, welcoming immigrants from around the world – signifying a mosaic of many peoples and faiths made beautiful by diversity.[28] Yet it is not a simple binary calculation, as is evident in tracing the development of the modern interfaith movement.

3.6   THE MODERN INTERFAITH MOVEMENT

Even though interreligious learning and encounter are not new, there is a modern history delineating the growth of a movement and an academic field that grounds our studies. It is important to recall that the prehistory was not merely a string of religious conflicts or a record of productive coexistence, but a complex combination of both – as well as mutual dependence and influence, woven together with all the factors that shape (and separate) societies. This more nuanced view facilitates contemporary efforts to analyze the impact of religious difference and to foster cooperation for the common good.[29]

Fighting for Equality. The birth of the modern interfaith movement is often traced to the 1893 World's Parliament of Religions, convened parallel to the Columbian Exposition in Chicago that attracted over twenty million visitors. It was an axial event in shaping attitudes toward religious diversity. Representatives of other traditions got to speak for themselves and were received in a spirit of understanding rather than polemic, providing many Americans their first contact with spiritual perspectives from Central Asia, Africa, and

[28] Richardson, *Strangers in This Land: Religion, Pluralism, and the American Dream* (Jefferson: McFarland & Co. 2010), 25–27. See also Tisa Wenger, *Religious Freedom: The Contested History of an American Ideal* (Chapel Hill: University of North Carolina Press, 2017).

[29] Parts of the movement history are adapted from Mikva, "Reflections in the Waves: What Interreligious Studies Can Learn from the Evolutions of Women's Movements in the United States," *Journal of Ecumenical Studies* 53, no. 4 (Fall 2018): 461–82, http://doi.org/10.1163/9789004420045_009.

the Far East. It sought to present similarities among different traditions and the collective value of religious life. This staking of
common ground, however, was self-consciously located in Christian
territory. Almost 80 percent of the papers were delivered by
Christians. John Henry Barrows, president of the Parliament, wrote
of the proceedings, "The Christian spirit pervaded the conference
from first to last. Christ's prayer was daily used. His name was always
spoken with reverence. His doctrine was preached by a hundred
Christians and by lips other than Christian. The Parliament ended
at Calvary."[30]

Christian privilege pervaded multiple aspects of American society in this era – with "blue laws" that restricted commercial enterprises on Sundays, religious tests for state and local public office,
control of the academic study of religion, and repeated calls to amend
the Constitution to declare the United States a Christian nation.
Religious minorities devoted significant communal energy to combatting religious discrimination; a key strategy was to emphasize
similarity with white mainline Protestantism, the dominant faith of
the nation. Interreligious prayer emulated Protestant worship, and
dialogue emphasized sameness: *Look at all we have in common!*

Despite America's First Amendment's protection of religious
freedom, adherents of minority traditions often had to combat a
virulent mix of racism and religious prejudice. Labor unions in the
northwest, for example, organized to prevent companies from hiring
"Asiatics," and mob violence chased "the Hindus" out of Washington
(1905–07). On the east coast, "No Irish Need Apply" frequently
capped help-wanted ads to exclude Catholics; Italian Catholics who
could not pass as white faced more substantial discrimination. Jews
were excluded from social clubs and hotels; they could not buy property in certain areas or purchase insurance for their businesses. They

---

[30] Barrows, "Review and Summary," in *The World's Parliament of Religions* (Chicago:
Parliament Publishing Co., 1893), 2:1578. See Eric J. Ziolkowski, ed., *A Museum of
Faiths: Histories and Legacies of the 1893 World's Parliament of Religions* (New
York: Oxford University Press, 1993), 3.

were regularly denounced in publications and were suspect as witnesses in judicial proceedings. Quotas were imposed on university admissions and, after the 1924 Immigration Act, on admission to the country as well – disguised as limits based on countries of origin (see Chapter 8).[31]

After the Shoah, the Christian world began to grapple seriously with the legacy of its centuries-long othering of Jews and Judaism. (Note: This volume generally does not use the term Holocaust, which refers to a burnt offering. Many people consider it offensive that the murder of millions could be equated with a sacrifice pleasing to God. The word Shoah means "utter catastrophe.") The World Council of Churches, in its first assembly in 1948, denounced antisemitism as a sin against God that is irreconcilable with Christian faith. In 1965, the Second Vatican Council issued *Nostra aetate*, a paradigm-shattering statement of kinship with diverse religionists. It acknowledges that Jews of today cannot be blamed for the death of Christ, and that God is still in covenantal relationship with them – for God's gifts and call are irrevocable (Romans 11:29). Islam, too, is dignified in the document by the manifold ways in which Muslims share Christian values.[32] Institutional investment by the Catholic Church substantially advanced projects of interreligious dialogue and related efforts. At the same time, with similarity as the foundational ground for equality, Christian normativity went substantially unchallenged.

Making Space for Difference. In the 1960s and 1970s a number of important developments took place. Degree programs and faculty positions in Religious Studies expanded significantly across US campuses. Explicitly interdisciplinary and comparative, it facilitated deeper study of religious difference. Ninian Smart, a key figure in the

---

[31] Naomi W. Cohen, *Jews in Christian America: The Pursuit of Religious Equality* (New York: Oxford University Press, 1992), 65–92; Leonard Dinnerstein, *Antisemitism in America* (New York: Oxford University Press, 1994).

[32] *Nostra aetate*, no. 1, www.vatican.va/archive/hist_councils/ii_vatican_council/ documents/vat-ii_decl_19651028_nostra-aetate_en.html. See Gavin D'Costa, *Vatican II: Catholic Doctrines on Jews and Muslims* (New York: Oxford University Press, 2014), 99–107, https://doi.org/10.1093/acprof:oso/9780199659272.001.0001.

popularization of such nonsectarian study, introduced a highly influential methodology that attempted to break free of Western/Christian frameworks for thinking about spiritual worldviews. Making room for nontheistic traditions, for instance, he identified doctrinal, mythological, ethical, ritual, experiential, institutional, and (later on) material dimensions of religion.[33] Similarly, Wilfred Cantwell Smith's 1962 controversial but now classic book, *The Meaning and End of Religion*, proposed an alternative framework in place of Euro-Christian constructions of religion. Out in the field, the interreligious movement similarly recognized and dignified difference, liberating encounter from lowest-common-denominator equations and reimagining dialogues to learn about the uniqueness of each tradition – even if conversation continued for a while to be dominated by white, male clergy.[34]

Institutional structures expanded, with the *Journal of Ecumenical Studies* broadening its focus to include interfaith issues, and the Dialogue Institute launching in 1978 to engage "religious, civic, and academic leaders in practicing the skills of respectful dialogue and critical thinking, building and sustaining transformative relationships across lines of religion and culture."[35] Theological schools like Hartford Theological Seminary (now Hartford International University for Religion and Peace) and Graduate Theological Union established programs and centers dedicated to interreligious relations.

Metropolitan-area interfaith councils multiplied, and religiously diverse groups formed to address social issues like civil rights and peace advocacy. The Clergy Consultation Service on Abortion organized over 1,000 religious leaders to help pregnant women before

---

[33] Smart, *The Religious Experience of Mankind* (Upper Saddle River: Prentice Hall, 1969).

[34] See, for example, Leonard Swidler and Marc H. Tanenbaum, *Jewish-Christian Dialogues* (American Jewish Committee, January 1, 1966), www.bjpa.org/Publications/details.cfm?PublicationID=14018.

[35] "Mission," Dialogue Institute, https://dialogueinstitute.org/mission-vision.

Roe v. Wade relegalized abortion as national policy in 1973; they referred women to abortion providers and arranged transportation to states where it was legal. Clergy Concerned About Vietnam was established in 1965 to challenge US policy in Southeast Asia. Religious activists like Rev. Dr. Martin Luther King, Jr. and Rabbi Abraham Joshua Heschel formed deep friendships and critical alliances.

Another momentous change was catalyzed by the 1965 Immigration Act, which expanded entrance to the USA for individuals from Asia and brought more substantial religious diversity to college campuses and communities. (It was signed into law by President Johnson in front of the Statue of Liberty.) Consequently, direct encounters with Hindu, Buddhist, Jain, and Sikh persons transformed ideas about Eastern traditions from exotic, essentialized religions of far away into dynamic, homegrown multiplicities. While the tendency to essentialize remains, the fields of Religious and Interreligious Studies strive to recognize that no lifestance is monolithic and lived tradition also varies from the reified "ism" one finds in books.

Transnational identity and cross-cultural influences added complexity to the unfolding narratives of religious diversity, as majority and minority religious cultures continually shape one another.[36] It is not surprising to learn how newer communities began to reorganize themselves to fit more comfortably into American ideas about religion and to qualify for the tax and organizational advantages of being a "church." In the other direction, however, Hindu teachings influenced the growth of transcendental meditation and yoga among people of diverse spiritual orientations – not to mention the impact of Mahatma Gandhi on Dr. King's philosophy of non-violent social

---

[36] See Diana L. Eck, *A New Religious America: How a "Christian Country" Became the World's Most Religiously Diverse Nation* (New York: HarperCollins, 2002); Robert Wuthnow, *America and the Challenges of Religious Diversity* (Princeton: Princeton University Press, 2005).

change. As different as we are, we cannot help but influence one another in our spiritual development.

The Birth of a "Field." The momentum of interreligious learning and engagement accelerated in the 1990s with a rapid expansion of their infrastructure. The Parliament of the World's Religions reestablished itself and convened thousands of people in Chicago for a centenary conference. Justice-oriented interpath organizations multiplied, like GreenFaith (1992), Interfaith Alliance (1994), Interfaith Worker Justice (1996), and Interfaith Power and Light (1998). Community organizations identified with a particular tradition, like the Inner-City Muslim Action Network (1997) and the Jewish Council on Urban Affairs (1964), regularly partnered to effect social change. UNESCO issued a Declaration of Principles on Tolerance (1995).

New kinds of projects emerged in this decade, like Scriptural Reasoning and building understanding through the arts. The Pluralism Project at Harvard University was born in 1991, investigating the changing religious landscape of American cities and analyzing how it complexifies our public life. Its founding director, Diana Eck, advanced the conviction that diversity alone does not constitute pluralism; learning and active engagement are required. Along with other academically rooted interfaith centers, such as the Center for Jewish, Christian and Islamic Studies at Chicago Theological Seminary and the Bernardin Center at Catholic Theological Union, it laid the groundwork for an emerging field of study. After September 11, 2001, and the London bombings in 2005, the movement grew exponentially. Hundreds of new initiatives broadened awareness of and investment in interreligious work – including the Interfaith Youth Core (now Interfaith America), nurturing interfaith learning and leadership on college campuses (2002); and President Obama's Interfaith and Community Service Campus Challenge (2011).

While most of the history in this section focuses on the United States, it is important to note that efforts were multiplying around the world. University ventures like the Cambridge Inter-faith Programme

(2002) and scholarly collaborations like the European Society for Intercultural Theology and Interreligious Studies (ESITIS, 2005); inter-governmental projects like the King Abdullah International Centre for Interreligious and Intercultural Dialogue (KAICIID, 2012); transnational coalitions like the African Council of Religious Leaders (2003, associated with Religions for Peace); a Muslim–Christian project called "A Common Word" that affirms shared values to cultivate understanding (2007); and community-based initiatives like the Cordoba Declaration (2017) that designated Latin America and the Caribbean as an "interreligious coexistence" zone – these represent only a few examples. Each was a response to the uniqueness of its context.

Amidst this flurry of activity, the academic field of Interreligious Studies was formally established. There were new degree programs, dedicated journals, and the formation of a section at the American Academy of Religion. Independently and in multiple consortia, scholars began to create foundational texts for the field, sketching its parameters and purposes. It is developing interdisciplinary tools to engage learning across the curriculum, intersectional lenses to account for multiple differences in identity, and a robust capacity for critical analysis – learning from and contributing to the history of the movement.

4 Ethical, Philosophical, and Theological Grounds of Parity Pluralism

Polls repeatedly demonstrate that a majority of Americans affirm that more than one religion may be "true" and even non-believers may find their way to eternal life in heaven. The questions tend to privilege Christian concerns for dogma and salvation, but the responses indicate a broad desire to interpret religious difference in ways that afford full dignity and equality to all people. Surveys in other religiously diverse countries such as India reveal similar findings.[1] Our working terminology for this perspective is "parity pluralism," where parity denotes comparable merit – *not* sameness: multiple lifestances are deemed equally sufficient and their variety is beneficial. For many people it is an ethical instinct, without detailed philosophical or theological analysis, and perhaps without much knowledge of other religious traditions. In the field of Interreligious Studies, however, there is substantial conversation about ethical, philosophical, and theological grounds for parity pluralism.

4.1 ETHICAL FOUNDATIONS

As discussed in Chapter 2, one can be a religious pluralist without affirming parity among diverse lifestances. Practically, pluralists recognize that religious understanding is necessary to prevent human beings from killing or harming each other based on differences of belief or practice. The discussion of history in Chapter 3 contains

---

[1] Pew Research Center conducts multiple surveys. See, for example, Justin Nortey, "Republicans More Likely Than Democrats to Believe in Heaven," November 21, 2021, www.pewresearch.org/fact-tank/2021/11/23/republicans-more-likely-than-democrats-to-believe-in-heaven-say-only-their-faith-leads-there/; Neha Segal et al., "Diversity and Pluralism," June 29, 2021, www.pewresearch.org/2021/06/29/diversity-and-pluralism.

examples of peaceful coexistence through the centuries. Pluralism demands more than tolerance, however; the reality of religious difference should not be presented as a burden to bear or a situation in which one party has disproportionate power to suffer the existence of another lifestance (or not).

Pluralism, even without a conviction of parity, requires that we privilege building human relationship. We must see religious others in their full humanity and respect their freedoms. While we need not compromise our truth claims or worldview, and we can share the passion that roots our spiritual lives, the goal of meeting one another is not to make our own perspective prevail. With hospitality, humility, and empathy, we seek to understand the experience of people who orient around religion differently – and to value their contributions to the collective experience of humanity. According to Catholic theologian Catherine Cornille, we also need to trust in our interconnectedness – affirming that religions have relevance for each other despite their irreducible differences.[2]

Communication Studies professors Charles Soukup and James Keaten illustrate how people can respond to religious otherness in humanizing or dehumanizing ways, no matter what their philosophical or theological convictions may be. They characterize humanizing responses as those that foster reciprocity, mutuality, self-reflexivity, authenticity, and compassion. Dehumanizing encounters sow fear, misrecognition, objectification, defensiveness, and a desire for control.[3] Theological exclusivists may recognize, for example, when their perspective makes others uncomfortable, and go out of their way to demonstrate respect for someone who believes differently. And parity pluralists may believe that everyone should embrace their point of

---

[2] Cornille, The Im-Possibility of Interreligious Dialogue (New York: Crossroad, 2008), 95.

[3] Soukup and Keaten, "Humanizing and Dehumanizing Responses across Four Orientations to Religious Otherness," in A Communication Perspective on Interfaith Dialogue: Living within the Abrahamic Traditions, ed. Daniel S. Brown, Jr. (Lanham: Lexington Books, 2013), 45–58.

view, demonstrating a desire for control, and they may misrecognize theological exclusivists as morally deficient.

What might a humanizing encounter look like for an evangelical Christian who meets me – a progressive Jew who believes in parity pluralism? The spirit of humility would preclude us both from presuming that we are more intelligent or more worthy than our dialogue partner. It should inspire us to be self-reflexive – recognizing that no one has a perfect understanding; even if we feel that our perspective is correct, there is something we can learn from one another. Empathy requires that, even if she is anxious to share the "good news" of her faith, she consider how I might be sensitive to the long and bloody history of Christians trying to convert Jews for the sake of their immortal souls. In place of persuasion, we pursue friendship.

Even though a conviction of parity pluralism is not required for humanizing encounter, the same principles of compassion and humility strike many as a compelling ethical foundation for affirming equality among lifestances. Some arrive at this conclusion simply because they know too many people whom they admire who identify with a different religion. They may also recognize a shared concern for ethics that establishes a claim of parity. The Jewish philosopher Moses Mendelssohn (1729–86), for instance, wrote an open letter to Swiss clergyman Johann Kaspar Lavater, rejecting pressure to convert to Christianity. It read in part:

> If a Confucius or a Solon were to live among our contemporaries,
> I could, according to my religion, love and admire the great man
> without succumbing to the ridiculous desire to convert him. Convert a
> Confucius or a Solon? What for? ... And as far as the general principles
> of religion are concerned, we should have little trouble agreeing on
> them. Do I think he can be saved? It seems to me that anyone who
> leads men to virtue in this life cannot be damned in the next.[4]

---

[4] Mendelssohn, "Letter to Johann Casper Lavater," in *Disputation and Dialogue: Readings in the Jewish-Christian Encounter*, ed. Frank Ephraim Talmage (New York: KTAV Publishing House, 1975), 269.

Today, in a globally connected world with continuous migrations, it goes beyond knowing "of" a Confucius or a Solon. Instead, people who orient around religion differently are our neighbors, colleagues, friends, and family members.

From a parity perspective, true equity and respect seem impossible when others' spiritual truths are dismissed as inferior; a hierarchy of lifestances establishes a hierarchy of humanity. Claims of ultimacy that often accompany exclusivist perspectives may link to other hierarchies regarding gender and sexual orientation (and, historically, race) – in conflict with the ethics of inclusion. As Michel Foucault persuasively demonstrates, truth claims readily become power claims.[5] Thus, parity pluralism seeks to accord respect to other human beings *and* affirm their spiritual choices. It maintains that we should see our lifestance as contributing to the world's store of sacred wisdom rather than owning it, counting among the world's faiths rather than triumphing over them. Encounter with difference is a call to learn, not a conflict to be resolved.

Yet most people assign degrees of parity, even if we do so subconsciously. We naturally prefer our own lifestance and perhaps see it as the medieval Muslim scholar ibn Arabi saw Islam: ours is the light of the sun and other traditions illuminate in lesser ways like the moon and the stars. Those that are close to us shine a bit brighter. Recognizing that these are personal judgments rather than absolutist claims, however, the ethics of parity can be maintained. Rabbi Arnold Jacob Wolf offers the analogy to marriage: we do not need to believe that our spouse is the most exceptional person in the world – only that they are the right person for us, the one who makes us better, the one who teaches us to love, the one who makes us whole. Besides, Wolf noted, we cannot really know what someone else's spouse is like without the intimacy of a life together.[6]

[5] See, for example, Foucault, *Power/Knowledge: Selected Interview and Other Writings, 1972–1977* (New York: Pantheon Books, 1980).
[6] Wolf, "The State of Jewish Belief," *Commentary* (August 1966), www.commentary.org/articles/jacob-agus-2/the-state-of-jewish-belief.

Ethical arguments for parity do not require that we abstain from judgment altogether. Instead, they frame the criteria in ethical measure. Theologians Marjorie Hewitt Suchocki and Paul Knitter have argued, for instance, that working toward the inclusive wellbeing of humanity is the fundamental criterion of value, and religions are true insofar as they orient people toward justice and liberation.[7] The Dalai Lama has urged us to focus on ethical teachings of the diverse lifestances as a way to both advance the flourishing of all living beings and cultivate common ground.[8] Ethics are culturally constructed, but non-ideological dialogue facilitates critical exploration of our respective norms.

4.2 PHILOSOPHICAL GROUNDS

Other arguments for parity pluralism move more into the philosophical realm. Perennial philosophy, richly expounded by Frithjof Schuon (1907–98) and popularized by Aldous Huxley, maintains that there is a unified reality or Godhead at the core of the world's religions. The *ein sof* (a reference to God, literally "without end") of Jewish mysticism, the *atman-brahman* of Hinduism, the *dharmakāya* of Mahayana Buddhism, the *Dao* (way), and so on – all grasp some transcendental element of a universal metaphysical truth.[9] Transcendentalism made a similar claim in the nineteenth century and its near-contemporary movement, the Theosophical Society, imagined that we should learn from each other's lifestances in order to evolve toward perfect universal understanding. (Opponents of religious pluralism sometimes try to paint the whole enterprise as an effort to construct a new universal religion, even though projects like that of the Theosophical Society are rare.)

[7] See their respective contributions to John Hick and Paul Knitter, eds., *The Myth of Christian Uniqueness: Toward a Pluralistic Theology of Religions* (Eugene: Wipf & Stock, 2005).

[8] Dalai Lama, *Towards True Kinship of Faiths: How the World's Religions Can Come Together* (New York: Three Rivers, 2010).

[9] Huxley, *The Perennial Philosophy: An Interpretation of the Great Mystics, East and West* (New York: Harper and Brothers, 1945).

These approaches, along with the more generic metaphor that all lifestances are different roads up the same mountain, have been criticized for erasing differences between the traditions or subsuming them in a comprehensive theory of religion. It has sometimes been called "identist" or "reductive" pluralism. John Hick, an influential twentieth-century philosopher of religion, is often included in this category. He certainly recognized the substantial differences between lifestances but believed that they conceptualize the same spiritual reality (the Real) in unique ways.[10]

Most contemporary articulations of philosophical parity take the enduring reality of difference as their starting point. Raimon Panikkar, a Roman Catholic priest of Spanish/Catholic and Indian/ Hindu heritage, offers the image of rivers, flowing in diverse regions of the earth and yielding life-giving waters to those who drink from them. The rivers never meet on earth but they do in the heavens, transformed into vapor or spirit, and then rain down again on all creation. The metaphor seeks to substantiate the abiding uniqueness of each lifestance, imagining their interrelatedness without essentializing them. Panikkar believes truth itself is plural.[11]

Such a concept may seem foreign to contemporary Western ears, but many philosophical perspectives have allowed for the plurality of truth. Plato, with his world of forms where what is real and true must be universal and timeless, represented only one school of thought. It became dominant in the wake of Immanuel Kant, who tied the principle to morality as well. These two giants of Western philosophical tradition helped to shape Enlightenment notions that goodness, ethics, and truth must be universal.

Yet philosophy both ancient and modern has grappled with the plural nature of truth. Heraclitus (6th century BCE) wrote about the unity of opposites. The Chinese school of Yinyang taught that

---

[10] Hick, *An Interpretation of Religion: Human Responses to the Transcendent*, 2nd ed. (New Haven: Yale University Press, 2005).

[11] Panikkar, *A Dwelling Place for Wisdom* (Louisville: Westminster John Knox, 1993), 112–14, 146–47.

apparently opposing forces are in fact complementary, and harmony between them contributes to the vital force (qi) of the universe. Abu'l Fadl (1551–1602), a court philosopher under the Mughal emperor Akbar, professed that truth is the inhabitant of every place; the sages themselves are evidence that it cannot be confined to one religion. Hegel critiqued Kant for ignoring how plurality and contradiction lead to understanding; everything involves a coexistence of opposed elements.[12]

Truth also has different measures and meaning depending on subject and context. Start with the semantic difference between "true friend" and "true story." To be judged true, observations need to be verified, mathematics require formulaic proof, and moral principles must cohere with a body of convictions. Then consider the dialectical insight that there are often competing truths, requiring us to navigate the tension between them. These reflections only begin to illuminate how truths are of diverse kinds. Spiritual lifestances deal in multiple types of truth, sometimes so diverse that "true" does not best describe their purpose.

Another philosophical foundation speaks about the pluralism of religious ends. In various formulations, scholars suggest that each lifestance is uniquely well-adapted in pursuit of its identified goals. With a superfluity of conflicting testimony, discrete pockets of evidence support specific interpretations. Christian theologian S. Mark Heim has written, "We can avoid the stale deadlock of the instrumental question over what will get you there – 'One way or many ways?' – by asking with real openness, 'Way to what?'"[13] This approach is not as tidy as one might wish: Buddhism, Sikhism, Jainism, and Hindu

---

[12] See Daniel W. Graham, "Heraclitus" and Robin R. Wang, "Yinyang" in the peer-reviewed *Internet Encyclopedia of Philosophy*, https://iep.utm.edu; Reza Shah-Kazemi, *The Spirit of Tolerance in Islam* (London: I. B. Tauris, 2012), 35–36; Georg Hegel, *Encyclopaedia of the Philosophical Sciences*, trans. and ed. Klaus Brinkmann and Daniel Dahlstrom (Cambridge: Cambridge University Press, 2010), Part 1: B.2.48.

[13] S. Mark Heim, "Dreams Fulfilled: The Pluralism of Religious Ends," *Christian Century* 118, no. 2 (January 17, 2001), 14.

traditions all pursue *nirvana*, for example, but identify the path and the purpose differently. Nonetheless, the pluralism of religious ends helps to establish parity by acknowledging that each lifestance has an internal coherence and value. They contribute to the categories of religious experience in unique ways.

A key aspect of Hick's pluralism rests on the fact that human experience of the world is ambiguous, leading to multiple culturally conditioned interpretations of ultimate reality. He maintains that no single lifestance is more effective at transforming lives than another or more demonstrable in its claims. This premise has been attacked as relativism: how can teachings of ultimate value have no ultimate truth? Some see it as a reflection of postmodernism's assertion that all knowledge is situated knowledge: it is fundamentally shaped by our experience, problematizing modernity's affection for scientific certainty.

The notion of epistemological limits, however, is not a recent innovation. Every rigorous analysis of learning has bumped up against the boundaries of human cognition. Religious discourse has taken this constraint to heart: Augustine and Nicholas of Cusa spoke of "learned ignorance," valorizing the admission of all we cannot know – especially when it comes to the nature of God. Other religious traditions have transmitted similar concepts, and have also presented doubt as an essential component of faith. Such manifold mysteries make room for parity, a presumption that diverse lifestances can each capture something invaluable, but none can claim exhaustive authority, exclusive knowledge, comprehensive understanding, or absolute certainty. The truths we are able to grasp are partial and provisional. Ambiguity liberates us from worrying that those who do not agree with us are intellectually or morally deficient. We may not be climbing the same mountain, but we are all still mid-ascent.

One can also argue that difference is necessary. There is the ontological observation: given the role of culture in religion and the breadth of human cultures, there must be a plurality of lifestances. There is also a qualitative reflection: monocultural entities tend to stagnate and can become tyrannical. Again, there is overlap in religious and philosophical arguments; Rabbi Jonathan Sacks reads the biblical story of the Tower of Babel as an anti-totalitarian text. Interpreting the dispersion as a rejection of the builders' imperial monoculture, Sacks argues that it is correction rather than a punishment or an etiology of cultural diffusion and conflict. The tower, with its unitary worldview and objective, runs counter to the natural proliferation of languages, cultures, and peoples described in the preceding chapter of Genesis – so God reestablishes difference. At the conclusion of the tale, Hebrew Bible begins the story of *one* people in relationship with its God in a world of plural particularities.[14]

As noted previously, sustainable ecosystems require diversity to thrive – a biological fact that applies to intellectual and spiritual life as well. Diversities expand our grasp of complexity and capacity to adapt. In Confucian philosophy, this is often described as *he*, or harmonization. Chenyang Li cites the ancient Chinese philosopher Shi Bo:

> Harmony (*he*) is indeed productive of things. Sameness does not advance growth. Smoothening one thing with another is called harmony. For this reason, things come together and flourish.[15]

In the Confucian conception, harmonization is an ongoing process, one that presupposes difference and the potential for conflict. Ideally, these dynamic forces are orchestrated to enhance all the components so they may achieve their individual optimal states.

This framework also highlights the role of history in the ongoing formation and reformation of lifestances, including the impact they have had on one another. Religions have always learned, borrowed from one another, and changed over time. Religious ideas

---

[14] Jonathan Sacks, *The Dignity of Difference: How to Avoid the Clash of Civilizations* (London: Continuum, 2002), 50–56.

[15] Chenyang Li, "Bring Back Harmony in Philosophical Discourse: A Confucian Perspective," *Journal of Dharma Studies* 2 (2020): 169, https://doi.org/10.1007/s42240-019-00047-w.

have never "always" meant anything; they have been fluid, multiple, and contested. Historical consciousness argues against privileging one path as if it has infallibly delineated the way for all humanity.

4.3   THEOLOGICAL AND SCRIPTURAL ARGUMENTS FOR PARITY

Boundaries between ethical and philosophical grounds for parity versus theological ones are blurry; discussions repeatedly intersect and scholars move between them. The categories of this chapter are heuristic. In this section, I assemble arguments that specifically draw on scriptural language or religious constructs, or that address theological obstacles to parity pluralism.

Many religious traditions delineate a particular path that is not intended to be universal, so they do not require a theology of religions that explains the multiplicity of lifestances. It is as natural as the diversity of flora and fauna on the earth. Given Christianity's universal aspirations and the dominance of Christian theology in the Western study of religion, however, its own work in this area has been very influential. Consider, for example, the exclusivist-inclusivist-pluralist paradigm that was mentioned in Chapter 2. It has been critiqued for privileging Christian questions of salvation, and for failing to reckon with the complexity of religious difference or nuances of religious thought. Paul Knitter proffers a fourfold structure in its stead with replacement, fulfillment, mutuality, and acceptance models.[16] Episcopal theologian Drew Collins resurrects the typology of Hans Frei, seeking a generous orthodoxy that changes the questions altogether.[17] Yet the earlier paradigm continues to shape numerous discussions of religious difference, including this one.

Most lifestances contain some teachings that support parity pluralism and others that press against it. The discussion here focuses

---

[16] Knitter, *Introducing Theologies of Religions* (Maryknoll: Orbis Books, 2012).

[17] Collins, *The Unique and Universal Christ: Refiguring the Theology of Religions* (Waco: Baylor University Press, 2021).

on the former. It is not organized by religion; rather it identifies various strategies for reading the traditions in pluralistic ways, using examples from multiple lifestances. As unique as the lifestances are, the ways they establish parity often overlap. This approach is inclusive but cannot be comprehensive in either depth or breadth. There are many published theologies of religions with rigorous analyses where one can turn for deeper study.

Divinely Intended Difference. One common thread is the notion that diversity is divinely intended, as indicated in Jonathan Sacks' reading of the Tower of Babel. This solves a theological conundrum for theists who believe in Divine Providence: it seems incomprehensible that God would allow countless people to be misled, so the diversity of lifestances must be part of God's plan. In the Hebrew Bible, the prophet Micah presents this eschatological vision: "For all the peoples walk, each in the name of its gods, and we will walk in the name of YHWH our God forever" (3:5). A covenant of Torah, which Judaism presents as its chosen path in relationship with the divine, is not intended to be the only way. Particularity is not exclusivity. Biblical texts portray God in relationship with many peoples, and rabbinic texts teach that the righteous of all nations will enter the world-to-come (t. Sanh. 13:2, b. Sanh. 105a).

Muslims can point to Qur'anic *ayat* (verses) that explicitly affirm a Divine purpose to multiplicity. In the passage cited in Chapter 3, the goal is not to prove who is theologically correct, but to demonstrate how your faith leads to right action: "We have appointed a law and a practice for every one of you. Had Allah willed, He would have made you a single community, but He wanted to test you regarding what has come to you. So compete with each other in doing good" (5:48). In 49:13, another purpose of diversity is identified: so that you may come to know one another.

Symbiotic Development. Mutual understanding has an instrumentalist value, namely peaceful coexistence. Many religious teachings also recognize, however, that engagement with difference is essential to the fullest development of our respective religions and

individual selves. Participants in interreligious dialogue and comparative theology repeatedly testify to this experience: encounter deepens
their understanding of their own lifestance in a coformative process.

In *I and Thou*, Jewish philosopher Martin Buber (1878–1965)
proposes that we can engage with all of creation, not only human
beings, in ways that transcend utilitarian experience and objectification. In place of this "I–It" relationship, we seek out the fullness of the
other in intersubjective meeting: "I–Thou." Buber also asserts that we
become our complete, actualized selves only by means of such I–Thou
relationships: "[A person] becomes an I through a You." To Buber, "all
actual life is encounter."[18]

These intuitions of coformation echo the Xhosa proverb,
"*Umuntu ngumuntu ngfubuntu* – a person is a person through other
persons." It is one common articulation of *ubuntu*, a concept that
embodies the African Indigenous values of humaneness, mutual
accountability, and an interdependency that is both spiritual and
physical.[19] Making it explicitly ontological, a teaching of the Buddha
asserts that nothing exists independently: "When this is, that is. From
the arising of this comes the arising of that. When this isn't, that isn't.
From the cessation of this comes the cessation of that" (*Assutava
Sutta, Samyutta Nikaya 12.2*). Thich Nhat Hanh (1926–2022), a well-
known contemporary Buddhist teacher, built on this foundation to
coin the term "interbeing" – an evocative framework for considering
the profound implications of our codependent existence and
development.[20]

The insight resonates across lifestances. Native American
emphasis on cosmic balance readily accommodates the premise that
the multitude of human spiritualities exist in productive tension and

[18] Buber, *I and Thou*, trans. Walter Kaufmann (Edinburgh: T. & T. Clark, 1970), 80, 62.
[19] James Ogude, *Ubuntu and the Reconstitution of Community* (Bloomington: Indiana University Press, 2019), 152.
[20] Nhat Hanh, *Interbeing: The Fourteen Mindfulness Trainings of Engaged Buddhism*, 4th ed. (Berkeley: Parallax Press, 2020).

symbiosis.[21] The Hindu monk Swami Vivekananda taught that a Christian is not to become a Hindu or a Buddhist, nor vice versa, but each assimilates the spirit of the others in order to grow in their own path.[22] Process thought, especially in the work of John Cobb, has inspired many Christian and other theologians to explore monotheistic frameworks of this principle. God is working in unique ways with all persons (indeed, all creation) to actualize goodness and beauty, and their diverse approaches are necessary for the fullness of our potential to emerge. Scripture and tradition are human, particular responses to this divine work. Marjorie Suchocki describes it as the "call and response" of creation and revelation: "[T]he peoples of the earth are being called by God to become a community of friends. Diversity, rather than being a hindrance to unity, is instead absolutely necessary for deepest community."[23]

Multiplicity Within the Divine. Ideas of the Trinity serve as foundations for pluralism (including parity pluralism) for Suchocki and other Christian theologians: there is an abiding multiplicity within God's own being. Those who reject parity still recognize that the Trinity establishes relational reciprocity as the very nature of God. It also models the practice of humility through *kenosis*, with Jesus' self-emptying act renouncing divine privilege in the incarnation.[24] Parity pluralists take it further. Diana Eck has written, "From a Christian pluralist standpoint, the multiplicity of religious ways is a concomitant of the ultimacy and many-sidedness of God, the one who

---

[21] See, for example, Rosemary McCombs Maxey, "Who Can Sit at the Lord's Table: The Experience of Indigenous Peoples," in *Native and Christian: Indigenous Voices on Religious Identity in the United States and Canada*, ed. James Treat (New York: Routledge, 1996), 47, https://doi.org/10.4324/9780203447437.

[22] Vivekananda, "Vivekānanda (1863–1902)," in *A Source-Book of Modern Hinduism*, ed. Glyn Richards (London: RoutledgeCurzon, 1996), 89, https://doi.org/10.4324/9780203990612.

[23] Suchocki, *Divinity and Diversity: A Christian Affirmation of Religious Pluralism* (Nashville: Abingdon Press, 2003), 18, 22.

[24] Wes Markofski, "Reflexive Evangelicalism," in *Religion, Humility, and Democracy in a Divided America*, ed. Ruth Braunstein (Bingley: Emerald Publishing, 2019), 47–74, https://doi.org/10.1108/S0198–871920190000036004.

cannot be limited or encircled by any one tradition."[25] Each religion realizes a vital aspect of the Divine and the fullness of God is revealed, not by suppressing or overcoming differences, but by living into them. For several Christian thinkers, this capaciousness is particularly fostered by the Holy Spirit, which rests both on those who believe in Jesus as Christ and those who do not. Humans are perpetually pulled to the transcendent, drawn to the spirit through difference in what the author of Ephesians calls the multicolored wisdom of God (3:10).

Jain tradition similarly speaks of the many-sidedness of reality and its reflections of the divine. Gandhi acknowledged that this teaching, from a tradition not his own, was transformative for him:

> I very much like this doctrine of the many-sidedness of reality. It is this doctrine that has taught me to judge a Muslim from his own standpoint and a Christian from his. Formerly I used to resent the ignorance of my opponents. Today I can love them because I am gifted with the eye to see myself as others see me and vice versa.

The Indian Supreme Court has ruled that Hinduism must by definition express itself through tolerance, recognizing that truth has many sides and paths toward it are many.[26]

Phenomenological approaches can lead to a similar conclusion. Druid and other neo-Pagan traditions, for example, generally privilege the experience of individuals in their encounters with the sacred over dogma or theological constructs. The riotous diversity of creation anticipates and affirms the multiplicity of our experience.[27]

Unity Amidst Diversity. Some religious perspectives emphasize an ultimate unity amidst diversity, mirroring the philosophical conviction of perennial philosophy that all religious experience is a

---

[25] Eck, *Encountering God: A Spiritual Journey from Bozeman to Banaras* (Boston: Beacon Press, 2003), 186.

[26] Jeffrey D. Long, "Anekanta Vedanta: Hindu Religious Pluralism," in *Deep Religious Pluralism*, ed. David Ray Griffin (Louisville: Westminster John Knox, 2005), 137, 146.

[27] Thorsten Gieser, "Experiencing the Lifeworld of Druids: A Cultural Phenomenology of Perception" (PhD diss., University of Aberdeen, 2008).

reflection of the One singular reality of the universe. The cosmology of Nigerian Igbo communities asserts the creator God as supreme, but sees all ancestors, spiritualities, and deities as serving the One in their own way. Hindu traditions have a long history of identist theology, conceived as many rivers that flow into one ocean. Ramakrishna Paramahamsa, a nineteenth-century Bengali saint, claimed to have practiced Hinduism, Christianity, and Islam – and discovered that the same God was directing his steps.[28]

At times, identist religious teachings are tied closely to the pursuit of peaceful coexistence. In the classic English collection of Bahá'í teachings, for example, the principle "Oneness of the world of humanity" is followed immediately by the "Oneness of the foundations of all religions." While the diversity of communities reflects splendor – "likened to the vari-colored flowers of one garden" where each enhances the beauty of the rest – the diversity of religions reflects unnecessary division: "The foundation underlying all the divine precepts is one reality. ... If we set aside all superstitions and seek the reality of the foundation we shall all agree, because religion is one and not multiple."[29]

Although this teaching portrays difference as misleading, other approaches embrace the paradox. Indonesia's national motto, *bhinneka tunggal ika* – unity in diversity, undergirded policies of religious tolerance in several Javanese ruling families going back to the seventh century. Facing destructive civil war, King Rajasanagara (fourteenth century) commissioned a reconciling *kakawin* (epic poem) by Mpu Tantular, who wrote, "It is said that the well-known Buddha and Shiva are two different substances – they are indeed different, yet how is it possible to recognize their difference at a glance – since the

---

[28] Kizito Chinedu Nweke, "Multiple Religious Belonging (MRB): Addressing the Tension between African Spiritualities and Christianity," *Theology Today* 77, no.1 (April 2020): 85, https://doi.org/10.1177/0040573620902412; Long, "Anekanta Vedanta," 137.

[29] Abdul Baha, *Abdul Baha on Divine Philosophy*, ed. Isabel Fraser Chamberlain (Boston: Tudor Press, 1918), 26–27.

truth of Jina (Buddha), and the truth of Shiva is one – they are different, but they are one, there is no duality in Truth."[30]

Mystical expressions of various lifestances set unity within diversity at the core of their metaphysics. Sufism speaks of *wahdat al-wujud*, the Unity of Being, in which only God truly exists. The world of ideas and things is but a fleeting shadow, reflecting a partial, temporary self-disclosure of Allah. The Jewish mystical tradition of kabbalah has a related premise: all of existence unfolds through the *sefirot*, a series of emanations of the Divine. All of existence is but a reflection of God, including our differences.

Limits of Human Understanding. Philosophy's reckoning with the limits of our comprehension also finds deep resonance among religions, which often identify epistemological humility as a virtue. The traditions are designed to cultivate faith, not certainty; its truths are truths to live by rather than absolutes. As described above, the concept of "learned ignorance" is an ancient one. Introducing a volume on intellectual humility in Judaism, Christianity, and Islam, James Heft describes it as "the acknowledgement of religious believers that what they try to understand – namely, God, and the ways of God – constantly transcends their ability to grasp fully and articulate adequately what they have experienced."[31]

From *via negativa* – the assertion that we can at best say what God is not, found among numerous Christian and Jewish thinkers – to Islam's teaching that we must wait for God to reveal the ultimate truth about areas of disagreement (*irja*), theologians repeatedly emphasize our limited understanding. Truth may be absolute and even singular, but we do not hold its fullness in our hands. This admission can be the ground of listening to and learning from one another. Jewish theologian Abraham Joshua Heschel (1907–72)

---

[30] As cited in Muhammad Imam Farisi, "*Bhinneka Tunggal Ika* [Unity in Diversity]: From Dynastic Policy to Classroom Practice," *Journal of Social Science Education* 13, no. 1 (Spring 2014): 47, https://doi.org/10.4119/jsse-687.

[31] Heft, "Learned Ignorance: An Introduction," in *Learned Ignorance: Intellectual Humility among Jews, Christians, and Muslims*, ed. James L. Heft, Reuven Firestone, and Omid Safi (Oxford: Oxford University Press, 2011), 4, https://doi.org/10.1093/acprof:osobl/9780199769308.003.0001.

maintained that the most urgent catalyst for engaging those who orient around religion differently is that our deepest experiences of faith reveal themselves to be "mere waves in the endless ocean of mankind's reaching out for God, where all formulations and articulations appear as understatements," and we become acutely aware of the tragic insufficiency of our grasp.[32]

Ethics. Ethical frameworks for parity pluralism also find expression in religious language. Values like hospitality and empathy are embedded in scriptural canons, for example: "Do not neglect to show hospitality to strangers; by so doing, some have entertained angels without knowing it" (Hebrews 13:2); "You know the heart of a stranger because you were strangers in the land of Egypt" (Exodus 23:9). Ethics as the measure of religious worth is threaded through religious narrative. One example is a story of the Buddha meeting with the Kalamas who are perplexed by the competing religious claims they encounter amidst the spiritual ferment of 6th–5th-century BCE India. He tells them to trust their discernment; they should not judge based on tradition or scripture or even logic – but on the ethical impacts that result from the teachings (*Anguttara Nikaya* 1.88–90).[33]

In some traditions, the litmus shifts toward piety – although hopefully true piety is linked to ethical action. Jerusha Rhodes notes that Qur'anic descriptions of religious difference are quickly followed by exhortations to manifest *taqwa* (God-consciousness). Incorporating this repeated trope in her analysis, she argues that Qur'an is not primarily a verdict on religious difference, but a guide to God-consciousness and proper behavior.[34] Similarly, the Sikh bedtime practice of *sohila*, reciting the prayers of three great gurus of the

---

[32] Heschel, "No Religion Is an Island," *Union Seminary Quarterly Review* 21, no. 2 (1966), 122.

[33] Judith Simmer-Brown, "Negotiating Conflicting Religious Claims through Inquiry: The *Kalama Sutta*," in *Words to Live By: Sacred Sources for Interreligious Engagement*, ed. Or Rose, Homayra Ziad, and Soren M. Hessler (Maryknoll: Orbis Books, 2018), 4–8.

[34] Jerusha Lamptey (now Rhodes), *Never Wholly Other: A Muslima Theology of Religious Pluralism* (Oxford: Oxford University Press, 2014), chap. 6–8, https://doi.org/10.1093/acprof:oso/9780199362783.001.0001.

tradition, promotes sincere faith rather than membership in the right group. Singing to the one of all forms and none, the devotee celebrates the gurus' teaching for making manifest the unifying light.[35]

Respect for the Spiritual Integrity of Others. Ethics also call for us to trust the spiritual instincts of others as an indication of respect for their intelligence and integrity. In part, it represents the desperate desire to exorcise religious sources of human oppression that so readily flow from claims of supremacy or supersession. It is also deeply rooted, however, in religious teachings. Islam's concept of *fitra* asserts that all humans are born with a purity of soul and a capacity to recognize both God and goodness (even though the tradition also states that people can be led astray). Hebrew Bible's charge to "love your neighbor as yourself" (Leviticus 19:18, cited in Matthew 22:39) can be interpreted to mean that, among other things, your neighbor's lifestance is to be honored as we would expect our own to be. The basic value of reciprocity – the golden rule – is found in almost every lifestance (Figure 2).

Many theologians see this as the natural and necessary implication of Divine love; the idea of limiting its fullness or its salvific potential to a single path seems improbable, even immoral. Liberation theology's assertion of God's preference for the poor often leads its advocates to affirm that the poor are God's people regardless of religious affiliation. Womanist theology likewise finds itself needing to make more room on the margins: love cannot be separate from inclusive justice. As Emilie Townes writes, "God's love moves out to grow in compassion, understanding, and acceptance of one another. It helps begin the formation of a divine–human community based on love that is pointed toward justice."[36] Ibn Arabi's medieval poem about following the religion of Love, cited in Chapter 3, evokes mystical dimensions of this conviction.

---

[35] Simran Jeet Singh, "Unity and Multiplicity: The Practice of Sohila and Sikh Theology," in *Words to Live By*, 148–54.

[36] Townes, *In a Blaze of Glory: Womanist Spirituality as Social Witness* (Nashville: Abingdon Press, 1995), 140.

FIGURE 2 "The Golden Rule"
© Encounter World Religions Centre, https://www.worldreligions.ca

In contemporary interreligious relations, parity pluralism often grows from the encounter itself, from the transformative impact of dialogue. A number of pioneers in the field began as exclusivists or inclusivists, but respect for their dialogue partners grew as did their appreciation for the beauty and wisdom found in other faiths. They subsequently sought theological foundations for parity. Prominent Christian examples include Wilfred Cantwell Smith, Raimon Panikkar, John Hick, Rosemary Radford Ruether, and Leonard Swidler.[37] Comparative theologians, at least those who recognize that such study must be done in ways that avoid essentialization or instrumentalization, often maintain that this sequence is obvious and perhaps preferred. Pluralism (parity or not) can be the fruit of dialogue even when it is not the starting point. The potential of this transformation, in fact, keeps some people away from interpath engagement – worried that the certainty of their belief will be diluted through encounter with religious difference.

Reimagining Tradition. Relationship with people of other faiths has also inspired theologians to reinterpret aspects of their tradition that seem particularly resistant to convictions of comparable value among lifestances. Historical critical study of scriptures that views them all as authored by human beings can diffuse absolutist claims for revelation. Yet many scholars elect to work *through* the texts, recognizing the powerful claim they continue to exert on adherents. Krister Stendahl has grappled, for instance, with John 14:3, "I am the way and the truth and the life. No one comes to the Father except through me," by examining the context. It is part of Jesus' farewell conversation with the apostles and they are tremendously fearful of what lies ahead. Jesus reassures them that there are many rooms in his Father's house, and that he is going ahead to prepare the way. When he tells them that they know the way to meet him, Thomas expresses uncertainty. Jesus' response is not intended to exclude; it is not the moment for grand theological claims. Rather, it is an intimate reassurance that they will know the way to God because they have known Jesus, and they have already experienced the truth of this mystery.[38]

---

[37] Perry Leukel-Schmidt, *Religious Pluralism and Interreligious Theology* (Maryknoll: Orbis Books, 2017), chap. 2.

[38] Krister Stendahl, "From God's Perspective We Are All Minorities," *Journal of Religious Pluralism* 2 (1993), 4, www.jcrelations.net/articles/article/from-gods-perspective-we-are-all-minorities.html.

The Qur'anic verse, "This day I have perfected for you your religion, and completed My Blessing upon you, and have approved for you as religion, Islam" (5:3), was often interpreted in supersessionary terms: Allah previously adjusted the teaching to fit particular historical contexts, but Qur'an is eternal and universal. Yet Looay Fatoohi, Tariq Ramadan, and others present more inclusive readings by focusing on the lexical meaning of *islam* (submission) rather than a "capital-I" faith; every religion revealed to the prophets or everyone who submits to God is on the right path.

No logic of parity will be satisfactory to everyone; despite some similarities, there are different issues within the various lifestances. The value in this summary is cumulative, demonstrating the creative possibilities that undergird parity pluralism.

4.4   CHALLENGES AND CRITIQUES

Arguments for parity among religious traditions also encounter substantial critique. The most obvious source is from scholars and theologians who feel that the reasoning distorts traditions in order to align with contemporary values. Religious teachings have always been interpreted and reinterpreted in response to their historical contexts, however. Every reading of tradition is selective, shaped by its spiritual inheritance, the will of the interpreter, and the influence of one's time and place. A close reading of almost any religion demonstrates that it was not "born" as an unequivocally exclusive path.

As mentioned above, identist strategies are criticized for failing to grapple adequately with the complexity of religious difference. Non-identist or "differential" approaches, tending carefully to the uniqueness of each lifestance, are sometimes faulted for lack of coherency and rigor. A related concern is that, by stripping out exclusivist claims, the stakes in the conversation that remains are severely diminished. It invites platitudes. One can rebut the latter charge by asserting that we have as high a stake in human harmony as we do in metaphysical truth. More broadly, however, these critiques frequently fail to engage the sophistication of the arguments for parity and the fullness of the interreligious discourse that unfolds.

(Remember that the summary of parity arguments here only scratches the surface.) While one can find facile reasoning and insipid discussion, they in no way typify the field.

Many of the challenges reflect those of Interreligious Studies as a whole. In trying to establish the ground of parity, for example, there is a tendency to essentialize religions – ignoring their internal diversity and the disparity between text and lived tradition. In addition, discussions may still privilege Christian concerns and conceptual structures. They may establish parity that works only for traditions that are theistic and scriptural, or neglect lifestances that have not been part of the "world religions" paradigm. This has implications for non-religious perspectives as well as neo-Pagans, Indigenous traditions, interspiritual identities, and others. When they do get included in discussions of religious difference, sometimes the demand for intelligibility according to familiar standards is just as problematic as neglect.[39] Another complicating dynamic, since these issues are intersectional, is that philosophical or theological hospitality may accompany cultural exclusion. Bias is generally grounded in race, ethnicity, caste, or class more than theology, so arguments for parity pluralism may fail to have the desired impact.

The potential to universalize parity pluralism as if it is a value-neutral theory of religion or the new "highest truth" presents an additional concern – still establishing hierarchies among religious values and systems. It risks replacing religious absolutisms with a reinvented Western cultural imperialism that continues to impose its values on the world's religions. Most of the publications and academic conferences promoting parity are based in North America and Europe, and it is no accident that the values align with the Enlightenment's emphasis on reason, unity, and egalitarianism. Even with self-critical attention to the dynamics of power, it is

---

[39] See, for example, Tracy Leavelle, "The Perils of Pluralism: Colonization and Decolonization in American Indian Religious History," in *After Pluralism: Reimagining Religious Engagement*, ed. Courtney Bender and Pamela E. Klassen (New York: Columbia University Press, 2010), 156–77.

potentially fraught to promote equality of religions without greater political, economic, and social equality among peoples and nations. The project may be blind to its own colonizing capacity.

Paul Knitter raises a different challenge: perhaps we are all inclusivists. We cannot help but privilege our own worldview and interpret other lifestances through our own lens. Constructing a theoretical framework for parity generally requires such acts of reinterpretation. Even if we recognize our perspective as a matter of personal preference rather than absolute value (as discussed in the section on ethics), we continuously process degrees of parity through our learning and encounters.[40]

Those who affirm parity pluralism, for instance, may have difficulty including among the "society of equals" those who see only their own lifestance as adequate. Including exclusivists might appear paradoxical at first, but almost all of the foundational logics of parity can make room for it. Epistemic humility suggests that we may all have something right, even if it is not the whole truth. Process thought sees God in relationship with *each* community in the ways that can transform their lives. Presumptions of our coformation press us to consider how certainty and ambiguity, boundaries and inclusiveness, illuminate each other.

Yet it is important to consider whether parity pluralism can or should include every lifestance. One seemingly straightforward criterion is to set those who advocate violence or coercion outside the bounds. There are other forms of harm, however, that occupy gray areas. Some might see gender equity as fundamental, thus excluding lifestances that advocate differentiated rights and roles or that insist on gender binaries. Others may question including a lifestance that allows abortion – or one that does not. They are not excluded from the interfaith "table," but moral non-negotiables can limit convictions of parity. Can the frameworks of parity withstand ethical as well as theological difference?

---

[40] Knitter, *Introducing Theologies of Religions*, 216–19.

These challenges do not undermine the foundations of parity, but they frame important questions for a self-critical position. The case below addresses parity in the civic sphere rather than the philosophical/theological one, but the issues are related. Individually and together, we have to navigate the question of boundaries.

Case Summary: "Invocation or Provocation?"[1]

Like many governmental bodies, the Chesterfield County Board of Supervisors in Virginia invites local religious leaders to offer brief invocations to start their meetings. When Cyndi Simpson asked to be added to the list in 2002, the clerk responded politely, "Sure, what church do you belong to?" Simpson replied that she was a Witch of the Reclaiming Tradition. Although the clerk took down her information, she received a letter two weeks later refusing her request. It read in part:

> As is the case with both the practice approved by the Supreme Court and the practice of the United States Congress, Chesterfield's non-sectarian invocations are traditionally made to a divinity that is consistent with the Judeo-Christian tradition. Based on our review of Wicca, it is Neo-Pagan and invokes polytheistic, pre-Christian deities. Accordingly, we cannot honor your request to be included on the list of religious leaders that are invited to provide invocations at the meetings of the Board of Supervisors.

Simpson's attorney sent a response urging the Board to discontinue the custom of religious invocations at their meetings since they could not honor the spiritual diversity of the community without discrimination. When the Board instead reaffirmed its policy, the ACLU filed suit in federal court claiming that it violated Simpson's First Amendment rights of free speech and freedom of religion, as well as the equal protection clause of the Fourteenth Amendment. (The Board did ask Christian clergy to cease invoking in the name of Jesus Christ, which had been common practice, to better comply with the stated policy of non-sectarian prayer.)

Simpson won in the district court but lost on appeal. The appellate decision cited *Marsh v. Chambers* (1983), asserting that the Board's policy is in line with its standard that "there is no indication that the prayer opportunity has been exploited to proselytize or advance any one, or to disparage any other, faith or belief." The US Supreme Court declined to review the case.

Questions for Consideration

1. Do you agree with the appellate court's decision that the Board's policy did not disparage a faith or belief? Why or why not?
2. Are there any lifestances that should not be given equal in the civic sphere? What criteria would you use?
3. Now shift to consider your own theological or philosophical perspective. Are there lifestances that you consider more or less "on par" with your own? Ones that are not? What criteria do you use and what do you need to learn to make that determination? How does your approach impact your engagement with religious difference?

[1] Adapted from Elinor Pierce, "Invocation or Provocation," The Pluralism Project (Harvard University, 2008), https://pluralism.org/invocation-or-provocation; and records of the Virginia American Civil Liberties Union, https://acluva.org/en/cases/simpson-v-chesterfield-county.

PART II **Meeting Spaces**

5   Meeting Difference Everywhere

Encounters with religious difference are everywhere, by accident and by design. This chapter discusses contexts of meeting in which encounter tends to be up close and personal, including family, congregations, college campuses, and the workplace. As diversity has grown in these spaces that were previously much more homogenous, it presents particular challenges as well as manifold opportunities for interreligious engagement – even without organized programs.

Diana Eck begins her book, *A New Religious America: How a "Christian Country" Has Become the World's Most Religiously Diverse Nation*, by describing houses of worship that dot the landscape: a mosque in Toledo, a Hindu temple outside Nashville, a Cambodian Buddhist temple and monastery south of Minneapolis, a Sikh gurdwara in Fremont, California. In the wake of the Immigration and Nationality Act of 1965, people from all over the world came to America and brought their spiritual lifestances with them.[1] The ongoing transformation of labor in rural areas, particularly the growth of agribusiness and food processing plants, brings some of this diversity to new places.

Canada similarly liberalized its immigration policies after World War II, and also increasingly recognized the spiritual diversity of the First Nations peoples who were already present. Europe's religious makeup changed as countries absorbed refugees and residents of their former colonies. Most Western nations have also witnessed substantial growth in secular humanist, agnostic, and spiritual-but-not-religious identities.

---

[1] Diana L. Eck, *A New Religious America: How a "Christian Country" Became the World's Most Religiously Diverse Nation* (New York: HarperCollins, 2002), 1.

North America and Europe, however, are *not* the most religiously diverse regions. While religious freedom is affirmed and a multitude of lifestances are represented, the historic dominance of Christianity remains because the percentage of people of different religions is still small. The sixteen most religiously diverse nations are in Asia, Africa, and Central or South America.[2] Encounters with religious difference in daily life have long been the norm in these places, and they are now the experience of those in the West as well.

So interreligious engagement is everywhere. We meet people of different lifestances in school, at work, and around town. Some people are delighted by this development; bringing the world to their doorstep enriches their lives. Many colleges and companies strive to create diversity, believing in its value. Other people are fearful, however, as it changes their sense of place. Or they simply fear making a cultural error, being uncomfortable or ill-equipped to navigate the differences that they face.

Meeting in the grocery store, the bank, or the park does not usually require much effort and the difference in lifestances may seem irrelevant. Yet there are non-religious institutional spheres where faith, praxis, and religious identity matter. In healthcare, for example, attitudes toward medicine, surgery, and end-of-life issues are frequently shaped by our spiritual orientation. Effective policing requires some understanding of religious practice about entering sacred spaces, gender, and dress. It is important to know, for instance, that Sikh men carry a knife (*kirpan*) as part of their ritual garb, not as a weapon. Foreign service officers should be familiar with religious communities where they are posted.

Professionals who encounter substantive lifestance diversity in their work increasingly receive some education to prepare them. The fields of social work and psychology try to incorporate cultural and religious sensitivity training and consultation. Chaplains learn to

---

[2] Pew Research Center, "Table: Religious Diversity Index Score by Country," April 4, 2014, www.pewresearch.org/fact-tank/2014/04/04/u-s-doesnt-rank-high-in-religious-diversity.

identify common human experiences like loss and healing, to lift up interconnected spiritual practices that can have meaning across boundaries, and to listen for particular needs that relate to people's lifestance.[3] Some of the most intensive settings for engaging religious difference, however, do not come with instructions.

5.1 FAMILIES AND CONGREGATIONS

As people increasingly mixed in social, academic, and work environments – and tolerance of religious difference grew – intermarriage dramatically increased. Partners discovered common values even amidst contrasting identities. In one survey, roughly half of all married Americans were wed to someone who came from a different lifestance, including half of those who identify as "none" who have married a "something." Although a percentage of spouses convert, approximately one-third of Americans remain with a partner of a different lifestance, and rates are higher among the more recently married. If one partner does convert, of course, it creates an interfaith family with the family of origin.[4]

The challenges are very real, yet encounter with religious difference through family is a powerful way to advance interreligious literacy and acceptance. Monica Coleman describes the multireligious nature of many African American families, magnifying the incentive for appreciative learning about a tradition other than one's own and forging deep understanding through sustained commitment to relationship. Harvey Cox describes his journey as a committed Christian married to a Jewish woman and raising Jewish kids as extraordinarily enriching. His exposure to Judaism is not simply what one might discover from books but a thick lived experience with nuclear and extended family as well as community. Daily life is saturated with the rhythms and rituals, songs and scents of Jewish life. It also makes him

---

[3] Dagmar Grefe, *Encounters for Change: Interreligious Cooperation in the Care of Individuals and Communities* (Eugene: Wipf and Stock, 2011), 138–39.

[4] Robert D. Putnam and David E. Campbell, *American Grace: How Religion Divides and Unites Us* (New York: Simon & Schuster, 2010), 148–54.

more reflective about his own faith – enriching his spiritual life in multiple ways.[5]

At the same time, family dynamics complicate things. As couples figure out how to navigate their differences, extended family often has a stake (and sometimes a say) in the matter. Weddings can be the first major challenge: will it be secular or religious? Who will officiate, where will it be held, and what tradition(s) will be observed? Many people object to intermarriage even if they harbor no ill feelings toward other faiths, and each lifestance has its own concerns. Islamic law permits a Muslim man to marry a Christian or a Jew (monotheistic "Peoples of the Book"), but a Muslim woman may not unless the partner first converts to Islam. The Church of Jesus Christ of Latter-Day Saints (LDS, frequently identified as Mormonism) teaches that families are not eternal unless they are headed by two LDS parents who were married in the church.

For a number of religious minorities in the USA, the issue is not primarily theological. People are concerned about assimilation, worried that their tradition will simply be swallowed up in the dominant culture. For Jews and others who represent miniscule portions of the world population, the threat is deeply existential: what if this lifestance completely ceases to exist? Even for traditions with hundreds of millions of followers around the globe, like Buddhism and Hinduism, families are deeply attached to religio-cultural traditions that root their identity; they want to pass them on to future generations.[6]

The desire to transmit one's spiritual identity to children often generates conflict for mixed couples. It is not unusual for individuals to discover the importance that their tradition holds for them once

[5] Monica A. Coleman, "Teaching African American Religious Pluralism," in *Critical Perspectives on Interreligious Education: Experiments in Empathy*, ed. Najeeba Syeed and Heidi Hadsell (Leiden: Brill, 2020), 14, https://doi.org/10.1163/9789004420045_003; Harvey Cox, *Common Prayers: Faith, Family, and a Christian's Journey through the Jewish Year* (Boston: Houghton Mifflin Harcourt, 2001), 2–4.

[6] Kate McCarthy, *Interfaith Encounters in America* (New Brunswick: Rutgers University Press, 2007), 127–34.

they are negotiating about how to raise their kids. Questions about religious symbols and rituals in the home, holidays, and affiliation become more freighted.

According to one survey, 35 percent of interfaith families elect to raise their children with no religious identity.[7] It may reflect indifference toward religion, a negative response to their own religious upbringing, a commitment to children choosing their own path when they are adults, or an inability to resolve the issue between the parents. Other couples pick one tradition for the children while honoring the second parent's path as distinct, but parents who are each deeply committed to their lifestance identities sometimes try to raise their children as "both." Religious leaders frequently discourage this choice, arguing that it is theologically confusing and foists onto the children a burden that the parents should have resolved, ultimately forcing children to choose between their parents.

Yet families raising children in two lifestances often report that the challenges are more practical than theological or psychological – how to resource the children's education, how to find time, what to do when schedules conflict, and so on. They are able to bracket truth claims, focusing on the relationships that cement family bonds and embracing religious practices that enhance spiritual or family life. There are some fledgling enterprises established to support interfaith families – most often Jewish-Christian blends. An organization called 18Doors, for instance, provides educational, organizational, pastoral, and other services to families and congregations. The rise of interspiritual identity, even outside of interfaith families, and growing awareness that blended identities have been common in many times and places, eases the path.[8]

Most interfaith families are not invested in broader interfaith community activities; they are just navigating life with the ones they

---

[7] Barry A. Kosmin and Seymour P. Lachman, *One Nation Under God: Religion in Contemporary American Society* (New York: Harmony Books, 1993), 248.

[8] See McCarthy, *Interfaith Encounters*, 148–55.

love. But religious pluralism is embedded in their being and it can have ripple effects on the extended family, committing them to pluralist values. Although religious bias still comes into play in some instances, the new traditions that have become part of their collective identity also inspire new learning and fresh attitudes. Karima Paustian shares her story as an example, noting that after she converted to Islam, her parents began to study the tradition. The whole family respected restrictions about pork and alcohol when gathered together – although for a while they assumed that, if her husband was not present, the rules did not apply. She acknowledges there were occasional ill-considered remarks, like disparaging religion as the opiate of the masses – but there was an effort to embrace the diversity newly embedded within the family.[9]

Because religion connects to politics, gender, and culture, almost any conversation can tread into sensitive territory. Congregations should also be aware of these sensitivities, since the increase in multifaith families means that the individuals assembled for worship or other activities do not necessarily share the same religious identity. Multifaith friendships mean that those assembled for lifecycle events represent a range of lifestances. Religious leaders should be aware of ways that texts and traditions present difference; scriptures or sermons that glorify the elect or demean non-believers now implicate loved ones. I tell my Christian students to imagine that I am sitting in the pews when they are preaching; it makes them read the anti-pharisaic polemic of Matthew 23 ("the seven woes") and other New Testament passages quite differently.

Congregations must also decide the limits of participation by family members who are not "of the faith." Can they vote? Can they hold office? Which rituals are accessible and which are not? What is the status of the children? Boundaries can kindle resentment and

---

[9] Karin (Karima) Paustian, "Interfaith Families: A Muslim Perspective, Part 1," *European Judaism* 53, no. 1 (March 2020): 93–97, https://doi.org/10.3167/ej.2020 .530112.

disagreements in the membership. Yet the presence of religious "others" within the community also stimulates individuals or segments of the congregation to retrieve resources within their tradition, like hospitality and humility, and foster intercultural competency.

In addition, congregations have historically been focal points for organizing interreligious efforts. They have developed partnerships with diverse religious organizations, established ongoing dialogues, hosted study programs and pulpit exchanges, worked together on common issues in the community, and more. Diversity within can help build bridges and deepen relationship between communities.

5.2   HIGHER EDUCATION

For many undergraduate students, time spent in college or university is their first or most intense encounter with difference. They meet people of diverse race, class, lifestance, sexual orientation, and gender identity; they also encounter a host of new ideas along with critical tools for thinking about them. Such experiences can be extremely challenging: "Research has shown that social diversity in a group can cause discomfort, rougher interactions, a lack of trust, greater perceived interpersonal conflict, lower communication, less cohesion, more concern about disrespect, and other problems."[10] Given this list of potential complications, why do most colleges and universities actively recruit a diverse study body?

Decades of research demonstrate that engagement with difference also makes us more innovative, diligent, and successful. In the context of higher education, diversity's most prominent value is how it prepares students to thrive in and contribute to the flourishing of a

---

[10] Katharine W. Phillips, "How Diversity Makes Us Smarter," *Scientific American* (October 1, 2014), www.scientificamerican.com/article/how-diversity-makes-us-smarter. Part of this discussion is adapted from Rachel S. Mikva, "The Change a Difference Makes: Formation of Self in Encounters with Diversity," in *Hearing Vocation Differently*, ed. David Cunningham (Oxford: Oxford University Press, 2019), 24.

multicultural world.[11] When General Motors filed an *amicus* brief on behalf of the University of Michigan to defend the school's affirmative action admission policies, for example, it argued that

> diversity in academic institutions is essential to teaching students the human relations and analytic skills they need to succeed and lead in the work environments of the twenty-first century. These skills include the abilities to work well with colleagues and subordinates from diverse backgrounds; to view issues from multiple perspectives; and to anticipate and respond with sensitivity to the cultural differences of highly diverse customers, colleagues, employees, and global business partners.[12]

Given the number of young adults who attend institutions of higher education, this formative work has a significant impact on society.

Schools vary regarding their investment in equipping students to navigate these differences; they also vary in their institutional commitment to a truly inclusive, equitable culture. Even in places that take this work seriously, religious difference often gets little attention among identity markers – despite the fact that it presents challenges for institutional identity, academic ceremonies, faculty representation, food service, housing, academic calendars, student group activities, distribution of resources, and more.

What do schools do about students whose holy days occur during registration, exam week, or instructional time? How well do they incorporate pluralist values into baccalaureate services and other

[11] See Sheen S. Levine and David Stark, "Diversity Makes You Brighter," *New York Times*, December 9, 2015, www.nytimes.com/2015/12/09/opinion/diversity-makes-you-brighter.html; Patricia Gurin, et al., "Diversity and Higher Education: Theory and Impact on Educational Outcomes," *Harvard Educational Review* 72 (2002): 330–67, https://doi.org/10.17763/haer.72.3.01151786u134n051.

[12] *Grutter v. Bollinger*, 137 F. Supp. 2d 821 (E.D. Mich. 2001), Brief of General Motors Corporation as *amicus curiae* in support of appellants, p. 2, https://diversity.umich.edu/admissions/legal/gru_amicus/gru_gm.html.

times or spaces that reflect a particular denominational history? Do cafeterias provide adequate food choices for people of diverse life-stances? How are minority religious viewpoints represented in curricula, syllabi, and library collections? Most schools have been slow to provide resources to minoritized religious groups; students often must rely on local volunteer clergy or provide leadership themselves. Humanist or atheist students rarely have chaplains, despite the rapidly growing cadre of "nones."

Meeting the needs of diverse groups can be complicated, as competing values often collide. In 2001, a group of orthodox Jewish students contested Yale University's policy that required all students to live in their coeducational dorms for the first two years of college; they felt it violated their religious commitment to *tzniut* (modesty). Conservative Christian student groups like the InterVarsity Christian Fellowship and Cru (formerly Campus Crusade for Christ) have bumped up against non-discrimination policies regarding LGBTQIA+ students as well as non-proselytizing agreements if they seek resources from the Spiritual Life Office. Denise Yarbrough describes an uneasy compromise they reached at the University of Rochester after extended deliberations with students and others: spontaneous conversations about religion or spirituality are encouraged, but evangelical students should not be "trained" to proselytize. They should not mislead or coerce their peers or use judgmental language (e.g., "damned to hell") – and they need to take no for an answer.[13]

How much support do schools provide in navigating these challenges? The American College Personnel Association (ACPA) Commission for Faith, Spirituality, Religion, and Meaning provides a schema that marks four postures schools take regarding religious difference: apathy, awareness, acceptance, and active engagement.

---

[13] Yarbrough, "Mapping the Discourse: A Case Study in Creating 'Interfaith Community' on a 'Multi-Faith' Campus," *Journal of Interreligious Studies* 13, no. 13 (2014): 50–66.

"Apathy" suggests that the school is largely mute about the role of religion, secularism, and spirituality in the education and experience of their students. Christian privilege goes unrecognized, and religiously minoritized individuals may interpret the indifference as hostility. The school likely espouses a commitment to inclusion but fails to reckon with substantive differences that exist and their importance.

An "aware" campus celebrates diversity and promotes tolerance, but students outside the normative lifestance are still guests. They may request time off for their holy days, for example, but there is no effort to examine the structural forces that continue to privilege certain lifestances and the impact on student experience. Minoritized students, faculty, and staff can tire of educating their peers and worrying that their actions shape how people think of their entire religion. Institutionally, religion is still seen as tangential, even though programs cannot adequately help students address questions of meaning while ignoring it.

"Acceptance" moves further along the journey, recognizing the value of lifestance diversity in pursuit of a liberal education – helping students understand multiple perspectives, privilege, and identity. Relationships between and among students, faculty, staff, and administration of diverse lifestances are characterized by respect, empathy, and serious engagement regarding the role of religion in their lives, their community, and the world. Members of minority lifestances have equal voice; they are partners in shaping the culture and spiritual life of the campus. In advancing religious pluralism, the schools seek "to dismantle religious privilege across institutional structures" and "to incorporate a wide variety of religious beliefs, not just ones that reinforce Christian assumptions about the nature of reality, deity, and humanity."[14]

---

[14] Dafina Lazarus Stewart, Michael M. Kocet, and Sharon Lobdell, "The Multifaith Campus: Transforming Colleges and Universities for Spiritual Engagement," *About Campus* (March-April 2011):10–18, https://doi.org/10.1002/abc.20049.

They address the increasingly pluriform nature of religious identity.[15]

"Active engagement" builds on the foundations of acceptance, recognizing the significance of religion across the curricular and co-curricular dimensions of campus life. Students develop competencies in interreligious literacy and engagement as a foundation for promoting pluralistic communities. They learn not only how to cultivate common ground and dignify difference, but also to address conflicts constructively.

Some topics are particularly sensitive on campuses today, such as the Israeli-Palestinian conflict. Megan Lane, who composed a case study about the issue, had to synthesize a hypothetical case based on multiple US campus incidents because the colleges she contacted declined to be profiled lest it exacerbate tensions. Here is a summary adapted from that case:

Case Summary: "When Causes Collide"[1]

Kinnamon University [fictional] has a reputation for social activism and takes its intersectional diversity work very seriously. The Movement for Black Lives (M4BL), organized in the wake of high-profile police killings of Black men in 2014, had widespread support on campus. One fall, as Nia Adams stepped into leadership of the Black Student Union (BSU), she began organizing a #blacklivesmatter march and sought multiple co-sponsors to showcase broad student solidarity in the fight against structural racism. After she presented the request at the Student Activities Council, the president of the Jewish Student Association (JSA), Rachel Cohen, committed her organization's support.

---

[15] See Rhonda Hustedt Jacobsen and Douglas Jacobsen, *No Longer Invisible: Religion in University Education* (Oxford: Oxford University Press, 2012), 26–27, https://doi .org/10.1093/acprof:oso/9780199844739.001.0001.

Nia promised to confirm with her and the other groups who offered to sign on after she secured authorization from BSU's Executive Board, a step required by their constitution for co-sponsored events. The Executive Board quickly approved the LGBTQIA+ Alliance, the Women's Center, and Students for Peace in Palestine. Nia recalled thinking that JSA was a natural partner, having been involved in many social justice causes on campus and faithful supporters of BSU efforts in the past. One board member, however, challenged the idea that a pro-Zionist organization could co-sponsor the march because the Movement for Black Lives platform explicitly affirms solidarity with the Palestinian people. There was some debate, but ultimately the board rejected JSA's co-sponsorship.

Nia was devastated by the decision and tried to convey the news gently to Rachel. She emphasized that it was meant to avoid divergence from M4BL's national platform and not to delegitimize JSA or depreciate its historical support of BSU. Rachel could see the care in Nia's message, but it still hurt. She forwarded it to JSA leadership, one of whom quickly wrote an opinion piece for the school paper.

Debate erupted throughout campus, much of it unfolding on Facebook. A Jew of color expressed fury at the assumption that all Jews benefit from white privilege and the way the debate forced him to bifurcate his identity. (Approximately 15 percent of American Jews are people of color, and about half the Jews around the world.) He also objected to the conflation of Jewish with Zionist, since not all Jews identify as both. Others argued that this decision was an affront to the long support of the American Jewish community for civil rights, and that one could support the need for the State of Israel *and* fight for Palestinian rights, as the JSA and many Jews on campus did. On the other side, students reiterated the M4BL platform, highlighted Israeli oppression of Palestinians, and protested the tendency to accuse critics of Israel of being antisemitic.

Questions for Consideration

1. How does this geopolitical conflict intersect with religion? How do assumptions that it is fundamentally a religious conflict distort the issues?

2. Imagine you are Rachel. Do you show up as an individual to support the rally anyway? What is your reasoning?
3. A Muslim student posted that JSA was the first to reach out when his mosque was vandalized. He understands that the national organizations may be at odds about Israel and Palestine, but he wants the campus community to find a way to stand together against violence and racism. What would you post in response?
4. Imagine you and a faculty colleague are the advisors for these student groups. How might you help transform this conflict into a learning opportunity for all involved?

[1] Lane, "When Causes Collide: Exploring Intersectionality and the Middle East Conflict," in *Educating about Religious Diversity and Interfaith Engagement: A Handbook for Student Affairs*, ed. Kathleen M. Goodman, Mary Ellen Giess, and Eboo Patel (Sterling: Stylus, 2019), 187–93.

It is important to recognize that the "4A" paradigm (apathy, awareness, acceptance, active engagement) presents markers along a journey rather than static postures. Also, colleges and universities are complex organisms, so various parts will be at different stages in their embrace of religious and other types of diversity.

Denominational or sectarian colleges can be anywhere along this path. In one regard, they start ahead of the pack because they recognize the importance of spiritual lifestance in student formation. While most of them historically had little religious diversity, that is changing. Some traditionally oriented Christian colleges, for example, draw theologically conservative students from other faiths who appreciate (or whose families appreciate) same-gender dorms, restrictions on drinking, and discouraging pre-marital sex. Even schools that elect to limit lifestance diversity – to reinforce particular values, deepen religious commitment, and encourage students to meet/fall in love with someone who shares their lifestance – can work with their students to advance interreligious literacy and the values of pluralism.

Recommendations are emerging to help schools advance along the spectrum.[16] They encourage making clear that the institution values all lifestances by incorporating the commitment into mission statements, diversity programs, and strategic plans. Senior administrative officials can highlight the importance of interreligious understanding and collaboration at major public events, show up for interreligious programs, and establish awards or internships that encourage interfaith leadership. Schools need to commit financial and human resources to support institutional progress along the path toward active engagement, a requirement that grows more urgent as multiple Religious Studies departments are being downsized or eliminated.

Policies should formalize academic accommodations, food and housing options, and other needs that regularly arise – along with clear procedures for addressing additional concerns. Conversations about broader issues of privilege, campus culture, and norms should include consideration of lifestances. Diversity training for faculty and staff should include it as well – not overlooking the important role of Student Affairs professionals (admissions, residence life, advising, financial aid, career services, and so on.).

Many schools are expanding interreligious programming in curricular and co-curricular approaches to student learning, and some are establishing requirements. Modules to advance interreligious cooperation or fluency are built into core courses across the curriculum – demonstrating relevance to health, journalism, business, social sciences, and other fields. Certifications of interreligious competency are available in graduate work. Professors are encouraged to factor lifestances into their syllabi and pedagogy. Course sequences, minors, and majors in Interreligious Studies are

---

[16] See, for example, Alyssa N. Rockenbach, et al., *IDEALS: Bridging Religious Divides through Higher Education* (Chicago: Interfaith Youth Core, 2020); Jacob Mitchell, *Interfaith Cooperation and American Higher Education: Recommendations, Best Practices and Case Studies* (Chicago: Interfaith Youth Core, 2017).

being established. Some schools offer campus-wide learning initiatives and collaborative partnerships across disciplines. Others have established intentional interfaith living communities or centers focused on interreligious understanding, akin to centers that represent other institutional commitments related to race, gender, or sexuality. Schools offer training in interreligious engagement for students, either for all those who are interested or particularly for Resident Assistants, orientation facilitators, and other student leaders.

While the work should not be limited to departments of Religious Studies, Offices of Spiritual Life, or co-curricular programs like Interfaith America, their leadership is critical. They are often best equipped to explore the complexity of religious identity and the diversity of lifestances on campus, foster meaningful exchange, and equip students to lead interreligious programs. Interfaith student groups have frequently taken the lead when a particular community has encountered hostility or there is religious conflict on campus. Students empowered to make change on campus will be able to make a difference in the world beyond higher education.

5.3 THE WORKPLACE

As mentioned above, many employers seek multicultural competency; it assists with global business and fosters strong client relationships. Religious difference plays a role not only in health care and other fields discussed in the introduction to this chapter, but also in banking, hospitality, and a variety of other settings. Do borrowers or lenders have religious concerns about charging interest? What services should a hotel provide for Sabbath-observant guests? What foods or food additives are ill-advised if marketing products to a largely Hindu population?

While such questions emerge across a variety of public-facing businesses, this chapter focuses on the more sustained engagement with difference in the workplace itself. Most Americans encounter religious diversity at work more than they do in other facets of their lives, and issues arise.[17] Accommodations for employees' religious needs can be a challenge for employers and co-workers. The culture of shared space often reflects the dominance of Christianity. Conscious and unconscious bias may make it difficult to establish a congenial environment for collaborative work and understanding. The role of religion in the workplace is in flux. Some companies undertake training for their employees, although most diversity workshops address race, gender, or sexuality more than lifestance. If you examine the educational materials for intercultural competency, you will discover that religion is still an undertreated difference of substance.

Title VII of the Civil Rights Act (1964) prohibits employment discrimination based on race, color, religion, sex, and national origin. Going beyond refusal to hire or promote based on religion, the Equal Employment Opportunity Commission (EEOC) issued guidelines that directed employers to accommodate reasonable religious needs if they do not cause undue hardship. "Reasonable needs" and "undue hardship" can be matters of interpretation, of course, so companies, courts, and the EEOC have been negotiating the meanings for decades. Here we do not focus on the legal standards but rather the kinds of issues that emerge in the workplace.

Lifestance-related conflicts surface a variety of competing concerns. Consider the following range of examples before we get to the case summary, recognizing that they are far more complex than can be relayed in brief outline. Notice where your initial sympathies lie in each instance and reflect on factors that influence your response:

- Meat-packing plants have attracted many immigrant workers. Somali immigrants, who are mostly Muslim, fought for breaks to accommodate prayer obligations. Managers entered into negotiations, but employees' departure from production lines can cause slow-downs and create burdens

---

[17] Molly Igoe, "Corporate America Leads in Exposing Americans to Diversity," *Public Religion Research Institute,* July 29, 2019, www.prri.org/spotlight/corporate-america-leads-inexposing-americans-to-diversity.

on other workers. Non-Muslim workers have at times complained that it is unfair to require them to pick up the slack (or, in one company proposal, all take a 15-minute pay cut).

- Seventh-Day Adventists, Church of God members, Sabbath-observant Jews, and others who alert their employers they cannot work on Saturdays have frequently been scheduled then anyway. Some employers are constrained by collective bargaining agreements or co-workers who resent filling in, making accommodation difficult, but others simply do not want to schedule around a Sabbath practice that is outside the "norm."

- Two Native American men in Oregon were fired from their jobs at a drug rehabilitation center because they ingested peyote as part of a tribal ceremony. When they applied for unemployment benefits, they were denied because peyote usage was considered a crime.

- A manager at a telemarketing firm who supervised several non-white employees claimed affiliation with the World Church of the Creator, which holds white supremacy as a central tenet. The company demoted him so he did not supervise other employees; although he did not act on his convictions at work, they were concerned that his beliefs created a hostile work environment.

- A Sikh employee of New York's Metropolitan Transit Authority refused to wear a hardhat over his turban in his job as a train car inspector, despite work safety requirements. MTA considered promoting him to a position that did not require a hardhat, but it violated the seniority provisions of their agreement with the union. Concerned that his vulnerability put other workers at risk as well, they terminated his employment.

- Abercrombie and Fitch declined to hire a young Muslim woman because her hijab conflicted with the company's "look policy" that did not allow headgear. Her family filed suit. A few years before, Costco terminated the employment of a young woman who would not comply with their "no facial jewelry other than earrings" policy that the company maintained was essential to convey professionalism. She claimed affiliation with the Church of Bodily Modification and sued, asserting religious discrimination.

- Pentecostal and other conservative Christian employees present a range of requests for accommodation. A therapist at a clinic asked, based on her religious beliefs, not to be assigned LGBTQIA+ clients or those having sex out of wedlock. A woman sought promotion to a job that required a coverall uniform but requested permission to wear a long skirt instead. A university employee refused to join the requisite union because he did not want to be part of their campaign for reproductive rights. A driver asked not to be assigned an overnight shift with a driver of the opposite sex. An office worker wanted to display religious imagery in her cubicle, and to distribute evangelical literature to co-workers. Another signed all her email messages, "Have a blessed day," and rebelled when one of the corporate accounts with whom she worked asked the company to keep religion out of the relationship.[18]

Religious values bump up against safety concerns, questions of fairness, comfort of clients and co-workers, company branding and profitability, and anti-discrimination commitments based on race, gender, and sexual orientation. Class and social power intersect, since pink- and blue-collar workers generally have less control of their schedule and less agency to shape their work environment. Politics also intersect, since political positions are often ostensibly grounded in religious values. One woman wore a button of an aborted fetus around the office, despite the objections of co-workers who supported reproductive rights and others who felt it was retraumatizing due to their experiences of miscarriage or infertility. She felt she was exercising her rights of free speech and religious expression.[19]

Courts frequently get pulled in to resolve such cases, adjudicating whether a religious claim is legitimate and whether companies suffer undue hardship in trying to accommodate it. Not surprisingly, the results are inconsistent. Most Sabbath and other holy day observance suits prevail; exceptions to dress codes often do not, but Samantha Elauf won her family's suit against Abercrombie in 2015. The peyote claimants lost and the World Church of the Creator adherent won, because his demotion was based on his beliefs rather

---

[18] See Raymond L. Gregory, *Encountering Religion in the Workplace: The Legal Rights and Responsibilities of Workers and Employers* (Ithaca: Cornell University Press, 2011), 15–20, 183–212; Douglas Hicks, *Religion and the Workplace: Pluralism, Spirituality, Leadership* (Cambridge: Cambridge University Press, 2003), 69.

[19] Hicks, *Religion and the Workplace*, 73–74.

than his actions at work. The truck driver and therapist lost, but the university employee won. At times, attitudes about particular life-stances seem to matter, but cases must work through the nitty-gritty of the legal codes.

Religion in the court system is addressed at greater length in Chapter 7. Here we take up a case that – like most issues of navigating religious difference at work – does not involve legal proceedings.

Case Summary: "Does Smudging Belong in the Workplace?"[1]

A man walked into an urban tribal office that serves the Native American community. He threatened to harm his ex-wife, who was onsite for the day attending an orientation meeting, and menaced staff and other clients as well before being arrested. The confrontation was deeply disturbing, and those present found themselves in heated discussions.

The next morning, an employee used a smudging ritual to cleanse the office of residual negative energy. Smudging is a long-standing practice of purification among many Native American peoples, burning traditional plants and resins (varying by tribe), so that the smoke displaces the troubling vibes and restores balance. One colleague immediately complained that the smoke aggravated her allergies. Others questioned whether the employee had been properly trained to do the ritual and was authorized by elders to perform it. There were questions about whether it belonged in an urban center outside of tribal land, and whether it belonged in a workplace setting at all. Two clients complained that it smelled like marijuana, comprom-ising their ability to remain clean and sober.

There were several employees, however, who argued that such rituals preserve Indigenous identity, values, and culture. It was import-ant for the center to uphold and model the traditions, so they felt that the smudging ceremony was a most appropriate response to the previ-ous day's disturbance.

Questions for Consideration

1. What are the competing concerns in this case?
2. If you were the supervisor, how would you manage the situation? What informs your choices, and what are the ramifications? Would you respond differently if it was a Native American employee in a non-Indigenous workplace?
3. Imagine a setting with intra- and interreligious diversity, where one employee requests an accommodation and others of the same lifestance think it is unnecessary or inappropriate. How do you respond? How else might intrareligious difference surface as a source of conflict?
4. What do you think about the argument that religion does not belong in the workplace?

[1] Toby Sawyer, "Does Smudging Belong in the Workplace?" Native Case Studies, https://nativecases.evergreen.edu/collection/cases/does-smudging-belong-in-the-workplace.

Unfortunately, encounters with religious difference in the workplace reveal not only competing concerns but discrimination as well. A 2016 survey found that 17 percent of Americans say they have experienced religious discrimination at work. The percentages for some groups are significantly higher: Muslim (44 percent), Hindu (41 percent), Jewish (30 percent), Mormon/LDS (26 percent), Atheist (25 percent).[20]

Religious bias that violates Title VII is frequently hidden in poor performance reviews, refusals to promote, unequal distribution of assignments or support, and/or social exclusion. Motives can be unclear and hard to prove. There are also cases of overt bias. Wallace Weiss was subjected to endless antisemitic verbal abuse at the hands of his supervisor and a co-worker at the US Defense Logistics Agency.

[20] Christopher P. Scheitle and Elaine Howard Ecklund, "Examining the Effects of Exposure to Religion in the Workplace on Perceptions of Religious Discrimination," *Review of Religious Research* 59 (2017): 10, https://doi.org/10.1007/s13644-016-0278-x.

After enduring it in silence for a long while, he complained to company executives. The antisemitic comments stopped, but he suddenly received negative performance reviews and was treated poorly in job assignments and blamed for delays. The company was aware of ongoing issues with his treatment but took no further action.[21]

This dynamic, in which explicit bias is limited to a couple of employees but the company shows itself to be broadly indifferent to the problem, is commonplace. Managers do not want to be bothered, or the culture favors the majority religion and minorities are seen as the source of conflicts. Accommodation issues also play out this way: people who want Sundays or Christmas off for religious reasons rarely have a problem because the national calendar is organized around Christian rhythms. (Countries with long-standing religious diversity often have calendars that reflect it. Eleven of India's fourteen national holidays are religious in origin: two Hindu, one Sikh, one Jain, one Buddhist, four Muslim, and two Christian. Singapore has ten public holidays: three secular, two Christian, two Muslim, one Buddhist, one Hindu, and one rooted in tradition Chinese religion.) Or consider how the presence of alcohol at social functions or Christmas trees in the lobby is often taken for granted as the norm, and the trouble is caused by those who suggest changing it. As discussed in Chapter 14, however, conflict itself is not the problem; it is often the only way to challenge existing power structures and rebalance the playing field.

Hostile work environments are generated in numerous ways. There may be disparaging looks and remarks, or simply an accepted practice that offends one's religious sensibilities. It might come from individuals or company policy. A Muslim manager continually sends Qur'anic passages to an employee who converted from Islam to Christianity. Posters of nude women adorn the walls in the common work area. An atheist is required to attend work meetings that begin with religious homilies and prayer. An employee frequently proselytizes, inviting co-workers to come to church and accept Jesus

---

[21] Gregory, *Encountering Religion*, 29–30.

Christ into their lives. Most of these behaviors are not designed with hostile intent, but intent is not the same as impact. The key questions are whether an employee experiences them that way and if it is a reasonable response.

Lifestance-related complaints to the EEOC comprise only a small portion of their caseload (4 percent in 2013), but it has been rising. Scholars attribute the growth to increased religious diversity as well as increasing interest of employees and employers to bring religion into the workplace.[22] Heightened visibility of both religious extremism and religious freedom claims likely contribute to the rise as well.

Growing interest in spirituality at work is spurred by several trends, including (1) baby boomers are aging, with spiritual questions becoming more important, (2) evangelical Christianity has forcefully engaged the public square, (3) the rise of unaffiliated individuals means that some turn to their workplace to fulfill needs historically tended by religious communities, and (4) there is cognitive dissonance between rampant materialism and deep knowledge that money cannot buy happiness. Humans search for meaning.[23] Making religion and spirituality a bigger part of work life may contribute to employee satisfaction, a sense of purpose or unity among co-workers, or improved performance – but it can also be a source of tension.

Some corporations encourage spiritual activities in the workplace: meditation sessions, classes, prayer groups, and company chaplains. They often try to establish a broadly inclusive generic spirituality or foster multiple avenues with lifestance-specific and interfaith employee resource groups (ERGs). The Religious Freedom and Business Foundation has for several years been ranking *Fortune 100* companies to encourage taking faith seriously as part of corporate

[22] Sonia Ghumman, Ann Marie Ryan, Lizabeth A. Barclay, and Karen S. Markel, "Religious Discrimination in the Workplace: A Review and Examination of Current and Future Trends," *Journal of Business and Psychology* 28, no. 4 (2013): 439–54, https://doi.org/10.1007/s10869–013-9290-0.

[23] Hicks, *Religion and the Workplace*, 28–38.

diversity initiatives. (In 2020, racial and ethnic diversity were mentioned over 1,000 times on the companies' public platforms, but religious diversity was mentioned only 92 times.) Its Religious Equity, Diversity, and Inclusion (REDI) index gives credit for faith-related ERGs, for addressing religious diversity in public documents and company policies, for communicating with employees and other businesses about best practices, and so on. They want companies to recognize the importance of faith in the lives of their employees.[24]

These efforts are not always as inclusive as they claim to be. Corporate chaplains are almost all Christian, with disparate capacities to think outside their own lifestance. The non-dogmatic nature of New Age traditions and aspects of Eastern thought may seem apt to introduce in the workplace, but they tread into issues of appropriation, and they still reflect the spiritual aesthetics of those who hold power in the institution. Religious individuals have sometimes resented the lowest-common-denominator approach; they feel it blurs particularity and trivializes religion.

There are also diverse attitudes about the appropriateness of religion in the workplace, including people who believe that it simply does not belong; although activities are optional, these employees may feel that their values are not respected. While a strictly secular workplace culture also represents a particular worldview, some efforts to accommodate religious difference slip into promoting religion. Freedom from religion is religious freedom too.

The benefits of fostering religion in the workplace can be debated. Just as civil religion is employed to form loyal citizens, workplace spirituality can be deployed to create loyal workers. If the office is the locus for exploring ultimate value, does it also become the place of ultimate giving – making it easier to take advantage of employees? Corporate chaplains present another issue. When employees have life crises or a co-worker dies, the chaplains can be very

---

[24] "Corporate Religious Equity, Diversity & Inclusion (REDI) Index," https://religiousfreedomandbusiness.org/redi.

helpful in processing grief. Yet they work for the employer; companies that provide chaplains to multiple businesses are explicit that chaplains are expected to side with the company in matters of conflict.[25] Growth of this corporate chaplain industry also raises the question of whether spirituality is perhaps not an adequate counterweight to materialism, but simply another human drive that has been commodified.

A percentage of companies do not strive to be inclusive, but seek instead to establish a particular religion; in the USA it is generally Christianity. Since they are not government institutions, it is not unconstitutional. You will find the identity expressed in mission statements, health insurance, décor, calendars, and other policies. "Honoring the Lord in all we do by operating the company in a manner consistent with Biblical principles" is the first article in Hobby Lobby's stated mission. It has led the company to refuse coverage of abortion or abortifacient contraceptives in employee health insurance (see Chapter 7), play Christian music in the stories, and close on Sundays.[26] Boston College, a Jesuit university that downplayed its Catholic identity for many years, decided in 2009 to install crucifixes and other iconography all over campus during a semester break. When people complained, the chair of the Christian art committee explained that they should be seen as a sign of welcome rather than exclusion, a message of God's forgiving love.[27] Two former employees of a North Carolina company filed suit in 2022, claiming they were fired for not attending mandatory Christian-based prayer meetings.[28] Employees who do not fit the mold can usually request accommodations, if appropriate, but the culture of these businesses is

---

[25] See Hicks, *Religion and the Workplace*, 27–47, 113–34.

[26] Alan Rappeport, "Hobby Lobby Made Fight a Matter of Christian Principle," *New York Times*, June 30, 2014, www.nytimes.com/2014/07/01/us/hobby-lobby-made-fight-a-matter-of-christian-principle.html.

[27] Jacobsen, *No Longer Invisible*, 10–11.

[28] Lateshia Beachum, "Two Workers Fired for Not Attending Company's Prayers, Lawsuit Says," *Washington Post*, June 29, 2022, www.washingtonpost.com/nation/2022/06/29/north-carolina-prayer-lawsuit.

proudly particular. Going beyond religion *in* the workplace, they promote religion *of* the workplace.

Most businesses, however – even those run by devout individuals – translate their religious values to a more pluralist idiom. Wegmans, a supermarket chain, is inspired by Catholic social thought to advance solidarity, subsidiarity, dignity of the human person, and care of the common good.[29] Jeff Swartz, the CEO of Timberland, asserted that he cut ties with a Chinese factory engaged in human rights abuses based on Torah teachings about treating all people with dignity.[30] The founding CEO of JetBlue, Jim Neeleman, claimed that his experience as a young Mormon missionary obliterated class distinctions for him and influenced many of the egalitarian decisions that typify the corporate brand.[31]

It is possible to have a faith-friendly workplace that pursues pluralist values. Tanenbaum, a non-profit dedicated to combatting religious prejudice, proposes a series of questions that businesses should ask themselves. Does the diversity policy include religious diversity? Does the company get to know employees well enough, including their lifestance, so that it can proactively address their needs and make them feel welcome? Does it readily accommodate distinctive dress as well as holy days and time during the workday for religious observance, making sure that employees know what flexibility is available and how to communicate their needs? Are individuals' religious observances taken into account when planning meetings and company events?[32] If food is provided, are the dietary

---

[29] Paul Marshall, "Can For-Profit Corporations Be Religious?" Religious Freedom Institute, July 25, 2020, www.religiousfreedominstitute.org/cornerstone/can-for-profit-corporations-be-religious.

[30] Drake Baer, "18 Companies That Are Extremely Religious," *Business Insider*, December 11, 2014, www.businessinsider.com/companies-that-are-extremely-religious-2014-12.

[31] Jeff Benedict, *The Mormon Way of Doing Business: Leadership and Success through Faith and Family* (New York: Warner Business Books, 2007), 1–22.

[32] "Religious Diversity Checklist," Tanenbaum Center for Religious Understanding, https://tanenbaum.org/about-us/what-we-do/workplace/workplace-resources/religious-diversity-checklist.

needs of participants sensitively addressed? How do policies foster inclusiveness when it comes to on-site affinity groups (ERGs), religious decorations in personal and shared workspaces, and office "holiday" parties? How are all these policies communicated, and how is the value of religious diversity embedded in the culture?

Fostering a pluralist workplace requires even more, of course. People at all levels should pursue interreligious fluency, and employers can provide opportunities for learning. We learn not only what might be taught in books, but also how the lifestance is lived out by those with whom we work – avoiding reductionism, and not asking them to speak for their whole tradition. We reach out with good wishes on their holy days. We recognize increasing inter- and intra-religious diversity, expanding our conceptions of "legitimate" life-stances. Inclusive language makes room for humanist lifestances as well. We become sensitized to social exclusion. If colleagues do not attend after-hours gatherings because alcohol is served, for example, do they miss out on the social networking that cements an office team? People should not be forced to compartmentalize and leave aspects of their identity at home, yet others' discomfort with religion in the workplace must also be respected.

Douglas Hicks, a scholar of economics and religion, promotes a respectful pluralism in which the presumption of inclusion incorporates limiting norms: non-establishment, non-coercion, and non-degradation. A Christmas tree in the lobby, for example, leans toward establishment of Christianity as the collective identity, but letting individual employees have religious symbols in their personal workspace does not. Non-coercion means that employees should not be required to participate in any religious activity as part of their job or have their absence counted as a deficiency. Even optional religious activities necessitate caution; if sponsored by a manager, for instance, those who participate may naturally become part of a more intimate circle with company leadership.

For non-degradation, Hicks offers the distinction between a "Jesus Saves" poster in an employee's personal office versus one that says, "Homosexuals Repent." Even though some people find both insulting, he believes the first passes muster – and a healthy office environment would allow for fruitful conversation about its intent and impact.[33] Where would the button with an image of an aborted fetus fall in this test? What about direct proselytization? Guidelines issued by the Clinton administration, still operative, are similar to the Rochester compromise discussed above: employees can invite others to join them for worship or offer literature but must also take no for an answer and do not persist. Yet how can any invitation not implicitly suggest that one lifestance is better than another? What about people who feel religion should remain a private affair? Hicks' approach does not promise a problem-free workplace, but it tries to find an equilibrium in our religiously plural world.

Juana Bordas maintains that fostering diversity and inclusion is a social responsibility, and that workplaces can be leaders in this commitment. Drawing wisdom from Latino, Black, and American Indian communities, she emphasizes the distinction between what she calls hierarchical pluralism and egalitarian pluralism – "come and fit in to the established culture" versus "your unique self becomes an integral part of our whole."[34] As corporate cultures become increasingly influential in society, the workplace becomes a powerful context for learning the basics of pluralism.

Families, congregations, campuses, businesses: Given that many contexts in the world today provide sustained encounter with religious difference, the work of interpath engagement extends far beyond designing formal interfaith programs like those discussed in Part III. Everything is interfaith now.

---

[33] Hicks, *Religion and the Workplace*, 173–79.
[34] Bordas, *Salsa, Soul, and Spirit: Leadership for a Multicultural Age* (Oakland: Berrett-Koehler, 2012), 203–04.

6 Media, Old and New

Media both reflect and shape the societies in which they are embedded. This chapter discusses diverse ways in which we meet religious difference in popular culture and information production – television, film, radio, museums, advertising, news outlets, websites, podcasts, social media networks, and so on. They all influence our perceptions of, provide information about, and at times facilitate contact with people who orient around religion differently. Reinforcing and confronting our biases (often simultaneously), they ultimately transcend their medium and impact interreligious engagement in the world at large.

We "meet" people of diverse lifestances through a variety of media. Television, film, newspapers, advertising, and other modes of mass communication have long delivered images and information that shape our imaginations. Newer media, transmitted through the Internet, augment the interactive possibilities and challenge traditional sources of authority by giving a platform to a vast range of new voices. Religion finds its way into each of these technologies. Suggesting a natural connection between media and religion, Singapore scholar Francis K. G. Lim invokes Heidegger's understanding of *techne*: "an application of knowledge that connects us intersubjectively with one another and with the material world, and in the process reveals to us our human essence."[1]

While each new technology has an impact on religion itself – the printing press gave access to sacred texts beyond clergy and

---

[1] Lim, "Charismatic Technology," in *Mediating Piety: Technology and Religion in Contemporary Asia*, ed. Francis Khek Gee Lim (Leiden: Brill, 2009), 2, https://doi .org/10.1163/ej.9789004178397.i-240.6.

scholars, for example – the focus here is on how the media impact *interreligious* impressions and relations. Here too, the medium matters. Consider the case of the geographically remote Hmong people in Vietnam: as they began to acquire radios in the 1980s, a Christian radio program – on the only station broadcasting in the Hmong language – led to the conversion of approximately 40 percent of the community.[2]

It is difficult to organize this chapter according to mode of delivery, however, because topics move rapidly between platforms. Categories of news and entertainment also repeatedly intersect. Pixar/Disney's 2017 film *Coco*, incorporating the Mexican celebration of *Día de los Muertos* (Day of the Dead) offers one example. Christian press (print and digital) debated whether parents should bring their children to see the film; some claimed it was not consistent with Christian spiritual teaching, but others valued how Catholic celebration of the saints was incorporated into Indigenous cultural traditions. News outlets addressed issues of religio-cultural authenticity, respect, and the potential for appropriation or exploitation. These questions, in turn, spawned exchanges on social media networks. And *Día de los Muertos* celebrations multiplied, including many people who were neither Mexican nor Catholic.

Given such multimedia interchange, the chapter is instead organized around three broad impacts that media have as they introduce religious difference. (1) They indelibly shape our impressions of religious others in ways that are deliberate and incidental, registering on conscious and subconscious levels. (2) They provide multiple forums for transmitting information, with varying quality and purposes. (3) They lead to interreligious contact and conversation – through online forums and comments, social media networks, fansites, and community organizing efforts.

---

[2] Ngo Thi Thanh Tam, "The 'Short-Waved' Faith: Christian Broadcasting and Protestant Conversion of the Hmong in Vietnam," in *Mediating Piety*, 139–58, https://doi.org/10.1163/ej.9789004178397.i-240.63.

The power of these interpath encounters is substantial, enhanced by their capacity to vivify religious difference through memorable images, sounds, spaces, and stories. They are particularly influential when the participants/recipients are not well-versed in traditions other than their own. Think of a lifestance that you do not know much about and discern how your basic view of them was formed. My first introduction to the Amish was through the film *Witness*, for instance, and my knowledge of Scientology is based on various news reports when someone leaves the fold. I have no personal relationships, focused study, or direct experience; my perspective is entirely formed by media.

The discussion of *Coco* above illuminates another important dynamic in considering the power of media, at least in societies where they are not government-controlled. Communication Professor Ruth Tsuria describes media as the locus of "Foucauldian discourse, a site of struggle, in which norms and concepts are negotiated."[3] Regarding religion, they create an important social space in which people and institutions argue the presentation of diverse lifestances, the challenges of interfaith encounter, the value of pluralism, and the meanings of religion itself. Disney is both a reflection of social norms and a shaper of them; its broad, multimedia impact makes it a natural mirror for us all to participate in this cultural negotiation.

The struggle is often implicit, constituted by differing images, discrete sources of information, and competing agendas. Material related to Islam in new media, for instance, ranges from polemical anti-Muslim websites and Twitter hate speech to content-rich explorations of Islamic traditions, from slick propaganda videos produced by Daesh/ISIS to the social media campaign #NotInMyName, from serious analysis about Islamophobia to the satirical #MuslimApologies thread that lampoons the continual demand for Muslims to go on

---

[3] Tsuria, "The Space between Us: Considering Online Media for Interreligious Dialogue," *Religion* 50, no. 3 (2020): 438, https://doi.org/10.1080/0048721X.2020 .1754598.

record against acts of terror. (The latter's humor is found in apologizing for everything that might connect to Muslims: "Sorry for trigonometry and astronomy," "Sorry for WW1 and WW2, just in case.") The contest is sometimes in the background, as was literally the case when graffiti artists were hired in 2015 to decorate a *Homeland* set with Arabic pro-Assad slogans. Instead, they inscribed messages critiquing the series for its demonization of Arabs and Muslims – but none of the producers knew the difference.[4]

It is through such contestation that society's dispositions take shape and evolve. Media both contribute to and are influenced by what sociologist Pierre Bourdieu calls the "habitus," the durable but not immutable norms that are shaped by past events and current conceptions, individual will and social structures. These dispositions are repeatedly reinforced (and occasionally challenged) through modes of cultural production and a person's feelings, thoughts, and actions.[5] Religious and interreligious elements constitute a substantial dimension of this habitus.

6.1   INFLUENCING PERCEPTIONS

The first question that shapes perceptions of religious difference is: Who is visible and who is not? Representation in news and popular culture matters; it is both an affirmation that you "count" in society and a window into understanding your worldview. In enables your voice to shape the habitus. The constellation of social media campaigns that protested the dominance of white men in media, including #OscarsSoWhite, Time's Up, and #WhiteWashedOUT, illustrates the importance attached to representation.

[4] Sophia Rose Arjana, "Monstrous Muslims: Historical Anxieties and Future Trends," in *Religion and Popular Culture in America*, 3rd ed., ed. Bruce David Forbes and Jeffrey H. Mahan (Berkeley: University of California Press, 2017), 94–95, https://doi.org/10.1525/9780520965225-007.

[5] Bourdieu, *The Logic of Practice*, trans. Richard Nice (Stanford: Stanford University Press, 1990), 52–65.

When minority lifestances do appear, it is hard not to oversimplify. A newspaper article has a limited number of inches; even online, editors must calculate for the limited attention span of most readers. A television series presents a finite number of characters that we care about in showcasing lived religion, so our understanding will be based on their perspective and our relationship to them. These constraints foster stereotypes – generalized beliefs about categories of people. They rely on the habitus to fill in the blanks.

Unfortunately, the habitus is replete with biases, many of them replicated unconsciously in the media. The simple choice of an ultra-orthodox Jewish man to represent Judaism visually – with his long black coat, *shtreimel* (fur hat), and tightly curled *peyot* (sidelocks) – reinforces conceptions of the religion's archaism and strangeness. The antisocial behavior and narcissism of Dr. Gregory House, the title character of a television series, confirms the prejudice that atheism is an amoral pathology.[6] These messages may be inadvertent, but they grow from the habitus of American culture. Language, too, draws from a socially constructed reservoir. Thus Western media generally refer to moderate or radical/fundamentalist Muslims, but identify Christians as progressive or conservative/devout. (For extended treatment of anti-Muslim bias, see Chapter 8.)

Minority stereotypes are frequently unflattering – neurotic Jewish men, Asian "tiger" moms, Muslim terrorists, and so on. Even positive images can be problematic, for example, the noble "savage" or the technically savvy secularized Hindu. The sexy, demon-battling witches of *Charmed* are an improvement on the warty, green villain of *The Wizard of Oz*, but neither is representative of real-life witches. News coverage of the "West Memphis Three" (1994), three teens convicted of murder, conflated Wicca with Satanism – a distortion that persists. Recognition of the problem prompted a rash of stories

---

[6] S. Elizabeth Bird, "True Believers and Atheists Need Not Apply: Faith and Mainstream Television Drama," in *Small Screen, Big Picture: Television and Lived Religion*, ed. Diane Winston (Waco: Baylor University Press, 2009), 30–32.

that "tamed witches into nature-loving, cookie-baking neighbors" by reporters who seemed more committed to eclipsing difference than equipping people to respect it.[7]

There is value in media that help us transcend religious difference. When Nadiya Hussain won *The Great British Bake-Off* in 2015, it was deeply humanizing for viewers to meet this hijab-wearing Muslim woman as a chef demonstrating her extraordinary skill rather than as a religious Other. When Nabil Abdulrashid won the Golden Buzzer in *Britain's Got Talent* in 2020, however, he was able to connect with the audience *in relation to* his Muslim identity, which he incorporated into his stand-up routine. A Black man of Nigerian descent, he used humor to mediate his multiple categories of otherness. Although both individuals dismantled stereotypes by jumping into the heart of British pop culture, actively engaging religious difference can be particularly effective in advancing interreligious understanding.

There are numerous examples in which media self-consciously try to challenge the public's conceptions of religious others. *Big Love* offered a sympathetic portrayal of a polygamous fundamentalist LDS family, raising broader social questions about what constitutes family, faithfulness, or normal. Coca-Cola's multilingual rendering of "America the Beautiful," an ad aired during both the Olympics and the Super Bowl, included visible religious difference to convey how the country's human diversity is part of its beauty; the company also ran a Ramadan campaign in the Middle East that included the slogan "Labels are for cans, not for people." When Balbir Singh Sodhi was shot in Phoenix on September 15, 2001, because the murderer mistook his Sikh garb for that of a Muslim, there was a flurry of news reports about Sikhs and Sikhism, trying to educate the American public.

Satirizing American illiteracy when it comes to religious diversity is another way of confronting the habitus, as demonstrated by the

---

[7] Sarah M. Pike, "Wicca in the News," in *The Oxford Handbook of Religion and the American News Media*, ed. Diane Winston (Oxford: Oxford University Press, 2012), 291, https://doi.org/10.1093/oxfordhb/9780195395068.013.0019.

character of Homer on the long-running cartoon, *The Simpsons*. In one episode, the family's Jewish friend comes over for dinner and offers a Hebrew blessing when asked to say grace; Homer bursts out laughing because he thinks it is just gibberish. A recurring Hindu character named Apu, who manages the Kwik-E Mart, shows Homer his shrine to Ganesha, the god of worldly wisdom. Homer's response is to offer the elephant-headed deity a peanut – a clear indictment of American ignorance about Hindu traditions and interreligious sensitivity.[8]

These efforts to confront the habitus can be found around the world. *Umm Haroun* (Mother of Aaron) is set in Kuwait in the 1940s and 1950s, when Jewish communities were still living across the Arab world. It portrays peaceful relationships between Muslim, Jewish, and Christian neighbors; interfaith love affairs; and Jewish midwives engaged by people of all faiths. MBC, a Dubai-based Saudi-owned satellite network, aired the show during Ramadan (2020) when television viewing is high as families break their day-long fast. They also aired *Makhraj 7* (Exit 7), a comedy series that includes an online friendship between a Saudi child and an Israeli child, creating space for the adult characters to debate the question of normalizing relations with Israel. Both shows ignited a fair amount of controversy, generating news reports and heated exchanges on social media. MBC's spokesman Mazen Hayek remarked, "If the choice is between a stereotypical image of the Arab world and one where MBC shows tolerance, mutual living and meetings between religions and cultures, then so be it ... At least we would be helping to heal wounds and bring people together."[9]

---

[8] See Bryan Stone, "Interfaith Encounters in Popular Culture," *Journal of Religion and Popular Culture* 25, no. 3 (2013): 406–07, https://doi.org/10.3138/jrpc.25.3.403.

[9] Lina Molokotos-Liederman, "The Role of Popular Culture in the Interfaith Encounter: A Soft Power?," Woolf Institute, June 15, 2020, www.woolf.cam.ac.uk/blog/the-role-of-popular-culture-in-the-interfaith-encounter-a-soft-power; Ali Younes, "Saudi TV Network Accused of 'Promoting Normalisation' with Israel," *Al Jazeera*, May 7, 2020, www.aljazeera.com/features/2020/5/7/saudi-tv-network-accused-of-promoting-normalisation-with-israel.

Not uncommonly, media simultaneously challenge and reproduce tropes about religious difference. My introduction to the Amish culture in *Witness*, for example, was sympathetic but definitely exoticized the community. *Pocahontas* defied the old narrative of primitive natives and white saviors and briefly acknowledged the exploitative ambitions of colonial conquest, but it perpetuated historical distortions, portrayed several native characters as animals, and stumbled into appropriation and romanticization. The film *Sex and the City 2* may have been trying to take on Western bias against Islam as it shuttled the dynamic quartet to Abu Dhabi. Yet Carrie could not help but stare at a woman wearing a *niqab* and eating french fries, amazed at the commitment required to lift the veil for each fry. The film reveled in its assumptions of Western cultural superiority as the group of Muslim women who rescued the hapless heroines from an ugly confrontation with men in the market (about sex, of course) revealed that they meet in a secret room to discuss American feminist literature and dress in high Western fashion. And it continued to fetishize Muslim women's garb as the friends escaped from the angry men by donning burkas – with one of the characters revealing a bit of leg to catch a taxi.

Efforts to introduce religious difference in popular culture are often more successful if they include *intra*faith diversity; the entirety of a tradition is not loaded onto the back of a single character. Introduction of Kamala Khan as the new Ms. Marvel in 2014 (comics) and 2022 (TV), a marketing and critical success, is a good example. A superhero teenage Muslim girl from Jersey City, Khan has a rich, multifaceted life; her faith matters but does not define her. Her world is populated by a range of Muslim characters, making it possible to explore interfaith and intrafaith issues with multiple perspectives – even though some commentators have expressed concern that the comic book heroine is too apolitical, an uncritical reflection of Western values. The Canadian television series *Little Mosque on the Prairie* (2007–12) was perhaps more daring in this regard, incorporating significant religious and political elements in its exploration of intrafaith difference and interfaith challenges. They were all played for humor, which creator Zarqa Nawaz thinks is one of the most effective ways to break down barriers.

It is not surprising that both projects mentioned above were created by Muslims. Without asserting that people should tell stories only about their own communities, we can readily affirm the value of diversified newsrooms and studios. Creators of media content who know lifestances from the inside – from hip-hop to feature films, from news desks to podcast productions – can complexify the images we see and hear.

Media's focus on conflict presents additional issues for meeting religious difference in this sphere. There is the news adage, "If it bleeds, it leads." Not all stories are quite that dire, but there is far more coverage of religious conflict than of projects promoting religious understanding. The rise of Hindu nationalism in India gets more coverage than the country's extensive interfaith work or the fact that over half its citizens see religious diversity as an asset. The role of the Russian Orthodox Church in the invasion of Ukraine is investigated more thoroughly than the role of faith in sustaining Ukrainian resistance. Religious leaders who turn out to be sexual predators get a lot more press than the vast majority who faithfully tend their communities. Hate speech makes news; words of interfaith solidarity rarely do. Religious hypocrisy also makes news, but loving faithfulness does not.

Focus on conflict is not restricted to physical violence and open hostility: the role of religion in contemporary culture wars provides plenty of fodder. Even the ethos of modern journalism to project objectivity through a "balanced" presentation of opinions sets up a framework of conflict. Differing religious views on reproductive justice or the climate crisis are set in opposition rather than as part of a pluralistic framework that makes room for difference.

Drama and humor also require the spark of conflict to shine. So in *Little Mosque on the Prairie*, religious diversity frequently appears as a problem to be overcome. Religion in general is a source of conflict when it is a significant element in characters' lives. Shows like *Greenleaf* try to present religion's potential for positive and negative impact, but its Memphis megachurch community is still rife with scandal, greed, adultery, and rivalry because that's what makes entertainment. It seems intuitive that the repeated presentation of religion and religious differences as conflictual – in both news and entertainment – complicates interreligious engagement. Yet it can also highlight the work that needs to be done and move people to confront the habitus, as illuminated by the film industry in Nigeria.

Case Summary: Change in Nollywood[1]

Nigeria developed a burgeoning film industry in the 1990s that has become one of the largest employment sectors in the country. It is dubbed "Nollywood," second only to India's Bollywood in the number of films released per year. *Living in Bondage* is identified as the first film to set the mold. Framed by Pentecostal sensibilities, the plot establishes African traditional religion (ATR) as primitive, superstitious, and tied to Satan, while Christian evangelical faith ultimately prevails in the existential war between good and evil. These tropes repeat in film after film for decades, seen by some not simply as entertainment but as actual spiritual warfare.

In recent years, however, scholars and media outlets have questioned whether this portrayal of ATR is self-destructive, denigrating Indigenous tribal customs and village life. Christian cultural dominance has been drawn into question as multiple Christian leaders have been caught in public scandals. Agnosticism is on the rise in Nigeria, along with increasing interest in traditional religious practices among Africans and descendants of Africans around the world. When Nigerian lawmaker Timothy Owoeye was exposed participating in a traditional ritual bath in 2018, the public rose to his defense asserting freedom of religion rather than turning from him in disgust as might have been the case only a few years before.

Nollywood has taken note. C. J. Obasi made a short film exploring juju (2021), not as an evil force but as a power like any other that can be used for good or ill. Later, raising funds to produce *Mami Wata* about a water spirit venerated in much of Africa, he wrote, "She is a water goddess who brings health, prosperity, goodwill. She is the symbol of the strength and power of the Black woman, but no thanks to religion and colonization, she has been demonized." Abba Makama's film *The Lost Okoroshi* (2019) reimagines the masquerade, an ancestral spirit often presented as malevolent, as a playful and benign entity that enables the protagonist to undertake a profound spiritual journey. In a self-reflective quip in the 2019 sequel to *Living in Bondage*, one character mocks the old way of debasing ATR, saying, "What do you think this is – Nollywood? We don't do those things anymore."

Questions for Consideration

1. Why would African filmmakers have demonized African religious traditions?
2. What are the obstacles in unlearning negative tropes?
3. In what ways does Nollywood reflect the dynamics discussed above regarding media as shaper and reflection of the habitus, the role of conflict, intersections of political and artistic forces, and so on?
4. Can you think of other examples in which media have been instrumental in perpetuating bias but then (at least some) come to challenge the habitus? What catalyzes the shift? How effective are the media's efforts to change minds and hearts?

[1] See Daniel Okechukwu, "Old Nollywood Demonised Traditional Religions: New Cinema Says 'No More,'" *African Arguments*, January 28, 2020, https://africanarguments.org/2020/01/old-nollywood-demonised-traditional-religions-new-cinema-says-no-more; Jeffrey Mahan, *Media, Religion and Culture: An Introduction* (London: Routledge, 2014), 142–43, https://doi.org/10.4324/9781315777061; Prisca Abiye Gobo, "Nollywood, Religion, and Development in Nigeria," Semantic Scholar, June 30, 2020, https://doi.org/10.37284/eajis.2.1.177.

Navigating difference in media, as in all places, involves questions of power. Religious Studies scholar William Scott Green notes, "A society does not simply discover its others, it fabricates them by selecting, isolating, and emphasizing an aspect of another people's life and making it symbolize their difference."[10] Those who hold power in society get to define themselves – and to define others as their (inferior) opposite. There is a striking scene in Salman Rushdie's *Satanic Verses* in which a man who had been a highly paid male model in Bombay is turning into a tiger. He bemoans his own fate along with that of a woman who is now mostly water buffalo, Nigerian businessmen who had grown tails, and a group of vacationers from Senegal who were doing no more than changing planes in London when they turned into snakes. Another character asks how this happened and he replies, "They describe us ..., that's all. They have the power of description and we succumb to the pictures they construct."[11] In Rushdie's style of magical realism, the power to define is literally brought to life.

Assertion of cultural dominance depends on the creation of an Other because self and other are mutually constituted. This means that minoritized communities and their lifestances are often portrayed in ways that reinforce narratives the dominant culture tells about itself. Consider the evolving image of Buddhists in American media (recognizing that this summary is necessarily oversimplified). *New York Times* coverage of a Buddhist conference in Paris in 1890 ridiculed their practices, and many newspapers had regular uncorroborated reports of barbarism that helped justify the colonial project. With a mix of racial and religious bigotry that reinforced the presumed cultural superiority of white, Christian America, the *Los Angeles Times* published this dispatch from Canton (Guangzhou), six

---

[10] Green, "Otherness Within: Towards a Theory of Difference in Rabbinic Judaism," in *To See Ourselves as Others See Us: Christians, Jews, "Others" in Late Antiquity*, ed. Jacob Neusner and Ernest S. Frerichs (Chico: Scholar Press, 1985), 50–51.

[11] Rushdie, *Satanic Verses* (New York: Random House, 1997), 173–74.

years after the Chinese Exclusion Act (1882) forbade entry of Chinese persons into the USA:

> They repel one in every way, and I watch them as I would the gambols of apes or the antics of some half-civilized missing link tribe of heathens ... If in the heat of the anti-Chinese excitements in America some shrewd politician had only come to Canton, watched, studied and pried into the life of this crowded city, he could have gone home with an illustrated lecture that would have been the most forcible argument for the Restriction Act, or an Expulsion or an Extermination Act.[12]

Chicago Tribune coverage of the 1893 Parliament of the World's Religions (see Chapter 3) was more positive. The newspaper reported on Buddhist scholars with respect and even cited Anagarika Dharmapala's rebuke of Christian missionaries, who "go into the temples of the ancient faiths, where gentleness and love are taught, and revile and insult its teachers and the principles which they teach." Ultimately, however, the Parliament and its media coverage were celebrations of American tolerance – again portraying self through representation of religious others. And still the press was incredulous when reporting on an American who had converted to the "effete religious mysticism of the East." The dominance of Western civilization presumably required a muscular religion.[13]

Although Buddhist and Shinto priests were portrayed as rabble-rousers within America's Japanese internment camps during World War II, hostility lessened in the 1950s as key American literary figures like Jack Kerouac and Allen Ginsberg popularized Zen teachings in affordable paperback books (a new media technology!). Buddhism began to appeal as a counterweight to the shortcomings of Christian-dominated societies. Its exotic power was magnified

---

[12] Nick Street, "American Press Coverage of Buddhism from the 1870s to the Present," in *Oxford Handbook of Religion and the American News Media*, 278, https://doi.org/10.1093/oxfordhb/9780195395068.013.0018.

[13] Street, "American Press Coverage," 277–79.

exponentially in 1963, when an elderly Vietnamese monk named Thich Quang Duc set himself on fire. He was protesting oppression by America's ally, the Catholic-dominated Diem government, that had brutally put down a Buddhist protest the week before and killed nine demonstrators. The "Oriental monk" meme was born.

East Asians still get portrayed as perpetual foreigners, but the Oriental monk became a template for assessing American interventionism, capitalism, and Western culture. Jane Iwamura, an expert on Asian American religions, race, and popular culture in the USA, describes the typology:

> The Oriental Monk serves as a colored "spiritual caregiver" to the West. And attraction to the icon on the part of American media makers and audiences alike reflect disillusionment with Western religious traditions and the hopes and fears attached with alternative spiritual traditions of the East. American consciousness plagued by the demands of modernity finds peace and resolution through the Oriental Monk. Also present in the narrative is the vision of the "new man," or more accurately, the "new West," that has learned its lessons well and combines Western initiative with Eastern spiritual know-how.[14]

The 14th Dalai Lama currently serves as the paradigm. Although his first appearance in US media (1977) asserted that he received CIA payoffs along with a rogues' gallery of bad actors – and Tibet's treatment of its citizens was abysmal long before the Chinese occupation – he became known for his commitment to human rights. He was awarded the Nobel Peace Prize in 1989 for non-violent resistance to Chinese occupation and preservation of his people's historical and cultural heritage. Hollywood A-listers joined the Free Tibet cause. Given that one-sixth of the Tibetan population has been killed and

[14] Iwamura, "The Oriental Monk in American Popular Culture," in *Religion and Popular Culture in America*, 65, https://doi.org/10.1525/california/9780520291447 .003.0003.

more are enduring forced labor, the majority of the land's virgin forests have been clearcut, its thousands of monasteries and temples have been looted and razed, and religious practice has been outlawed – Tibet's Oriental monk par excellence makes a perfectly non-threatening spiritual caregiver to the West.

The Oriental monk is a popular figure in entertainment as well, including *Kung Fu*'s Kwai Chang Caine, Mr. Miyagi in *The Karate Kid*, Yoda in the Star Wars saga, Splinter in *Teenage Mutant Ninja Turtles*, *Kung Fu Panda*, *Avatar: The Last Airbender*, and *Xiaolin Showdown*. It is a notable improvement on yellow-peril hordes, sinister Fu Manchu characters, inscrutable Dragon Ladies, and a variety of gangsters – but the figure still serves as a tool to examine, define, and improve the Western self and society.[15]

6.2   PROVIDING INFORMATION

People are not simply passive recipients of media, of course; they make choices about what to consume. When they go online or turn to other media to get information about religion, it is most often about their own lifestance or their own formation.[16] There are many sources to which people can turn for inspirational and intellectual teachings through the lens of a particular tradition: videos with sermons and text studies, television and radio programs, sectarian newspapers and magazines, denominational and congregational websites, blogs and podcasts.

Although you can learn quite a bit about religious others by exploring materials produced for their internal consumption, the focus here is on media designed to introduce people to religious difference. Some have a conversionary agenda, such as Cru's Internet outreach ministry and Scientology's Super Bowl ads. Some are polemical: there are numerous efforts, particularly utilizing new media, that carefully curate information or disinformation to discredit

---

[15] Iwamura, "The Oriental Monk," 52–53.

[16] Díez Bosch, Míriam, Josep Lluís Micó Sanz, and Alba Sabaté Gauxachs, "Typing my Religion: Digital Use of Religious Webs and Apps by Adolescents and Youth for Religious and Interreligious Dialogue," *Church, Communication and Culture* 2, no. 2 (2017): 132, https://doi.org/10.1080/23753234.2017.1347800.

a lifestance. Hate groups that focus on religious Others often have professional websites, they produce films and podcasts, and they are active on social media networks. The influence campaign that goes by the name Project Nemesis disseminates material via their website, a Telegram channel, YouTube, Twitter, and Instagram. Identifying as a campaign against Israel that does not discriminate based on race or religion and giving the appearance of reasoned discourse, they nonetheless utilize antisemitic tropes, target individuals, and distort facts; their messages are regularly shared by alt-right groups.[17] (Criticism of Israeli policy is not antisemitic; see Chapter 8.)

The Southern Poverty Law Center follows several anti-Muslim hate groups such as ACT for America and the Center for Security Policy, both of which use media very effectively to spread their disinformation. There are also information sources that fall into the category of apologetics, such as the website Answering Islam, written by evangelical Christians who strive to demonstrate the superiority of Christianity. Their research is careful and their tone is generally respectful, but their agenda is clear.

These examples highlight the need for information literacy as well as religious literacy to discern the objectives and reliability of media sources. Watchdog organizations flag especially problematic websites and other media, but the range of purposes in producing religiously related content is broad. We are most interested in those dedicated to advancing interreligious literacy and the public understanding of religion. This work includes providing knowledge about lifestances and their practitioners, reporting news in which religion or religious difference is a significant element, fostering pluralism and interpath understanding, giving voice and visibility to religious minorities, exploring spiritually rooted values, and analyzing the role of religion and religious difference in our common life.[18] Examples

---

[17] Lev Topor, *ISGAP Report: Antisemitic Influence Campaigns: Project Nemesis*, Institute for the Study of Global Antisemitism and Policy, June 26, 2022, https://isgap.org/wp-content/uploads/2022/06/Project-Nemesis-Report-Lev-Topor-1-1.pdf.

[18] Adapted from Brie Loskota, "Understanding Religious Literacy Content Creators and Providers in Education, Journalism, and New Media: A Report for the Arthur

abound throughout the many modes of media, from professionally produced documentaries and major museum exhibitions to obscure podcasts and individual blogs.

There are many challenges in this work, including familiar questions like who gets to speak about a community, what lifestances are made visible, and how we balance understanding of lived religious experience with what textbooks teach about specific lifestances. Critique is a particularly sensitive issue, with many pluralists wary of saying anything negative about religious others. In addition, people usually want to present their own perspective in a positive light – so what is the role of self-critical faith in media designed for broader consumption? Avoiding criticism runs the risk of flattening under-standing and letting harmful ideas go unaddressed, but it is difficult to do well. (See Chapter 7 for further discussion.)

Bias also complicates the work. Implicit bias blinds people to discriminatory aspects of information they produce or consume. Confirmation bias leads to seeking out sources that affirm our opinions. Mark Twain offered the somewhat cynical insight: You can ignore the news and be uninformed. Or you can pay attention and be misinformed.[19] For those who report the news, the paradoxical challenges are more complex. Consider these examples:

Case Summary: When Is Religious Difference "News"?

In 2007, the Swiss People's Party (SVP) campaigned on the slogan "Switzerland instead of Sharia." It was a brazen anti-Muslim trope, conjuring the idea that Muslim immigrants were a threat to traditional Swiss culture, and it received a lot of negative press. Nonetheless, it

Vining Davis Foundations," Center for Religion and Civic Culture, August 31, 2021, https://crcc.usc.edu/understanding-religious-literacy-content-creators-and-providers-in-education-journalism-and-new-media.

[19] Barney Zwartz, "Religion in the Media: How Has It Changed, Where Is It Going, Why Does It Matter?," ABC News, August 24, 2016, www.abc.net.au/religion/religion-in-the-media-how-has-it-changed-where-is-it-going-why-d/10096622.

kept SVP in the news, and they won the most seats of any party in Parliament. (Its leader was not elected head of the coalition by Parliament members, however.)

In 2016, Swedish Green Party elected representative, Yasri Khan, placed his hand over his heart instead of shaking hands with a female reporter. To make physical contact would violate his practice as a Muslim, he explained. It made news. Members of his party were unhappy. Khan argued that respect is what is required, not a specific form of greeting, but he ultimately resigned.[1] The same year, Swiss school authorities refused to grant Muslim boys an exemption from shaking a female teacher's hand. A previous ruling had granted the exception, but media coverage created a national uproar, since shaking the teacher's hand is considered a traditional sign of respect in Switzerland.[2]

Questions for Consideration

1. How do you navigate the tension between the need for the public to know about dangerous hate speech and the media's potential to magnify its impact?
2. What role did media play in MP Khan's resignation? Should it have been a news story?
3. How do you navigate the tension between local customs/culture and religious diversity?
4. How might reporting about efforts to accommodate diversity create blowback? Can you think of other examples? How might media best navigate this problem?

[1] "Politician Quits After Refusing to Shake Women's Hands," *The Local*, April 20, 2016, www.thelocal.se/20160420/swedish-politician-quits-after-refusing-to-shake-womens-hands.

[2] "No Handshake Exemption for Muslim Students, Swiss Canton Rules," *Middle East Eye*, May 25, 2016, www.middleeasteye.net/news/no-handshake-exemption-muslim-students-swiss-canton-rules.

Media face another critical challenge: newspapers have been struggling to survive and have had to cut back on staff. Despite the significant role of religion in many news events, religion reporters were among the first to go. Journalists who are left frequently lack the training or knowledge necessary to understand religious perspectives, intrafaith diversity, and the thick, complicated ways in which spiritual lifestances are factors in the news.

Even language can lead to misunderstanding. When Pentecostal Christians gathered at the Capitol for a rally about abortion and family values, a *Washington Post* journalist covered the event, reporting, "At times, the mood turned hostile toward the lawmakers in the stately white building behind the stage." The article then quoted an onstage remark from one of the religious broadcasters: "Let's pray that God will slay everyone in the Capitol." It appears that the reporter and editors did not understand the expression as hope for an inbreaking of the Holy Spirit, presenting it instead as a call for God to execute America's elected representatives.[20] Journalists try to compensate for their limited religious knowledge by developing a contact list of experts, but the diversity of lifestances today demands a substantial network, and they still need to know what questions to ask.

Numerous projects attempt to address this problem. Sacred Writes equips American scholars of religion to translate their research for a broader audience, and funds partnerships between scholars and media outlets. The American Academy of Religion also tries to connect journalists with scholars who can provide essential background and insight. The website *Get Religion* focuses on how mainstream media cover religion and tries to elucidate what they do not "get." The Religion News Foundation (RNF) and other organizations offer training for journalists to improve religious literacy.

The Conversation is a non-profit news organization that invites scholars in a range of fields, including religion, to write academically informed but publicly accessible articles on current issues. Articles are published on its own website under a Creative Commons license, allowing other news outlets to reproduce them. Established in

---

[20] Terry Mattingly, "Getting Religion in the Newsroom," in *Blind Spot: When Journalists Don't Get Religion*, ed. Paul Marshall, Lela Gilbert, and Roberta Green-Ahmanson (Oxford: Oxford University Press, 2009), 147, https://doi.org/10.1093/acprof:oso/9780195374360.003.0009.

Australia in 2011, there are also editions in Africa, Canada, France, Indonesia, New Zealand, Spain, the United Kingdom, and the United States.

Efforts dedicated to religion reporting frequently have interreligious understanding embedded in their mission. *Religion News Service* was founded in 1934 as an independent affiliate of the National Conference of Christians and Jews, and it continues to strive for balanced, non-sectarian journalism. Now a subsidiary of RNF, it publishes on a widely viewed website and provides stories to newspapers, news magazines, online outlets, broadcasting firms, and religious publications.

Sustainability is a challenge. Although various religion media projects have had short stints in the for-profit world, most are non-profit and require foundation support. Lilly Endowment has invested millions of dollars in the Religion News Foundation and The Conversation US to facilitate a Global Religion Journalism Initiative. Other organizations, such as the Public Religion Research Institute (PRRI), the Pew Research Center, and the Association of Religion Data Archives receive substantial foundation support to provide quality data and analysis related to religion.

A few universities have dedicated centers, like NYU's Center for Religion and Media and the University of Colorado at Boulder's Center for Media, Religion, and Culture; these support valuable research at the intersections of media and religion. NYU's center also publishes *The Revealer*, which brings together the voices of scholars and journalists to explore complex questions regarding religion's role in society, geared to a non-academic audience; they look at how religion shapes and is shaped by race, sexuality, gender, politics, history, and culture.

Harvard University's Pluralism Project has long been a leader in the field, focused on public-facing information – from their online publication of *On Common Ground* to their rich curation of news and introductory material as well as their innovative case study initiative. The center's commitment to advancing *inter*religious understanding is evident. Many media projects also make this goal explicit, such as National Public Radio's (NPR) "Interfaith Voices," the *Interfaith Observer*, the *Journal of Interreligious Studies*, and the relatively new *Interfaith America* online magazine. Every non-profit dedicated to interpath understanding uses media in some fashion to build its brand and spread its message, sharing knowledge about diverse lifestances, amplifying voices of their practitioners, and publicizing worthwhile interfaith efforts.

Another challenge in the media and religion universe is the ephemeral nature of popularity. *Newsweek* and *The Washington Post* collaborated on a blog called "On Faith" that was one of their most popular projects. *USA Today* had similar success with Cathy Lynn Grossman's "Faith and Reason" blog – but both projects faded after a while.[21] So I might mention the popular podcast *Keeping It 101: A Killjoy's Introduction to Religion*, which has cleverly sourced itself for various college courses in religion. Or *Weird Religion*, in which the hosts (both professors) have found a magic blend of religion, strangeness, and popular culture to capture the current *Zeitgeist*. By the time of this book's publication, however, they may be forgotten. Especially in this age of new media, religion information sources must continually reinvent themselves and lure new audiences to have an impact. (NPR's *On Being*, a popular program hosted by Krista Tippett since 2003, might be an exception – although it has also had to adapt, for example, changing its name from *Speaking of Faith* to expand its view beyond organized religion.)

The continuous intertwining of religion and politics makes the religion and media landscape rockier. Coverage of the "Moral Majority" and other conservative Christian groups beginning in the 1980s increasingly made it appear that religious and conservative were synonymous in the USA. *Religion Dispatches* was explicit in its founding (2007) that it sought to challenge the dominance of conservative religion in media. It is not always clear how religion

---

[21] Debra L. Mason, "Religion News Online," in *Oxford Handbook of Religion and the American News Media*, 163, https://doi.org/10.1093/oxfordhb/9780195395068.013 .0010.

information sources navigate this terrain and how it shapes their content, however, and the rocks are always shifting.

Case Summary: BeliefNet and Patheos

In 2000, BeliefNet was launched with an enviable $26 million in venture capital funding. The goal was to produce deeply informed reporting on religion and to become a forum for America's intellectuals to debate the profound political and religious dimensions of critical issues facing the nation. Despite being the only major player in online religion news and reporting one million unique viewers per month, the organization declared bankruptcy two years later.

It had already shifted away from news as its central focus (a costly labor-intensive endeavor), and when it emerged from bankruptcy after several months, the site was transformed into a locus for sharing feel-good spirituality – although one could still find relatively reliable information on a wide variety of lifestances. It was owned for a few years by Rupert Murdoch's News Corp, and then purchased by BN Media in 2010, a company with evangelical ties. At that point, BeliefNet's content was reportedly sanitized and Christian material was displayed more prominently.[1]

Patheos was born in 2009, another noble attempt to provide high-quality material on religion. It began by publishing peer-reviewed articles and then expanded with lifestance-specific blogs. In 2017, it was also purchased by BN Media. There was an exodus of Pagan and other writers shortly after. The company had issued replacement contracts demanding editorial control and forbidding any negative coverage of Patheos or related companies. One of those companies, it turns out, is Affinity4, which helps raise funds for organizations including the National Rifle Association, Focus on the Family, and the American Center for Law and Justice; the last of these actively supported a law in Uganda imposing the death penalty for "aggravated homosexuality." Writers who pushed back had their blogs summarily deleted, as did a long-time Christian blogger in 2018 who frequently reported on scandals in the Protestant church.

Another exodus unfolded in January 2021 after Patheos instructed its non-religious bloggers that they could stay at Patheos as long as they focused on how to live a good life within their own lifestance and did not write posts critical of religion. The lead story on the website as they departed was "Don't Stop Believing: Faith for the New Year."[2] As an example of Patheos' non-critical stance, a search for Scientology yields numerous blogposts written by adherents about relatively uncontroversial aspects of their church, while any headline that suggests an oppositional stance has been disabled, linking instead to a generic page telling readers how wonderful it is they found their way to Patheos.

BN Media then created Radiant Foundation as an umbrella organization for its non-profit media ventures, including Patheos, BeliefNet, and several other wellness and spirituality platforms. Its homepage proclaims, "Every individual, every community and every society is enriched by faith. The Radiant Foundation seeks to create a healthier, more unified world by promoting authentic expressions of God-centered spirituality in personal and public life."[3]

Questions for Consideration

1. Do you believe that eliminating all critique of religion is the best way to cultivate interreligious understanding? Does it make too much room for dangerous religious ideas and too little room for secular lifestances? Is promoting pluralism at odds with deep religious understanding?

2. What is required for due diligence in vetting online media sources? What are your go-to sources about religion?

3. How do you address your own confirmation bias as a consumer of media information?

4. Do the evangelical ties of BN Media or its connection to right-wing groups discredit the sources in your mind? If so, what sources do you trust that might make someone else nervous?

---

[1] Mason, "Religion News Online," 158.

[2] John Halstead, "Why Did Over a Dozen Bloggers Leave Patheos?," *Huffpost*, February 6, 2017, www.huffpost.com/entry/why-did-over-a-dozen-writers_b_14603506; Dan Wilkinson, "Patheos Removes Blog of Christian Whistleblower," *Unfundamentalist*, May 28, 2018, http://unfundamentalists.com/2018/05/patheos-removes-blog-of-christian-whistleblower; Yonat Shimron, "What Happened to the Nonbelief Channel at Patheos?" *Religion News Service*, January

4, 2022, https://religionnews.com/2022/01/04/what-happened-to-the-nonbelief-channel-at-patheos.

[3] Radiant Foundation, www.radiant.org.

Many religious organizations produce their own media. The Mennonite community's work is fairly typical in this regard. Third Way Café was established in 1998 to provide online information about Anabaptists and Mennonite tradition. Denominational websites followed and Third Way has merged with the Mennonite Publishing Network to create MennoMedia with a variety of online and printed material. The United Methodist Church has a production company to help local congregations and community projects create content – mostly for internal consumption. They provide a recording studio, web services, and communications training to their members. Deseret Digital Media, owned by the Church of Jesus Christ of Latter-Day Saints, operates newspapers and websites as well as radio and television stations. The latter affiliates with a national network, inserting LDS broadcasts sporadically through its schedule and occasionally declining network programs that do not reflect its religious values.

There are advantages and disadvantages to these sources in terms of public understanding of religion. Appreciative learning abounds – clarifying how they would like to be understood – but there is little demonstrated self-critical capacity. A fair amount of self-produced media content seeks to proselytize or validate more than to inform. Still, they are frequently close to the communities about which they speak, avoiding traps of trying to teach from 30,000 feet.

6.3 FACILITATING CONTACT

Media sources of information can also facilitate connection. Individuals from small or minoritized lifestances often find each other online. Chinese Christians use social media to forge virtual communities and to create a space for exploring religion in their daily lives.[22] In the USA, three formerly religious individuals producing content on YouTube connected in 2018 and established the Faithless Forum. They had each been exploring how to talk to religious people they love about their atheism, embracing science as a mode of understanding the world, investigating oppressive aspects of various cults and religions, and grappling with how people come to believe what they do. One of them fled his hometown in West Virginia after posting a video critical of a local teacher for infusing religion into his daughter's health class; the hate messages on- and offline were terrifying. Atheists frequently encounter hostility, so Faithless Forum is designed to support atheist content creators, promote collaboration, and build a secular community. They have convened groups online and in person.[23]

Interreligious connections also unfold. Simran Jeet Singh has described Twitter as a way to follow what is going on the Sikh community, to educate others about Sikhs and the issues they face – and as a tool for advocacy, frequently reaching across lines of difference to engage people around shared concerns.[24] He currently serves as Executive Director of the Aspen Institute's Religion and Society Program, which utilizes diverse media to foster pluralism and examines the impact of faith on democracy and equity. The team not only produces research, however, but also draws scholars, funders, and activists of diverse lifestances together through their information-

[22] Francis K. G. Lim and Bee Bee Sng, "Social Media, Religion, and Shifting Boundaries in Globalizing China," *Global Media and China* 5, no. 3 (July 15, 2020): 261–74, https://doi.org/10.1177/2059436420923169.

[23] Nidhi Upadhyaya, "Atheists Find Community on YouTube – and in Person," *Religion News Service*, December 3, 2021, https://religionnews.com/2021/12/03/atheists-find-community-on-youtube-and-in-person.

[24] Walter Smelt, "Promoting Religious Literacy in a Digital Age," *Harvard Divinity Bulletin*, August 18, 2016, https://news-archive.hds.harvard.edu/news/2018/08/18/promoting-religious-literacy-digital-age.

producing efforts; their Powering Pluralism Network emphasizes community-building to amplify impact.

Media projects are frequently designed to forge interpath connections. In the wake of the 9/11 attacks, BeliefNet established multiple moderated forums to dialogue about Islam. There was a lot of monologuing as well, but it was an effort to connect people who orient around religion differently to work through difficult questions together. Interreligious organizations use media to expand their networking capacities. Webinars, all the rage especially during the COVID-19 pandemic, embrace the translocal nature of virtual meetings to advance literacy and pluralism on a global scale. Many are set up in open "rooms" so that those present are visible to each other. Zoom, Facebook Live, and similar platforms enable participants to connect via comments and chat.

Media messaging can also be a form of public diplomacy, a way of reaching out to religious others. Organizations, religious and secular, frequently disseminate greetings on major holidays, for example. The "Dear Hindu Friends" letters discussed in Chapter 2 constitute but one example. Even though the connection may be abstract, it is intended to affirm the value of one community relating with another.

Media can facilitate interreligious contact in less expected ways as well. Mel Gibson's *Passion of the Christ* sparked controversy with its negative portrayal of Jews, prompting a number of Jewish and Christian congregations to organize shared viewing experiences followed by conversation. Online fan groups of various pop culture productions with religious content or overtones stimulate sometimes substantive spiritual exchanges. Contact is not always friendly, however. Anonymity in online spaces and the faceless quality of communication can invite incivility. Creators of media content may find hate mail or worse if they strike a nerve.

People bring the media messages they have been absorbing into actual spaces of meeting – for better and worse. In our media-saturated world, we are often unaware of the elements in which we swim. Like the fish when asked, "How's the water?," we reply "What's water?" Interreligious encounters will already have a history, fashioned by information about and images of one another found in media.

7   Interreligious Encounter in the Public Square

In a religiously plural society, the role of religion in public life becomes an interreligious issue in itself. This chapter discusses various positions on the relationship of religion and state, and explores how interpath encounters play out in public discourse, public policy, public services, public space, and public schools. Because context is critically important, the focus is narrowly drawn – limited almost exclusively to the United States – while many of the issues obtain more broadly as well. Although there are many interreligious projects that focus on the public square, most of the encounters under discussion here flow from the natural ways we meet one another in shared society.

While the First Amendment also safeguards freedom of speech, the press, assembly, and the right to petition government, it begins with two interdependent principles to protect the freedom of religion. The "establishment clause" prohibits the US government from instituting an official religion and has served as the foundation for separation of religion and state. The "free exercise clause" promises that individuals may practice their religion without legal impediment. While these guarantees initially applied only to the federal government – and many states had official religions – its protections were gradually extended to restrict state and local governmental action as well. Translating these commitments to civic life, however, remains an ongoing challenge. The United States currently has the most diverse collection of lifestances on the planet and, among developed countries, it is the most religious. There has never been consensus on the role of religion in the public square, and associated issues figure prominently in contemporary culture wars.

Separation of religion and state serves a vital role in preserving American democracy and creates broad space for spirituality to flourish. Roger Williams, James Madison, and Alexis de Tocqueville all understood that keeping religion out of state affairs – and government control out of religion – fosters the vitality of religious life. It still allows people to vote for religious reasons and officials to act for religious reasons. At the same time, it protects minority beliefs from the tyranny or simple ignorance of the majority and allows freedom *from* religion as a viable lifestance as well. As discussed in Chapter 2, Danièle Hervieu-Léger offers an understanding of secularism in which religion is not eradicated from the public sphere. Instead, it shares the space with diverse beliefs, and no institution can lay claim to a monopoly of meaning.

Yet some people believe that the establishment clause has made the public arena an *anti*-religious space, compromising their free exercise. Experiencing the two clauses in tension rather than symbiosis, they argue that "religious citizens are forced to split off vital components of their personalities," and that religious expression "has been pushed to the margins, to a sort of cultural red-light district, along with other unfortunate frailties and vices to which we are liable."[1] Richard John Neuhaus predicted in 1984 that the "naked public square" – excluding religious influence from the civic arena – would also result in the death of democracy.[2]

These competing views make the public square contested turf, with both principles and power at stake. Another complicating factor is that America's civil religion – the national mythology, symbols, heroes, and rituals that theoretically draw its population together – is just as contested. Is it a mosaic of many peoples or a melting pot designed to eliminate difference? Is the flag a holy object that must not be mutilated, or does a commitment to freedom mean that one

---

[1] Stephen L. Carter, *The Culture of Disbelief: How American Law and Politics Trivialize Religious Devotion* (New York: Anchor Books, 1994), 230; Wilfred M. McClay, "Two Concepts of Secularism," in *Religion Returns to the Public Square: Faith and Policy in America*, ed. Hugh Heclo and Wilfred McClay (Baltimore: Johns Hopkins University Press, 2003), 33.

[2] Neuhaus, *The Naked Public Square: Religion and Democracy in America* (Kentwood: W. B. Eerdmans, 1984).

may burn it in protest? Is Columbus Day for celebrating the "New World" or for mourning the Indigenous world his journey helped to destroy? Is taking a knee during the National Anthem a symbol of patriotic concern for the enduring stain of racism, or a scandal of disrespect? In truth, these questions require more than either/or response. They take on a religious aspect because civil religion, like other lifestances, addresses questions of meaning and is woven into the spiritual fabric of American society. In addition, the politicization of faith – with people using religion for partisan advantage and politics for sectarian gain – makes it hard to separate these conflicts from intrareligious and interreligious strife.

Most Americans remain proud of the nation's aspirations regarding religious freedom. They are grateful that the Bill of Rights provides recourse for those who feel unduly burdened by the law. High-profile gestures of inclusivity, like a Passover seder and a Ramadan iftar at the White House, receive broad support. Two-thirds of Americans affirm that we can successfully work across racial and religious divides.[3] Yet many decisions regarding how we discuss, enshrine, and embody religious values in our collective civic life remain controversial.

7.1 PUBLIC DISCOURSE

Toward the end of the twentieth century, political philosopher John Rawls introduced an influential proposition that we should utilize "public reason" rather than religious beliefs in arguing policy positions. The rules that regulate our common life should be based on arguments to which we all have equal access, framed so that diverse people might reasonably be expected to agree.[4] Progressives seemed to

---

[3] "Americans Deeply Divided by Party on Ideals of Religious and Ethnic Pluralism," PR Newswire, February 21, 2019, www.prnewswire.com/news-releases/new-prrithe-atlantic-survey-americans-deeply-divided-by-party-on-ideals-of-religious-and-ethnic-pluralism-300799351.html.

[4] Rawls, *Political Liberalism* (New York: Columbia University Press, 1993). In the 2005 expanded edition, he made additional room for religious speech (l–liv). Aspects of this discussion are adapted from Mikva, *Dangerous Religious Ideas: The Deep Roots of Self-Critical Faith in Judaism, Christianity, and Islam* (Boston: Beacon Press, 2020), 89–90, 176–78, 197–98.

cede their public religious voice; it was not for lack of religious conviction, but rather for liberal commitment to pluralism and Rawlsian public reason. Unfortunately, it gave the erroneous impressions that political liberalism was hostile to religion, that religious voices were being pushed out of public debate, and that "religious" increasingly meant "conservative."

Urging progressives to reclaim public religious discourse and "tap into the moral underpinnings of the nation," President Obama (then a senator) declared:

> When we discuss religion only in the negative sense of where or how it should not be practiced, rather than in the positive sense of what it tells us about our obligations toward one another ... others will fill the vacuum, those with the most insular views of faith, or those who cynically use religion to justify partisan ends.

He went on to assert in Rawlsian style, however, that democracy requires religiously motivated individuals to translate their convictions into universal values, "accessible to people of all faiths, including those with no faith at all."[5]

Robert Audi proposed a somewhat different approach to make space for religious discourse in public life while also protecting against its potentially oppressive power. It is a notion of theo-ethical equilibrium: "Where religious considerations appropriately bear on matters of public morality or of political choice, religious people have a *prima facie* obligation" to seek a balance between those convictions and a broader responsibility to our common life.[6] It is not a matter of translation, à la Rawls. Religious reasoning has a place in public discussion, but people must stand both inside and outside their lifestance to examine its impact. It requires self-critical faith and

---

[5] Obama, "Call to Renewal", *New York Times*, June 28, 2006, www.nytimes.com/2006/06/28/us/politics/2006obamaspeech.html.

[6] Robert Audi and Nicholas Wolterstorff, *Religion in the Public Square: The Place of Religious Convictions in Political Debate* (Lanham, MD: Rowman and Littlefield, 1997), 37.

reclaiming the complexities of religious thought. This balancing act facilitates our efforts to shape a common civic virtue as we come to understand each other's values, while still defending against dominant religious voices legislating morality for everyone. Secular ethics and reasoning can exist alongside religious discourse rather than instead of it.

Fleshing out this more "conversational" model of public discourse means that individuals and communities are encouraged to share their religious perspectives on public policy, but without expectation that they operate as a trump card. They may claim to speak *from* a tradition but not to speak exclusively *for* it, since it is evident that people interpret the same spiritual inheritance in diverse ways. They may present teachings that shape their values as people of faith, but they function in public space as ideas rather than authoritative religious truths. Protected but not privileged speech, public religious discourse can also be challenged as we address critical issues in our body politic.

To illuminate these dynamics, consider the example of Jeff Sessions. When he was serving as Attorney General in 2018, he invoked the New Testament to justify separation of families for asylum seekers and other undocumented migrants who were detained trying to cross the border. "I would cite you to the Apostle Paul and his clear and wise command in Romans 13, to obey the laws of the government because God has ordained the government for his purposes," he opined during a speech to law enforcement officers.

It is not uncommon for religious and political leaders to cite scriptural passages as prooftexts, hoping to use their moral authority to advance a policy position. Legal experts cried foul, however, since there was no law authorizing the separation of families; the administration was actually looking for a way to circumvent the rule that families with children could not be incarcerated for more than twenty days. Historians quickly noted that it was a favorite verse of British loyalists during the Revolutionary War and of slaveholders in the antebellum South. Theologians argued that he missed the biblical context of trying to avert a nationalist revolt against Rome; he also neglected the conclusion in which Paul asserts that love is the fulfillment of the law because it does no harm to neighbor (13:10). Interfaith activists bemoaned the furor that would likely arise if a US official tried to cite the Vedas, Confucius, or Qur'an that way. Defenders of the separation between religion and state claimed there was no place for such arguments in public policy discussions (and the verse itself could be read as a message to keep religion out of politics).

Others, however, thought it was fair game since many religious leaders were vocal about the unethical implications of the policy, citing the Bible's profound commitment to the stranger (e.g. Leviticus 19:33–34). Sessions' foray into biblical exegesis was not particularly skillful, and some people found the episode scandalous or absurd, but it provided a taste of critically engaged religious ideas as part of public discussion. The family separation policy was ended, at least officially, the following month.

It may seem logical to manage religious diversity by avoiding argument when possible. Interreligious leaders should not only be able to cultivate common ground and dignify our differences, however; they should also be able to facilitate conflict in constructive ways. Interreligious encounter in public discourse can promote understanding of what drives the convictions of our neighbors. Civil debate can advance deeper exploration of texts, beliefs, and praxis – and diminish the temptation of moral certainty. It can also distinguish Christian religious ethics that might otherwise pass as universal, excavating a richer diversity in our social fabric.

Religious ideas must be subjected to critical scrutiny without succumbing to bigotry or reigniting medieval battles between claimants of the "true faith." We can express strong disapproval without characterizing opponents as despicable. We can develop language to challenge specific ideas rooted in faith when they impact the common good, without impugning the faith from which they grow.

One strategy for crafting more constructive public discourse is to utilize Diana Eck's distinctions regarding each person's multiple voices. In response to the Southern Baptist conference when it issued a pamphlet describing Hindus as lost in total darkness, for example, she offered a nuanced, layered critique. As a scholar of Hinduism, she argued that they seriously misrepresent Hindu traditions. As a fellow American, she defended their right to believe and to say the derogatory things they do. And as a Christian, she maintained that their views are not well grounded in the Gospel of Christ, as she understands it.[7] Eck did not claim to speak for all of Christianity, but she staked her ground. She did not disparage Southern Baptists, but she challenged the disrespect embedded in their approach. Careful deployment of our multiple voices helps navigate the difficult terrain of religion in public discourse, affirming freedom of religion even for ideas that offend while continuing to promote interreligious understanding.

7.2   PUBLIC POLICY

Despite the Constitution's establishment clause that generally separates matters of religion and state, numerous issues related to religious difference require legislation, administration, or adjudication.[8] Governments regulate ritual slaughter of meat and what kinds of cases can be taken to religious courts. Prisons determine which life-stances they will accommodate for inmates in terms of dietary restrictions and daily practice. The Selective Service System judges whether one's conscientious objector claim is legitimate. Municipalities decide which holidays to grant as paid days off.

Many of these incursions seem unavoidable, but some laws tread on uncertain ground. Not surprisingly, the courts have been drawn in to determine the boundaries of establishment on numerous occasions. "Blue laws" that require stores and other facilities to be

---

[7] Eck, "Prospects for Pluralism: Voice and Vision in the Study of Religion," *Journal of the American Academy of Religion* 75, no. 4 (2007): 771, https://doi.org/10.1093/jaarel/lfm061.

[8] See Winnifred Fallers Sullivan, *The Impossibility of Religious Freedom* (Princeton: Princeton University Press, 2005).

closed on Sundays, or to restrict sale of certain items like alcohol, have been challenged for forcing Christianity's Sabbath on the entire population. Shopkeepers who needed to close on Saturdays for religious reasons and on Sundays because of the law complained that they could not earn a living. In 1961, the Supreme Court ruled that such laws (which were much more common and restrictive than they are today) are constitutional because they have a secular purpose: "to set one day apart from all others as a day of rest, repose, recreation and tranquility – a day which all members of the family and community have the opportunity to spend and enjoy together, a day on which there exists relative quiet and disassociation from the everyday intensity of commercial activities" (*McGowan v. Maryland*).

In other cases, the courts have set limits on establishment of religion in public policy, even when the government has a compelling interest. A now controversial but still influential ruling flows from the 1971 Supreme Court case *Lemon v. Kurtzman*. It set three criteria to pass constitutional muster: (1) the law must have a secular purpose, (2) its primary effect must neither advance nor inhibit religion, and (3) it must not foster excessive entanglement between government and religion. More recent decisions have tried to address some of the trouble spots in the "Lemon test," given the ambiguity of such determinations.[9]

Religion shapes public policy in other ways that raise concerns about establishment. America's long-standing debate about reproductive justice is one example. The movement trying to make abortion illegal in most or all circumstances is largely funded and driven by Catholic and evangelical Christian organizations. Their success in overturning *Roe v. Wade* led to a raft of state legislation severely restricting or outlawing abortion, establishing their religious perspective about the beginning of human life as the law of the land – even though many religions teach it does not begin at conception.

---

[9] Valerie C. Brannon, "No More Lemon Law? Supreme Court Rethinks Religious Establishment Analysis," *Congressional Research Service*, June 21, 2019, sgp.fas.org/crs/misc/LSB10315.pdf.

The free exercise clause raises its own challenges, with ongoing tensions between freedom *of* and freedom *from* religion, between religious freedom and governmental interests, and between the rights of individuals versus religious groups. Do restrictions on proselytizing in airports abridge religious freedom? How about restrictions on euthanasia? Does the government infringe on the religious freedom of parents by requiring that they vaccinate their children or on that of congregations by making them cease in-person gatherings during a pandemic? Does the state have a compelling interest in regulating substances (e.g., peyote, ayahuasca) used in religious rituals – or is this another instance of using the law to deny Indigenous peoples' rights? Does the government infringe on the rights of a business or religious group to require that they cover contraception in their health insurance plan, or compromise the rights of individuals if the groups are exempted? *Burwell v. Hobby Lobby* (2014) provides a useful case study to illuminate this last question.

Case Summary: Burwell v. Hobby Lobby Stores, Inc.[1]

The Green family owns and operates Hobby Lobby Stores, Inc., a national arts and crafts chain. The family has sought to run the business in a way that aligns with their Christian faith. Because they believe that use of contraception is immoral, they objected to the requirement of the Patient Protection and Affordable Care Act (ACA) that employment-based group health care plans must provide certain types of preventative care – including FDA-approved contraceptive methods. While non-profit religious institutions could seek an exemption, for-profit institutions such as Hobby Lobby could not.

In 2012, the Green family sued to challenge the requirement that their employee health plan cover contraception, arguing that it violated the free exercise clause of the First Amendment as well as the Religious Freedom Restoration Act of 1993 (RFRA). Eventually the case made its way to the Supreme Court. The government argued that religious beliefs must not impinge on the rights of third parties, in this case employees who do not share the Greens' convictions about contraception and who seek insurance coverage for their needs. Additionally, they argued that freedom of religion protections do not extend to for-profit corporations and, in any event, freedom of religion is not violated when the impact is an incidental consequence of an otherwise valid statute; namely, the ACA is not designed to discriminate against religious persons. With a 5-4 decision split along political ideological lines, the Court determined that the ACA infringed on Hobby Lobby's freedom of religion.

Without presuming legal expertise, we can explore a variety of interpath questions raised by the case.

Questions for Consideration

1. What do you think of the Court's decision? Should corporations, even "closely-held" family businesses, be included under the First Amendment protection of religion? What are the broader implications of such a decision?

2. The Constitution protects freedom of religion only from government interference, but what do we do when someone's free exercise conflicts with someone else's? Is your approach the same when it is a conflict between an institution (house of worship, business, denominational office) and an individual versus a conflict between two individuals?

3. Conscientious objectors to military spending have tried to argue (to no avail) that tax law infringes on their religious beliefs by allotting part of their payment to fund the military. What do you think of this argument?

4. Can you call to mind other examples in which public policy and religious freedom collide?

5. As you brainstorm, notice whether there are there particular lifestances that predominate in your list. Consider contextual, historical, and personal factors that might influence your examples.

[1] The summary is drawn from news reports, but Timoth Ewest, David M. Miller, Kacee Garner, and Holly Huser wrote it up as a case for Harvard Business School, "Faith and Work: Hobby Lobby and AutoZone," https://hbsp.harvard.edu/product/W14680-PDF-ENG.

Similar issues arise in relation to public services. Title II of the Civil Rights Act (1964) and other laws prohibit discrimination based on race, color, religion, or national origin when it comes to providing public accommodations. Hotels, restaurants, retail establishments, and other businesses must serve everyone equally. The Fair Housing Act (Title VIII, 1968) prohibits discrimination in renting or selling a dwelling. People generally associate the Civil Rights Act with the formal end of racial segregation, but there were significant implications for religious difference as well. An innkeeper could not refuse to rent the facility for a non-religious wedding ceremony. Jews and other religious minorities could no longer be legally barred from moving into certain neighborhoods. Buddhist monks could not be denied service in a restaurant for wearing religious robes.

It is worth calling to mind the significance of religious and interreligious activism in the long struggle for civil rights. Such coalitions remain significant in the ongoing fight for recognition of religious rights in public policy and services – as in the protests at Standing Rock resisting the Dakota Access Pipeline, and in airports around the country in response to the Trump Administration's "travel ban" that targeted mostly Muslim-majority countries.

Yet individuals and businesses sometimes seek religious exemptions to non-discrimination laws. Does it infringe on the rights of a county clerk to be required to issue a marriage license for a same-sex couple if her religious beliefs reject the legitimacy of same-sex marriage? Should a baker be free to refuse to make a wedding cake for that couple for similar reasons? As the Supreme Court has grown more politically conservative, it has become more receptive to such claims.[10]

But what about the rights of the couple to equal treatment under the law, and what about their religious beliefs? Conflicts have

---

[10] Marcia Coyle, "The Supreme Court's Religion Conundrum," Interactive Constitution, February 8, 2021, https://constitutioncenter.org/interactive-constitution/blog/the-supreme-courts-religion-conundrum.

arisen in relation to pharmacists who oppose contraception or abortion, adoption agencies receiving state funds that want to place children only with families of a particular religion, health care providers with religious reservations about transgender individuals, and taxi drivers who feel they should not transport passengers carrying alcohol. (This last issue, which arose in Minneapolis-St. Paul, is discussed in Chapter 14.) As we consider these questions, most readers will be more sympathetic to one perspective than another, but the deep challenge of democracy is how to best balance competing rights and responsibilities.

7.3 PUBLIC SPACE

The majority of interpath encounters in public space go unnoticed – simply sharing parks, airports, streets, and government buildings with people who orient around religion differently. When issues do arise in the United States, they frequently have to do with questions of Christian privilege or the separation of religion and state. Former Chief Justice of the Alabama Supreme Court, Roy Moore, triggered one such case when he installed a monument of the Ten Commandments in the lobby of the state judicial building after announcing at his swearing-in, "God's law will be publicly acknowledged in our court." It was viewed by many as an unconstitutional effort to establish state religion and several lawyers filed suit. After Moore refused to comply with a court order to remove the monument, he was eventually removed from office in 2003.[11]

In Bladensburg, Maryland, there is a forty-foot cross that stands as a World War I memorial; the Appellate Court ruled that it "excessively entangles the government in religion because the cross is the core symbol of Christianity and breaches the wall separating church and state," but the Supreme Court reversed the decision in 2019

---

[11] Kent Faulk, "Roy Moore Timeline: Ten Commandments to Gay Marriage Stance," May 7, 2016, www.al.com/news/birmingham/index.ssf/2016/05/roy_moore_timeline_ten_command.html.

(*American Legion v. American Humanist Association*). Christmas displays are erected on public property, sometimes publicly funded. Come December, the songs and symbols of the holiday are every-where – gratifying many people who enjoy the spirit of the season, and marginalizing others by making Christianity the "norm."

Examining public space more closely, however, we see other religious symbols, sounds, and events that are not Christian. Statues of Moses, Confucius, and Solon adorn the US Supreme Court building, standing as great lawgivers of the ages. Figures on the roof of the New York State Supreme Court Appellate Division include these three, plus Zoroaster, Manu, Justinian, Lycurgus, Alfred the Great, and Saint Louis. It had a statue of Muhammad as well, which was removed in the 1950s after ambassadors from Egypt, Pakistan, and Indonesia objected to displaying an image of the prophet. In some US towns, not only do church bells sound on Sundays, but the Muslim call to prayer (*adhan*) also echoes through the streets when the times for *salat* arrive.

Non-Christian festivals also occupy public space. Ganesha Chaturthi, for example, is a nine-day celebration of the Hindu god's birthday that has become a tradition in Flushing, NY:

> The highlight of the festival is the Ratha Yatra ... The people place Ganesha on the chariot, decorated to be a portable temple, and pull the chariot through the streets of Flushing. Musicians take the lead, playing the reedy instrument called the *nada-swaram*. Devotees by the hundreds lend a hand to pull the Lord's chariot by its long ropes. There is dancing and chanting, the singing of devotional *bhajans*, all along the parade route.[12]

Such events require public support in the form of permits, street closures, police presence, facilities, clean-up, and so on. Many people

---

[12] Diana L. Eck, *A New Religious America: How a "Christian Country" Has Become the World's Most Religiously Diverse Nation* (New York: HarperCollins, 2001), 121–22.

feel that it is a worthwhile investment in the vibrant mosaic of American spiritual life.

Looking at public-access private space, we see how religious and ethno-religious enclaves shape the sights, sounds, and smells of neighborhoods across the USA. At the center of Little Saigon in Southern California, for instance, is the upscale Asian Garden shopping mall, with statues of Buddha and the three gods representing good luck, prosperity, and longevity (*Phúc Lộc Thọ*). Upstairs, there is an area set aside for ritual and prayer.[13] Religious institutions that use traditional Vietnamese architecture shape the skyline, and the smell of incense wafts from shops and street vendors with their own shrines to Buddha, Catholic saints, and family ancestors. Such areas form organically or by design to create places where people can find the foods, goods, services, institutions, and like-minded souls to support their spiritual life. From Amish, Muslim, and orthodox Jewish communities to the multifaith subcultures of the Indian diaspora – such religiously identified neighborhoods dot the American landscape.

It can be argued that these are simply exotic accents and that most American spaces remain de facto Christian, but some Christians have adopted the approach of minority traditions to create their own communities with more explicit identities. Domino's Pizza founder Tom Monaghan, for example, invested hundreds of millions of dollars to create a Catholic town in southwest Florida called Ave Maria. Since its founding in the early 2000s, it has struggled with a number of scandals, and the current website does not refer to its Catholic identity – but many of the original residents were drawn by the idea of living in a community that explicitly embodies Catholic teachings.[14]

Religion in public space is significant because it communicates the values of that place and who belongs there. Religio-political

---

[13] Sanjoy Mazumdar and Shampa Mazumdar, "Planning, Design, and Religion: American's Changing Urban Landscape," *Journal of Architectural and Planning Research* 30, no. 3 (Autumn 2013): 226–27.
[14] Sarah E. Jones, "A Catholic City?" *Church and State* 68, no. 1 (January 2013), 12–13.

conflicts around the world have led to the destruction of sacred shrines, religious icons, and houses of worship – rejecting the idea that they (and the people to whom they are important) belong. Most struggles do not involve violence, however. Switzerland banned the construction of minarets lest it change the traditional skyline of its towns. Other European countries forbid wearing a burka in public space. Some American cities have refused requests to broadcast the *adhan* or to grant a building permit for a mosque. Hostility to the proposed Cordoba House/Park 51 project – called the "Ground-Zero Mosque" by those opposed to its construction – argued that a Muslim organization did not belong anywhere close to the place where a handful of Muslim extremists had murdered so many Americans, even though Imam Rauf and other organizers of the project were Americans too, dedicated to interfaith understanding. These examples unfold within the context of anti-Muslim bias in the West (see Chapter 8), but space communicates identity and belonging in every context.

Again, religion is generally one part of a more complicated story. Consider the case of a public art installation at the commuter rail station in Baldwin Park, CA, called *Danzas Indegenas* (Indigenous Dancers). Commissioned in 1993, artist Judy Baca mixed evocations of the area's Franciscan missions with dancing figures of the Indigenous Tongva and Chumash tribes. There is a prayer mound dedicated to Toypurina, a Tongva medicine woman who revolted against the San Gabriel Mission in 1785 to protest forced Indigenous labor. One side of the installation's central arch honors the languages and cultures of this past; it includes an excerpt from *Borderlands/La Frontera* by Gloria Anzaldúa: "The land was Mexican once, was Indian always, and is, and will be again." The arch's other face focuses on the present and future, quoting diverse residents as they reflect on their community.

Twelve years later, an anti-immigration group called Save our State (SOS) tried to use the installation to raise its own profile and to stir up trouble for this primarily Latinx town. SOS claimed that the art was anti-American, that the white, European story of America was being eclipsed by immigrants and multicultural perspectives. They did not care about Indigenous spirituality. Like the Park 51 uproar, it had more to do with history and politics than religion. Baldwin Park residents responded with a community art festival and a mobile mural project called *You Are My Other Me* – seeing the meeting of religions and cultures in public space as an opportunity to enhance civic life.[15]

Sensitivity to issues of inclusivity in public space has grown in recent decades. At the same time, some individuals feel that public space has become oppressively secular. There are Christians who might support the addition of Hanukkah or Kwanzaa symbols as part of a municipal winter display, for example, but express outrage about a "war on Christmas" if instead traditional Christian symbols are removed. They do not perceive secular space as neutral space and feel that their faith is being driven out of the public square. The challenges of balancing competing interests and identities is illustrated by the controversy in Santa Monica, California about nativity scenes in public space.

Case Summary: Nativity Scenes in Public Space[1]

Since 1953, the city of Santa Monica, California has allowed the display of nativity scenes in Palisades Park – even voting at one point to identify as City of the Christmas Story. The life-size dioramas depict discrete moments in the New Testament narratives, including Joseph's Dream, Rest on the Road, Nativity. When erected side-by-side, they fill approximately one city block.

The City Council enacted various regulations regarding installations in the park over the years, always making official or unofficial exceptions for the nativity scenes. In 2003, as a way of respecting

---

[15] Erika Doss, "Public Art Controversy: Cultural Expression and Civic Debate," *Monograph* (October 2006): 8–10.

content neutrality, they initiated a lottery system if the demand for space was greater than the two blocks allotted for "Winter Displays" – the only unattended overnight installations allowed at the time.

In 2010, Damon Vix applied for space, electing to install a sign with a quote from Thomas Jefferson, "Religions are all alike – founded on fables and mythologies." In 2011, applications exceeded the available space. A loose confederation of people opposed to religious displays on public property received eighteen slots in the lottery, the local Chabad organization received one, and the group sponsoring the nativity display received two. It made national news.

The city attorney submitted two reports to the Council in 2012 laying out their options: they could continue with the lottery system or eliminate the exception for "Winter Displays" in the park. She recommended the latter option, which would preserve the ocean vista for which the park was renowned and save hundreds of hours of staff time related to the lottery – a concern that was likely to grow as various groups threatened to flood the system. The City Council accepted her recommendation and unanimously voted to disallow all unattended, overnight displays on park property. The decision was controversial, prompting heated letters on all sides of the debate.

Hunter Jameson, head of the Santa Monica Nativity Scenes Committee that organized the displays, told a television reporter, "What a dog in the manger, what a Grinch-like, mean-spirited attitude for the Christmas season." The group's lawyer William J. Becker, Jr. accused "liberal Irish Democrats" and left-wing factions on the City Council of buckling to pressure, likening the decision to communist China: "It's the People's Republic of Santa Monica."

The group failed to get a preliminary injunction and lost their case in court because the law had secular justifications and did not discriminate against Christianity or religious expression. The nativity scenes have since been erected on private church properties.

Questions for Consideration

1. What issues are involved here? Be sure to explore underlying questions of identity/belonging, religious/secular, and other concerns.

2. What do you think of the City Council's decision? Today, objectors would label it part of a war on Christmas; how do you respond to this discourse – or the freighted attacks like those of Becker?

3. If you were an interfaith leader in the community, how might you engage this controversy? What is your goal and how will you assess whether you achieve it?

4. There are still many religious symbols in public space, some supported with public funds; which ones come to mind? Some localities present multiple traditions; others distinguish between overtly religious displays and more generic symbols. What are the strengths and weaknesses of these approaches?

[1] *Santa Monica Nativity Scenes Committee v. City of Santa Monica*, US Court of Appeals 9th Circuit (2015); Nicole Pellegrini, "Nativity Scenes in Public Spaces: The Controversy Continues," accessed August 19, 2022, https://wizzley.com/nativity-scenes-in-public-spaces-the-controversy-continues; Rory Carroll, "Atheist Victory in California as Surf City Loses Its Nativity Display," *Guardian*, December 1, 2012, www.theguardian.com/world/2012/dec/01/santa-monica-nativity-scene-atheist.

7.4   PUBLIC SCHOOLS

Students in K–12 spend a substantial percentage of their waking hours in school, and the experience profoundly influences their formal and informal learning. Consequently, parents and society at large have an enormous stake in what happens there. Charged with the mission of forming young citizens, public schools are a key battleground in the culture wars, and religion plays a part. Religious difference shows up in relation to school policy and also as students individually navigate the diversity of lifestances. The former includes questions about curriculum, school menus, academic calendars, dress codes, holiday customs, prayer, bathrooms, and accommodation of religious groups or private practices.

Some policies perpetuate Christian privilege, and others make conservative Christians feel marginalized. There is enduring tension between people who are eager to accommodate religion whenever possible and those who feel that religion has no place in public educa-tion. There is discrimination against religious minorities, often imposed by rendering their lifestances invisible. School customs like the Pledge of Allegiance ignore the experience of atheists who cannot affirm a nation "under God," and Jehovah's Witnesses who reject the idea of saluting a flag. Common school projects like Native American dream-catchers appropriate religio-cultural symbols. Teachers may know little about the diverse lifestances of their students and may be ill-equipped to shepherd a multicultural classroom. At the same time, public schools are often among the most religiously diverse spaces in a young person's life – and careful, collective deliberation can model inclusive environments, respectful communication, and deep learning from one another's experience.

Many contemporary conflicts in US schools have long histories. Horace Mann (1796–1859), considered by many to be the father of American education, advocated for the establishment of "common schools" where all could study without paying tuition. He hoped to forestall the rigid class hierarchies of Europe and to equip students to sustain a vibrant democracy. In place of sectarian education, he advo-cated "universal" Christian principles; early public education included prayer and Bible recitation. When the Catholic student population grew, there was argument about which Bible to use, but the role of Christian faith in public education went substantially unchallenged.

When the theory of evolution was introduced into science cur-ricula, however, a major controversy erupted; some legislatures passed laws forbidding state-funded schools from teaching it, privil-eging the belief that the word of God is revealed in the Bible and takes precedence over all sources of human knowledge. In 1925, *The State of Tennessee v. John Thomas Scopes* (commonly known as the "Scopes Monkey Trial") made front-page news, with William Jennings Bryan arguing on behalf of the state and Clarence Darrow defending the high school teacher who asserted the right to teach evolution in class. Even though Scopes lost the trial, the conviction that scientific knowledge rather than faith should determine science curriculum eventually became the legal standard. The debate has never fully subsided, however, and religiously conservative voices today advocate that "intelligent design" be taught as a competing or corollary theory. This approach has also been ruled religious rather than scientific, and therefore disallowed, but some school districts are responding by trying to bypass the restrictions with guidelines on teaching "controversial issues."[16]

Other curricular conflicts arise when parents want to exempt their children from various activities like sexual education, co-educational gym, or military training that they feel undermine values they are teaching at home. Representing a range of religious and political perspectives, families have expressed concerns about text-books, assignments, and materials in the classroom or library. Some parents remove their children from public education altogether, opting to teach them at home or to enroll them in private schools, most of which are religious. There is no consensus on whether families should receive vouchers to subsidize the cost: people who prioritize support for public education and/or separation of religion and state contest with inner-city families fleeing failing schools as well as conservative and liberal families living in places where the school culture does not support their worldview. Relying on a 2002 Supreme Court decision (*Zelman v. Simmons-Harris*) that it does not represent unconstitutional support for religion, approximately one third of US states allow parents to receive vouchers to send their children to parochial schools. Such questions about subsidizing religious education are not new. White flight from cities in the 1960s, along with rising costs for the many Catholic schools left behind, prompted a number of states to seek ways to help the institutions

---

[16] James Fraser, *Between Church and State: Religion and Public Education in a Multicultural America*, 2nd ed. (Baltimore: Johns Hopkins University Press, 2016); "Fighting Over Darwin, State by State," Pew Research Center, February 3, 2014, www.pewforum.org/2009/02/04/fighting-over-darwin-state-by-state.

survive – prompting a decade of legislation and litigation to tease out reasonable parameters.[17]

Prayer in public education has been another enduring conflict. A landmark Supreme Court ruling, *Engel v. Vitale* (1962), determined that facilitating prayer in the classroom – even if it is nonsectarian – violates the establishment clause. Thirty years later, another case ruled that it is unlawful to have outside clergy offer prayers at school graduations and similar occasions. Some communities still seek ways to include prayer at school events, however. A Santa Fe high school, for example, invited students to vote at the beginning of each year whether to include student-led prayer at the start of football games. In 2000, the Supreme Court issued a 6-3 decision forbidding the practice, arguing that it is still school-endorsed prayer and that constitutional rights cannot be forfeited by majority vote. Yet in 2022, a more politically conservative court ruled in favor of a former high school football coach who took a knee in prayer at midfield after games and invited the team to join him.

Lower courts have tried to work out the ramifications of these and other rulings, but the legal parameters are a bit blurry. Moments of silence with a secular purpose have passed muster, as have some student expressions of prayer that had no oversight from the school, but it is not consistent. Teachers and coaches comprise a particularly challenging category, with private and professional roles; they have personal freedom of religion but also a potentially coercive power over students – even if wielded only through modeling a particular lifestance.

Support for extra-curricular groups has also been an issue. In 1984, the US Congress passed the Equal Access Act, requiring public secondary schools that receive federal financial aid not discriminate against religious or political viewpoints. So religious clubs have an

[17] Ira C. Lupu, David Masci, and Robert W. Tuttle, "Religion in the Public Schools," Pew Research Center, October 19, 2019, www.pewforum.org/2019/10/03/religion-in-the-public-schools–2019-update.

equal right to school facilities and to any subsidy or administrative support offered to other groups. Outside periods of classroom instruction, students are free to participate in religious activities, alone or together, just as they may for secular ones. Of course, every answered question yields several others in its wake. What happens, for instance, when a religious student group violates a school's non-discrimination policy? What if the members want to proselytize in school? What if their activities are hurtful to other students?

The experience of New York City schools, an enormous system with a broadly diverse population, provides another example of complexity. They added the Lunar New Year plus Eid al-Fitr and Eid al-Adha to the school holiday calendar. The decision sought to respect the needs of Chinese and Muslim students, to encourage everyone to make space for difference, and to provide teachable moments for students to learn from one another's faith. Yet some conservative Christian families complained that multiculturalism is a religion in its own right, being established in the public schools. The district's decision also encouraged Sikh, Hindu, Buddhist, and other families to wonder why they were still invisible. (Rosh Hashanah and Yom Kippur, two significant holidays in Jewish tradition, have been included in the New York City calendar since 1960 because so many teachers were Jewish that the schools could not easily function on those days.)

Schools, legislatures, and courts continue to struggle with new issues as they arise. The case of transgender students fighting to use gym and bathroom facilities that align with their gender identity has made headlines since 2016. While not a religious question per se, some families who are fighting against accommodation claim religious foundations for their objections. Conflicts about Wiccan practice are less well known. Although the US Court of Appeals (4th Circuit, *Dettmer v. Landon*) affirmed in 1986 that Wicca is a religion deserving First Amendment protection, practitioners continue to face significant suspicion and challenges in public education and elsewhere. The American Civil Liberties Union (ACLU) successfully sued on behalf of a high school student outside Detroit so she would be allowed to wear a pentacle as a religious symbol, yet the issue has subsequently arisen in other schools.[18] In early 2000, Shari Eicher was suspended from her high school teaching position in North Carolina when community leaders protested to the school board after learning that she was involved with a coven. On the same day that she lost her job, the board allegedly voted to post the Ten Commandments in the schools, seeming to reinforce the difference between acceptable and unacceptable religion.[19] Young children in Wiccan families have been disturbed by depictions of witches as green, warty, cruel individuals – or being told by a teacher that their parents are going to hell. As students get older, they frequently encounter bullying by their peers based on their beliefs.[20]

This last problem highlights the fact that, whatever a school's policies, students still need to navigate religious difference on an interpersonal level. It is equally true, however, that student behaviors often reflect broader social values and biases. Schools, as mediators of culture, are consequently essential instruments for building bridges of understanding amidst diversity.

The courts have made a relatively clear distinction between activities designed to inculcate religious teachings, which represent an unconstitutional establishment of religion, versus teaching *about* religion. The latter is not only legally permissible but increasingly recognized as a valuable method to help children (and the adults they will become) constructively engage religious difference. Since fear often festers within ignorance, interreligious cooperation requires

---

[18] "Michigan School Change Policy on Honor Student Witch," ACLU, March 25, 1999, www.aclu.org/press-releases/michigan-school-changes-policy-honor-student-witch.

[19] Steven Lubet, "Witch Hunt in a Public School," *SFGate*, April 16, 2000, www.sfgate.com/opinion/openforum/article/Witch-Hunt-in-a-Public-School–2764193.php.

[20] Olivia Monforte, "After Receiving Backlash For Her Religion, One Student Reclaims Her Identity as a Witch," *Mustang News*, February 3, 2020, https://mustangnews.net/after-receiving-backlash-for-her-religion-one-student-reclaims-her-identity-as-a-witch.

religious literacy.[21] There have been several recent efforts to flesh out constitutionally acceptable ways to teach about religion in public schools.

In 2000, the Clinton administration's Department of Education distributed the first set of national guidelines to school principals delineating the legal safe harbor for navigating issues of religion in public education. In 2010, the American Academy of Religion published *Guidelines for Teaching about Religion in K–12 Public Schools in the United States*. Presenting religion as internally diverse, dynamic, and embedded in all aspects of culture, it helps teachers reimagine a sphere in which everyone has a seat at the table and students learn from their differences.

In 2007, the First Amendment Center published *Finding Common Ground*. Resulting from years of collaboration with educators and religious leaders, the project recognizes that focusing on court cases might not be the most generative method for cultivating understanding and collaboration for the common good. Legal contests always have a winner and loser. Drawing from the Williamsburg Charter of 1988, which celebrated the bicentennial of Virginia's call for a bill of rights, the book focuses instead on "the 3 R's" of rights, responsibilities, and respect. They have become the foundation for policy and curriculum in several states:

- *Rights:* Religious liberty, or freedom of conscience, is a precious, fundamental, and inalienable right for all.
- *Responsibilities:* Central to the notion of the common good is the recognition that religious liberty is a universal right joined to a universal duty to respect that right for others. Rights are best guarded and responsibilities best exercised when we guard for all others those rights we wish guarded for ourselves – "the Golden Rule for civic life."
- *Respect:* Conflict and debate are vital to democracy. Yet if controversies about religion and schools are to reflect the wisdom of the First Amendment

---

[21] Diane Moore, *Overcoming Religious Illiteracy: A Cultural Studies Approach to the Study of Religion in Secondary Education* (London: Palgrave McMillan, 2007), https://doi.org/10.1057/9780230607002.

and advance the best interest of the disputants and the nation, then how we debate, and not only what we debate, is critical.[22]

The volume also offers specific guidance for public school policies and procedures, as well as tips for parents and teachers to communicate constructively about religious concerns. It presents foundational principles and strategies endorsed by national religious, educational, and legal institutions.

The pathway to achieving these goals is still contested, of course. Compare the Bible Literacy Project's *The Bible and Its Influence* to the materials of the National Council on Bible Curriculum in Public Schools. While the former appears to be a faithful attempt to teach *about* the Bible, the latter curriculum "attempts to re-shape the collective memory of American origins and encourage the notion that the American character is quintessentially conservative Protestant."[23] People imagine the meaning of rights, responsibilities, and respect in different ways, and they frequently collide in multidimensional intersections, as evident in the following case.

Case Summary: Freedom of Speech, Freedom of Religion, and Freedom from Harm[1]

The Gay Straight Alliance student group at Poway High School in California organized a Day of Silence in 2003 to promote tolerance for diverse sexual orientations. Students supportive of the effort tried to refrain from speaking in school. In the days surrounding the project, some students made comments and wore clothing condemning

---

[22] Charles Haynes and Oliver Thomas, *Finding Common Ground: A First Amendment Guide to Religion and Public Schools* (Nashville: First Amendment Center, 2007), 18.

[23] Mark A. Chancey, "A Textbook Example of the Christian Right: The National Council on Bible Curriculum in Public Schools," *Journal of the American Academy of Religion* 75, no. 3 (September 2007): 557, https://doi.org/10.1093/jaarel/lfm036.

homosexuality, resulting in several verbal and physical altercations. When the Gay Straight Alliance sought permission to repeat the Day of Silence the following year, the principal required that they first work together to strategize ways to reduce tensions.

On the Day of Silence in 2004, a sophomore named Tyler Harper wore a T-shirt on which he had written, "I WILL NOT ACCEPT WHAT GOD HAS CONDEMNED" and "HOMOSEXUALITY IS SHAMEFUL, ROMANS 1:27." The next day he wore a similar shirt, with a slightly revised message on the front, "BE ASHAMED – OUR SCHOOL HAS EMBRACED WHAT GOD HAS CONDEMNED." When students began to talk about the T-shirt in class, a teacher asked Harper to change, explaining that the shirt was inflammatory and created a negative and hostile working environment for others. When he refused to remove his shirt and asked to speak to an administrator, the instructor gave him a dress code violation card to take to the front office.

Several administrators spoke with Harper that day. They explained that the school was not promoting homosexuality but rather tolerance, and they encouraged him to express his opinions in more positive, non-confrontational ways. Harper continually refused to remove the T-shirt and twice asked to be suspended. Instead, the administration had him spend the day in the office doing his home-work; they explained that he could not return to class wearing the T-shirt due to its potential to hurt other students and to disrupt learning.

His family sued the school, claiming that it interfered with Harper's free speech. They lost a preliminary injunction; the court cited a 1969 decision, *Tinker v. Des Moines Independent Community School District* that schools can restrict a student's free speech to prevent disruption of school activities. On appeal, Harper lost again. The majority opinion ruled that the determinative issue was "the impermissible intrusion on the rights of gay and lesbian students." It relied on another aspect of the *Tinker* opinion that allows school officials to prohibit student speech that invades the rights of others: "Speech that attacks high school students who are members of minority groups that have historically been oppressed, subjected to verbal and physical abuse, and made to feel inferior, serves to injure and intimidate them, as well as to damage their sense of security and interfere with their opportunity to learn."

One judge on the panel disagreed, arguing that free speech could be restricted only if the injury it would otherwise inflict was assault, defamation, invasion of privacy, extortion, or blackmail. Students do not have "an affirmative right not to be offended." The case came before the US Supreme Court in 2007 (*Harper v. Poway Unified School District 20*), by which time Harper had already graduated. It declared the case moot but vacated the previous decisions so that the underlying issues could be relitigated.

Questions for Consideration

1. Several competing values come into conflict here. How would you identify them, and how would you balance them in this case?
2. How might the balance shift if you move the issues out of a public high school – into a parochial school, a university setting, or the (adult) public square?
3. Imagine that you are part of the group trying to reduce tensions in advance of the 2004 Day of Silence. What strategies would you suggest and how would you manage the process? Be sure to examine all the ways your ideas could go wrong!
4. Imagine that you are the editor-in-chief of the school paper. Draft an editorial that might be published after Harper spends the day in the office, or after the family files suit against the school.
5. Thinking about "rights, responsibilities, and respect" as an operating principle, how do you cultivate civic virtue in public education?

[1] US Court of Appeals 9th Circuit, *Harper v. Poway Unified School District 20* (2006), https://caselaw.findlaw.com/us-9th-circuit/1356455.html.

8   Antisemitism and Islamophobia

The places we meet religious difference are not empty lots; they are full of history that shapes our encounter – not always in positive ways. Two tragic phenomena with substantial impact in Western contexts are antisemitism and Islamophobia. This chapter presents working definitions and a brief history, along with a framework for thinking about prejudice. Examining the complex, intersectional, and inter-woven dynamics of these dangerous hatreds, we reckon with their ongoing influence and explore the role of Interreligious Studies in dismantling them.

Human beings learn through difference. Consider how *Sesame Street* uses the sorting song, "One of these things is not like the others ..." to teach basic cognitive skills. We can mark difference without viewing it as evidence of inequality, but people frequently conflate the two. Research in social identity theory has demonstrated that group membership, even if arbitrarily assigned, is sufficient to cata-lyze favoritism for members and discrimination against those out-side.[1] Groupings are not necessarily stable, however. Paul Hedges offers the example of a Christian and a Muslim who see each other as "Other," differing on substantial theological and cultural grounds. If a Buddhist joins them, the first two may feel more aligned as theists. And if an atheist engages the group, the three who identify with a faith

---

[1] Henri Tajfel and John Turner, "An Integrative Theory of Intergroup Conflict," in *The Social Psychology of Intergroup Relations*, ed. William G. Austin and Stephen Worchel (Monterey: Brooks/Cole, 1979), 33–47. Parts of this chapter are adapted from Rachel S. Mikva, *Dangerous Religious Ideas: The Deep Roots of Self-Critical Faith in Judaism, Christianity, and Islam* (Boston: Beacon, 2020), 98, 120–34.

may feel they now constitute the in-group together, and set the non-believer outside.[2]

Since religious identity marks differences that matter, biases can take more extreme form, leading to antipathy, persecution, and violence. Sadly, history is full of interreligious hatreds. This chapter focuses on two examples that have plagued Western culture for a long time: antisemitism and Islamophobia. They are not confined to the West, and they are not the only biases of consequence, but their impact here is profound and ongoing – making interreligious encounter fraught with background.

8.1   DYNAMICS OF PREJUDICE

Todd Green, the Executive Director of America Indivisible, defines Islamophobia as "the fear of and hostility toward Muslims and Islam that is rooted in racism and that results in individual and systemic discrimination, exclusion, and violence targeting Muslims and those perceived as Muslim."[3] You could substitute Jews and Judaism for Muslims and Islam, and you would have a working definition of antisemitism – although one might find mistrust rather than fear as the anchoring negative emotion. Definitions can be controversial, and this one requires unpacking, a process that begins here and continues in the specific discussions of antisemitism and Islamophobia.

Like other forms of prejudice, these antipathies manifest in thinking, feeling, and action. They rely on stereotypes that malign the group and strip those assigned to it of their individual character. Because these biases exist in the social fabric, they affect everyone – even those who explicitly reject the prejudice. Stereotypes, media messages, and social norms all shape how we process information.

Let's try an exercise to illustrate the problem of implicit bias. Can you guess what percentage of terrorist incidents in the United

---

[2] Paul Hedges, *Religious Hatred: Prejudice, Islamophobia and Antisemitism in Global Context* (London: Bloomsbury Academic, 2021), 33.

[3] Todd H. Green, *Fear of Islam: An Introduction to Islamophobia in the West*, 2nd ed. (Minneapolis: Fortress Press, 2019), 9.

States were carried out by Muslim extremists between 2008 and 2016? You may try to select a low number to resist the unfair association of Islam and terrorism – but you may still be too high. The answer is 14 percent. Seventy-one percent of domestic terrorist attacks in the USA during that period were perpetrated by right-wing extremists, and 15 percent by left-wing extremists (largely eco-terrorism). So why do most people imagine a higher number? There are several factors. Attacks by Muslims are almost always prosecuted as terror attacks (84 percent), while comparable attacks by right-wing Christians are not (9 percent). Terror attacks by Muslims get 357 percent more media coverage than those committed by non-Muslims. And both news coverage and fictional stories about Muslims usually portray them in a negative light, disproportionately associated with violence.[4]

As Green notes in his definition, the prejudices play out not only at an individual level; they also infect institutions and systems. These are often the most dangerous manifestations, leading to exclusion, exploitation, and extermination. Jewish experience in the West has included all of these, taking different forms through history. Jews have been excluded from social clubs, universities, neighborhoods, and entire countries. They have been exploited as middlemen between medieval European gentry and peasants so that hostility from the lower classes would attach itself to the Jews; they have been engaged as lenders whose loans were later repudiated, and as merchants and tradesmen brought in to establish commerce in new territories only to be expelled once their utility was diminished. They

---

[4] Erin M. Kearns, Allison E. Betus, and Anthony F. Lemieux, "Why Do Some Terrorist Attacks Receive More Media Attention Than Others?" *Justice Quarterly* 36, no. 6 (2019): 985–1022, https://doi.org/10.1080/07418825.2018.1524507; Eric Bleich and A. Maurits Van der Veen, "Media Portrayals of Muslims: A Comparative Sentiment Analysis of American Newspapers, 1996–2015," *Politics, Groups, and Identities* 9, no. 1 (2018): 20–39, https://doi.org/10.1080/21565503.2018.1531770; David Neiwert, "Far Right Extremists Have Hatched Far More Terror Plots Than Anyone Else in Recent Years," *Reveal*, June 22, 2107, https://revealnews.org/article/home-is-where-the-hate-is.

have been murdered in small- and large-scale assaults on their very existence, most catastrophically in the Shoah with the extermination of six million Jews (two-thirds of those who lived in Europe, over one-third of all the Jews in the world).

Systemic bias incorporates rationalizations that deflect accusations of prejudice. People deny responsibility, claiming that they are simply following orders or they cannot be held liable for the actions of the state. They may disregard the consequences entirely – seeing only the way policies impact their own interests. Systemic bias also enables people to minimize their assessment of harm done. It allows them to view their actions as beneficial even if they are exploitative, such as slaveowners who saw themselves as kindly caretakers of "their Negroes" or colonialism's self-image as a civilizing project. People often claim that victims bring it upon themselves, part of a process of dehumanization that eventually makes their suffering seem inconsequential.

In thinking about prejudice, it is important to remember that those with greater social power generally determine which differences matter and what they mean. In fact, continuing dominance is often contingent on creation of an "Other." The distinctions are cast in moral binaries of good and evil to justify the bias, even though the catalyst is generally a desire for social, economic, and political control.[5] Self-defense is a common claim: "they" are threatening our security, our culture, or our way of life. Immigrants, for example, are frequently demonized, portrayed as criminals and job-stealers. The Trump administration portrayed travelers from Muslim-majority countries as potential terrorists in imposing a "travel ban." (A few non-Muslim countries were added to the original list to help it pass constitutional muster.)

Religious values, beliefs, and narratives have frequently been involved in these exercises of justification – but we will see that they

---

[5] Alar Kilp, "Religion in the Construction of the Cultural 'Self' and 'Other,'" *ENDC Proceedings* 14, no. 2 (2011): 197.

can also be deployed to *challenge* prejudice, to empathize with and humanize people who are different.

8.2   ANTISEMITISM, THE LONGEST HATRED

Although there are many important connections between antisemitism and Islamophobia, each has its own history and typology, so we address them separately. First, a note about the spelling of antisemitism. It is often written as "anti-Semitism," but scholars contend that it is not a hatred of Semitism or Semites; it is a hatred of Jews. In fact, there is no such thing as Semitism. There are speakers of Semitic languages like Arabic, Amharic, and Hebrew – but the prejudice does not attach to most of them. Wilhelm Marr coined the term in the late nineteenth century in a hate-filled tract, "The Victory of Germanicism over Judaism." He wanted to include Jews who were no longer practicing or who converted to Christianity, believing that there was a sickness in the blood – a racialized pseudo-science that has been thoroughly discredited. By removing the hyphen and using lower-case letters, the current spelling recognizes the nature of this prejudice without perpetuating the racist construct.

Some of the earliest expressions of antisemitism were directed more against Judaism than against Jews, but the racialization of religion transformed its focus. As George Fredrickson explains:

> Anti-Judaism became anti-Semitism whenever it turned into a
> consuming hatred that made getting rid of Jews seem preferable to
> trying to convert them, and anti-Semitism became racism when the
> belief took hold that Jews were intrinsically and organically evil
> rather than merely having false beliefs and wrong dispositions.[6]

Racism here does not refer to skin color since people of every race are Jewish. Religion gets "raced" when otherness is defined not by

---

[6] George Fredrickson, *Racism: A Short History* (Princeton: Princeton University Press, 2002), 19.

religious praxis or conviction – or even culture – but by some innate, unalterable quality.

The New Testament, unfortunately, has historically been a significant source of hostility to Jews and Judaism in the Christian world. It can be read to blame Jews throughout the ages for Jesus' death (Matthew 27:25), even though he was crucified by Roman authorities for treason against the empire – and even though Christian theology asserts his death was necessary. The Gospel according to John associates Jews with the devil (John 8:44). Various Epistles inveigh against legalistic distortions of God's teaching, an argument used for centuries to claim that the Jewish covenant has been superseded (e.g., Galatians 4:21–31, Hebrews 8:13).[7] Although Jesus, the apostles, and early followers of the movement were all Jewish, the main streams of Judaism in Late Antiquity were condemned for denying Jesus as messiah – accused of being blind to the meaning of their own scriptures (e.g., Romans 11:7–10). Criticism of the Pharisees was polemical; representing a reform movement similarly interested in drawing out the practical, ethical, and spiritual import of biblical teachings, the Pharisees constituted the closest competition and suffered the most withering reproach (e.g., Matthew 23).

Supersessionism, also called replacement theology, undergirds Christian anti-Judaism. It was Augustine (354–430 CE) who provided a theological rationale to explain the continuation of Judaism after Jesus theoretically rendered the Jewish covenant obsolete. He affirmed that God chose Israel and gave them the Torah, yet Jews remain in what Augustine viewed as a fossilized form to serve as witnesses to the truth of Christianity; they must live in misery to demonstrate that there is no salvation without Christ. As Augustine's strategy became normative, it promoted a certain tolerance, but it also

---

[7] E. P. Sanders' 1977 book *Paul and Palestinian Judaism* began a movement away from this supersessionary reading and the stark demarcation between faith and deeds.

painted Jews as the quintessential Other whose fate was dangerously woven into narratives of Christian vindication.

The tone of anti-Jewish discourse grew more strident once Christianity was officially recognized within the Roman Empire and subsequently became the religion of the state. John Chrysostom's *Adversos Judaeos*, a series of sermons delivered in Antioch in 386–87 CE, paints a particularly hateful portrait. Challenging Christians who were attached to elements of Jewish practice, he called the synagogue a whorehouse and a dwelling of demons and declared Jewish souls full of demons too. He identified them as "the common disgrace and infection of the whole world," urging Christians not even to exchange greetings with them. Within the first sermon alone, he accused Jews of overpowering lust, plundering, covetousness, abandoning the poor, stealing, dishonesty in business, and more. Unwilling to "pull the plow" of Christ's teaching, they become like animals fit only for slaughter. Chrysostom cited the end of a parable in Luke 19:27 as prooftext: "As for these enemies of mine who did not want me to be king over them – bring them here and slaughter them in my presence." Scholars contextualize his remarks within the genre of *psogos*, a no-holds-barred polemical style. Unfortunately, however, accusations like these became staples in the history of antisemitism.

Rhetorical violence and polemic led to physical violence and discriminatory legislation. Once the Roman Empire became Christian, legal restrictions included prohibitions against Jews proselytizing, intermarrying, owning slaves, building new synagogues, practicing law, serving in the imperial administration, testifying against a Christian, receiving public honor, or holding office. Some of these disabilities extended to everyone who was not Christian according to current orthodoxy, but Jews served as the foil for construction of the elect Christian self. In later periods, persecution included prohibitions against owning land, exclusion from many trades, forced disputations, public burnings of the Talmud, special taxes, identifying garb, ghettoization, expulsions, libels, and pogroms.

Libels against the Jews were preposterous, but many Christians believed them. Blood libels imagined that Jews murdered Christian children to use their blood for religious rituals; these lies repeatedly sparked mob violence against Jewish communities. After the Fourth Lateran Council (1215) declared the Eucharist actually becomes the body of Jesus, stories were concocted that Jews desecrate the host to renew the agonies of the Passion. The accused was often burned at the stake; sometimes entire Jewish communities were exterminated. In the fourteenth century, Jews were falsely blamed for the bubonic plague that killed 100–200 million people in Eurasia and North Africa. Again, Jewish communities were attacked and their populations massacred or expelled.

Jews were expelled for a variety of reasons. After a priest converted to Judaism in Mainz (Germany) in 1012, Henry II forced all the Jews in the province to leave. They were allowed to return soon after, but the expulsion from England in 1290 lasted 365 years. Causes driving this expulsion were more typical: a chance for nobility to confiscate property and renege on debts combined with broad embrace of libels and general antipathy. At different times and for differing durations, Jews were expelled from the majority of territories in Europe.

Even when Jews had official protection, they were often the target of violence. The Crusades of the eleventh–thirteenth centuries were primarily intended to combat the Islamic Empire, especially to wrest the Holy Land from Muslim control. En route, however, soldiers ravaged Jewish communities in the Rhineland and elsewhere – extorting property, forcing conversion, murdering residents. King Henry IV issued an order protecting the Jews, as had several popes, and a few local officials took steps to defend the local Jewish populations. They could not restrain the marauders, however, fired by hatred and charges of deicide; 12,000 Jews died during the First Crusade alone.[8]

---

[8] See Robert Chazan, *The Jews of Medieval Western Christendom 1000–1500* (Cambridge: Cambridge University Press, 2006), https://doi.org/10.1017/CBO9780511818325.

During the Middle Ages, life was often much better for Jews living in the Muslim world. They had the status of *dhimmi*, a term with a semantic range that includes Divine favor and mutual faithfulness; it established religious freedom and civil rights for "Peoples of the Book" (*Ahl al-Kitab*). While the designation also entailed a broad range of disabilities, Jews were not generally singled out for negative attention. The Pact of Umar, for example, dealt with the largely Christian inhabitants of conquered cities in Syria (seventh century, although records are later). In exchange for peace and protection, they were not allowed to build new religious facilities or repair old ones in Muslim areas; proselytize or hold public religious ceremonies; display crosses or Christian books in Muslim thoroughfares; dress like Muslims, adopt their naming customs, ride on saddles, bear weapons, or strike a Muslim; they were required to wear the *zunnar*, a belt that identified them as Christian. These stipulations constituted typical elements in the regulation of *dhimmi* populations, along with collection of a special *jizya* tax.

Nonetheless, there are records of anti-Jewish sentiment. Ibn Ḥazm (eleventh century) wrote a vituperative polemic against the Jews, dismissing their claim of being chosen for sacred purpose:

> There is no greater wonder than that they make themselves children of God. All who know them know that they are the dirtiest of nations in clothing, the most inane in appearance. They are the most wretched, abominable, perfect in wickedness. They are the greatest in deceit, most cowardly of spirit, strongest in despicableness, most deceitful of tongue, weakest of determination, and most frivolous of character. God forbid this foul election.[9]

Even during periods of relative tolerance and robust cultural exchange between Jewish, Christian, and Muslim populations, such as *La*

---

[9] Theodore Pulcini, *Exegesis as Polemical Discourse: Ibn Ḥazm on Jewish and Christian Scriptures* (Atlanta: Scholars Press, 1998), 133.

Convivencia in al-Andalus, there was still sporadic violence against Jews (see Chapter 3).

8.3 THE EMERGENCE OF MODERN ANTISEMITISM

After Christian rulers had retaken most of the Iberian peninsula and shortly before they expelled Jews and Muslims in 1492, there was a significant development in shaping racialized antisemitism. Beginning in 1449 in Toledo and spreading throughout Spain, laws were enacted that prevented Conversos and Moriscos (Jews and Muslims who had converted to Christianity, often coerced) from holding public office. The statutes were named *limpieza de sangre* (purity of blood), promoting the idea that the taint of Jewish or Muslim ancestry carried on for generations. Religious identity was racialized, even though modern conceptions of race had not yet fully developed.

The layers that Fredrickson described – anti-Judaism, antisemitism, and racism – fed one another. Jews who converted were suspect, prompting populist pogroms and official Inquisitions. Those who did not convert were pressed into ghettos, beginning with Venice in 1516. As commoners gained rights in Europe, Jews were still excluded. Seen as the unassimilable Other, they were not granted citizenship until the late eighteenth to mid-nineteenth centuries (varying by place), a stage in Jewish history referred to as emancipation.

In 1523, Martin Luther composed an essay, "That Jesus Christ Was Born a Jew," arguing that Jews had not converted in large numbers because they were treated poorly and shown only a popish mockery of Christianity: "If I had been a Jew and had seen such dolts and blockheads govern and teach the Christian faith, I would sooner have become a hog than a Christian. They have dealt with the Jews as if they were dogs rather than human beings; they have done little else than deride them and seize their property."[10] When Jews failed to

---

[10] Martin Luther, "That Jesus Christ Was Born a Jew," www.uni-due.de/collcart/es/sem/s6/txt09_1.htm.

embrace Luther's reformed tradition, however, he composed *On the Jews and Their Lies* (1543). Abandoning efforts to convert them, Luther advocated "merciful severity" – burning down their homes and synagogues and stripping them of legal protections. His antipathy was less about religion or culture; although it began there, he came to attach unalterable, undesirable qualities to "the Jews."

Jews became a stand-in for whatever one wished to condemn in society. Historian David Nirenberg identified "vast stockpiles of anti-Jewish stereotypes" as "the product of conflicts between Christians, conflicts in which each party strove to claim the mantle of 'true Israel' for itself, and to clothe the other in the robe of 'Jew.'"[11] Jews are still cast in this dangerous position today, used to define in-group and out-group and to lend legitimacy to the former. It explains why today Jews may get blamed for the abuses of both communism and capitalism, accused of both parochialism and globalism, secularism and religious obscurantism – depending on who is making the argument and for what purpose.

In the early twentieth century, a new trope emerged – the fabricated notion that Jews are part of a global conspiracy to control the world. The most notorious and widely distributed purveyor of this lie is a pamphlet first published in Russia, *The Protocols of the Elders of Zion*. Pretending to be minutes from secret meetings, it portrays Jews plotting to manipulate the economy, control the media, and magnify religious conflict. After the Russian Revolution in 1917, anti-Bolshevik émigrés spread these charges across the world. The text was translated into dozens of languages and spawned additional antisemitic tracts like Henry Ford's *The International Jew*.

In 1921, *The London Times* definitively proved that the *Protocols* were false; in fact, the material was borrowed from a French satire, *Dialogue in Hell between Machiavelli and*

---

[11] David Nirenberg, "Slay Them Not: A Review of Paula Fredriksen's *Augustine and the Jews*," *The New Republic* 240, no. 4 (March 18, 2009): 42–7, https://newrepublic .com/article/64630/slay-them-not.

Montesquieu, that did not even mention Jews. Nonetheless, the pamphlet continued to circulate, playing a key role in Nazi propaganda. In the Arab world, it is still often presented as factual. A forty-one-episode series based on the text was produced in Egypt; it was broadcast on twenty-two Arabic-language channels during Ramadan in 2002. In the USA and Europe, the text is promoted by neo-Nazis, white supremacists, and other extremists. It has even been published in countries that have very few Jews, like Japan.[12]

While the Nazis' attempted genocide represents racialized antisemitism on a scale never imagined, they built on existing tropes and began with familiar policies. They passed the Nuremberg Laws (1935), stripping German Jews of citizenship and forbidding them to marry or have sexual relations with those of "German blood." (These laws later included Roma and Black people; Nazi racism was not limited to Jews.) Additional decrees excluded Jews from many occupations and public establishments, confiscated or boycotted their businesses, and deprived them of most political rights. They were pressured to leave (until 1940, when it was no longer allowed), forfeiting the bulk of their property to the state. Personal assaults increased, leading to the nationwide pogrom called *Kristallnacht* (Night of Broken Glass) in November 1938. Jews were sequestered in ghettos and sent to concentration camps designed for forced labor in inhumane conditions. It was not until 1941 that the Nazis proposed and implemented the "Final Solution" aiming to exterminate all Jews in the expanding Third Reich.

Nazism's genocidal campaign worked with standard kinds of justification for their antisemitism. They portrayed Jews as a cultural, economic, and biological threat to German welfare – responsible for all the ills of the nation – and claimed the nation must act in self-defense. They dehumanized Jews, literally calling them *Untermenschen* or subhumans, so people would be unconcerned

---

[12] United States Holocaust Memorial Museum, "Protocols of the Elders of Zion," https://encyclopedia.ushmm.org/content/en/article/protocols-of-the-elders-of-zion.

about their welfare. Images in newspapers, film, textbooks, and public displays always conveyed a parasitic quality: leeches, lice, bacteria, rats. Even the language of extermination suggests an infestation.[13]

For the Nazis, Jewish identity was not determined by religion. It was a manufactured racial identity, determined to be inferior to the white race. If three or more of your grandparents were born Jewish, you were categorized as a Jew – even if your family all identified as Christian. Nazi pseudo-scientific theories projected that mixing of the races would be the downfall of Western civilization. Aryan identity was the purest of the white race, they believed, and Jews the most degenerate – the most polluted of bloods.

8.4   ANTISEMITISM TODAY

Antisemitism in the world today grows from these roots, with echoes of all the historical tropes. It is possible to trace slanderous accusations about Jews and money, for example, back to Judas (even though all the apostles were Jewish) and dehumanization of the Jews all the way back to the John's Gospel testimony. Even though most Christian denominations have repudiated anti-Judaism and antisemitism, churches still read texts that seem to blame Jews for the death of Jesus and treat Torah (which means "teaching") as burdensome "law." Some Christians still imagine that Jews have horns. They may believe that God has rejected the Jews for rejecting Christ. Numerous seminaries and congregations actively work to challenge these calumnies because they will not disappear by themselves.

Social clubs no longer officially prohibit Jews, and redlining neighborhoods to exclude them is now unlawful. Discrimination in hiring is less common, and percentages of non-Jews in Europe and North America who hold strongly antisemitic views shrank toward the end of the twentieth century. Antisemitic expression is illegal in many European countries, as is the baseless effort to deny the Shoah

---

[13] See Martin Gilbert, *The Holocaust: A History of the Jews of Europe during the Second World War* (New York: Henry Holt & Co., 1985).

or minimalize its devastating impact on the Jewish people. Nonetheless, over 30 percent of Europeans believe that Jews were responsible for the 2008 global financial crisis; approximately one in six Americans believes that they have too much power in the business world and essentially run the television and film industries. Sixty percent of religiously directed hate crimes in the USA are against Jewish targets.[14]

There is also a kind of "soft" antisemitism that lurks in other stereotypes: the Jewish American princess, the nice Jewish boy, the guilt-inducing Jewish mother, the idea that Jews are good with (or all have, or think only about) money, that they are pushy or cheap or clannish or more loyal to Israel than their own country. Academic feminist circles have blamed Judaism for patriarchy and activists have isolated Jews in intersectional causes.[15] Because these biases circulate broadly in the culture, they help sustain the hard-core antisemitism expressed by a smaller percentage of the population.

Antisemitism often uses coded language. Repeated accusations against George Soros as a sinister monied figure behind whatever it is that people do not like – Black Lives Matter protests, the "caravan" of migrants traveling toward the Mexico–US border in 2018, European immigration policies – serve as a way to blame the Jews. None of the conspiracy theories have any validity, but he is a convenient bogeyman because he is a Jewish American born in Hungary who contributes to left-wing organizations. The charges echo the instrumental antisemitism that David Nirenberg addressed, using hostility toward

---

[14] Anti-Defamation League, "Antisemitic Attitudes in the U.S.," January 27, 2020, www.adl.org/resources/report/antisemitic-attitudes-us-guide-adls-latest-poll; "Survey: 31% of Europeans Blame Economic Crisis on Jews," Ynet News, February 10, 2009, www.ynetnews.com/articles/0,7340,L-3669706,00.html; Federal Bureau of Investigation, "2019 Hate Crimes Statistics," https://ucr.fbi.gov/hate-crime/2019/topic-pages/victims.

[15] See Lauren Post, "Anti-Semitism in the Feminist Movement Is Nothing New," *The Forward*, May 5, 2017, https://forward.com/community/371071/anti-semitism-in-the-feminist-movement-is-nothing-new; Judith Plaskow, "Blaming Jews for Inventing Patriarchy," *Lilith*, June 5, 1980, https://lilith.org/articles/debut-2.

Jews to discredit the cause and hatred for the cause to deepen hostility toward Jews.

Coded language presents a veneer of deniability and creates in-group affinity for those who understand the signals. Neo-Nazis are fond of the numbers 88 (standing for "Heil Hitler") and 109 (representing their count of countries that have expelled Jews), among others. They use symbols as obscure as ancient runes, as familiar as the German SS logo, and as commonplace as the OK hand gesture to signify white supremacy. Certain tokens have been compared to gateway drugs, like Pepe the Frog that began as an ironic figure but morphed into a representation of extreme ideology.

Antisemitism is at the heart of white supremacism, so it is not surprising that the Capitol insurrection in 2021 had a flood of Nazi paraphernalia. Similarly, the "Unite the Right" rally in Charlottesville, Virginia, in 2017 saw large numbers of antisemitic banners, clothing, and tattoos as marchers chanted the Nazi motto "blood and soil" and "Jews will not replace us." The latter slogan echoes the conspiracy theory that Jews are out to dilute the white race, now by encouraging liberal immigration policies. It is this anti-semitic manifestation of the "Great Replacement" falsehood that propelled the terrorist who walked into the Tree of Life Synagogue in Pittsburgh and mowed down eleven Jews on a Shabbat morning in October 2018. He hated Jews, clearly, but his motivation was political. Committed to an ideology of white supremacy, he believed Jews were enabling migrant "invaders." His final social media post read, "I can't sit by and watch my people get slaughtered. Screw your optics, I'm going in." It was a flammable mix of religious, national, and racial prejudice, ignited by a culture of violence and manufactured sense of peril.[16]

---

[16] Ben Lorber, "Taking Aim at Multiracial Democracy: Antisemitism, White Nationalism, and Anti-Immigrant Racism in the Era of Trump," Political Research Associates, October 22, 2019, https://politicalresearch.org/2019/10/22/taking-aim-multiracial-democracy.

8.5   THE ISRAELI-PALESTINIAN CONFLICT

Although the Israeli-Palestinian conflict is primarily geopolitical rather than religious, the sides are drawn in religious terms and it ignites passion among people of diverse lifestances. Interfaith engagement efforts around the world frequently stumble into it.

There was antisemitism in the Arab world before the rise of modern Zionism, but most Jews living there had good relations with their neighbors. As Jews began to return to the Land of Israel in the nineteenth century as part of a movement for self-determination and statehood in their ancestral homeland, however, things began to change.[17] The Grand Mufti in Jerusalem (Islamic jurist in charge of the city's Muslim holy sites) during World War II openly admired Nazi ideology and lent religious credibility to antisemitism. After Israel was established in 1948, Jews living in most Arab countries were expelled (750,000). Sayyid Qutb, an influential Egyptian Islamist intellectual, wrote *Our Struggle with the Jews* (1950), spinning a story of animosity that goes back to the very beginning and distorts the history of relationship.[18] Even outside the Middle East, Muslim hostility has grown; in 2003, the Malaysian prime minister's party distributed Ford's *The International Jew* at campaign rallies – although almost all Malaysian Jews had already been pressed to leave by state-sanctioned antisemitism in the 1970s.

Antisemitism often masquerades as anti-Zionism, but not all criticism of Israel is antisemitic, and the boundaries between the two are contested. There have been several efforts to distinguish when something crosses the line. One of the more nuanced versions is the

---

[17] See Michael Stanislawski, *Zionism: A Very Short Introduction* (London: Oxford University Press, 2016). Christian Zionism is different; for one perspective, see Robert W. Nicholson, "Evangelicals and Israel," https://tikvahfund.org/uncategorized/what-american-jews-dont-want-to-know-but-need-to.

[18] See Abdelwahab Meddeb and Benjamin Stora, eds., *A History of Jewish-Muslim Relations: From the Origins to the Present Day*, trans. Jane Marie Todd and Michael B. Smith (Princeton: Princeton University Press, 2013).

Jerusalem Declaration on Antisemitism (JDA, 2020), composed in response to the 2016 International Holocaust Remembrance Alliance (IHRA) statement. JDA sought to clarify IHRA's definition and to protect more space for debate about Israel and Palestine. It identified these tropes related to Israel as antisemitic:

- Applying symbols, images, and negative stereotypes from classical antisemitism to the State of Israel
- Holding Jews collectively responsible for Israel's conduct, or seeing Jews as agents of Israel
- Requiring Jews to publicly condemn Israel or Zionism
- Assuming that non-Israeli Jews are more loyal to Israel than to their own country
- Denying the rights of Jews in Israel to exist and flourish, dismissing their human rights as unimportant[19]

Examples might be helpful. Israeli officials are frequently depicted in cartoons with stereotypical Jewish features or cast as Nazis. The trope of blaming Jews for social ills or accusing them of manipulating world events is often transferred to Israel. Some claim that Israel is responsible for US police violence against people of color, for instance, pointing to Israeli anti-terrorism training for several American police departments. Sadly, police brutalization of African Americans precedes existence of the State of Israel by a long shot. Amidst the violence that spiked between Israel and Hamas in May 2021, pro-Palestinian groups started physically attacking Jews around the world.

In 2015, a Jewish UCLA student was initially rejected for the Student Council's Judicial Board, with a majority of delegates concluding that her affiliation with Hillel and a Jewish sorority meant that she would be biased about questions related to Israel. Later that year, advocates of the Boycott, Divestment, and Sanctions (BDS) campaign against Israel persuaded the organizers of the Rototom

---

[19] "Jerusalem Declaration on Antisemitism," https://jerusalemdeclaration.org.

Sunsplash music festival in Spain to cancel a performance by Matisyahu, a Jewish American reggae/rap singer, unless he signed a declaration supporting a Palestinian state. A boycott is not antisemitic (although the BDS movement frequently utilizes antisemitic tropes), and there are millions of Jews who support a Palestinian state. Yet Matisyahu was singled out among 250 artists because of his Jewish identity. Both of these actions were reversed, but they illustrate patterns of behavior that discriminate against Jews because of Israel.[20] (Note that Muslims who have criticized Israel have sometimes been disinvited to events as well, a similarly problematic policy.[21])

Additions to the JDA list could include denying Jewish history in the land (e.g., "alleged" Temple in Jerusalem) and using Zionist as a code-word for Jew or Israeli to demonize them or to reject the reality of Israel among the world's nations. But supporting the Palestinian demand for political, national, civil, and human rights is *not* antisemitic. Neither is evidenced-based criticism of Israel (as opposed to fabricated conspiracy theories); many Jews, including Israeli Jews, are vociferous critics of policies that sustain the Occupation and harm Palestinians. One can advocate for strategies like BDS or adding strings to US military aid – or even oppose the idea of Zionism as a national liberation movement – without being antisemitic. Political speech does not need to be measured or reasonable; criticisms that use words like "apartheid," "massacre," or "ethnic cleansing" are provocative but not necessarily antisemitic. One may even apply a double standard to Israel because people always choose where to focus their justice concerns. Consideration of these dialectical tensions can help guard against antisemitism without silencing criticism of unjust Israeli policies.

---

[20] See Deborah E. Lipstadt, *Antisemitism Here and Now* (New York: Schocken Books, 2019).

[21] See, for example, Omid Safi, "The Asymmetry of Interfaith Dialogue," October 29, 2015, https://onbeing.org/blog/the-asymmetry-of-interfaith-dialogue.

8.6   ISLAMOPHOBIA

Discussion of Islamophobia similarly needs to begin by addressing terminology. After the Runnymede Trust in the United Kingdom issued a report, "Islamophobia: A Challenge for Us All," in 1997, the term spread quickly – but it is contested.[22] Some say it is misleading because the prejudice does not necessarily manifest as fear, and it is not a psychiatric condition. Phobia also emphasizes personal bias rather than systemic and institutional discrimination, when clearly the problem exists on all levels. While these criticisms make sense, there are other terms we use in similar manner, such as homophobia and xenophobia.

The word Islamophobia is also challenged by those who complain that it silences legitimate critiques of Islam. Others object that the targets of hostility are really Muslims themselves, not Islam; learning the Five Pillars does not tend to assuage anti-Muslim bias. Like antisemitism, Islamophobia racializes religious identity. Race never was a true biological category; rather, culture, history, and territory are mapped onto bodies to group peoples hierarchically and sustain/repress power.

The Runnymede report identifies eight characteristics of Islamophobia: Islam is viewed as (1) monolithic and static, (2) separate from and counter to Western culture, and (3) inferior to Western religion and culture. Muslims are seen as (4) hostile, aggressive enemies who (5) manipulate systems to magnify their power (e.g., "creeping sharia"). This perspective presumes that (6) racist treatment of Muslims is acceptable (e.g., profiling), (7) Muslim critiques of Western culture are invalid, and (8) anti-Muslim discourse is natural.

These attitudes did not suddenly develop after the attacks on September 11, 2001, or the Madrid train bombings in 2004, and they are not limited to the modern era. Hostility to Muslims and Islam in the West traces back to the encounter of empires in the seventh

---

[22] The Runnymede Trust, "Islamophobia: A Challenge for Us All," 1997, www .runnymedetrust.org/publications/islamophobia-a-challenge-for-us-all.

century. (Although it is not accurate to dichotomize Islam and "the West," given that Islam has been very much a part of Western culture, we use the familiar categories here.) Things did not start off too badly. Qur'an critiques some Christians and aspects of the faith, but also affirms the Gospels (*Injil*) as genuine teaching by God and Jesus as a significant figure, along with many prophets from Hebrew Bible. Early biographies of Muhammad record him dispatching a group of followers to take refuge from Quraysh persecution by going to the Christian king in Abyssinia. The monarch was particularly impressed by Qur'an's teaching about Jesus and offered them protection. After Muslim armies took Jerusalem in 638, Umar promised protection of the holy sites and elected to pray *outside* the Church of the Holy Sepulchre to demonstrate respect.

Nonetheless, Christians under Muslim rule were *dhimmi*, and animosity grew as Islam's rapid spread revealed a new tradition with universal theological and imperial ambitions to rival Christendom's. Muslims frequently presented their scripture as the final and uncorrupted revelation, superseding Christianity just as Christians had imagined superseding Judaism. Early Christian records grappled with the theological implications of an expanding Muslim empire. The first instinct was self-critical: many saw it as a temporary scourge to purify the Christian community, or a sign of imminent apocalypse. They composed apologetics to defend Christian Scripture and doctrine against charges of textual distortion, idolatry, and irrationality.

Yet they also produced substantial amounts of polemic. John of Damascus (676–749) portrayed the religion of the "Ishmaelites" as a Christian heresy and forerunner to the Antichrist. The ninth-century *Risâlat al-Kindi* presented Muhammad as an oversexed, materialistic idolater who enriched himself through trade, raiding, and marriage to a wealthy patron. The author claimed that Muhammad pretended to be a prophet to rule over his tribe, and that Qur'an was a product of satanic law written by Muhammad himself. Rites such as washing before prayer and fasting during Ramadan were seen as useless efforts to purify the body while the soul remained corrupt. Written primarily for Christian readers to confirm their status as God's elect, even if subject to Muslim rule, such works were designed to highlight the superiority of Christianity.

During the Crusades, Christian rulers collaborated to wrest territory from Muslim control, particularly the Holy Land; Catholic and Orthodox Christians, continually at odds with one another, saw themselves allied against a common enemy. In his call to arms at Clermont (1095), Pope Urban II reportedly characterized Muslims as "an accursed race, a race wholly alienated from God" who invaded Christian territory – pillaging and burning the towns, torturing and killing the inhabitants, defiling and destroying the churches. He proclaimed the Crusade was a holy war, commanded by Christ, capable of remitting sins and guaranteeing salvation.[23]

There was certainly polemic coming from the Islamic world as well; each side saw the other as the aggressor, the infidel, the barbarian. It calls to mind the classic "us vs. them" analysis as drawn by Tom Gauld (Figure 3).

Even though this was really a clash of empires fighting for power and resources, populated by soldiers eager for plunder and glory, religion was deployed to mark difference and to justify violence.

It is in this period that the fundamental anti-Muslim mythological framework solidified. Despite multiple caliphates and schools of Islamic thought, Islam was viewed as monolithic. Even though it continued to develop theology, jurisprudence, philosophy, and Qur'anic interpretation, it was seen as static. Islamic culture was identified as alien and inferior despite substantive contributions to Western culture, literature, philosophy, mathematics, and science. Aristotle, for instance, was virtually unknown until Latin translations of ibn Rushd's (Averroës) commentaries emerged in the twelfth century. Western sailors adopted Arab technology like the astrolabe,

---

[23] Quoted in Paul Halsall, "Urban II (1088–1099): Speech at Council of Clermont, 1095, Five Versions of the Speech," Internet Medieval Sourcebook, December 2017, https://sourcebooks.fordham.edu/source/urban2–5vers.asp#robert.

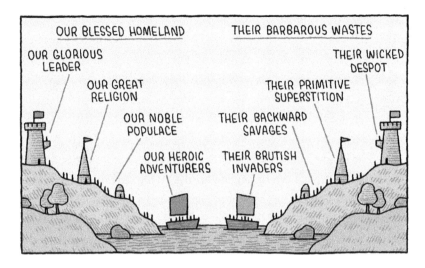

FIGURE 3 "Our Blessed Homeland"
©Tom Gauld (2015)

which aided navigation, and the triangular sail that improved maneuverability. Arabic numerals, the decimal system, algebra – all were absorbed by Muslims in their encounters with Indian and other cultures, and from there made their way into Europe. Muslims led major advances in surgery, anesthesia, and antiseptic hygiene; hospitals in Baghdad and Cairo transformed care by treating diseases rather than merely tending the afflicted. The first universities were established in the Muslim world. Literary forms and narratives in Europe borrowed heavily from Arabic. In fact, the idea of "Christian Europe" is a distortion, since there were Muslim populations and/or rule in the Iberian peninsula (until 1492), Turkey, Poland, and the Balkans.[24]

8.7   THE EMERGENCE OF MODERN ISLAMOPHOBIA

These misperceptions, embedded within mutual religio-political hostility, would not have the contemporary influence they do except for

[24] See Ahmed Essa, *Studies in Islamic Civilization: The Muslim Contribution to the Renaissance* (Herndon: International Institute of Islamic Thought, 2012); John Esposito, ed., *The Oxford History of Islam* (Oxford: Oxford University Press, 1999), https://doi.org/10.1093/acref/9780195107999.001.0001.

the impact of European colonialism. Adventures across the Atlantic prospered, with much of the native resistance killed off by European diseases. Gold poured into Spain and Portugal from South America. Trade in tobacco, rice, furs, and indigo from North America enriched Britain and the Netherlands, as did footholds in the Asian spice trade. These developments magnified a period of decline in the Muslim world.

The beginning of the end of Islam's "golden age" is often identified as the Mongol siege of Baghdad in 1258. Mongol rulers converted to Islam two generations later, but the damage was done. This city of tremendous culture and learning, capital of the Abbasid caliphate since 762, was destroyed. The historical narrative as shaped in the West frequently exaggerates this decline, with Islam entering modernity only because of European (read: white, Christian) colonization of Muslim lands at the end of the eighteenth century. It ignores the Ottoman Empire, which gained territory and influence during this period, defeating Constantinople and the Byzantine Empire in 1453. It ignores tremendous intellectual and political creativity demonstrated across the Islamic world throughout the eighteenth century, preceding Western influence. Instead of recognizing how European colonial rule disrupted Muslim systems of education, jurisprudence, and governance, this narrative presents the fall of the Islamic empire as the inevitable result of cultural and religious deficiencies.[25]

While medieval anti-Muslim sentiment was generally expressed as religious conviction or rhetorical polemic, modern versions often take the form of scholarship. (Antisemitism was similarly couched in "scientific" inquiry.) The field of study called Orientalism has become an epithet precisely for this biased view that passed for academic rigor in the nineteenth and much of the twentieth century. Ernest Renan's 1883 talk at the Sorbonne, "Islam and Science," is reflective of the problematic assumptions at work:

---

[25] Ahmad S. Dallal, *Islam without Europe: Traditions of Reform in Eighteenth-Century Islamic Thought* (Chapel Hill: University of North Carolina, 2018).

From his religious initiation at the age of ten or twelve years, the Mohammedan child, who occasionally may be, up to that time, of some intelligence, at a blow becomes a fanatic, full of a stupid pride in the possession of what he believes to be the absolute truth, happy as with a privilege, with what makes his inferiority ... The Muslim has the most profound disdain for instruction, for science, for everything that constitutes the European Spirit.[26]

Notice how he treats "the Mohammedan" as a singular, essentialized being whose faith and values are completely other than and inferior to those of Christian Europe.

Edward Said's 1978 book *Orientalism* helped to expose this prejudice built into the academy, where power defines knowledge. In the Orientalist imagination, Europe represented everything good: democracy, peace, egalitarianism, liberalism, reason, education, tolerance, modernism. Islam represented everything bad: autocracy, violence, gender oppression, fanaticism, unreason, obscurantism, intolerance, and backward traditionalism. Of course, these assumptions are all deeply flawed. Not only does Islam share many of the positive qualities associated with Christian Europe in that analysis; it is also clear that fanaticism, gender-oppression, and anti-democratic tendencies exist in the West. The academy has tried to take this critique to heart, reshaping the way it presents Islam as well as other non-Christian traditions, but it is a work in progress.

8.8   CONTEMPORARY ISLAMOPHOBIA

Islamophobia today manifests on multiple levels – within media and political discourses, individual actions, institutional mechanisms, and state policies. There are verbal and physical assaults against Muslims and people perceived to be Muslim. There are attacks on mosques, Islamic centers, and stores owned by Muslims that become

---

[26] Zachary Lockman, *Contending Visions of the Middle East: The History and Politics of Orientalism* (Cambridge: Cambridge University Press, 2010), 79, https://doi.org/10.1017/CBO9780511804342.

victims of vandalism or arson. Anti-Muslim demonstrations and efforts to block Muslim religious groups from incorporating or getting construction permits continue. Bias in hiring and housing is well-documented, as is sustained disparagement in the public square. And there are policies at every level of government targeting Muslims, directly and indirectly. African American Muslims must grapple with the problematic combination of Islamophobia and anti-blackness, suffering discrimination on both counts, even from within the Muslim community.

While openly hostile actions are committed by a small percentage of people, they are acting out broadly shared prejudice. Half of those living in Germany and Switzerland and 40 percent of those in the United Kingdom view Islam as a threat. In Spain and France, 60 percent say that Islam is incompatible with the West. As with Jews before the Shoah, there is a perception that Muslims represent an unassimilable Other that imperils European culture.[27]

Media framing contributes to these attitudes, impacting conscious and subconscious perceptions (see Chapter 6). A huge percentage of stories – real and fictional – are about Islamic terrorism or Islam oppressing women. Even stories that seem to break the mold, like coverage of Malala Yousafzai, reinforce the stereotypes. Yousafzai, a teenage advocate for female education in Pakistan, was shot by the Taliban in 2012. She survived, recovered, and continued her work – giving speeches at the United Nations and becoming the youngest recipient of the Nobel Peace Prize. Of course, the story behind her story was one of Muslim violence and misogyny. More insidiously, the Taliban's actions were presented as religious (if extreme) Islam – but Yousafzai's commitments to education, personal courage, and ethics were not generally portrayed as reflections of her Muslim faith.

Popular television shows like *Homeland* and *24* were rife with Muslim terrorists and veiled women. The occasional counter-

---

[27] Roland Benedikter, *Religion in the Age of Re-Globalization: A Brief Introduction* (Cham: Palgrave Macmillan, 2022), 112, https://doi.org/10.1007/978-3-030-80857-0.

examples were generally characters working for the United States against Muslim terrorists, suggesting that there are only two kinds of Muslims: bad Muslims who try to destroy "us" and good Muslims who help us stop them. Media also tend to erase the long history of African American Muslims, present from before the country was established, perpetuating the idea of Muslim as foreigner.[28] Recognizing the power of television and film to shape attitudes, producers in the USA, Europe, and Canada have been working to offer more positive, diverse images of Muslims, for example, *All-American Muslim, Community, Little Mosque on the Prairie,* and *EastEnders*. They generate controversy because the image of Islam is freighted with centuries of baggage.[29]

Binaries of good Muslims who support Western values and bad Muslims who attack them are also visible in political discourse, higher education, and other public arenas. One such false dichotomy pits Islam against free speech. Good Muslims support Western privileging of speech even when it is offensive. Bad Muslims take to the streets with violence and angry epithets when insulting images of the Prophet Muhammad appear in Danish cartoons – and the worst shoot up the offices of the publisher. We can complicate this binary by recognizing there were significantly more peaceful demonstrations than violent ones, but they did not get news coverage. We can acknowledge that restrictions on free speech exist, including European prohibitions against antisemitic discourse – which some Muslims see as a double standard. There is a deeper public conversation to be had about why insulting the Prophet is considered so egregious, and why free speech is considered so sacred – but all this is eclipsed in the dichotomization.

Muslims in the West are often considered suspect if they intimate that Western colonialism and ongoing geopolitical interference

---

[28] See Amir Hussein, *Muslims and the Making of America* (Waco: Baylor University Press, 2017).

[29] Evelyn Alsultany, *Arabs and Muslims in the Media: Race and Representation after 9/11* (New York: New York University Press, 2012).

have created many of the problems ascribed to "the Muslim world," or that Western nations are not the egalitarian bastions they imagine themselves to be. Gender issues can be particularly fraught. Ironically, European states have increasingly legislated what Muslim women *cannot* wear (niqab, hijab, etc.) in the name of women's equality. Gayatri Chakravorty Spivak once speculated that white men saving brown women from brown men is the animating collective fantasy of Western imperialism.[30]

Wearing *hijab* has become a political act. In Canada, a study found that women wearing hijab were subjected to discrimination when applying for a job. Many were told to remove it during the interview, or that they would not be allowed to wear it at work if they want the position. In 2017, the Quebec legislature passed Bill 62, making it illegal for people to wear face coverings (*niqab*) when giving or receiving a service from the state. Women could not wear *niqab* to ride the bus, teach or learn in a public school, or check out a book from the library. A citizenship guide promoting gender equality speci-fied that Canada's religious tolerance would not extend to barbaric practices like honor-killings or female genital mutilation. Such prac-tices are indeed abhorrent, but not really religious in nature; the guide promotes Islamophobia and false civilizational divides – and also fails to reckon with the patriarchy and violence against women that has always existed in Canada (and other Western nations).[31]

Most discriminatory policy stems from Islamophobic associ-ations of Muslims with violence. Nations must be concerned with security issues, but state actions need to be balanced with democratic values. Legislation targeting Muslims is not an acceptable response to the global scourge of terrorism. In the wake of a Muslim who opened fire in Vienna in November 2020, for example, Austria passed a law

---

[30] Gayatri Chakravorty Spivak, "Can the Subaltern Speak?," in *Can the Subaltern Speak? Reflections on the History of an Idea*, ed. Rosalind Morris (New York: Columbia University Press, 2010), 48–49.

[31] Jasmin Zine, "Introduction," in *Islam in the Hinterlands: Exploring Muslim Cultural Politics in Canada*, ed. Jasmin Zine (Vancouver: UBC Press, 2012), 9–10.

requiring all imams to register with the government and pushed for the European Union to do the same. Even though only one-fifth of attacks in Europe are religiously motivated and only a fraction of those are committed by Muslims, Muslim piety and identity are being associated with terrorism.

Beginning on the first anniversary of the September 11 attacks, the United States authorized "special registration" of men over the age of sixteen who were visiting from selected Muslim-majority countries. They were required to be fingerprinted, photographed, and interviewed under oath about their beliefs and their politics, with the information entered into a national database. It was not an effective antiterrorism policy (especially since the majority of attacks on American soil are committed by native-born, white, Christian, right-wing extremists), but it continued until 2011.[32]

The Patriot Act (2001) significantly expanded surveillance powers, which have been disproportionately directed against American Muslims. At one of my first interfaith conferences, I noticed that most of the Muslims had tape over their laptop cameras. Until that experience, I did not understand the degree to which the entire community was being watched. People were asked to inform on their mosques, and some were threatened with being put on the no-fly list if they did not cooperate. Simply transferring funds back home to family in Pakistan or Syria can raise red flags. Donors to charity organizations get charged as "unindicted co-conspirators" if there is any paper trail to any organization that might be linked with terrorism. These policies contribute to politicizing and marginalizing Muslim identity.

Another factor is the growth of an Islamophobia industry that has flourished by selling fear of Muslims, with hundreds of millions of dollars distributed to misinformation centers and activists. There are over one hundred organizations in the United States alone devoted to

---

[32] Rachel S. Mikva, "In Reactionary Times," in *Interreligious Studies: Dispatches from the Field*, ed. Hans Gustafson (Waco: Baylor University Press, 2020), 191.

disseminating biased information about Islam and Muslims; many of them have been designated hate groups by the Southern Poverty Law Center. A few of the groups proclaim their bias in their names, such as Jihad Watch and Foundation for Advocating Christian Truth. Some may be trying to lure unsuspecting folks with names that approximate Muslim non-profits; if you cannot quite remember "Council on American-Islamic Relations" (CAIR), for instance, you might accidentally end up at the Bureau of American Islamic Relations, an anti-Muslim hate group. The majority of these organizations, however, try to convey noble purpose with names like ACT for America and the Center for Security Policy.

Leaders of these organizations have concluded that there is political and financial profit in selling bias against Muslims and Islam. They promote each other's work and serve on each other's boards – and many earn six-figure incomes. They gain notoriety by saying outlandish things, like Robert Spencer's (Jihad Watch) complaint that Christmas is "under siege because there are large numbers of Muslims in the West. That is the sole and only reason. The responsibility lies with those who admitted them without regard for Islam's doctrines of religious warfare and supremacism." Or Brigitte Gabriel's (ACT for America) fabricated statistic that 15–25 percent of Muslims are radicalized, meaning "180 million to 300 million people dedicated to the destruction of Western civilization."[33] Their voices get amplified in an echo chamber of right-wing politicians, media, religious leaders, and grassroots organizations. Their messages infect public discourse, so that schools, landlords, Hollywood, law enforcement agencies, and the rest of us become witting or unwitting accomplices.

Consider the movement for anti-sharia legislation in the United States. It serves no legal purpose: the Constitution already forbids the

---

[33] Southern Poverty Law Center, www.splcenter.org/fighting-hate/extremist-files/ individual/robert-spencer; Alexander LaCasse, "How Many Muslim Extremists Are There? Just the Facts, Please," *Christian Science Monitor* (January 13, 2015), www .csmonitor.com/World/Security-Watch/terrorism-security/2015/0113/How-many- Muslim-extremists-are-there-Just-the-facts-please.

authority of foreign law, and no Muslim group has tried to impose sharia in America. Other religious groups have religious courts that deal with ritual matters; they are not deemed threatening. Yet in the 2010s over two hundred bills were introduced in state legislatures, and at least twenty were enacted – all based on model legislation titled "American Laws for American Courts," drafted by David Yerushalmi and promoted by multiple Islamophobic groups. The campaign was designed to spread the idea that Islam is dangerous; using the Islamophobic trope that Muslims manipulate systems to magnify their power, they conjure a stealth strategy of sharia domination – persuading approximately one-third of Americans that Muslims want to establish sharia law in the USA. These baseless concerns have proven useful for gathering funding and political support.[34]

Yerushalmi is one of several Jews who are prominent in the Islamophobia network. Although American Jews rank among the highest groups in having *positive* views of Muslims, some are significant contributors to anti-Muslim groups (and a portion of those funds are directed through donor-advised funds administered by Jewish communal agencies). Concerns about Muslim opposition to Israel is often cited as a motivation.[35]

Professional Islamophobes are scattered throughout the West. In the Netherlands, for example, an obscure parliamentarian named Geert Wilders gained great notoriety by comparing the Qur'an to *Mein Kampf* and trying to have it banned, seeking to block immigration from Muslim-majority countries and construction of mosques, and

---

[34] See Green, *Fear of Islam*; Matthew Duss et al., "Fear Inc. 2.0: The Islamophobia Network's Efforts to Manufacture Hate in America," Center for American Progress, 2015; "Learn More: Sharia Law," America by the Numbers, August 24, 2016, www .americabythenumbers.org/learn-sharia-law.

[35] Dalia Mogahed and Azka Mahmood, "American Muslim Poll 2019: Predicting and Preventing Islamophobia," Institute for Social Policy and Understanding, May 2019, www.ispu.org/wp-content/uploads/2019/04/AMP-2019_Predicting-and-Preventing-Islamophobia.pdf; Benjamin Gladstone, "For Jews, the Fight Against Islamophobia Must Begin at Home," *Tablet*, August 30, 2017, www.tabletmag.com/sections/news/articles/for-jews-the-fight-against-islamophobia-must-begin-at-home.

other provocations. After making *Fitna*, a film that expanded on his Islamophobic views, his party almost tripled its number of seats in the parliament. While it is difficult to tease apart religious and political motivations, religion adds a dangerous ultimacy to the equation.

Anti-Muslim sentiment is not confined to the West. Around the world, Islamophobia utilizes a toxic formula of ethnic nationalism, religious bigotry, and fear-mongering to advance political power. We see it deployed against the Rohingya in Myanmar and the Uighurs in China, and embedded in Hindu nationalist pressure in Kashmir. Taliban destruction of Buddhist shrines in Afghanistan and the growth of Muslim militant groups in Southeast Asia deepen fear and hostility.[36] There is not room to address all these concerns, however, so we shift to consideration of ways that Interreligious Studies and interfaith activism may combat antisemitism and Islamophobia.

8.9   CHALLENGING ANTISEMITISM AND ISLAMOPHOBIA

Interreligious efforts can be particularly effective in challenging anti-semitism, Islamophobia, and other forms of religious bias. While encounters with religious diversity sometimes spark hostility and violence, many people see opportunities for mutual enrichment instead. Individual voices throughout history have resisted our tendency to "mis-recognize" people whose lifestance is different than our own. Jesus tried to expand his listeners' conception of neighbor in the parable of the good Samaritan. Muslim officials convened *majalis* to compare religious convictions in a reasoned manner (see Chapter 2). Philo, Nicholas of Cusa, ibn Arabi and others spoke of the presence of God in all religious experience, sensing a unity that transcends difference without erasing it.

By the twentieth century, the record of religiously endorsed hatred was so terrifying that scholars began to challenge it in earnest. Rosemary Radford Ruether wrote a groundbreaking study of Christian antisemitism, demanding educational, social, and theological

[36] See Hedges, *Religious Hatred*, 218, 225, 278.

reconstruction to unwind the teachings of contempt (*Faith and Fratricide*, 1974). Martin Buber, Emmanuel Levinas, Mary Boys, and Thich Nhat Hanh are among scores of religious scholars who composed theologies that model ways to humanize the Other.

Organizations were established to combat religious bias. The Anti-Defamation League, for example, was founded in 1913 "to stop the defamation of the Jewish people and to secure justice and fair treatment to all." The National Coalition of Christians and Jews (1927) was created when anti-Catholic rhetoric swelled during Al Smith's run for the Democratic presidential nomination; its mission was to reduce anti-Catholic and anti-Jewish prejudice. The American Jewish Congress (1918) fought against restrictions in housing, employment, and education – rallying for equal rights regardless of race, religion, or national ancestry. In 1945, the founding charter of the United Nations included non-discrimination on the basis of religion.[37]

Vatican II's *Nostra aetate* (1965) was a transformative Catholic statement of interfaith fraternity. While the Church conceives of its own path as the fullest expression of religious truth, the statement affirms the Jewish covenant with the assertion in Romans 11:29 that God does not revoke Divine promises, and expresses regard for Muslims' submission to the one God. A significant number of Protestant denominations have issued statements repudiating antisemitism; numerous Jewish and Christian groups in the West have publicly denounced Islamophobia as violations of their spiritual values. Muslim and Jewish community leaders have reciprocated with declarations and outreach efforts of their own.

Beginning with a "social relations" model of making change through relationship-building and community education, religious and interreligious organizations later expanded their strategies to include public advocacy, legislation, and litigation to protect the

[37] See Rachel S. Mikva, "With No One to Make Them Afraid: A Jewish Perspective on Safeguarding Religious Freedom," *Cultural Encounters* 16, no. 1 (2021): 23.

rights of all religious minorities. People also respond to hatred with direct action. In 2010, an extremist church in Gainesville, Florida, advocated burning the Qur'an to commemorate September 11. A man who was present at one of these conflagrations grabbed the Qur'an that the group was going to burn and ran off with it. He made a video to ridicule the hate and it went viral. There were also groups that responded by advocating "Read the Qur'an" day instead or by donating a copy of the text to the Afghan army for every one that was burned.

Jews and Muslims have volunteered to protect each other as they gather in their sacred spaces in the wake of attacks or times of particular vulnerability. Interreligious coalitions have formed as solidarity movements; they publicly and vocally stand up for individuals and communities under assault. Emphasizing our shared values of religious freedom, they transform the story; it is no longer Us vs. Them but rather a broader understanding of the Us.

Often, the most dramatic change occurs when we develop relationships with religious others. If we can cultivate hate through our religious teachings, we can elect to cultivate empathy instead. The chapters that follow flesh out multiple methods in which Interreligious Studies and engagement seek to do precisely that.

PART III **Modes of Engagement**

9   Practices of Interreligious Engagement

As described in previous chapters, interreligious engagement happens all over the place. We now turn to orchestrated projects to cultivate relationship and understanding among people with differing lifestances, using various modalities. Part III of the book discusses projects that focus on (a) dialogue; (b) study and spiritual encounter; (c) community-based service, organizing, and advocacy; and (d) utilizing the arts. There is also a chapter on conflict transformation, which can be relevant to programs of all sorts. Before detailing each in a subsequent chapter, however, we discuss common objectives and core practices for shaping these diverse modes of interreligious engagement.

Terms can be elastic, and "dialogue" is attached to various forms of encounter. In 1984, the Pontifical Council for Interreligious Dialogue described four modes that have become frequent points of reference:

- *Dialogue of life*, describing our efforts to live in an open and neighborly spirit as we meet one another in the world;
- *Dialogue of action*, in which people of diverse lifestances collaborate for the development and liberation of all;
- *Dialogue of theological exchange*, where specialists share their religious heritages, coming to appreciate each other's spiritual values and enrich perspective on their own;
- *Dialogue of religious experience*, where persons of faith share their spiritual riches as they relate to prayer, contemplation, and other aspects of their experience.[1]

---

[1] Pontifical Council for Interreligious Dialogue, "Dialogue and Proclamation" 3.42, www.vatican.va/roman_curia/pontifical_councils/interelg/documents/rc_pc_ interelg_doc_19051991_dialogue-and-proclamatio_en.html.

While these forms of encounter are interrelated, I tease them apart to examine each in detail. Many aspects of the dialogue of life were discussed in Chapters 5–7. The dialogue of action is covered in Chapters 12 and 13. The dialogue of theological exchange and dialogue of religious experience are addressed in Chapters 10 and 11 – distinguished as projects that focus on conversation versus those that utilize shared study or spiritual encounter. Rather than assuming that dialogue about religious ideas is restricted to specialists while other participants are limited to sharing rituals or personal faith journeys, however, interreligious dialogue has been largely democratized. It no longer looks like it sometimes did in 1950s America, with a handful of white, male clergy talking about their religious ideas in front of an audience. More focused on the dynamic meeting of persons rather than comparing traditions, more inclusive and collaborative, more capable of exploring difference, interreligious "dialogue" is a robust enterprise with a plethora of modalities.

Another framework that you see is the dialogue of head, heart, and hands. It aligns nicely with an organizing structure suggested by Mark Heim based on three yogas or paths for human liberation delineated in the Bhagavad Gita: *jnana* (knowledge), *bhakti* (devotion), and *karma* (action).[2] The categories still slip and slide into each other: learning together clearly involves the pursuit of knowledge, but in rabbinic tradition, it is also considered a spiritual endeavor. Studying sacred texts or other materials in the presence of one another – when we have deliberately gathered across religious difference – has profound experiential, affective dimensions. Dialogue, understood in the narrow sense of planned programs for conversation, is both educational and deeply devotional. And *karma* may seem best embodied in interreligious community service or advocacy, but all our efforts to meet one another involve action. So before presenting chapters that

---

[2] S. Mark Heim, *Salvations: Truth and Difference in Religion* (Maryknoll: Orbis Books, 1995), 99–100.

take up individual strategies for engagement, we explore the rationales and core practices that these yogas share.

9.1   THE WHY OF INTERRELIGIOUS/INTERPATH ENGAGEMENT

Rather than refer to all the modalities as dialogue, this volume speaks of coordinated programs for encounter across religious difference as interreligious or interpath *engagement*. (As noted in Chapter 2, "interpath" was coined in the dialogue world to be more inclusive of people who come to the table with secular, cultural, or philosophical perspectives, as well as individuals who identify as interspiritual or spiritual but not religious.) "Engagement" tries to capture the deliberateness of the encounter – meeting across difference for a purpose.

Still, it is helpful to begin by thinking about dialogue, which intimates something more substantial than mere conversation. Through (*dia-*) speech (*logos*), we connect, come to appreciate, and become responsible to/for one another. Dialogue is significantly different than other types of speech. It is not debate because the object is to understand rather than persuade; we come ready to listen and learn. It is not negotiation or mediation because it is not designed to engender agreement or compromise among the parties (see Chapter 14 for conflict transformation). It is not testimony; although sharing one's experience, understanding, and aspirations is part of the process, dialogue is not the same as alternating monologues. There needs to be a transformative shift, crossing into the empty space between and "inhabiting" the world of the other. Lastly, dialogue is not therapy; although personal growth is a natural outcome, it is not the primary goal.

Building on this reflection, we consider the goals of interpath engagement. The foundational objective is to understand people of diverse lifestances more authentically and deeply, nurturing relationships of mutual respect and appreciation. In the process, we advance the common good. It happens through sharing wisdom, generating creativity, and strengthening our capacity to live as good neighbors.

Some projects go further, undertaking additional acts of world repair. We also come to know ourselves more fully as we explain ourselves to others, see our lifestance through their eyes, and recognize how their worldview illuminates our own in fresh ways. We discover questions we would not have considered. If our own growth becomes the center of the encounter, however, it diminishes the humanity of our partners by making them objects rather than subjects, and it also tends to distort how we interpret what they say.

What does faith contribute to the equation? Identifying a diversity of lifestances as the organizing impulse potentially adds a spiritual element that opens hearts and allows for deeper human bonds. It provides moral and ritual frameworks to weave our developing understanding into our daily lives and social fabric, and it offers institutional structures for mobilizing others. It brings to bear the teachings from multiple traditions that highlight the ethics of speech and values like respect, compassion, empathy. And it brings out into the open differences regarding what theologian/philosopher Paul Tillich called our "ultimate concern[s]," differences that significantly impact our common life, so they can be tended with care.

As a crucible of difference with established tools for building bridges, interpath engagement is a means to foster cohesion in our increasingly fragmented society – navigating intersected issues around race, gender, or politics as well as lifestance. We live amidst great diversity, as is evident in the daily news and in our own communities. It is also a time of polarizing forces: nationalism, authoritarianism, militant fundamentalism, culture wars, and violent conflicts around the world divide us so intensely that even issues which could bring us together – the climate crisis, refugees, a global pandemic – only exacerbate the problem. These circumstances create a dialogical imperative. While religion at times contributes to the divides, it can also be an organizing force in healing them.

It is critical that we do not simply *imagine* differences but rather *meet* them. Invented otherness is almost always threatening, fashioned from stereotypes and social anxieties. When Shakespeare wrote the sinister Jewish character of Shylock in *The Merchant of Venice*, for example, he did not actually know any Jews; they had been expelled from England over 300 years before. According to social scientists, knowing people with a different lifestance generally fosters more positive perspectives on the group. Also, one meaningful relationship with a person who had previously seemed "other" can improve attitudes about a range of differences. A recent study of college students demonstrated that meaningful interaction with people of diverse lifestances is instrumental in developing the skills and attitudes necessary to bridge ideological divides.[3]

The work of interpath engagement unfolds on multiple levels. It is possible to effect social change by changing minds, shaping interpersonal relations, improving institutions, changing laws, empowering communities, challenging systems of oppression, creating systems of support and more. The relational dimensions of engagement, however, remain primary. As Jennifer Bailey, founding Executive Director of Faith Matters Network, teaches: Social change moves at the speed of relationship, and relationship moves at the speed of trust.[4]

Relationship and trust develop naturally when people's bonds are stronger than their differences or when they have a common task. When they have no connection or their association is marked by ignorance and mistrust, however, engagement requires careful and collaborative planning. Here are some of the foundational practices of interreligious engagement.[5]

---

[3] Alyssa N. Rockenbach, et al., *IDEALS: Bridging Religious Divides through Higher Education* (Chicago: Interfaith Youth Core, 2020); Robert Putnam and David Campbell, *American Grace: How Religion Divides and Unites Us* (New York: Simon & Schuster, 2010), 533.

[4] Jennifer Bailey, *To My Beloveds: Letters on Faith, Race, Loss, and Radical Hope* (St. Louis: Chalice Press, 2021), 104. See also https://thepeoplessupper.org.

[5] See also Eleazar S. Fernandez, ed., *Teaching for a Multifaith World* (Eugene: Pickwick, 2017), chaps. 2 and 5.

9.2   DEEP LISTENING

Deep listening – sometimes described as compassionate or generous listening – is a core practice of interpath engagement. It involves fullness of presence and the capacity for empathy, the ability to reason and feel from experiences other than our own. This is less about standing in someone else's shoes (which is still about what we see) and more about how they see themselves. Emotional intelligence recognizes our own feelings and the feelings of others; generous listening requires that we use the information only to comprehend, not to exert power. We set aside possible feelings of self-defensiveness or self-interest and try to understand how our partners' convictions are true for them. We resist making assumptions about why they say what they do; the questions we ask are designed to deepen understanding rather than challenge their perspective or control the conversation. Listening does not have an agenda. Even so – if people feel heard, they may in turn be more open to hearing stories of those with whom they disagree.

In Buddhist tradition, deep listening is essential as a means to relieve suffering. Several *bodhisattvas*, individuals capable of achieving nirvana who chose to remain in this world to ease the burdens of others, are revered for their capacity to listen from the heart as a healing practice.[6]

You may have learned about "active" listening; it involves evident attention, reflecting back what you heard, and demonstrating a commitment to stay engaged. Generous listening builds on this foundation and adds a hermeneutic of grace, identifying strengths rather than weaknesses. When people say things we find troubling, we seek clarification without disparagement. Questions like "Can you flesh out that idea or tell me a story to illustrate what you mean?" or "Can you share why you say that?" establish a tone of openness. We avoid turning differences into dichotomies where one perspective

---

[6] Thich Nhat Hanh, *The Heart of the Buddha's Teaching* (New York: Harmony Books, 2015), chap. 12.

is good and any other is necessarily bad. It does not mean sacrificing your values, but the goal remains understanding rather than persuasion.

In interreligious engagement , it is important to make room for our partners to change. They may say something toward the beginning of the process that seems closed-minded or uninformed; we cannot lock them into that perspective or it will hinder growth and relationship. When trying to navigate difference, errors are common; it is healthy to assume good will when others make mistakes and try to learn from our own. Practice the pause: waiting before responding can help us react to errors in a constructive way. It also inculcates deeper listening so we truly hear our partners instead of formulating our replies while they are speaking. The content sinks in so we become aware of our feelings that have been stirred and take time to explore their meaning. It can cool tempers and warm hearts as the space allows us to see the human being before us.

9.3   WE ARE THERE TO LEARN

Some people approach interpath work eager to dispel misunderstanding about their lifestance or community. They may even be motivated to study their tradition at greater depth so they can be better informed and thoughtful in what they share. It is critical, however, that all parties come to the table with an interest in learning about the lifestance of others, not only in teaching about their own. This is the foundation for mutuality.

There are limits, of course, to understanding someone else's lifestance. As outsiders, we are ultimately excluded from the experiential histories, intersected conceptual terrain, and spiritual imprint that root its meaning. We may discern similarities-in-difference through analogy, but this imaginative exercise sometimes casts others too much as reflections of ourselves. Nonetheless, learning in the company of those who are willing to share their journeys and refining our understanding within relationship is the best way to navigate this challenge.

Participants must also have the capacity for self-critical faith. Belief transformed into ideology becomes vapid. Philosophers and theologians through the ages have insisted that we must recognize the limits of our knowledge and challenge our own convictions in order to ask questions of substance that help us grow in understanding. Contemporary scholarship highlights the need for reflexivity, appreciating how our social location shapes our worldview and even how we learn. It does not matter whether we see ourselves as progressive or conservative along the theological spectrum; the roots of self-critical faith grow deep in the soil of spiritual lifestances, designed for us to cultivate. Even scriptural traditions that suggest adherents hold God's word in their hands, for example, demonstrate awareness of multivocality in their sacred texts, the provisional nature of truth and the human role in interpreting the Word, historical change and its impact on religious meaning, epistemological humility and the role of doubt in faith. Identity and openness to learning or change are not diametrically opposed.[7]

Some adherents worry that doubt is a sign of inadequate devotion, but it is really a measure of humility. A volume of interreligious scholarship, *Learned Ignorance: Intellectual Humility among Jews, Christians, and Muslims*, demonstrates the importance of this quality within religious thought and practice.[8] Another interreligious group of scholars, working together on a Just Peace paradigm, discovered how self-critical faith can also be transformative in establishing trust. They were struggling to articulate the need for the project, all insisting that their religion was one of peace. Then they agreed to bring each other their "worst text" – a text that revealed the violence embedded in each of their scriptural traditions – and suddenly a path opened before them.

---

[7] See Rachel S. Mikva, *Dangerous Religious Ideas: The Deep Roots of Self-Critical Faith in Judaism, Christianity, and Islam* (Boston: Beacon Press), 35–82.

[8] James L. Heft, Reuven Firestone, and Omid Safi, eds. *Learned Ignorance: Intellectual Humility Among Jews, Christians, and Muslims* (Oxford: Oxford University Press, 2011), https://doi.org/10.1093/acprof:osobl/9780199769308.001.0001.

[I]t made us each less defensive and more open. Muslims and Jews did not have to say, "You Christians have used the New Testament to justify killing many of us" – the Christians had already said that. Christians did not have to accuse the others of justifying persecutions or attacks based on their holiest texts – Muslims and Jews had already said that... We each developed a hermeneutic – a method of interpreting scriptures – that showed respect for those problem passages but did not use them to cause harm.[9]

Self-critical faith requires a willingness to risk vulnerability and inhabit ambiguity – qualities that can be transformative because acknowledging that we do not have all the answers illuminates how much we need one another. This shared struggle is the essential glue of a diverse society. Social power intervenes here; it is easier for privileged religious voices to admit the ugly stuff. But no tradition can remain vital, and they can certainly not thrive together, without continuing to cultivate these capacities.

9.4   SPEAKING *FROM* A LIFESTANCE RATHER THAN *FOR* IT

Swami Tyagananda and others have suggested that interfaith dialogue is not designed to talk about religion but to facilitate the sharing of religious selves; this can be extended to other types of interpath engagement.[10] Speaking *from* a lifestance rather than *for* it is a core practice, even though the older model of specialists' theological exchange frequently operates in the "speaking for" mode. Cumulative tradition is too vast to be neatly summarized; individuals

---

[9] Susan Brooks Thistlethwaite, "Introduction," in *Interfaith Just Peacemaking: Jewish, Christian, and Muslim Perspectives on the New Paradigm of Peace and War* (New York: Palgrave Macmillan, 2012), 3, https://doi.org/10.1057/9781137012944_1.

[10] Swami Tyagananda, "Doing Dialogue Interreligiously," in *Interreligious Dialogue: An Anthology of Voices Bridging Cultural and Religious Divides*, ed. Christoffer H. Grundmann (Winona: Anselm Academic, 2015), 59–73.

can represent only a piece without masking the multiplicity and complexity embedded within.

The idea that we speak for ourselves and receive others as speaking for themselves, without expectation that they represent a whole group, is both a caution and a reassurance. Many people do not feel sufficiently knowledgeable to speak broadly about their tradition, but they are experts in their own experience. Participants get to define themselves – not constrained by how media, textbooks, or religious hierarchies see them. They describe their relationship to tradition and their understanding of it with clear caveats that their statements reflect their own perspective. They may try to introduce a multiplicity of voices within their lifestance – still recognizing how they are filtered through their own lenses.

We not only speak in this individuated mode; we listen in it as well. In reflecting back what we hear, we present a portrait based on what our partners have shared. At the same time, we do not make their viewpoint stand for the whole, and we resist making broad assumptions based on limited knowledge. Participants are certainly not responsible for anything terrible that people of their lifestance have done, and no group should be judged based on the actions of a few individuals. Although we may ask how they interpret aspects of their tradition that we find troubling, we should not press them to defend or disavow them.

There is one way in which it is productive to see our partners as potentially representative of their lifestance. When people admire individuals from a tradition they consider suspect, it is common to mentally divide the group into good and bad adherents or to identify the people they know as exceptions. A theist may believe that one must believe in God to be an ethical person, for example. Then they meet an ethical atheist. Assuming that this person is an exception does little to further interpath understanding. Instead, the encounter should trouble assumptions about the group and the cognitive dissonance should prompt them to consider how their original expectations were formed.

Commitment to individuation also facilitates humanization. Our partners are people, a realization that reinforces the next core practice.

9.5 MUTUAL RESPECT IN SPEECH AND ACTION

Mutuality in relationship operates as a virtuous circle, with trust begetting trust. Participants know that they will not be purposely insulted and their integrity will not be violated – but respect runs deeper than politeness. As mentioned in Chapter 4, Martin Buber's I–Thou paradigm is often invoked as a model for recognizing the irreducible humanity of those we encounter: we seek out the fullness of one another's being in intersubjective meeting where respect is not a favor but a realization. His coformative insight that we become our complete, actualized selves only through such I–Thou relationships is found in multiple Indigenous traditions. The Lakota say "*mitakuye oyasin*," roughly translated as "we are all related." The Mosquito peoples on the Caribbean coast of Nicaragua greet one another with "*kupia kumi*" (we are one heart), as they put their hand on their own heart. Juana Bordas describes "I am another yourself" as the Mayan golden rule.[11] This foundation of mutuality allows for vulnerability, authenticity, even playfulness.

In interreligious engagement programs, respect is an operating principle – demonstrating concern for those in the out-group as much as for the in-group. In other contexts, where respect is not expected, it is often transformative. Offered unilaterally, it may nonetheless catalyze reciprocity. Once mutuality is established, the power of "transgressing" established boundaries can seed transcendent movements of liberation. Rev. angel Kyodo williams, a Zen priest, calls this insurgence rooted in love "radical dharma."[12]

---

[11] Bordas, *Salsa, Soul, and Spirit: Leadership for a Multicultural Age* (Oakland: Berrett-Koehler, 2012) 15, 162, 167.

[12] angel Kyodo williams, Rod Owens, and Jasmine Syedullah, *Radical Dharma: Talking Race, Love, and Liberation* (Berkeley: North Atlantic Books, 2016).

While the capacity to recognize and honor the Thou in interpath engagement is fundamentally an attitude, there are practices that cultivate and express it. We allow people to finish talking without interruption and strive to share "airtime" evenly. We do not ask partners to share more than they are comfortable doing; they can pass or pass for now. We choose words carefully, for example describing a practice as unfamiliar rather than strange – and in general try to anticipate how our comments may be received. We do not compare our ideals to others' messy reality; instead, we relate ideals to ideals, practice to practice. We plan *with* our partners rather than for them. We speak as honestly as possible, not relying on habitual responses, stale scripts, or dictates from the past that we have not stopped to consider in a critical way. I have a Zoroastrian colleague who describes this type of honesty as rooted in *asha*, a polysemous term that links truth, existence, justice, and doing right; she sees it as an organizing principle of existence that diminishes the power of evil and reveals the beauty of what *is*.

Learning the vocabulary and communication norms of those with whom we are working is a demonstration of respect. It is not correct to refer to a synagogue or gurdwara as a church, for example. Even "house of worship" is not appropriate for the gathering place of every lifestance. If our partners have a scripture, we should know or ask its name. Also, if we use insider language from our own tradition, we should explain what it means. (At the same time, we should make room for the possibility that some of our partners are well-versed in other traditions.) Since we are meeting in order to learn and should resist making assumptions about the person in front of us based on what we read in a book, we need not memorize huge amounts of information. Instead, we recognize that our religious language is not universal even if we are communicating in a common tongue, and we ask questions in ways that deepen mutuality.

We should also consider dissimilarities in communication norms. In my experience of Jewish culture, for instance, interruptions and rapid exchanges of thoughts represent positive engagement;

prolonged silence may be interpreted as ignorance or disinterest. In most Native American communities, however, interruptions are extremely rude and silence is valued for many of the reasons discussed above related to the pause. Silence also demonstrates respect for the person who has just spoken. Some cultures resist addressing conflictual issues; others may not be adept at non-confrontational dialogue. Cultural approaches to time also vary; beginning and ending on time is a requisite of respect in some circles, but it is not universal. These differences need to be understood. Many facilitated dialogue efforts work together to establish communication norms for the group toward the beginning of the process. In this exercise, we listen to diverse cultural perspectives even if some are set aside. The idea that interrupting people is a sign of active engagement, for instance, is generally rejected as a norm but it is helpful for participants to know if it is "normal" for some. Cultural differences impact how people communicate, what they are willing to talk about, how they learn, and what kinds of engagement feel suitable, so groups must always be attentive to submerged aspects of identity.

9.6 EQUALITY

Equality is an aspiration in interpath engagement even though the project is necessarily marked by power constructs that make true equity difficult to establish. For one thing, interreligious programming is inherently exclusive. Who sets the table, who sets the rules, and who controls access? The power to convene is substantial, often providing outsized influence over place, representation, language, and agenda. We compensate for this by working with people of diverse lifestances in planning and facilitation and by always asking whose voice is not being heard. Habits of "discounting" voices of lay people or those who come to the table without a recognized religious identity should be resisted, and programs need to make space for less familiar lifestances. Even efforts that seek to be collaborative in planning, however, find that some sponsors have more financial or human resources to invest. Vulnerable and minoritized communities are often overloaded when it comes to interreligious work. Equality must be tended at every turn, recognizing intersections with race, gender, age, and class.

Numerous issues related to power were discussed in Chapter 2: European colonialism shaped the way we think about religion and the relationship between lifestances. Christian majorities are common in the context of Western culture, meaning that Christian questions, values, and norms are prominent, and Christian voices may dominate the conversation. Broad inter- and intrafaith diversities generally make equal representation unfeasible; often only Christianity is presented as internally diverse. Certain groups are routinely underrepresented or invisible, such as African American Muslims or Jews of color, Pagans, Humanists, and Indigenous traditions. Women's voices are marginalized in some lifestances, raising a paradoxical dilemma: is it even possible to establish both gender equity and equality among faith traditions?

Government-sponsored interreligious engagement efforts, common in Europe, raise additional issues of power. Some participants feel that the national culture is party to the dialogue as the convener, but without the requisite willingness to learn and change; they worry that the underlying purpose is to assimilate "foreign" religious cultures. If only some participants are seen as carriers of difference, that is not equality. Even the value of tolerance suggests that some parties have disproportionate power to decide whether or not to abide religious others and to determine what qualifies as intolerance.[13]

Identifying power dynamics and being sensitive to these challenges help to advance equality, even if it remains elusive.

[13] Anne Hege Grung, "Interreligious Dialogue: Moving between Compartmentalization and Complexity," *Approaching Religion* 1, no. 1 (May 2011): 25–32, https://doi.org/10.30664/ar.67467; Schirin Amir-Moazami, "Dialogue as a Governmental Technique: Managing Gendered Islam in Germany," *Feminist Review* 98 (2011): 9–27.

9.7   ACCOUNTABILITY

Philosopher Emmanuel Levinas (1905–95) discussed the "face" of the other as it makes a claim on us; encounter manifests vulnerability and calls forth our mutual responsibility. Acknowledging that inequalities are always present in encounter, he posited that the most urgent demand is "Do not kill me" – the beginning of our accountability to one another. Levinas challenged the idea that we should rely on finding commonalities to cultivate responsibility because someone will always be set outside that circle of concern. God is revealed in otherness rather than sameness, he believed, and difference is the essence of encounter; if we absorb the otherness of a person into some similarity to self, we erase that person's essential particularity (killing them a different way).[14] Levinas' insight aligns with current best practices in interpath work to go beyond cultivating common ground; we must excavate and navigate differences that matter. Dignifying difference is a foundation for accountability.

Part of response-ability is simply about showing up – being a faithful partner in engagement projects. It involves patience with a sometimes slow-moving process and resilience when encountering rough spots. While this commitment is necessary simply to sustain the relationship, its influence may be more substantial. Studies of Malerkotla for example, a religiously diverse town in the eastern part of Punjab, explore why no one there was killed during partition of Muslim-majority Pakistan and Hindu-majority India at the end of British rule. Even during this period of intense violence, formal and informal dialogue sustained congenial relations; they were fostered by generations of open public festival rites, exchanges of food on holy days, shared sacred sites, and large multifaith wedding receptions that accommodated the religious needs of diverse communities.[15]

---

[14] Emmanuel Levinas, *Totality and Infinity: An Essay on Exteriority*, trans. Alphonso Lingis (Dordrecht: Kluwer Academic Publishers, 1961).

[15] Anna Bigelow, "Muslim–Hindu Dialogue," in *The Wiley-Blackwell Companion to Inter-Religious Dialogue*, ed. Catherine Cornille (Chichester: John Wiley & Sons, 2013), 287, https://doi.org/10.1002/9781118529911.ch17.

Accountability is also essential in the stories we tell. Scriptures often mention other religious lifestances, not always in positive ways, and historical narratives portray others in a particular light. Liturgies, holidays, and folklore all speak of people who are different than "us," powerfully shaping the spiritual psyche. In interpath engagement, we come to see more clearly how our stories implicate others. At one Jewish-Christian-Muslim gathering, the organizers asked a member from each tradition to share an object of religious significance. A Christian presenter discussed a jar of soil from a sacred spot. A Jewish presenter shared the intricate symbolism wrapped in the *tzitzit* (fringes) of the prayer shawl. A Muslim presenter explained that Muslims cannot equate any object with Allah, because it is *shirk* – a serious violation of Islamic theological commitments. It might have been a last-minute cover for forgetting his assignment and having no object in hand, but it also implicated the other presenters. Had he just suggested, by accident of course, that their words bordered on idolatry? He could have brought prayer beads, a *mihrab* that points the way to Mecca, or another Muslim ritual object – since no one had equated their items with God. Even when teaching about our own tradition, our stories say something about those with a different lifestance.[16]

Interreligious projects do not take place in a vacuum, so it is important to recognize how participants may also feel accountable to broader communities. Some may be moved to affirm LGBTQIA+ equality as relationships develop in a group that includes queer participants, for example, but feel constrained by their home community. Others may believe that they need to justify their participation by making space to proselytize or criticize – even though these are generally considered out of bounds in Western interpath encounter. A long-time Muslim leader in dialogue with the Jewish community,

---

[16] See Rachel S. Mikva, "Six Issues That Complicate Interreligious Studies and Engagement," in *Interreligious/Interfaith Studies: Defining a New Field*, ed. Eboo Patel, Jennifer Howe Peace, and Noah J. Silverman (Boston: Beacon Press, 2018), 129.

for instance, was invited to speak at a synagogue's Friday evening Sabbath service. It ended up being during an Israeli ground invasion in Gaza and he felt compelled to speak out against Israeli policy. Even though many members of the synagogue also objected to the assault, they were taken aback by their invited guest's vociferous critique. If he had not done so, however, his own community would have protested that his presence was tacit approval. Jewish-Muslim tensions regularly arise around Israel and Palestine – even though their shared experience as minorities in Western countries also provides fertile common ground to explore.

History – not only current events – can weigh heavily in inter-religious engagement. Sometimes we need to figure out how to be accountable to the "ghosts" in the room, the experiences of violent conflict or theological dispute that leave traces of anxiety and resentment. Part of being response-able to one another is to recognize the sensitivities that partners bring into the space of encounter. Even though *dia-* does not mean "two," dialogue projects frequently involve only two lifestances because the particular history of relationship and current circumstances need room for unpacking.

Participants are also accountable to one another for the success of their project; if they do not feel collectively responsible, it will most likely fail. The vision for what success means is forged together, with appropriate tools to document the work and harvest what is sown. Meeting notes, artistic representations, video, social media engagement, and other methods can record the work. It is essential, however, that along the way participants reflect together on the value of what they are doing, what they are taking away with them, and what they will do with it.

Bridges are not permanent; to maximize impact, there must be mechanisms to sustain relationship and hard-won gains when formal programs conclude. The face of the other makes a claim on us to take our new perspectives back to our own families and communities. At the same time, partners do not want to violate confidentiality, so each project should set a policy. Often "what someone says" is private, but you are encouraged to share "what you learned" with others. Sometimes groups decide that it is appropriate to share what was said, just not who said it. Most important, we find ways to live into what we have learned.

9.8   MUTUAL HOSPITALITY

Hospitality is not simply a warm invitation to participate, but a careful fashioning of supportive space. Mutuality matters; it is best if partners can alternate being guest and host. Some groups seek out a neutral location; although there can be great benefit in coming into each other's spiritual homes when that is an option, there are participants who may feel that entering someone else's sacred space violates their tradition. A hospitable space should be comfortable – physically and spiritually – and it should offer room that is conducive to focused listening. Small gestures, like name tags and time for substantive introductions, go a long way in establishing relationship and building community. Invite interaction. Use open-ended questions. Create opportunities for participants to explore their own questions, needs, and purposes. Recognize people's diverse learning styles, physical abilities, and cultures in structuring the program. These all help to create an aura of hospitality.

In planning, we need to communicate about dietary needs if food will be served (as well as attitudes about alcohol or caffeine), greeting protocols (e.g., some people do not shake hands with those of a different gender), and other religious concerns. Sometimes values collide here; one culture may feel it is rude not to serve meat or alcohol when feeding guests, while others may find it ethically problematic to be present if they do. While asking rather than presuming is generally the best approach, a Muslim colleague confided to me that, if he is asked whether it is okay for alcohol to be present, he feels obliged to say yes – but believes that the onus should not be put on him. We strive to abstain, forego, and accommodate for each other in a spirit of hospitality rather than simple obligation.

Of course, no program can be all things to all people. There often need to be multiple "tables" for interpath engagement. Some people feel they should not be present if there is no opportunity for proselytizing (*dawa*, evangelizing, etc.); they may argue that prohibiting it actually promotes a theology – that of pluralism. Others disagree, teasing apart pluralism from parity pluralism as was done in Chapter 4. They point out that conversion efforts (implicit or explicit) prevent others from sitting at the table. Jewish tradition, for example, teaches that presence amidst proselytizing could mislead others by making it seem you are considering conversion, so it is discouraged. Most Western dialogue projects preclude proselytizing, but different contexts have different rules. The Programme for Christian–Muslim Relations in Africa (PROCMURA), for instance, generally considers the opportunity to convert others as a tool to attract participants.

Disagreement about the basic rules of engagement can take other forms as well. A few scholars of Interreligious Studies have opined that dialogue without concern for questions of truth seems barren, even inauthentic – but others feel that this criterion privileges particular lifestances and invites debate even if the premise is a common search. Some have argued that engagement must be a meeting of commitments, where people speak from identified spiritual lifestances.[17] Others, however, believe that the language of invitation needs to resist closed notions of cultural and religious belonging – seeking a more dynamic discourse of inclusion that transcends static notions of difference and grapples with cultural complexity. While there does not need to be unanimity in how we understand interpath norms, each of these differences can make the encounter feel less hospitable to those whose preference or perspective is set aside.

---

[17] See, for example, Catherine Cornille, *The Im-Possibility of Interreligious Dialogue* (New York: Crossroad, 2008), 64; "Meaning and Truth in Dialogue," in *The Question of Theological Truth: Philosophical and Interreligious Perspectives*, ed. F. Depoortere and M. Lambkin (Leiden: Brill, 2012), 137–55, https://doi.org/10.1163/9789401208284_008.

There are times when potential participants themselves feel mutually exclusive. Dialogue and other interreligious efforts recognize a need for the inclusion of conservative religious voices. A bigger tent complicates issues like gender and LGBTQIA+ rights, however, and potentially exposes historically marginalized individuals to additional harmful experiences. Yet it is possible to embody respectful encounter even with contrasting theo-ethical convictions. The opportunity to meet in the humanizing process of dialogue, study, spiritual experience, and world repair is invaluable, so we navigate the surprisingly complex waters of hospitality with a spirit of transparency and care.

10 Dialogue

Dialogue, in its narrow sense of planned programs for conversation, is one of the oldest models of interpath engagement. This chapter explores many of the models, methods, and tools for dialogical encounter, even as they continue to multiply. It also discusses reservations that people may have and related challenges.

Some people assume that talking to each other cannot make much of a difference. Since religious bigotry, oppression, and even violence continue, dialogue has not solved the problem. The multitude of interpath dialogue projects, however, present a counterpoint. Anecdotes abound that suggest they have been essential in keeping situations from deteriorating further, and participants have felt the transformative impact in their own lives. Even though much of the work proceeds in small-scale projects, the broader aspirations align with Meg Wheatley's affirmation:

> I believe we can change the world
> if we start listening to one another again.
> Simple, honest, human conversation.
> Not mediation, negotiation, problem-solving,
> debate, or public meetings.
> Simple, truthful conversation
> where we each have a chance to speak,
> we each feel heard, and we each listen well.[1]

In the process of dialogue, we obviously learn about each other – but we learn how to dialogue as well. Its value goes beyond knowledge,

---

[1] Margaret Wheatley, *Turning to One Another: Simple Conversations to Restore Hope to the Future* (San Francisco: Berrett-Koehler, 2002), 3.

forming the attitudes and character that make us better neighbors in our multifaith world.

10.1   MODELS FOR DIALOGUE PROJECTS

There are too many variations to be comprehensive in discussing dialogue models, but these examples provide a starting place for exploration. Some convene as a conversation among adherents of two or more specific lifestances; others gather simply based on geography or focus around a theme. A shared difference can be an effective organizing structure. Women often feel a powerful sense of solidarity, for instance, in discussing their experiences with patriarchy and its residue in their diverse traditions. Transgender people of faith, individuals with disabilities, or people of color who are minoritized within their religious communities can similarly bond in their struggle for visibility and equity.

A common template for dialogue utilizes a one-program format with brief presentations followed by Q & A. It provides an opportunity to learn about diverse lifestances, presumably from adherents, and is generally easy to access – but it provides little opportunity to engage in more sustained, transformative relationship-building. It may also shut out significant voices and experiences, with men frequently overrepresented among the speakers, and with perspectives that focus on mainstream forms of familiar lifestances. Even more participatory and inclusive programs cannot have substantial impact with a single encounter. Since these projects are often sponsored by a collection of congregations, schools, and/or community organizations, however, those that collaborate regularly for such programming eventually establish institutional relationships that can be valuable – especially in the wake of divisive issues or events that arise in the community.

Another template initiates a dialogue framework with no pre-established end. Participants remain engaged for a short or long period of time, but the dialogue continues. Such extended projects naturally develop deep connections among participants: the Buddhist–Christian Theological Encounter, known informally as the Cobb–Abe group (named after John Cobb and Masao Abe, who helped birth the effort), was an invitation-only affair that gathered primarily scholar-practitioners for five days every eighteen months – a small but transformative project that lasted for twenty years. Local efforts commonly take the form of two or more religious communities hosting a monthly gathering for facilitated conversation; they often include breaking bread together to deepen a sense of connection. National and international networks like the Sisterhood of Salaam-Shalom support local chapters that sponsor their own programs, while the national office coordinates more ambitious efforts like conferences and study tours to explore interreligious issues as they unfold in various contexts. Individuals have also initiated interreligious relationships, going on to write books and launch speaking tours, as did the authors of *The Faith Club* and *Interfaith Amigos*, the partners in Stand Up for Peace and the Israeli-Palestinian Comedy Tour. Their modeling can inspire others to reach out across difference in their own communities – but the most profound impact is on the authors and speakers who do this work together for years.

There are models that utilize a middle ground, designed for sustained engagement over a defined period of time. Chicago Theological Seminary and other schools frequently run year-long programs with graduate students of diverse lifestances; the dialogue undergirds a coformative process that deepens their commitments to their own traditions and makes them better religious leaders in America's multifaith culture. (Some faith-based training, like Clinical Pastoral Education [CPE], is regularly done in multifaith cohorts in the USA.) Retreats and multipart workshops are also common, including in areas where religion has been embedded in geopolitical conflict like Bosnia, Ireland, Israel/Palestine, and Myanmar. Distinct from conflict transformation projects, these efforts do not generally address the conflict directly or attempt to negotiate a resolution. Instead, they focus on relationship-building – humanizing people who are seen as enemies.

Some colleges and universities have established interreligious living communities for students who want to learn about the daily practices and perspectives of peers through the intimacy of a shared home. Interfaith America works on multiple campuses to develop student leadership, curricula, and other initiatives that incorporate interreligious dialogue – reaching young adults at a formative period in their lives.

As is evident from the discussion so far, there are a variety of sponsors for interreligious dialogue. Religious institutions are frequent initiators; larger ones like the Catholic Church establish offices to catalyze or participate in regional dialogue projects. The Church of Norway, representing the majority-Lutheran population, established the Christian–Muslim Contact Group – even fostering the Islamic Council so it could have a suitable partner. On a smaller scale, local congregations also collaborate to create pulpit exchanges, shared programs, and dialogue groups. Colleges and universities, recognizing the challenges and opportunities of students facing significant religious diversity, frequently dedicate staff and resources to interpath programming.

Some projects are coordinated or funded by government agencies. Article 17 of the Treaty on the Functioning of the European Union formalized a dialogue with churches, religious associations, philosophical and non-confessional organizations; in 2021, the Council of Europe passed a comparable resolution for interreligious and interconvictional dialogue. The Council for Religious and Life Stance Communities in Norway, founded in 1996, is an independent but publicly funded agency. In the USA, President Obama launched an annual Interfaith and Community Service Campus Challenge.

Although state involvement always raises certain concerns, it can have significant impact. Saudi Arabia's King Abdullah sponsored an interreligious conference in Madrid in 2008. His initiative – along with conferences in Alexandria, Qatar, Cairo, Islamabad, Istanbul, and Jakarta – has helped to disarm theological objections to interfaith work in the Muslim world. The Doha International Centre on

Interfaith Dialogue (DICID) and the KAICIID Dialogue Centre (established by Austria, Saudi Arabia, and Spain, with the Holy See as a founding "observer"), supported by government funds, stand as enduring institutions that continue to generate momentum for international interreligious dialogue.

NGOs of all sizes contribute to the work of dialogue. The Parliament of the World's Religions periodically convenes thousands of people from around the world to meet, talk, learn, and eat together for a few days. The Institute for Interfaith Dialogue in Indonesia arranges programs throughout the country. Urban non-profits pursue dialogue to address particular struggles in the community. The Inner-City Muslim Action Network (Chicago and Atlanta), for example, used this approach with African American neighborhood leaders and largely Muslim immigrant store-owners to work through tensions around food justice. Individuals also launch projects, like the Buddhist-Evangelical dialogue established by Kyogen Carlson and Paul Metzger in Portland, Oregon; prompted by controversial ballot measures in one election cycle, it lasted for over a decade.

Dialogue efforts can productively engage a diversity of life-stances without necessarily having a distinctly religious focus. "Hands Across the Hills," for example, connects communities in Leverett, Massachusetts, and Letcher County, Kentucky, over three long weekends; constructed around political and geographic divergence, spiritual lifestances (interfaith and intrafaith) nonetheless emerge as a significant carrier of difference. Similarly, a multifaith book group that reads broadly without putting religion at the center of its agenda can still accomplish many of the objectives of interpath dialogue; lifestances emerge as a filter that shapes how we encounter the world. There is a workbook called "Dialogue That Enlarges: Bridging Ideological Divides through a Faith Lens" from the Better Arguments Project that guides individuals or groups to reflect on how their lifestances shape their worldviews and can also help them forge relationships across difference.

Dialogue work can be done virtually. The Tony Blair Foundation, for example, sponsors a Face to Faith program connecting 12–17-year-olds from around the globe via video conferencing. A number of services offer comparable updated versions of pen pals to students at various stages in their education – easily adapted for interpath dialogue. Dialogue can even be asynchronous. In 2007, 138 Muslim scholars and leaders initiated a significant project called "A Common Word." Launched as a reconciling endeavor in response to Pope Benedict XVI's Regensburg speech that referenced a fourteenth-century characterization of Muhammad's message as inhuman and violent, it invited Christian leaders to explore common elements of faith. "A Common Word" has catalyzed over a decade of substantive engagement, with letters of response, signatories, publications, and educational programs. Most of the dialogue is indirect, but face-to-face conversations and relationships have grown from the project as well.

10.2   TOOLS FOR INTERRELIGIOUS DIALOGUE

There are manifold tools for shaping dialogue. Dialogue circles are familiar to most people as a way to encourage balanced participation and generous listening – but there are multiple modalities that are easily adapted for interreligious encounter. We can borrow the 4-D strategies of appreciative inquiry, for example.[2] Participants *discover* the best of what exists in interreligious cooperation, *dream* about what could be, *design* how it might come to pass, and *deploy* their best ideas. The World Café method of table conversations has been developed with hosting kits and guidelines that work well with inter-religious dialogue; it uses question prompts and facilitated small-group discussion, followed by sharing highlights in the large group. Open Space Technology democratizes planning to some extent by having participants propose session topics related to a theme; then everyone chooses which conversation(s) to join. Collaborative mind-

---

[2] See AI Commons, https://appreciativeinquiry.champlain.edu.

mapping helps groups brainstorm and organize thoughts around a central theme, drawing out compelling similarities and distinctions in perspectives along the way. "Speed-faithing" creates multiple one-on-one interfaith exchanges, each 5–10 minutes, with suggested questions as participants engage diverse interlocuters over the course of the program.

Guides like *The Art of Hosting, Crucial Conversations: Tools for Talking When the Stakes Are High*, the Public Conversations Project's *Fostering Dialogue Across Divides*, and National Public Radio's *Better Conversations* are excellent tools to cultivate best practices, and dialogue projects like "The People's Supper" and "Fear+Less Dialogues" work well with interpath frameworks. There are also evaluative guidelines like "What Works? Evaluating Interfaith Dialogue Programs," published by the US Institute of Peace.

Collaborative tasks are useful in drawing groups closer. Chapter 12 addresses those projects that are designed to advance the broader public good, but dialogue groups can benefit from simply planning a meal or visiting sacred sites together, sharing a blog, or designing opportunities for cross-cultural immersion. Coordinating the work develops their cooperative sinews and strengthens their sense of purpose. The concrete results may also provide justification for those whose families or communities are skeptical of the value of engagement. Sometimes the synergy begins with a task and moves to dialogue. After bloody clashes in Egypt between Muslims and Christians in 1996, for example, the European Union sponsored efforts that brought the communities together to work on urgent agricultural projects – and dialogue developed.

Case study discussions can be an excellent exercise as part of interpath dialogue. There are real conflicts that arise in interreligious engagement, even when everyone comes to the table wanting to make it work. They emerge out of the multiple ways we meet each other in daily life, and occasionally as accidental side-effects of formal interfaith efforts. As we see from case summaries included in this volume, real-world examples make the issues come alive. Human stories cultivate empathy, the case structure fosters problem-solving skills, and the gradual unfolding of events invites readers to consider how they would respond along the way. Through discussing the cases, participants come to understand something about their partners' perspectives – and may hear the critically important internal dialogue *within* lifestances, since people do not interpret or embody their tradition the same way.

Stories in the news can be useful for this exercise, as they have immediate relevance. At the same time, carefully constructed cases detailing past incidents are especially effective tools to explore the complexities and ambiguities of interreligious issues in a way that simple summaries cannot. Ultimately, the process of case study analysis also demonstrates how conflict can be generative, encouraging stakeholders to imagine a new story together. As mentioned in Chapter 1, the Case Study Initiative at Harvard University's Pluralism Project provides multiple cases and other materials available for public use, an invaluable resource for further study.[3]

10.3   SHARING OF STORIES

Storytelling is an essential tool in dialogical encounter. Religion cannot be reduced to doctrines, scriptures, or even "what I believe" testimonies; it comes to life through stories, those we inherit and those we live. In dialogue, we prompt stories of self-introduction – "Share a story about your family growing up ..." or "Tell a story of a time when ..." – as an effective means of building relationship. It empowers participants to be teachers since they are scholars of their own experience. When we share personal stories, it is not designed to teach spectators a lesson; instead it invites partners into our lives.

---

[3] https://pluralism.org/case-studies. Elinor Pierce is also publishing a book of cases. Ethics case studies infrequently have religious dimensions but are worth exploring; see the APPE Intercollegiate Ethics Bowl, www.appe-ethics.org/cases-rules-and-guidelines; National High School Ethics Bowl, https://nhseb.unc.edu/case-archive; National Center for Principled Leadership and Research Ethics, https://ethicscenter.csl.illinois.edu/research-ethics-resources/educational-materials/rcr-training-materials.

Valarie Kaur, for example, relates a story of when she was sixteen years old. She had been told by well-meaning Christians on more than one occasion that her Sikh faith condemned her to hell and that her inability to accept Jesus as her Lord and Savior was confusion cast upon her by the devil. Joining her grandfather at the gurdwara one Sunday, she describes an urgent need to challenge this presumption:

> I feel the blood of warriors and soldiers course through me, and I don't want to beg or plead anymore. My grandfather once told me of Mai Bhago, a great Sikh woman warrior who led armies into battle. I want to fight like her. I want to defend my family and community against those who condemn us, starting here and now. Where can I find them?[4]

She runs down the street to a nearby church, ready to take on the local priest – but the door is locked. A woman practicing the organ lets her in and she finds herself deeply moved by the music and the art, experiencing an overwhelming sense of Oneness among seekers of God. When the organist pauses, she sees the girl's tear-stained face and asks if she is okay. Valerie blurts out that she does not believe it possible God would be exclusivist. The woman regards her with profound compassion and responds, "I don't either."

When Kaur tells this formative tale, where her battlefield turned into a sanctuary and God opened up the gates of Oneness, as readers we experience her hurt, her fury, her surprise, her transformation. This is why stories change minds more readily than arguments. Stories move from competing notions of truth to varieties of human experience, with elements that are both infinitely varied and profoundly shared. It is important to be careful with assumptions about shared experience, however. Imagine a largely white Catholic-Jewish group, for example. They could decide to invite people to relate

---

[4] Kaur, "Doubled-Edged Daggers," in *My Neighbor's Faith: Stories of Interreligious Encounter, Growth, and Transformation*, ed. Jennifer Howe Peace, Or N. Rose, and Gregory Mobley (Maryknoll: Orbis Books, 2012), 172–76.

their immigrant stories – thinking of all the people who came from Europe over the centuries. But this would erase the very different experiences of African Americans from both groups, since most could hardly call their arrival on this continent "immigration." Shared experience is not universal experience.

Reflect for a moment on how much of religious and cultural teaching is done through story, and brought to life through ritual or retelling. The values of interreligious engagement are themselves communicated in stories within the diverse traditions: the Good Samaritan reminds us to recognize the full humanity of people outside our group, and the Two-Row Wampum illustrates the ideal of a fruitful co-journey without trying to make other people into copies of ourselves. The best preaching comes across as a story – not "this once happened to me" but "hear how my story involves you too" – like Dr. King's vision of having been to the mountaintop, a spiritual ascent weaving together Moses' final chapter and our collective journey on civil rights. Asking people to share a story from their lifestance that they find meaningful can be very revealing. We understand ourselves and our world by the construction and reconstruction of narratives.

There are many ways to invite participants to share their stories. Prompts can be directed specifically toward our spiritual selves: an experience that inspired gratitude, a favorite ritual, or something you struggle with in your lifestance. Social justice educator Linda Christensen discovered a poem by George Ella Lyon, "Where I'm From," that inspired a template for her students; it is readily adapted as a jumping off point for interreligious dialogue.[5] Ask people to complete a list of words and phrases, and it becomes a poem with multiple stories to unpack in pairs or small groups. (It is helpful to use Lyon's poem or create your own as a model.)

---

[5] Christensen, *Reading, Writing, and Rising Up: Teaching About Social Justice and the Power of the Written Word* (Milwaukee: Rethinking Schools, 2000), 18–20.

I AM FROM (items/smells/sounds from the home, yard, neighborhood where you grew up)

I AM FROM (names and brief descriptors of relatives/others who shaped you)

I AM FROM (familiar expressions you recall growing up, in any language)

I AM FROM (foods and traditions from family gatherings)

I AM FROM (influential characters, experiences)

With only a modest amount of reflection, the exercise opens up conversations on culture, lifestance, and identity formation. Participants get to be creative and feel that their stories are being heard.

10.4 RESERVATIONS ABOUT DIALOGUE

While religious perspectives contribute powerful insights into the principles of dialogue, they also convey substantive concerns. Some leaders worry that investment in interreligious dialogue will detract from their mission to strengthen their own communities, absorbing time and resources. While the tension is real, communities have also reported that the participants bring revitalizing energy back "home," or that they were grateful to be able to rely on vital friendships at a difficult time.

Some adherents fear that exposure to diverse paths will weaken commitment to their own faith; if all lifestances are respected, what happens to their identity? Although it is a reasonable fear, scholars and practitioners in the interfaith movement have long known that substantive dialogue most often deepens participants' sense of identity and commitment. They become more conscious of their own religious particularity and more adept at narrating their journey within it, refining their ideas through the sharpening lens of encounter. They gain new insight as others ask questions and reflect what they have heard.

At an interfaith conference in Japan, for example, a Catholic missionary met an expert in Shinto tradition who taught him about the development of the written character for *kami* (god, spirit, essence). The missionary had previously believed that Shintoism always taught there was divinity in all things (panentheism). From this encounter, however, he came to understand something different – that any part of the world may awaken human awareness of the reality of god – and this enlivened his own sense of reverence for the created world as a Roman Catholic. His respect for Shinto beliefs deepened rather than diminished his commitment.[6]

In some ways, religious identity is like one's mother tongue. Learning about another tradition in dialogue is like learning to speak another language; it does not diminish one's capacity with the first but provides a powerful tool of translation for generative and creative exchange between the two. At the same time, mutual transformation is often presented as an expectation or goal of dialogue. Consider, for instance, Leonard Swidler's seven stages of deep dialogue:

- Radical encounter with difference;
- Entering the world of the other (self transformed through empathy);
- Inhabiting the world of the other (self transformed into the other);
- Crossing back with expanded vision;
- Dialogical/critical awakening (self inwardly transformed);
- Global awakening (the paradigm shift matures);
- Personal and global transforming of life and behavior.[7]

For one endowed with self-critical faith, dialogue does involve change – but it is not about diluting faith. Rev. Rob Schenck, an evangelical pastor who for decades led the fight against abortion, described his experience when he stepped back from his activism to talk with pregnant women and others:

> Instead of shouting at people with different opinions than my own, I learned to listen to them. As a result, I decided to quit arguing and start asking questions. Thinking of how the perfect Jesus stepped into our sinful existence by taking on human flesh, I decided to step into the pain, shame, and fear of those I had once physically blocked

---

[6] Seamus Cullen, "Shinto in Japan," Columban Interreligious Dialogue, https://columbanird.org/shinto-in-japan.

[7] Leonard Swidler, Khalid Duran, and Reuven Firestone, *Trialogue: Jews, Christians, and Muslims in Dialogue* (New London: Twenty-Third Publications, 2007), 33–36.

at clinic doors and marginalized through my lobbying efforts. The experience was life changing.[8]

He realized that he had neglected the welfare of pregnant women and lost sight of the "greatest commandments" of loving God and loving neighbor; in fact, he acknowledged that he had lost sight of all that is required to be "pro-life" including beyond the womb. He admitted to getting caught up in culture wars, in the rightness of his cause, and in the glorification of his own reputation – helping to birth a movement that is evidently *not* pursuing common good because it resorts to violence and sidelines its other ethical commitments. He still believes that fetal life should be protected, but not at the expense of women, and he is ready to wrestle in that tension. He even explored what Judaism, as the faith of Jesus, teaches about the beginnings of life. These encounters made him a better Christian in his mind, but they did not leave him unchanged.

While the potential for personal transformation can be inspirational for some, it is terrifying for others. Many people who identify as theologically conservative find it particularly problematic. If they feel that they already have "the truth," transformational dialogue threatens to confuse matters. Further, if proselytizing is off the table, the value of engagement may seem diminished – perhaps even a violation of their charge to spread the faith. They point to verses from their scriptures or examples by their teachers that eschew interpath dialogue or warn followers not to trust outsiders.

However, advocates of dialogue point to counterverses, such as Jesus teaching, "In my Father's house are many dwelling places. If this were not so, I would have told you" (John 14:2), and the Qur'an's assurance that the multiplicity of lifestances is by Allah's design, so that we come to know one another and compete with one another in doing good (5:48, 49:13). Given the multivocal nature of the traditions, we should acknowledge that each perspective represents a selective

---

[8] Rob Schenck, "What's Gone Wrong with Evangelicals #7: Abortion and Its Politicization," September 9, 2020, www.revrobschenck.com/blog/2020/9/7/whats-gone-wrong-with-evangelicals–7-abortion-and-its-politicization.

reading – and listen carefully to the particular concerns of those resistant to dialogue.

Traditional voices are not the only ones to express reservations about the expectation of respect for diverse perspectives. There are those who argue that the broad commitment to tolerance means accepting intolerance, a sacrifice that suppresses necessary debates about religion and violence, patriarchy, homophobia, and free speech. Respect for the person, however, does not require agreement with the ideas. Outside of the dialogue context, we can continue to advocate vociferously for our positions. Ideally, our relationship with those who think otherwise can make us more thoughtful in our campaign and able to promote our position without contempt for those who disagree.

Some dialogues result in misunderstanding, with a chasm too immense to bridge or a simple inability to communicate clearly. Even so, the effort to humanize people of diverse lifestances – even if we do not fully understand them – is considered worth the risk. Even if people have reservations, they join interreligious dialogue and other efforts because they realize the dangers of ignorance and fear. It is still far too easy to demonize people who orient around religion differently.

Some dialogue efforts explicitly make space for addressing contentious disagreements. Common sense usually advocates that the relationship not start there, even if the issue is present from the outset as an "elephant in the room." Eboo Patel suggests that if people challenge why it is not being addressed right away, we should explain that there are other animals at the zoo.[9] If you focus only on that one animal, you miss all the other possibilities of discovery. It may even distort your perspective, so that everything starts to look like an elephant.

When groups do convene to address issues that perpetuate distrust between communities, there are several common strategies. One is to insist on the "listening to understand" rather than "listening to persuade" principle. Can they then learn to tell a new story together? Another is to identify relevant aspects of the conflict

---

[9] Patel, *Interfaith Leadership: A Primer* (Boston: Beacon Press, 2016), 108.

about which people agree, those on which they will never agree, and those that are in the middle – and then focus on that last column to see whether they can enlarge the space of understanding. A different approach is to encourage people to make their case, but only by calling in, not calling out – candor with compassion. This means that arguments must focus on the positive reasons for your position rather than the harm of the contesting one, and affirm your partners' ethics and goodness in the process. Seek the shared values that might invite them to accept part of your argument. The guidelines of nonviolent communication (see Chapter 14) provide useful foundations.

Interreligious dialogue has on occasion been mischaracterized, claiming that it fosters a lowest-common denominator religion that everyone can affirm, rather than honoring the particularities of individual lifestances; or that it blurs boundaries and elides difference. Some projects likely make this error, but most are committed to highlighting and dignifying the particularities of diverse lifestances and the unique ways that participants embody them.

Case Summary: A Campus Convening[1]

The interfaith leadership team on a Canadian campus convened a retreat with a new crop of fellows – students who committed to working and talking together over the course of at least one year. Participants had been asked to prepare a story, a small but significant part of their spiritual biography. In sharing them, a number of issues and potential conflicts came to light.

- A First Nations student shared his family's story of forced relocation and Christian missionary education that stripped them of their Chippewa language, culture, and traditions. A couple stories later, when an LDS student spoke how inspired he was by his two years of missionary work, there was notable squirming in the group.
- A Muslima student talked about her hijab jihad, and some participants were visibly taken aback. She explained jihad as struggle, most often a personal spiritual one, and shared that the hardest part was that her father did not want her to wear hijab, but she felt a strong desire to do it. One of the students

responded that she thought the struggle would have been the other way, and she felt chastened by her assumptions.

- Several students' stories had an overlapping theme of exclusion in interfaith work. A young woman who grew up in an interfaith family claimed both her Baptist and her Yoruba heritage. She expressed frustration that interpath programs usually expected her to choose, to show up with a single identity – and also tended to ignore the impact of race in interreligious engagement. A non-binary student related a story of going to an interfaith program on gender and being rendered invisible. An international student from China who identified as Daoist struggled with the complete lack of knowledge about his tradition in North America, so much of the language and focus of inter-faith efforts did not really include him in a substantive way. He worried that he was invited to participate as an "exotic."

- One student shared her theology of religious pluralism, talking about many paths up the same mountain. Another student listened respectfully, but then acknowledged that he could not embrace the image because he felt it dimin-ished the utter uniqueness of diverse lifestances. (See Chapter 4 for discussion of this tension.)

Questions for Consideration

1. What issues do you see emerging through these stories and initial reactions?
2. If you were one of the co-conveners, how might you guide participants to constructively unpack these conversations during the retreat in ways that honor the core practices of dialogue?
3. How might these issues inform programming through the year?

---

[1] This case is a composite of various stories and experiences, including my own, along with Dana Graef, "Learning the Language of Interfaith Dialogue: The Religious Life Council at Princeton University," *CrossCurrents* 55, no. 1 (Spring 2005): 106–20; Joel Lohr, "Finding Myself in the Other: Learning from Those Outside My Faith," in *Deep Understanding for Divisive Times: Essays Marking a Decade of the Journal of Interreligious Studies*, ed. Lucinda Allen Mosher, et al. (Newton Centre: Interreligious Studies Press, 2020), 53–60; Denise Yarbrough, "Mapping the Discourse: A Case Study in Creating 'Interfaith Community' on a 'Multi-Faith' Campus," *Journal of Interreligious Studies* 13 (2014): 50–66.

11 Study and Spiritual Encounter

Interreligious spiritual encounters are organized around national holidays, shared tragedies, coalitions for social change, and community events. These programs often adapt Protestant models of worship, with a series of prayers, songs, and scriptural readings. Other forms of ritual practice can be shared as well, inviting people to observe or participate. Both approaches rely on spiritual affect to deepen our capacity for connecting across difference. Learning together can stimulate a similar bond. This chapter explores models of interreligious engagement that use study and spiritual encounter as the foundation for developing relationship and understanding.

11.1 STUDY

Interreligious literacy is nurtured by the study of different traditions, but there is a difference between learning *about* and learning *with*. Learning in the presence of people who orient around religion differently can be extraordinarily powerful. Whether we are studying texts, concepts, practices, or history, the experience provides both cognitive and affective impact. It develops our understanding of diverse lifestances, fosters accountability, provides insider/outsider perspectives on texts and traditions, illuminates intrareligious diversity, and invites deeper consideration of our own beliefs and practices.

Interreligious study projects cannot be comprehensive in breadth or depth. They offer a textured particularism that is specific to the individuals assembled, the influences that shape them, and the program that draws them together. Nonetheless, they develop our capacities to engage diversity. We learn to shift perspective and appreciate different viewpoints without experiencing them as a threat to what we think or believe. We ask open-ended questions designed to advance our understanding rather than prove a point. We develop greater tolerance for ambiguity.

Intellectual diversity and respectful disagreement have a generative value. As the author of Proverbs wrote, "Like iron sharpens iron, so one person sharpens the wit of another" (Proverbs 27:17). There is inspiration in receiving testimony from others about aspects of their traditions that they find significant. Their experiences, and their questions about ours, catalyze more fertile engagement with our own lifestance and its teachings. When Anantanand Rambachan teaches his class about Hindu mystical practices, it sends his students scurrying to discover the threads of mysticism in their own traditions.[1] In a History of Christian Thought course at Chicago Theological Seminary, a non-Christian woman who grew up in India innocently asked on day one, "Who is Paul?" – and it launched a phenomenal discussion as the professor and Christian students tried to respond. Identity and openness are not opposed to one another; they are essential complements in nurturing dynamic, self-reflexive faith.

Further, interreligious study offers a method to decolonize our mind. We do not study others as curiosities; we meet them as human beings. They are embodied rather than hermeneutical others – pressing us sometimes to unlearn what we think we know. "Colonization" might seem an overwrought term for well-intended study *about* religions, but consider this reflection by Māori scholar Linda Tuhiwai Smith about the inextricable link between academic research and European colonialism, and its impact on Indigenous peoples:

> It appalls us that the West can desire, extract and claim ownership of our ways of knowing, our imagery, the things we create and produce, and then simultaneously reject the people who created and developed those ideas and seek to deny them further opportunities to be creators of their own culture and own

---

[1] Judith A. Berling, *Understanding Other Religious Worlds: A Guide for Interreligious Education* (Maryknoll: Orbis Books, 2004), 117.

nations ... This collective memory of imperialism has been perpetuated through the ways in which knowledge about Indigenous peoples was collected, classified and then represented in various ways back to the West, and then, through the eyes of the West, back to those who have been colonized.[2]

Studying alongside those who orient around religion and other markers of identity differently is a necessary guardrail against the colonization of knowledge.

Interreligious study programs also provide a logical strategy of response to concerns about religious hostilities. One cause of enmity is ignorance – both of diverse lifestances and the people who identify with them. To build toward mutual understanding, education and relationship are both essential.

11.2   MODELS FOR STUDY

Many programs still follow the model of subject-matter experts from two or more lifestances speaking about a common theme, followed by questions and answers. As with this model of dialogue, it is sometimes maligned for privileging male voices, essentializing traditions, and ignoring internal diversity. Nonetheless, there remains a place for such programs and certain best practices apply.

Planning should be collaborative so individuals from diverse lifestances contribute to topics of interest, appropriate speakers, timing, desiderata for creating a hospitable environment, and other details. Sensitivity to power dynamics and representation is important. Unlike academic religious studies, which sometimes privilege "objective" or etic approaches, the speakers are usually adherents, encouraging attendees to understand a tradition from the inside. Numerous regional interfaith groups regularly run programs together; even if attendees vary from event to event, there is sustained

---

[2] Smith, *Decolonizing Methodologies: Research and Indigenous Peoples* (New York: Zed Books, 2012), 30–31.

relationship that develops between the organizations involved in planning that can yield long-term benefits.

A related approach invites a subject-matter expert of one life-stance to teach in the congregational or educational context of another. An imam co-teaches a course on mysticism at a Christian-affiliated college. A swami teaches about Hindu holiday customs or a rabbi teaches about life-cycle events in a series of classes at a local gurdwara. It might be a simple pulpit exchange, with clergy preaching in each other's house of worship. Such programs sometimes incorporate conversation between the leader of the host institution and the invited guest to catalyze deeper reflection and model appreciative learning. They actualize encounter. Podcasting presents a newer context for such conversations, with numerous religious and interreligious organizations offering programs.

These efforts demonstrate institutional commitments to learn about religious others with a disposition of respect and sincere interest – not apologetics or proselytization. Trust is key; a willingness to be vulnerable and to ask hard questions strengthens the learning. As always, it is important that presenters speak *from* rather than *for* the entirety of their traditions and that they share aspects of internal diversity. Inviting several speakers from the same lifestance can bring to life the multiplicity of lived tradition.

Still, these programs provide relatively passive models of engagement, emulating what the prominent Brazilian educator Paulo Freire called "banking education": the instructor is expected to deposit knowledge in learners.[3] In its stead, current wisdom in Interreligious Studies (and in the field of education) promotes active pedagogies and student-centered, multidirectional, intersubjective learning. People become agents in their own growth.

It is possible to enhance presentational programs with active-learner elements. Facilitated table conversations after a panel

---

[3] Freire, *Pedagogy of the Oppressed*, trans. Myra Bergman Ramos (New York: Bloomsbury, 2014), 72.

discussion, for example, invite attendees to become active participants. (In this case, it is useful to have a mechanism to ensure that
people do not end up sitting with those they already know.) There are
also numerous modalities that employ active learning in their basic
structure. Book groups and film clubs, cooking classes and musical
exchanges, field trips and case studies, can be part of self-directed
dialogue projects with learning about religion embedded within them
to catalyze deeper exchange.

Active learning does not mean sacrificing a teacher or guide.
Study tours offer transformative possibilities for experiential learning
and relationship-building, as do shorter retreats. In the latter, exploring a shared challenge often generates a strong glue among participants. LGBTQIA+ individuals might want to study aspects of their
diverse traditions that are more liberative than the "clobber verses"
one often hears, or groups may gather to explore how religious teachings can inspire collective action on the climate crisis and to grapple
with religious resistance. While interreligious learning can be done in
person, online, or even through epistolary exchanges, the value of
face-to-face interaction should not be minimized. And, as always,
sustained practice is more impactful.

A fruitful aspect of interpath study is that numerous lifestances
have particular pedagogical traditions that can also be shared. The
"how" of learning becomes as transformative as the content of it.
Native American teaching, for example, tends to be non-linear and
relational, with knowledge transmitted through stories; each iteration
is shaped according to the storyteller and recipient at the time of
telling. In rabbinic tradition, students work in pairs (*chevruta*), often
reading texts aloud to each other and asking questions as they wrestle
with the possibilities of meaning. The latter modality is readily
adapted for interreligious learning, with pairs drawn from diverse
lifestances; the impact of learning together in this intimate format
is profound.

Scriptural traditions share long histories of textual interpretation, prompting a broadly successful interreligious learning project

beginning in the 1990s called Scriptural Reasoning (SR). Interested individuals gather to study sacred texts of their distinct traditions that relate to a common theme. Although adherents are invited to provide context and those who understand the original language may read it aloud to convey its rhythms and sounds, or provide insight about the nuances of specific translations – the exercise invites all to explore their meanings and relevance without regard for who "owns" the text. This approach highlights an important distinction between SR and comparative religion; the exercise is one of shared reasoning rather than comparative study. Ideally, there is more than one person who identifies with each tradition so the conversation reveals internal diversity. Participants may differ about interpretations and about the authority of the text. SR acknowledges that scriptural study can be a source of conflict as well as a foundation for bridge-building, so it cultivates better disagreement.

While the practice began among university scholars from Jewish, Christian, and Muslim traditions, it has expanded in many ways. Organizations have facilitated SR conversations in primary and secondary schools. Pre-packaged materials and guidelines are available from the Internet and groups have popped up around the world. In China, it has included Buddhist, Confucian, and Daoist individuals and texts. David Ford, one of the developers of SR, remarked that he knew it was successfully translating to this new cultural context when it generated both argument and laughter.[4]

In Israel/Palestine, the methodology has been utilized among hospital staff; the medical profession is often held up as a paradigm of coexistence, but the common mission is still strained by violence and politics in the broader society. Further, the professional context often suppresses religious and cultural identity, leaving essential differences unaddressed. SR provides opportunities to acknowledge their

---

[4] Ford, "Flamenco, Tai-Chi and Six-Text Scriptural Reasoning: Report on a Visit to China," Cambridge Inter-Faith Programme, October 2012, www.interfaith.cam.ac.uk/resources/lecturespapersandspeeches/chinavisit.

particularities in respectful interchange. Setting political differences aside without denying them, participants develop deeper understanding of and connection with each other.[5]

Another creative mode of scriptural study that has begun to penetrate the world of interreligious engagement is roleplay. It may involve stepping into the shoes of a person within the text, exploring our own feelings and choices in the events that unfold before them. It can also mean stepping into the world of ideas. Ecclesiastes 3, for instance, describes a dialectical tension in our reality, with a time to weep and a time to laugh, a time to gather stones and a time to scatter them, and so on. "What time is it for you right now?" the guide asks, inviting people to share their choices and their reasons. These exercises are less about interpreting the text and more about seeing ourselves in the sacred stories, an embodied pedagogy that can draw us closer together as it draws us into the scriptures.[6]

Scriptures are not the only texts worthy of study together. Stories from different lifestances provide low-hanging fruit for learning together. Human beings are natural interpreters of story. Texts summarizing a religious concept can also be fruitful: imagine a group of religiously diverse, Western-trained therapists exploring how the Buddha's Four Noble Truths might stimulate new therapeutic approaches. Simply re-languaging an idea in diverse lifestances unlocks possibilities of meaning for words we assume we understand. "Conscience," for example, expands through the Confucian concept of good-knowing and the Muslim concept of *fitra* (innate nature). Utilizing simulations in this broader framework for study, Religious Studies professor Celine Ibrahim proposes specific scenarios to identify learning targets: what would public health officials and religious

---

[5] Miriam Feldmann Kaye, "Scriptural Reasoning with Israelis and Palestinians," Cambridge Inter-Faith Programme, www.interfaith.cam.ac.uk/resources/ scripturalreasoningresources/srwithisraelisandpalestinians.

[6] See, for example, Peter Pitzele, *Scripture Windows: Toward a Practice of Bibliodrama* (Los Angeles: Torah Aura Productions, 1998); The Elijah Interfaith Institute, "The Elijah Educational Network and Bibliodrama," https://elijah-interfaith.org/bibliodrama.

leaders need to know, for instance, to talk about congregational adaptations during the coronavirus pandemic? Her students each step into a role and begin to explore together key rituals from different traditions and how they might be adapted. They discover a depth of theological and cultural understanding necessary to do the work, and research how various communities responded.[7]

Other efforts to develop sustained relationship through interreligious study reveal substantial coformative power. The Institute for Islamic, Jewish, and Christian Studies in Baltimore, for example, sponsors cohorts for religious leaders and lay leaders from these three traditions; it also trains secondary school educators to address religious diversity in their classrooms. The KAICIID Fellows Programme brings together leaders and teachers from a broad array of lifestances for training in intercultural communication and dialogue facilitation. These projects provide real skills, but an essential part of their value is the fellowship of diverse learners doing sustained work together. Congregations and individuals have also established interreligious study groups, some of which last for decades. Campus environments, designed for learning together and constituted with rich intersecting diversities, can be ideal laboratories for interreligious study projects – engaging young adults at a formative stage of their lives.

A number of transformative efforts unfold as part of graduate theological education. Hebrew Union College-Jewish Institute of Religion has long had Christians doing doctoral work, integrating Jewish scholarship and living Jewish tradition into their formation as scholars of Christianity. Some of these graduates were central in reshaping academic discourse to understand Jesus as a Jew. Numerous seminaries and divinity schools, historically Protestant or Catholic, have undertaken substantive interreligious study as part of their curricular or co-curricular offerings. Others have become multifaith.

---

[7] Ibrahim, "Simulation-Based Pedagogy for Interreligious Literacy: Critical Thinking Exercises for Teens and Young Adults," in *The Georgetown Companion to Interreligious Studies*, ed. Lucinda Mosher (Washington, DC: Georgetown University Press, 2022), 398–99, https://doi.org/10.2307/j.ctv27qzsb3.43.

They grapple with dismantling Christian privilege in the content of their courses and the basic structure of their degree programs – reimagining how to think and talk about pastoral care, spiritual formation, public theology, and other subfields that were established with Christian language and norms.

The goal of interreligious study programs is not only the pursuit of knowledge; it is also a pursuit of wisdom. Wisdom is about forming dispositions, attitudes, and character – an inner knowing – for constructive engagement in a multifaith world. "Who is wise?" asked the rabbis of the second century CE. Their response: "The one who learns from every person" (m. Avot 4:1).

II.3 SPIRITUAL ENCOUNTER

Making a distinction between programs of study and spiritual encounter is somewhat artificial. The former can be spiritual, the latter is often educational – and both dimensions are essential to understanding. As Jeanine Hill-Fletcher notes, you may be conversant with Hebrew Bible and some of Jewish interpretation. Without also experiencing the ritual element, however – seeing the ways that Torah is read, paraded, debated, and enacted in the synagogue and beyond – your appreciation for its role in Jewish life is incomplete.[8] Recognizing the overlap, the categories still help us think about various starting points for interreligious engagement.

Spiritual encounters happen outside of formal programs, of course. Chaplains work with people of diverse lifestances and try to meet their spiritual needs. Jewish families often invite people of different faiths to their Passover seder, and Hindu families bring non-Hindu friends to celebrate Diwali with them. *Chado* (literally "the way of tea"), influenced by Zen practice, creates an interfaith

---

[8] Cited in Marianne Moyaert, "Inappropriate Behavior? On the Ritual Core of Religion and Its Challenges to Interreligious Hospitality," *Journal for the Academic Study of Religion* 27, no. 2 (2014): 229, https://doi.org/10.1558/jasr.v27i2.222.

ritual whenever one who stands outside the tradition is welcomed with a tea ceremony.

Those who work in interreligious engagement incorporate spiritual encounters in programming because they provide a strong glue for building relationship. Rituals operate on complex symbolic planes, evoking history, experience, emotions, and commitments – reaching deep aspects of our being. They are generally quite particular, but they share a transcendent element that can erase boundaries and bind our hearts together. Rituals are means for distilling meaning and beauty, embodying vulnerability, healing hurts, drawing close, and discovering joy. While they are acts by which we cement our lifestance identity, they can also fashion bridges between us.

By naming this approach to interpath engagement as "spiritual" and talking about "rituals," we may imagine that it necessarily eliminates people who consider themselves secular. But we are all ritual beings, whether it be the sequence of our morning habits or our preferred practices for reflection and connection. When my atheist friend speaks of hiking in the wilderness, for instance, he recognizes how it feeds his spirit and moves him to unique levels of consciousness.

11.4   MODELS FOR SPIRITUAL ENCOUNTER

One common model for interreligious spiritual encounter is an interfaith service. Catalysts include national holidays, shared tragedies, coalitions for social change, and community events such as a campus baccalaureate, dedication ceremony, or public meeting. Many local interfaith organizations in the USA, for example, sponsor a joint Thanksgiving service – and several have published pamphlets with best practices for interreligious worship. As an aspect of civil religion, such gatherings strengthen the social fabric of religiously diverse communities. They provide opportunities to root shared experiences within language of the spirit – speaking to the moment in ways that open our hearts to one another with care for our common life.

The boundaries of interfaith prayer are sometimes contested. When the Arizona House of Representatives had an atheist offer the opening prayer in 2016, a group of Republicans who were angry he had not invoked God called on a Baptist minister to present an additional prayer. For the 2004 National Day of Prayer service in Troy, Michigan, the mayor's invitation to a Hindu resident to offer a prayerful greeting from her tradition set off a firestorm. The next year, the organizers' request for a permit specifically identified a "Judeo-Christian" observance, language that served as cover for an exclusively Christian ecumenical gathering.[9] Chapter 4 discusses a case in which a Wiccan was refused permission to offer an invocation for a county board meeting on the grounds that it would not represent the community's values. Even when there is no active hostility to certain lifestances, representation is a challenge: a community's true diversity is often underestimated, intrafaith differences are overlooked, and many perspectives are simply rendered invisible.

Some interfaith services emphasize common ground. They focus on unifying themes and seek language that people might use to pray together. Many lifestances share a common "grammar" so that prayers evoking hope, forgiveness, comfort, compassion, service, thanksgiving, or love can resonate in diverse ways. Such programs sometimes suffer from "lowest-common-denominator" spirituality that is not particularly impactful, however, and they presume a commonality that still leaves people out. With a Protestant-infused model of prayers, music, and scriptural readings – invoking a monotheistic deity – for example, atheists and polytheists are unlikely to feel fully included. Quakers might prefer a gathering of silence and spontaneous testimony; even the presence of prayer leaders may seem somewhat strange. Others worry that the "common faith" approach threatens their particular aims and claims. Nevertheless, these efforts utilize

---

[9] For an interesting treatment of this case, see Elinor Pierce, "Trouble in Troy: The National Day of Prayer," https://pluralism.org/trouble-in-troy.

spiritual modes of encounter to bridge religious difference, celebrate our diversity, and create a meaningful shared experience.

A more supple approach encourages individual voices to speak out of their particular lifestance (again *from* rather than *for* it). It does not require diminishment of their commitments and does not presume others do or should share them. A Protestant minister, for example, may close a thematic prayer with something like, "I offer this in the name of Jesus, whom I have come to experience as Divine, even as others approach the transcendent in their own way." A Buddhist monk can sound his Tibetan singing bowl, explaining its significance and initiating a minute of meditative silence without imposing a specific focus or belief. Although some observers would describe this as gathering to pray rather than praying together, participants hopefully experience profound moments of connection in the assemblage of spiritual traditions.

The choice between a singular prayer portrait and a collage of particulars need not be binary. The invitation for particular expressions can be accompanied by a thematic reading that fleshes out the common ground. Both models also provide an opportunity for deep learning if planned collectively: Are your rituals generally fixed or spontaneous? Do you have leaders? Is there a place for petitionary prayer? How do you foster practices of gratitude?

Interreligious spiritual encounters can focus on drawing specific communities together. Going beyond pulpit exchanges among clergy, some inter-congregational friendships include inviting one another to visit for a prayer service. Rather than representing diverse traditions, such services speak in a single tradition – sometimes teaching a bit along the way so that guests might appreciate its particular beauty. They may observe and/or participate, as feels appropriate. At times its very foreignness is the most compelling aspect – chanting from scripture in a foreign language, the mystery of Catholic mass, the relentless spinning of the Sufi dervish, and so on. Often, however, it is the surprise discovery of resonance that opens the heart.

Many Interreligious Studies courses require students to visit worship services from traditions other than their own, to experience the embodied tradition brought to life.[10] Some people do this on their own, drawn by a desire to celebrate or mourn the life-cycle passage of a friend or neighbor – or simply to appreciate the rich spiritual fabric of their community. *How to Be a Perfect Stranger: The Essential Religious Etiquette Handbook*[11] offers guidance on being a good guest, with information about various lifestances. General best practices suggest attending with an acquaintance who affiliates with the congregation if possible. If not invited, request permission to attend and ask if there is anything you should know about dress or behavior. Do some homework in advance, both to demonstrate respect and to deepen understanding of what you witness. Be aware of how the congregation fits in the intrafaith diversity of the lifestance, perhaps visiting more than one.

Viewing sacred spaces from different lifestances can be a spiritual event by itself, without participating in or observing ritual practice within. Such spaces are set aside as liminal, designed to move or transport you. These experiences may include a journey to someone's holy land or holy city, a site of pilgrimage, or it can be the neighborhood Jain temple. For some traditions, such sites are found in nature. At Stonehenge or Sequana (the Celtic sanctuary at the source of the Seine river) one can still feel the traces of those who established the sacred site.

In East Asia, it is common for individuals to visit shrines of multiple religious traditions as part of their personal spiritual practice. At the Church of St. Antony in Chennai, India, for example, there are long lines of non-Christians who come to honor the saint and seek favors. Not constrained by the Greek philosophical tradition of non-contradiction, this popular religiosity reflects the reality of long-

---

[10] See Henry Goldschmidt, "Being There: What Do Students Learn by Visiting Houses of Worship?" *CrossCurrents* 68, no. 3 (September 2018): 1–18.

[11] Stuart M. Matlins and Arthur J. Magida, eds. *How to Be a Perfect Stranger: The Essential Religious Etiquette Handbook*, 6th ed. (Woodstock: Skylight Paths, 2015).

standing religious diversity in the region as well as the "contagious" nature of sanctity. When our neighbors invest a place with special meaning, the accumulation of transcendent human experience lingers. (Besides, as the patron saint of lost things, who does not occasionally need help from St. Anthony?)

Sacred space is ordinary space transformed. While the perspectival shift is often sparked by architectural or natural beauty, the anomalous can also open such a doorway. The Bedouin tent set in the garden of St. Ethelburga's Centre for Reconciliation and Peace in London is one example. Assembled on the ruins of a church that was blown up by the IRA in 1993, it was a response to the attacks of September 11, 2001, and subsequent events. It sits incongruously in the shadow of a medieval Catholic church to establish a space without hierarchy in which diverse sacred stories and beliefs can fruitfully co-inspire.

Many efforts to create sacred space are designed to be used by individuals and communities of diverse lifestances. They can be mundane airport chapels or stunning spiritual life spaces on college and university campuses. Gandhi established multifaith ashrams. Congregations of differing lifestances have set out to share buildings or campuses, like the Tri-Faith Initiative in Omaha, to interweave the spiritual lives of their communities. They become acutely aware of each other's calendar and customs, and usually attempt formal programming together as well.

Sacred places have also been sites of conflict. The Swiss referendum against building minarets, Malaysia's destruction of Hindu shrines to make way for "necessary state projects," the squabbles between diverse Christian sects over every square inch of the Church of the Holy Sepulchre in Jerusalem, and the controversy over the idea of a Muslim community center near Ground Zero in New York City – all reveal the stakes of creating or claiming holy space, even if they also reflect concerns about social or cultural dominance more than religion. Corporate power also shapes conflict over space, as evident in the struggle of Native Americans to preserve sacred lands against pipelines, ranching, and commercial development.

Many approaches to interreligious spiritual encounter do not revolve around worship or sacred space. They generate new rituals or experiment with practices that evoke soulful engagement in different ways. Participants bring an object of significance to them, for example, and tell its story. Or they craft squares of a quilt evoking a concept from their lifestance that they value. A group gets together to write and share spiritual memoirs. A walking meditation evokes our multifaith concern for the damage to our mother earth. The possibilities are endless.

Case Summary: Walk for Peace and Reconciliation[1]

The Khmer Rouge in Cambodia initiated a systematic campaign to erase Buddhism from the country. Although Buddhist thought and practice had served as the foundation for Cambodian spirituality for more than six centuries and there were over 65,000 monks and novices, with *wats* (monasteries) in almost every community, the Khmer Rouge saw it as a foreign influence. During the 1970–75 civil war, over one-third of the *wats* were destroyed. By the time Pol Pot's Khmer Rouge government was forced out in 1979, there were probably only 100 monks left, most living in exile in Vietnam.

In the 1990s, violence resumed. The supreme patriarch of Cambodian Buddhism, Maha Ghosananda, was known as the Cambodian Gandhi. Having lost his entire family to the brutality of the Khmer Rouge, he recognized the ongoing need for healing and reconciliation so he began leading an annual walking meditation called the *Dhammayietra*, the pilgrimage of truth. In English it is generally known as the Walk for Peace and Reconciliation.

He walked across Cambodia's minefields and deforested land. The monks who accompanied him immersed flowers in water and sprinkled it on shops and homes as they walked through the towns. In 1993, as they walked through open fighting, Ghosananda announced, "We must remove the land mines in our hearts which prevent us from making peace – greed, hatred, and delusions. We can overcome greed with weapons of generosity, we can overcome hatred with the weapon of lovingkindness, we can overcome delusions with the weapon of wisdom."

Questions for Consideration

1. What makes ritual a particularly effective modality for peacebuilding, or for healing from trauma (personal and collective)?
2. Can you think of other examples of trauma or conflict for which interreligious ritual or study might be an effective catalyst for healing or reconciliation?
3. The walk is also a political act. How does its frame as ritual shape its impact?
4. What challenges and possibilities do you see in utilizing rituals in interreligious engagement?

<hr/>

[1] Lisa Schirch, "Ritual, Religion, and Peacebuilding," in *The Oxford Handbook of Religion, Conflict, and Peacebuilding*, ed. Atalia Omer, R. Scott Appleby, and David Little (Oxford: Oxford University Press, 2015), 522, https://doi.org/10.1093/oxfordhb/9780199731640.013.0020.

Many traditions have literature and processes for spiritual development. These make fertile ground for interreligious learning that is also spiritual encounter, deeply rooted in particular ethical and theological teachings while also relatable to other perspectives. Shantideva's *Bodhicaryavatara*, a Mahayana Buddhist text written in India around 700 CE, focuses on enlightenment through the six perfections (including patient endurance, joyous effort, and wisdom). The *Spiritual Exercises* written by Spanish priest Ignatius of Loyola in the sixteenth century provide a model for individuals to work at living fully into their relationship with the Divine.[12] In Jewish tradition, the nineteenth-century Musar movement established contemplative practices intended to cultivate one's soul through ethical and spiritual

<hr/>

[12] Thomas Cattoi, "Reading Ignatius in Kathmandu: Toward a New Pedagogy of Interreligious Dialogue," in *Teaching Interreligious Encounters*, ed. Marc A. Pugliese and Alexander Y. Hwang (New York: Oxford University Press, 2017), 208–19, https://doi.org/10.1093/oso/9780190677565.003.0015.

work with focused objectives like patience, generosity, gratitude, trust. Jain monastic tradition teaches about the three *guptis* (care in thought, speech, and action) and the five *samitis* – rules of conduct to avoid doing harm. Secular lifestances have a variety of philosophical constructs for moral development.

Focusing on spiritual and ethical practices that sustain us highlights difference without focusing on issues that divide us. In fact, this approach emphasizes our common commitment to cultivating character. Interreligious programs may invite participants simply to teach, in pairs or small groups, about an aspect of their practice that is particularly meaningful or formative for them. What is its history and how does it relate to their practice? How is it woven into their life and what impact has it had? Participants may consider whether it is appropriate to show as well as tell, either demonstrating or inviting others to join.

The beauty of spiritual traditions also leads to instances of borrowing when one has *not* been invited in. Examples of such appropriation were mentioned in Chapter 2, yielding Buddha statues as garden ornaments, "Native American" totem poles made in China, dreamcatcher art projects, and church seders that transform the Jewish Passover tradition into a "last supper" experience.

Other manifestations fall into a gray area, but they deserve inquiry. Yoga is a very popular practice among people of diverse lifestances, for instance, yet we should consider its roots. It was first mentioned in the *Rigveda* (1.18.7, 1.30.7, 10.114.9) and then discussed broadly in the *Upanishads*, eventually becoming an established school of Hindu philosophy. Various iterations were incorporated in Buddhism and Jainism. What do we make of yoga's current commercialization – practiced by many with little notion of its origins? In 2008, the Hindu American Foundation launched a "Take Back Yoga" movement aiming to visibilize the connection to ancient faith traditions, but even this modest goal stirred controversy. What about the secularization of bindis, Christmas trees, maypoles, and lacrosse? (The last of these has Onandaga roots, considered by some a sacred exercise.) We can debate who owns traditions, or how and why symbols or rituals get unmoored from their religious anchors – but we ought to at least ask the questions.

Intent matters. For interreligious engagement programs, a clear criterion is that they are designed to further interreligious understanding, not co-opt someone else's traditions for our own purposes – whether they be athletic, aesthetic, or spiritual. Even with the best of intentions, however, the impact may be hurtful for those whose traditions are in play.

Some people are not comfortable with interreligious spiritual encounters, no matter the form or substance. They may believe it transgresses their own lifestance's boundaries simply by being present in the sacred space of another or seeming to condone something that they see as idolatrous. When Rev. David Benke participated in an interfaith service of solidarity at Yankee Stadium shortly after 9/11, the Lutheran Church-Missouri Synod suspended him for almost a year. They felt that his appearance with an imam, a rabbi, a cardinal, and Sikh and Hindu holy men gave the impression that there might be more than one God.[13]

Some people believe that interreligious spiritual encounters are impossible; the depths of meaning cannot translate across the boundaries of our differences. Others worry that acknowledging the beauty of other lifestance rituals may draw people away from their roots, or encourage them toward syncretism. And some individuals simply do not like the discomfort of the unfamiliar, with its sense that they do not belong. For them, the experience of difference only deepens the gap.

Despite these objections, and even with the consistent risks of superficiality or distortion, the draw of interreligious spiritual encounters remains strong. In services, retreat, workshops, and site visits, they invite us to share deeply, to build trust rather than simple tolerance. They provide ways for living out what is learned.

---

[13] Ruth Langer and Stephanie VanSlyke, "Interreligious Prayer: An Introduction," *Liturgy* 26, no. 3 (2011): 5–6, https://doi.org/10.1080/0458063X.2011.562448.

12 Community-Based Service, Organizing, and Advocacy

While pursuit of interreligious understanding is itself an act of world repair, there are numerous efforts to engage spiritually diverse individuals and groups in common action for the common good. These projects include providing services within communities, messaging to change hearts and minds, organizing for systemic change, and advocating for policies to advance human and environmental flourishing. This chapter examines the relationship of interpath engagement and social action, exploring different strategies for change and the issues that arise.

If you think of movements for social change through history, religious leaders and organizations were frequently at the forefront. Quakers were among the first white people to denounce slavery, and the Society of Friends spearheaded international campaigns against the slave trade. Social welfare projects, striving to support the "cast-offs" of society, included thousands of religiously inspired activists like Britain's Samuel and Henrietta Barnett in the late nineteenth century. Archbishop Óscar Romero and other Catholic priests fought courageously against human rights violations in El Salvador and elsewhere.

The scale of these efforts often required diverse religious actors to collaborate. After the Shoah, Jewish leaders and organizations grappled with the catastrophe that had murdered one-third of the world's Jews by joining with Christians around the world to advocate for universal human rights in the United Nations Charter, including nondiscrimination on grounds of religion. Together they fought to enshrine freedom of thought, conscience, and religion in the Universal Declaration of Human Rights (1948) and the International

Covenant on Civil and Political Rights (1966).[1] The Civil Rights Movement in the United States and the campaign against the Vietnam War, the anti-apartheid movement in South Africa, and other long-term struggles were sustained in part by coalitions of committed religious groups.

Justice-oriented convictions flow from a multitude of life-stances, sometimes influencing one another as well. Consider the practice of nonviolent resistance to oppression, for example, which is both a spiritual practice and a strategic choice. As Thich Nhat Hanh wrote in summarizing a Buddhist nonviolent response to the Vietnam War, "Nonviolent action, born of the awareness of suffering and nurtured by love, is the most effective way to confront adversity."[2] It was evident in transcendentalist Henry David Thoreau's call for civil disobedience (1849), the Māori response to colonial conquest at Parihaka (1880s), Gandhi's Hindu-rooted Satyagraha (literally "holding onto truth") movement in India (1917), Abdul Ghaffār Khān's leadership of the Muslim community there (including founding the Khudai Khidmatgar movement in 1929), Dr. King's approach with the Southern Christian Leadership Conference (1950s–60s), and other transformational figures. King repeatedly acknowledged the impact of both Jesus and Gandhi on his commitment to nonviolence.

There are multiple approaches to world repair, and the interreligious world utilizes most of them. Projects of community service are perhaps the most visible: feeding and housing people who cannot afford these basic necessities, supporting individuals who were previously incarcerated or struggling with addiction to find jobs and get their lives back on track, aiding refugees, tutoring, and so on. We also see substantial interreligious efforts to change the culture on the

---

[1] Michael Galchinsky, *Jews and Human Rights: Dancing at Three Weddings* (New York: Rowman and Littlefield, 2007), 29–32. See Rachel S. Mikva, "With No One to Make Them Afraid: A Jewish Perspective on Safeguarding Religious Freedom," *Cultural Encounters: A Journal for the Theology of Culture* 16, no. 1 (2021): 23.

[2] Thich Nhat Hanh, *Love in Action: Writings on Nonviolent Social Change* (Berkeley: Parallax Press, 1993), 39.

climate crisis, to protest the exponentially expanding wealth gap, to dismantle systemic racism, and other broad societal challenges. Often these projects are about messaging, about changing hearts and minds. But they can go further, advocating with policymakers and organizing within communities to take concrete action. I use the term "social action" to refer to the full gamut of approaches.

The strategy should match the objectives. If a coalition wants to end hunger, it is not sufficient to staff a soup kitchen and food pantry – but if the group seeks to alleviate suffering in the community, then it is part of the requisite work. If a local interfaith council wants to get rid of lead in their city's water pipes, they will need to organize and mobilize, lobby politicians and advocate with corporations, ally with scientists, learn from previous efforts, and build common cause with related civic organizations.

Faith-based groups sometimes default to the service-providing model or other activities that play to their strengths. Scholar of applied theology Howard Dean ("Doc") Trulear has suggested, only half in jest, that if Rosa Parks was arrested today for refusing to go stand at the back of the bus, the church would offer to pray for her, or organize a van ministry, or launch a study group, or suggest that she pray to Jesus for a car. Prayer, service, study, fostering faith in God's blessings – these are fine things for religious groups to do. But the prophetic voice, he argues, is the one that changes the society in which we live and breathe for the better. Parks' allies did provide alternative transportation during the Montgomery bus boycott, but they also fought to change the system.[3]

To do this work, we may be guided by the insight of Bryan Stevenson, founder of the Equal Justice Initiative. He is speaking about world repair in general, not interreligious efforts, but the

[3] Trulear, "Theological Education and Social Justice as Vocation." Presentation at *Current and Future Trends in Theological Education*, June 2018. This paragraph is adapted from Rachel S. Mikva, "Readings for Resilience: Reflections on the COVID-19 Pandemic and Beyond," in *Doing Theology in Pandemics: Facing Viruses, Violence, and Vitriol*, ed. Zachary Moon (Eugene: Wipf & Stock, 2022), 160.

wisdom translates. *Get proximate*: work closely with people of other lifestances and with those who are impacted by an issue. *Change the narratives*: fear and anger drive too many of our cultural assumptions, leading to apathy, dehumanization, and despair. *Find your hope*: this work is generally long and slow, so we need resilience to see it through. Spiritual imaginations have always been agile in imagining the world that could be. *Risk being uncomfortable*: there are things we have never done, things we do not know, people whose experience is very different, problems that seem intractable, forces that will try to stop us – and we will be most effective if these do not scare us away.[4]

12.1   THE WHAT AND WHY OF SOCIAL ACTION IN INTERPATH ENGAGEMENT

We can define this realm of interreligious work as common action for the common good, but the simplicity is misleading because we do not all agree on the common good. Most religious and political progressives would likely not view interreligious efforts to discriminate against same-gender loving or transgender individuals, to limit reproductive rights, or to divert public education funds to parochial schools as advancing the common good. Political conservatives might not see interfaith efforts on behalf of criminal justice reform, immigration, or "green" climate policy that way. In the USA, even the words "social justice" have become tainted by partisan politics. Nonetheless, we share a common expectation that our lifestance – the framing of our ultimate concerns – should somehow seek wholeness in a broken world. We can talk about interreligious strategies to dismantle that which obstructs the flourishing of the planet and all its inhabitants, and to promote that which helps them thrive, even if we do not agree on what they may be.

---

[4] Martin Saunders, "Bryan Stevenson: Four Steps to Really Change the World," *Christianity Today*, July 16, 2015, www.christiantoday.com/article/bryan-stevenson-four-steps-to-really-change-the-world/59211.htm.

Sikh scholar and activist Rahuldeep Gill reflects on the need to shift between two kinds of interreligious engagement. To achieve civic harmony, he sometimes works with people whose ideas of justice conflict with his own. To pursue a more equitable world, however, he also works over against some of his interreligious partners on matters of policy. Their joint efforts that "keeps potholes filled, schools running, [and] the homeless fed" also create the relationships and the civic glue that prevent political conflict from spilling over into violence.[5]

What is the relationship between interpath engagement and social action? Paul Knitter argues that they need each other. We cannot adequately address the challenges of the world, global and local, large and small, if we disregard the power of religion to shape spirits, organize community, and inspire action.[6] Madelaine Albright, a career diplomat and the first female American Secretary of State, acknowledged that she came late to this understanding. Having been trained to avoid religion in approaching international relations, she increasingly recognized that it was too important in people's lives and in the course of human history to ignore.[7]

The complementary argument, that interreligious engagement needs social action, has several facets. Knitter takes seriously the Marxist/Humanist critique that religion serves as an opiate for the masses, that it has too often perpetuated injustice by siding with the oppressors or stifled dissent with promises of a better world in the afterlife or other distractions. He recognizes the role that religious difference sometimes plays in conflict. As a consequence, he insists that we must collaborate so our diversity of lifestances also contributes to solving the world's problems. Citing South African scholar

---

[5] Gill, "'Whatever Pleases the One:' Guru Nanak's Response to Violence and Warfare," in *Words to Live By: Sacred Sources for Interreligious Engagement*, ed. Or Rose, Homayra Ziad, and Soren M. Hessler (Maryknoll: Orbis Books, 2018), 198.

[6] Knitter, "Inter-Religious Dialogue and Social Action," in *The Wiley-Blackwell Companion to Inter-Religious Dialogue*, ed. Catherine Cornille (Chichester: John Wiley & Sons, 2013), 133, 140, https://doi.org/10.1002/9781118529911.ch9.

[7] Albright, *The Mighty and the Almighty* (New York: HarperCollins, 2006).

Farid Esack, Knitter laments that too many interreligious efforts are like "tea parties," meeting in universities and hotel conference rooms far removed from human suffering. Interreligious understanding is a necessary but insufficient goal for encounter.[8]

In addition, the work of social action is an essential gateway for interpath connection. In some instances, such as the fight against HIV/AIDS in Malawi, it becomes a catalyst for bridging religious differences that seemed irreconcilable.[9] It identifies values that we share without denying our differences and naturally makes room for secular and religious approaches. For many, particularly young people, it is the core of their lifestance commitments and the only compelling mode of interpath engagement. There is a deep desire to ground our worldview in efforts to improve the world, to see our principles bear fruit.

The crucible of faith and praxis is vital to religious traditions. As Dr. King taught, "Any religion that professes to be concerned with the souls of men but not the slums that damn them, the economic conditions that strangle them, and the social conditions that cripple them is a dry-as-dust religion."[10] On the interreligious plane, educator Maria Hornung frames the interdependency this way: "Interreligious and interideological dialogue that does not eventuate in action will grow hypocritical and ineffective. Action that does not invest in deeper communication and greater understanding and acceptance will grow sterile and give way to apathy. Neither dialogue nor action can survive on its own."[11]

It is difficult to maintain a balance between the work of social action and substantive interreligious engagement. In some cases, the structure affords little interaction because individual congregations

---

[8] Knitter, "Inter-Religious Dialogue," 139.

[9] Lewis Ndekha, "Ambivalence in Interreligious Relations in Malawi: Is an African Model of Interreligious Relations Possible?", www.academia.edu/10682091.

[10] Martin Luther King, Jr., *Stride Toward Freedom: The Montgomery Story* (New York: Harper, 1958), 36.

[11] Maria Hornung, *Encountering Other Faiths* (Mahwah: Paulist Press, 2007), 27.

sign up for particular time slots or organize in their own communities. As Religious Studies scholar Kate McCarthy notes in her study of the Chico Area Interfaith Council, the service commitments also take a lot of time and energy. Although the organization's by-laws direct an equal balance between social action and dialogical relationship-building – and there is always interest in the latter when it happens – it is often eclipsed by the goal-oriented requirements of the former.

McCarthy also explores some of the factors that keep religious leaders or groups away from interfaith social action. Smaller and less wealthy congregations often do not have the bandwidth; even a couple of the partner organizations do not come to meetings or participate much given other priorities. Some traditions lack the institutional structure that would make them visible to the council.

During McCarthy's research, the pastor of the large evangelical church in town explained his community's non-participation with other concerns: he felt that the theology of the group was necessarily a "many roads up the same mountain" view, and he did not want to compromise his Christian convictions. He also believed that the group was too politically activist and too progressive, and he resisted the formality of regular meetings instead of just making a couple phone calls to get things done. He thought "it would be 'awesome' to sit and talk with a Muslim or other non-Christian and could think of no reason why people of different faiths shouldn't work together on issues of hunger and homelessness in the community," but he was "not especially interested in the community structure that makes such dialogue and such collaborations possible."[12] The theology of religions and the politics of the council were more diverse than he imagined, but these assumptions often keep conservative groups away. To move past these objections, it requires personal outreach and conversation rather than an open invitation.

---

[12] McCarthy, *Interfaith Encounters in America* (New Brunswick: Rutgers University Press, 2007), 94–101.

12.2   COMMUNITY-BASED SERVICE

Cities all over the USA have local interfaith councils that do vital work in their community – often the first place people turn when they are hungry or homeless. Geography determines the interpath partners, congregations are their engine (although individuals may participate without one), and secular non-profit organizations are their allies. The Greater Chicago Food Depository, for instance, partners with religious and interfaith food pantries and soup kitchens, supplying food and information, because the faith-based groups are embedded in local communities where there is need.

Even though policies around poverty prompt political debate, efforts like these can generally fashion inclusive tables – groups with conservative *and* progressive politics or religious convictions. Neighborhood clean-ups, tutoring programs, and ancillary support for people with disabilities are similarly uncontroversial. The main question is whether potential partners have the human and material resources to contribute, making sensitivity regarding class and race as important as insight into the interreligious dimensions of the coalition. Other direct service projects create more limited coalitions because of political or theological divides. Sometimes the teams surprise you, however, as when political conservatives who are opposed to immigration show up to help settle refugees.

The desire to help others as expressions of our lifestance is broadly embraced, and gathering interreligiously to provide services feels like a win-win. "Service" can be a loaded word, however. Service-providers by definition have the resources and hold power within the relationship. Efforts to compensate for this imbalance include hiring individuals who had previously (or currently) required the support, providing avenues for feedback so recipients influence the shape and substance of the service, and recognizing the value of their expertise and experience in thinking about the issues. International service organizations are often fastidious about identifying themselves as followers, not the leaders of projects.

Community-engaged service-learning (CESL) is a common practice in higher education and some of it is done in interfaith fashion, incidentally or by design. The valuable benefits of these programs explain their popularity. They call students to an ethic of service and cultivate their sense of civic/social responsibility. They develop leadership skills and provide supportive contexts for navigating difference. They have the potential to transform teaching and learning, creating a student-centered integration of theory and praxis. They contribute in modest ways to world repair.

The critique of CESL is equally compelling. At the most basic level, the experience of parachuting in for a short while limits effectiveness and tends to obscure the structural dimensions of social injustice. Students develop truncated understandings of societal issues and strategies for change. It also runs the risk of becoming about the students and their experiences rather than the work that needs to be done. Projects that require students to traverse race and class differences frequently end up reinforcing hierarchical structures, setting up the largely white middle- and upper-class students as the saviors or social superiors. Informed by post-colonial criticism like sociologist Meyda Yeğenoğlu's caution about taking "a detour through the other," scholars and activists have raised concerns about cultural tourism, especially efforts that "commodify People of Color for the benefit of white people and white-serving institutions."[13]

In the interreligious arena, these risks are definitely present. Inside and outside higher education, however, the involvement of diverse congregations and individuals increases the likelihood of fashioning projects that are authentically embedded in the communities they serve. In addition, the practice of creating space for

---

[13] Lauren Irwin and Zak Foste, "Service-Learning and Racial Capitalism: On the Commodification of People of Color for White Advancement," *Review of Higher Education* 44, no. 4 (Summer 2021): 419; see David K. Seitz, "'It's Not About You': Disappointment as Queer Pedagogy in Community-Engaged Service-Learning," *Journal of Homosexuality* (October 2018): 305–14, https://doi.org/10.1080/00918369.2018.1528078.

relationship-building opens opportunities to deepen self-awareness about the place of self and others in the ecology of mutual care.

Another issue that arises around faith-based service providers relates to government support. In the USA, it was generally expected that religious agencies receiving public funds to provide services had to provide those services to everyone, regardless of religion. Consequently, organizations rooted in a single tradition such as Catholic Charities or Jewish Child and Family Services were "interfaith" in the communities they served, operating with intercultural sensitivity and without proselytizing. Even so, we should acknowledge the "power of the purse" for organizations that receive such funds.

Of late, the issues have grown more complicated. In 2022, a three-judge panel in Tennessee allowed a Methodist adoption and foster care agency that receives public funds to refuse service to a Jewish couple, arguing that the couple was able to secure the service elsewhere in the state. It is not yet clear how this "separate but equal" ruling will impact faith-based service organizations but, as discussed in Chapter 7, religious freedom is increasingly being upheld as grounds for discrimination.

12.3   MESSAGING

Spiritual lifestances draw creatively on sacred events in their histories to inspire and motivate action. It can be relatively straightforward, as with the American Jewish World Service materials distributed around Jewish holidays that tie the themes to global concerns, such as Passover and the refugee crisis or world hunger. Since it is important to capture people's attention in this world of information overload, Auburn Seminary talks about the utility of "ethical spectacle." They co-sponsored an "ark" float at the 2014 Climate March, a powerful symbol for people who value the story of Noah as a message about our potential to destroy/preserve creation. When the Trump administration implemented a family separation policy for undocumented immigrants (to circumvent the rule that families with children could not be incarcerated for more than twenty days), a number of churches built a different kind of crèche that Christmas. They locked Joseph, Mary, and baby Jesus in separate cages – a provocative protest.

Religious symbolism can be very powerful. In 1991, a Buddhist monk in Thailand named Phra Prachak "ordained" trees in the Dong Yai forest to protect them from logging – wrapping them with the holy yellow threads of Buddhist clergy. Although he was prosecuted by the government for this work and eventually forced to forfeit his status as a monk, the ordination gave the villagers courage to stand up to government forces and corporate interests. The trees are now part of the officially protected Dong Phayayen-Khao Yai Forest World Heritage site (2005).[14]

The climate crisis illuminates several challenges in social action messaging. The easy part is excavating teachings from diverse lifestances that urge us to reimagine our relationship with the natural world; there have always been alternative visions to the politics of fear, greed, conquest, and extraction. Spiritual lifestances also provide deep reservoirs of hope – not as idle optimism but as active faith that the world can be different than it is and that we have a part in shaping it. Hope is essential because if you announce that something must be done or we are all going to die, most people strangely choose the latter. Succumbing to what theologian Catherine Keller calls "a critically plausible nihilism" and others have named futilitarianism, leads to the same place as denial. "I can't do anything about it" or "It's too late" yields to consumption and distraction just as readily as "It's not happening."[15]

Yet religion also contributes to inaction. Some religious communities are particularly resistant to climate science. Apocalyptic

---

[14] Noel Rajesh, "Monks Battle to Save Forest," *Down to Earth*, September 15, 1992, www.downtoearth.org.in/news/monks-battle-to-save-forest-30134.

[15] Rachel S. Mikva, "Does Interreligious Understanding Matter if the World Is Coming to an End?" in *Deep Understanding for Divisive Times: Essays Marking a Decade of the Journal of Interreligious Studies*, ed. Lucinda Mosher, et al. (Newton Centre: Interreligious Studies Press, 2020), 13.

expectations, faith that God has a plan, and the blurring of political/ religious identities play a part. As Clive Hamilton, a professor of public ethics, puts it, "Denial is due to a surplus of culture rather than a deficit of information."[16] So faith-based and interfaith efforts abound to change the culture. Green Muslims, Hazon, EcoSikh, Brahma Kumaris Environmental Initiative, A Rocha and hundreds of other non-profit organizations associated with individual lifestances promote sustainability through education, congregational organizing, and advocacy. Interfaith organizations have also emerged, including Interfaith Power and Light, GreenFaith, the Interfaith Center for Sustainable Development, Interfaith Rainforest Initiative, Australian Religious Response to Climate Change, National Religious Partnership on the Environment, the South African Faith Communities Environmental Institute, and more. Existing interfaith institutions like the Parliament of the World's Religions and United Religions Initiative have dedicated arms working on the climate crisis.[17]

It is still unclear what the impact of these messaging efforts may be in generating the requisite global commitment to sustainability. Pope Francis' 2015 encyclical *Laudato si'* eloquently made the case for our common home in peril, the human roots of the crisis, and the abuse of creation as sin. The Catholic Church rolled out substantial ancillary teaching materials and publicity. When surveyed, however, only 18 percent of Catholics reported having any discussion about climate at church, and three-quarters said they never talk about it – the same percentage as the population at large. Five percent said they trusted the pope less because of the encyclical.[18]

---

[16] Hamilton, "What History Can Teach Us About Climate Change Denial," in *Engaging with Climate Change*, ed. Sally Weintrobe (Abingdon: Routledge, 2013), 16–32, https://doi.org/10.4324/9780203094402.

[17] See Tatiana Brailovskaya, ed., *Faith for the Earth: A Call to Action* (Nairobi: United Nations Environment Programme, 2020), 105–07 for a partial list of organizations.

[18] George Marshall, "Communicating with Religious Communities on Climate Change," *Journal of Interreligious Studies* 19 (Summer 2016): 28.

The Evangelical Environmental Network has a resonant message of creation care and has been advocating within the community since 1993, but white evangelicals are still the most resistant to climate science. There is an Interfaith Forum that meets parallel to the G20 international conference each year (IF20), designed to provide substantive input and insight from diverse religious communities to guide policymakers on climate change and other issues. The impact it can have in this interstitial role between state and non-state actors is promising, but has not yet been fully realized.

Given that attitudes to the climate crisis are determined by culture more than science, by values and identity, it seems that religious engagement is essential to generating sufficient momentum for change – despite the unconvincing progress to date. The way life-stances influence our vision of the cosmos, our ethics, and our way of life matter. And because the fate of the earth is a global concern, it is inherently interreligious.

The message itself can be a challenge. Some ecologists argue that the language of sustainability is insufficient because it suggests perpetuating the present state of affairs into a stable future rather than cultivating resilience in the face of inevitable revolutionary change.[19] In addition, the urgent claims of environmental justice – to address the disproportionate exposure of poor and marginalized communities to harms from extraction, industry, and waste, alongside other gross inequities in environmental resources – contend with the climate crisis for prioritization.

Messaging is generally considered one component in organizing for social change but, given exponentially increasing social media communication and its influence, it has become a mode of action in its own right. Some non-profits talk about digital organizing and are undertaking substantial research to improve effectiveness. ReThink

---

[19] See Kevin Minister, "An Ecological Approach to Interreligious Studies," in *The Georgetown Companion to Interreligious Studies*, ed. Lucinda Mosher (Washington, DC: Georgetown University Press, 2022), 163–64, https://doi.org/10.2307/j.ctv27qzsb3.20.

278 COMMUNITY-BASED SERVICE, ORGANIZING, AND ADVOCACY

Media, for example, received a grant to determine the most effective messaging to combat Islamophobia in the USA and to train interreligious influencers to utilize it. They learned to lead with values like freedom of religion, shared identity as Americans, the Golden Rule, and a sense of strength through unity. This positive and aspirational approach resonated with a broader swath of the population than focusing on discrimination or myth-busting. It also captured the high moral ground, where they advocate using strong language, for example, "We do not ban people from our country because of how they worship. That is not the America we aspire to be." Some takeaways from the research, like advocating positive action, seem obvious but others are more subtle: focus on shared identity before explaining differences, and acknowledge people's fears and dispel them with information rather than judgment.

Tips for communicating on social media in general are proliferating, although the digital natives dominating the sphere today hardly need them. Keep it short. Use strong images, concise sentences, and active verbs. Ask questions periodically to get comments and conversation going. Use the right platform for your topic, your timing, and your intended audience. Share content from other sources, expanding your network's connections. The list goes on.

12.4 COMMUNITY ORGANIZING AND ADVOCACY

Alexia Salvatierra and Peter Heltzel talk about faith-rooted organizing, "based on the belief that many aspects of spirituality, faith traditions, faith practices and faith communities can contribute in unique and powerful ways to the creation of just communities and societies."[20] Coming from the Christian organizing world, they explain that the goal is not simply to organize people of faith but also to help them dig into their traditions and spiritual practices as the foundation for their action.

[20] Salvatierra and Heltzel, *Faith-Rooted Organizing: Mobilizing the Church in Service to the World* (Downers Grove: IVP Books, 2013), 9.

There are some interesting differences between classic organizing theory and this approach. Saul Alinsky, arguably the "father" of community organizing, maintained that self-interest is the primary motivation for participation. Getting activists to identify their self-interest preempts white saviors and callous manipulators, and helps people remember why they are in the fight. Salvatierra tells a story, however, of unlearning this truism, guided by a group of mothers risking death to participate in a march in the Philippines. They laughed at her framing of the cause in terms of self-interest and explained that they were motivated by love for their children – by which they meant everyone's children. In faith-rooted organizing, self-interest can still be a useful consideration, but without neglecting the emphasis many lifestances place on love and obligation to others.[21]

Another substantive difference between the two methods is the conception of one's adversary in the struggle for justice. Classic organizing theory generally treats them as targets; faith-rooted organizing sees them as children of God, capable of transformation. We call them in, more than call them out, trusting that there is a spark of virtue and compassion that can set us on the same page.[22] Critique is powerful because it exposes the harm done by existing systems, purposeful and incidental, but organizing efforts need also to project what a better system looks like and how we might build it together. By focusing on what we are advocating, those who advocate something else cease to be our enemy. They are not even the problem; the problem is that we have different strategies for moving forward but we live or work in the same place. Framed this way, we may become problem solvers together.

Salvatierra and Heltzel relate several organizing successes that integrate faith-rooted values. A family in Southern California owned a

---

[21] Salvatierra and Heltzel, *Faith-Rooted Organizing*, 133–34.
[22] Helene Slessarev-Jamir, *Prophetic Activism: Progressive Religious Justice Movements in Contemporary America* (New York: New York University Press, 2011), 111.

number of malls and outsourced cleaning services to the lowest bidder; the workers did not earn a living wage or benefits and did not even have protective equipment. So in 2002, Clergy and Laity United for Economic Justice (CLUE) invited numerous clergy to sign a letter to the family explaining the problem. Since the signatories included their own senior pastor, they sat down with the clergy in their home church and ultimately committed to a living wage. In San Diego, the Interfaith Committee for Worker Justice (ICWJ) joined with numerous other organizations to advocate for living wage legislation. The coalition used public comment time to press their talking points. ICWJ folks, however, used their time to pray – for the poor, for the community, for the City Council. When a journalist asked one of the unlikely supporters of the bill why he voted for it, he replied that he could not stand being prayed for anymore. "He had armed himself against the talking points, but he had no armor against the prayer. The prayer reached his heart."[23]

Many faith-based and interfaith organizations still rely on Alinsky's approach, and many of the core strategies are useful in any event. The "one-to-one" is a fundamental tool in any organizer's work because building relationship is key to building power for a successful grassroots movement. Schedule a time to meet and talk with someone who might be an ally. We share part of our story, including what draws us to the cause, and invite them to share their story, values, and interests. What do they want to see changed, and what do they see as their role? Each person we engage is another link in the ever-expanding network.

Religious and interreligious organizing efforts display compelling assets. Some are intangible, like the trust engendered in healthy relationships between decision-makers and their clergy – as evident in the case of the mall owners. Political scientists Robert Putnam and David Campbell note that religious congregations are vital institutions because their members are more civically active; they are incubators for civic energy and leadership skills, then released into society

---

[23] Salvatierra and Heltzel, *Faith-Rooted Organizing*, 73, 95.

at large.[24] They can also be very effective in mobilizing their constituencies, although many congregational leaders lack confidence in their capacity for organizing and advocacy.[25] As discussed in Chapter 14, interreligious efforts are useful in conflict transformation (even though religion can also be a source of conflict). Teachings of nonviolence and reconciliation, processes of repentance and forgiveness, notions of interdependence and transcendence, commitments to personal responsibility and collective wellbeing can be the infrastructure of necessary bridge-building.

Yet organizing and advocacy also become more complicated in interreligious space. Broad-based interfaith organizations often avoid issues like abortion, LGBTQIA+ rights, or Israel/Palestine. Even issue-specific coalitions periodically miscalculate as they try to find common ground among difference on controversial issues. The example below describes my own experience, so I offer a more personal rendering:

Case Summary: Making Space for Difference[1]

Long before *Roe v. Wade* was overturned in 2022, I invited a friend to attend a rally planned by the Religious Coalition for Reproductive Choice. RCRC describes itself as "a broad-based, national, interfaith movement that brings the moral force of religion to protect and advance reproductive health, choice, rights and justice through education, prophetic witness, pastoral presence and advocacy."[2] They gather Buddhist, Catholic, Hindu, Jewish, Muslim, Protestant, and Universalist Unitarian perspectives supporting reproductive justice. Since individuals and organizations on the other side of the debate

---

[24] Putnam and Campbell, *American Grace: How Religion Divides and Unites Us* (New York: Simon & Schuster, 2010), 454–58.

[25] Justus Baird, "Educating Religious Leaders for Faith-Rooted Social Justice Work," Auburn Seminary, July 2013, https://auburnseminary.org/report/educating-religious-leaders.

often try to assert an exclusive claim on religious values, I appreciate RCRC's affirmation of reproductive rights as a matter of religious freedom.

The rally unfolded as you might expect. Speakers from different lifestances emphasized the importance of women and families making reproductive health decisions without shame, stigma, or legal coercion. They shared their traditions' teachings about abortion – a varied and nuanced chorus of religious insight. They spoke about all the issues that are part of reproductive justice – sexual education, food security, paid leave, affordable childcare, health care – not simply keeping abortion safe and legal. Then someone introduced a song composed for the occasion, "An Acorn Is Not a Tree," and my friend began to fume.

He had come to support women's bodily autonomy and religious freedom, including the right to choose what they believe about the beginnings of life. But he did not personally distinguish between a fetus and a human. In the analogy of the song, he believed an acorn is morally equivalent to a tree – but he refused to impose his religious convictions on others. He saw himself as both pro-choice and pro-life. How could the organizers erase him from the coalition?

As we reflected together on this experience, we recognized the risks in making assumptions about what brings people to a cause. Interreligious collaboration to advance the common good is crucial, but we cannot presume that allies share our religious or ethical perspectives just because they are on our side. The most obvious strategy to avoid this error is to ask questions. Invite people's stories. What brings you to the table, and how is it informed by your lifestance?

Questions for Consideration

1. I was moved that this young man with sincere religious feeling committed himself to the value of a religiously plural society – making room for diverse convictions about things that matter most. What values in your own political or spiritual lifestance might conflict with relational values in interreligious work? How do you navigate that tension?

2. We live and learn through working together toward world repair. Have you ever been part of a social action effort with noticeable interfaith missteps? What would you do differently, and why?

3. How do you speak within rather than for a coalition? Does it dilute the message?

4. Ali ibn Abi Talib, the fourth of the rightly guided caliphs and a key figure in Shi'ite tradition, says that justice rests on four pillars: deep comprehension, abundant knowledge, blossoms of wisdom, and flowerbeds of restraint.[3] How might you apply this insight to reflect on the rally or another interfaith social justice project?

[1] This case is adapted from Rachel S. Mikva, "An Acorn Is Not a Tree," in *With the Best of Intentions: Interrogating Interreligious Mistakes*, ed. Lucinda Mosher, Elinor Pierce, and Or N. Rose (Maryknoll: Orbis Books, forthcoming 2023).

[2] Religious Coalition for Reproductive Choice, https://rcrc.org.

[3] Hussein Rashid, "Opening the Door: Imam Ali and New Conversations in Interreligious Dialogue," in *Words to Live By*, 165.

Despite the challenges of effective social action, we conclude this chapter with the encouraging words attributed to anthropologist Margaret Mead: "Never doubt that a small group of thoughtful citizens can change the world. Indeed, it is the only thing that ever has."

13 Arts

Almost any mode of art can become a vehicle for interreligious engagement – music, pictorial arts (painting, drawing, photography, printmaking), sculpture, ceramics, poetry and creative writing, crafts and folk art, theater, film/TV, dance, and more. Some artistic expressions, like architecture, material objects, and ritual performance play central roles in spiritual identity and praxis. This chapter discusses the relationship of art and religion, the promise that arts show for advancing interreligious understanding and collaboration, the range of objectives and projects that one may find, and challenges that arise.

13.1 ART AND RELIGION

Religions have long and complex histories with artistic expression. Most lifestances have a rich material culture; the buildings they construct and the ritual objects they use reveal key values within their tradition. Art itself can be a ritual, whether it be creation of a mandala, the dance of the dhikr, or a song in worship. Every mode of artistic expression has religious examples because the role of creativity in spiritual life is profound. From a Hindu perspective, aesthetic experience is "not merely entertainment but epiphany, a manifestation of bliss (*ānanda*) which comes from the absolute reality (*brahman*)."[1] This conviction influences Hindu artistic culture, with images of all sorts – human beings, animals, plants, divine figures – rendered in rich, sensuous forms.

Religious teachings promote beauty, as taught by the Prophet Muhammad in a *hadith*: God is beautiful and loves beauty (*al-Mu'jam*

---

[1] Melanie Barbato, "Interreligious Art in Light of Hindu and Buddhist Thought," *CrossCurrents* 68, no. 3 (September 2018): 342.

al-Aswat 6906). The aesthetics of writing and reciting Qur'an, the development of graphic art, and the architectural splendor of many mosques testify to this belief. Judaism speaks of *hiddur mitzvah*, fulfilling the commandments with as much beauty as is possible – leading to artistic investment in ritual objects, religious music, and other elements of Jewish practice. Bahá'í thought emphasizes the unity of inner and outer beauty, so its stunning buildings and gardens are meant to foster a spiritual complement, ultimately expressed through amity among all peoples.

Yet art can also be a source of conflict as it intersects with religious ideology. Aniconic traditions have resisted representation of divine or human figures, art has prompted charges of blasphemy or triggered violence, and religious leaders have often condemned new musical styles, both secular and religious. (If you visit Cleveland's Rock & Roll Hall of Fame, be sure to view the early television programs with people excoriating the genre as deriving from the devil.)

Art reveals the ongoing influence of religions on one another as well. Many motifs are simply adopted or adapted, such as the halo surrounding the heads of Jesus and the saints in Christian art – drawn from images of the Greek god Apollo and indirectly from depictions of the Egyptian sun god Ra. The decorative elements of Christmas – fir trees, ornaments, mistletoe – reflect the holiday's roots in Druid and other Pagan traditions. Medieval Jewish poetry in Spain was heavily influenced by Arabic forms and themes of Muslim verse. Music often travels freely, with new words set to borrowed melodies.

Religious hybridity is made visible in art, as in the ancient caves of Ajanta and Ellora northeast of Mumbai. Ellora's Cave 29, for instance, has a figure of the Hindu god Shiva with Jain earrings and a Buddhist hand salute.[2] Hindu texts, sculpture, and pictorial art often portray Buddha as an avatar of Vishnu. Imagery from Rastafarian and

---

[2] Richard Kearney, "Introduction: A Pilgrimage to the Heart," in *Traversing the Heart: Journeys of the Interreligious Imagination*, ed. Richard Kearney and Eileen Rizo-Patron (Leiden: Brill, 2011), 4, https://doi.org/10.1163/ej.9789004183803.i-504.7.

other hybrid traditions visually manifests their unique fusions. Depending on one's perspective, these expressions may be seen as radical hospitality, creative adaptation, or transgression of significant boundaries.

Even with this complex relationship of art and religion – or perhaps in part because of it – the arts offer a fertile field for interreligious engagement.

13.2   THE VALUE OF THE ARTS IN INTERPATH ENGAGEMENT

Ethnomusicologist Roberta King recounts a concert of Middle Eastern music to support Syrian refugees in Southern California, hosted at an evangelical church. It begins with a Senegalese *griot* playing his *kora*, a 21-string harp-lute. He dedicates his song to the refugees – many of whom are present – and, as always, to honor Allah; it is an act of solidarity with this community of Christians, Muslims, and others coming together to repair the world. The final performer, a Jordanian Palestinian immigrant who plays the *oud*, starts with two simple Christian hymns and encourages the audience to participate. As they sing *Salaam, salaam, yarabi salaam* ("Peace, peace, O my Lord peace"), it evokes a wistful longing.

> Then it happens. The singer launches into a well-known Arabic folk song as the dynamics of the evening shift dramatically. The music slips off the stage and ripples throughout the audience. Faces light up with delight as Middle Easterners recognize one of their beloved songs. The song evokes a nostalgia of better times and of home. With growing momentum, the Middle Eastern newcomers move toward the front of the sanctuary and start to line dance, men clasping hands, holding them high in the air with large smiles on their faces. Now the church members and the local community gingerly come forward, attempting to join in. The young women in their *hijabs* bring out their smartphones to capture the excitement. It's a spontaneous moment breaking down multiple barriers. Joy

and delight abound. But wait – as the music and dance begin to subside, there is weeping in the room. A lovely Syrian mother in silk headscarf reaches down to her tearful three-year-old daughter. Crying through her tears, she asks, "Why does the music have to stop?"[3]

What is it about music and other artistic expression that is so moving, it leaps across difference and touches our souls? Interreligious arts projects have many of the benefits that other efforts do. They expand our perspective, helping us see what we cannot see alone. They invite appreciative inquiry and cultivate empathy. They dismantle stereotypes, celebrating both our meaningful differences and our common humanity. But the arts have unique ways of working their magic.

Moving beyond cognition and reason, art helps us discover new ways of knowing and unknowing, of finding ourselves and losing ourselves. Encountering people of different lifestances, we not only look, listen, and think together; we *feel* together. Appreciation for music and art transcend culture because we do not necessarily need to understand them for us to feel their joy, pain, fear, or desire. And still, artistic ventures are meaning-making exercises that elicit deep connections. They can even be world-making exercises – especially fiction and film – utterly transforming our imaginations and shaping our lives.

Imagination awakens curiosity, making it a "special agent of interreligious hospitality."[4] Art thus enhances our receptivity to the unknown. It is comfortable with ambiguity, in the gaps between tradition and translation, revealed and hidden, intention and impact. In a theological sense, it is akin to Paul Tillich's discussion of mystery. More than simply something we do not yet know, mystery

---

[3] King, "Performing Witness: Loving Our Religious Neighbors through Musicking," in *The Arts as Witness in Multifaith Contexts*, ed. Roberta R. King and William A. Dyrness (Downers Grove: InterVarsity Press, 2019), 41.

[4] Richard Kearney, "Introduction: A Pilgrimage to the Heart," *Religion and the Arts* 12 (2008): 3.

contradicts ordinary cognition and does not cease to be mysterious once it is revealed. The object is not to resolve it but to live in it.[5] This kind of openness involves risk-taking, which is a dynamic present in all interreligious engagement. With the arts, risk is multiplied: the world of feeling exposes our soft spots, and co-creators of art become invested in the product and its reception. Because the arts always involve risk, however, perhaps the interreligious dimensions themselves seem less frightening.

The sense of interdependence that grows through sustained encounter is accelerated in artistic ventures. Whether one is a co-creator of the art, a viewer/listener, or setting up the chairs for an event, there is a sense of collective endeavor. Consider musicologist Christopher Small's neologism "musicking": a form of human encounter "in which all those present are involved and for whose nature and quality, success or failure, everyone present bears some responsibility."[6] Art also expands the reach of interpath work: some people engage the projects because of their artistic components, getting drawn into interreligious relationship as a by-product.

Multivocality, prominent in most interreligious contexts, unfolds somewhat differently through artistic expression. Disagreement is expected and embraced; there is no wrong answer because each contribution or response contributes to the experience and understanding of the whole. Artist Sonia Delaunay's description of visual art can be a metaphor for the vivifying power of meeting religious difference: "One who knows how to appreciate colour relationships, the influence of one colour with another, their contrasts and dissonances, is promised an infinite variety of images."[7] Art is

---

[5] See Cindy Beth Johnson, with Jann Cather Weaver, "Letting the Arts Lead," in *Teaching for a Multifaith World*, ed. Eleazar S. Fernandez (Eugene: Wipf & Stock, 2017), 179–98.

[6] Small, *Musicking: The Meanings of Performing and Listening* (Hanover: University Press of New England, 1998), 10.

[7] Cited in Christopher Longhurst, *Pictorial Art for Interreligious Dialogue* (KAICIID Dialogue Centre, Vivid Publishing, October 2021) *frontispiece*, www.vividpublishing.com.au/pictorialart.

created to be a dialogue. It also embeds the principle of speaking from rather than for a tradition; art reveals what a person says, not what a religion says.

These unique qualities of artistic expression have been deployed for a variety of projects and purposes in interreligious engagement.

13.3 PROJECTS AND PURPOSES

The most common purpose is as a bridge. Because the arts are emotionally evocative and multiperspectival, readily creating shared experience, they are effective vehicles to foster interreligious relationship. Artists from diverse lifestances may collaborate in curating or creating something together. In "Out of One, Many" three Middle Eastern artists – a Jew, a Christian, and a Muslim – each made five paintings that interpret parts of Abraham's life and legacy in their tradition. Touring Europe and the United States, they used the common ground and unique perspectives to foster cultures of harmony.

"Artist" does not need to be a professional identity for bridge-building. Poetry Pals guides elementary school children to use their creativity to navigate religious differences, cultivating empathy and understanding as they share their work.[8] "In the Name of the Fathers" drew together men who were immigrants from Muslim countries and native Dutch working-class men to create a play addressing violence in their communities, drawing on their shared experiences as fathers.[9] Creative writing and photography, quilting and poetry slams, improv and mural painting readily involve all participants as artists. Focused on personal stories, spiritual questions, or a collective vision, an

---

[8] See www.oncaravan.org/abraham; http://olivetreeartsnetwork.org/programs/poetry-pals.

[9] Eugene van Erven and Kate Gardner, "Performing Cross-Cultural Conversations: Creating New Kinships thru Community," in *Acting Together: Performance and the Creative Transformation of Conflict*, ed. Cynthia E. Cohen, Roberto Gutiérrez Varea, and Polly O. Walker (Oakland: New Village Press, 2011), 2:10–20.

interreligious art project can explore diverse worlds of learning and feeling.

There are multiple ways to involve people in the creative process. Playback Theater, an improvisational project with hundreds of companies in over seventy countries, uses professional actors but the stories of participants. A member of the troupe interviews audience members about significant moments in their lives. Then the actors immediately dramatize the story/stories – using music, movement, and dialogue to bring them to life – followed by discussion. Easily tailored to interreligious engagement, the process surfaces critical issues, fosters openness, and builds trust.[10]

Individual artists also use their gifts to invite bridge-building, at least in the viewers' or listeners' imaginations. Some, like Judy Chicago's "Rainbow Shabbat," require no previous knowledge to receive its message of universal friendship. Others are more subtle: Mizuho Matsunaga's "Shangrila and Schlaraffenland" series, for instance, uses Zen and Rococo sacred art to excavate the shared human longing for escape from bondage – but it would likely be lost on those not versed in art history.[11] While these works do not directly foster interreligious engagement, it is a relatively simple matter to create a program that presents art for shared experience, learning, and discussion. It can be designed to display multiple religio-cultural traditions, focus on critical issues, or explore visions of harmony.

A related purpose of numerous interreligious art projects is conflict transformation – building bridges to heal harm inflicted by war, bigotry, or structural violence. The impact is generally most substantial on the artists. Pontanima, an interfaith choir in Sarajevo, began in 1996 after tremendous interreligious and interethnic violence tore apart the Balkans. Father Ivo Marković acknowledges that, when they first tried to sing Serbian or Muslim songs, participants

---

[10] Sarah Halley and Jonathan Fox, "Playback Theater," in *The Change Handbook*, ed. Peggy Holman, Tom Devane, and Steven Cady (San Francisco: Berrett-Koehler, 2007), 561–72.

[11] Barbato, "Interreligious Art," 345.

balked; they felt disgust at singing music of the enemy. So they started with a Jewish song, which carried less baggage. In just a couple months, however, choir members had built relationships strong enough to see the beauty in each other's music – and to sing it together.[12]

A shared experience of being in the audience can also be powerful. In Yogyakarta, the 2010 concert "Common Sounds: Songs of Peace and Reconciliation," conveyed hope for the diverse peoples of Indonesia: "It was a mesmerizing moment of harmony of sound as musicians from different nations and different faith traditions set aside their religious and ethnic differences, yet remained true to their religious and musical beliefs, and locked their hearts together to sing for peace." Later in the concert, when children from different communities performed together a mime/dance embodying harmony, conflict, and transformation, it touched hearts even more deeply. Christian and Muslim women also sang together, moving the audience with a message of women's empowerment alongside one of peace.[13]

Arts can help to transform conflict even if they are a small part of the engagement. John Lederach, an expert in conflict transformation (see Chapter 14), asserts that even five minutes devoted to artistic experience,

> when it is given space and acknowledged as something far beyond entertainment, accomplishes what most of politics has been unable to attain: It helps us return to our humanity, a transcendent journey that, like the moral imagination, can build a sense that we *are*, after all, a human community.[14]

---

[12] "Sarajevo's Choir That Bridged the Ethnic Divide," www.bbc.com/news/av/stories–43472897.

[13] Roberta Rose King and Sooi Ling Tan, "Prologue: From Beirut to Yogyakarta," in *(un)Common Sounds: Songs of Peace and Reconciliation Among Muslims and Christians*, ed. Roberta Rose King and Sooi Ling Tan (Eugene: Cascade Books, 2014), 7–12.

[14] John Lederach, *The Moral Imagination: The Art and Soul of Building Peace* (Oxford: Oxford University Press, 2005), 153–54, https://doi.org/10.1093/0195174542.001.0001.

Conflict transformation can also take the form of protest and resistance to structures of violence or oppression. These projects are frequently created by an individual or group with a shared religious identity, speaking out and hoping that people of diverse lifestances and cultures will notice, care, and change. *The Hijabi Monologues*, for example, collected and performed vignettes of Muslim women's experience of bigotry. While the stories are diverse in tone, each illustrates how the woman's actions and personhood were reduced to her religion, in the way that racial minorities' actions are viewed through the lens of race.

Diverse groups of artists have also come together in acts of resistance. In 2015, a public art collective in San Francisco took action after an anti-Muslim hate group ran bus ads implying a link between Islam and Nazism. The bus company said that free-speech protections prevented them from refusing the ads, so members of the collective plastered over the images with large reproductions of the new Ms. Marvel (Kamala Khan, a popular Muslim teenage comics figure) and replaced the tag line with creations of their own, for example, "Calling all bigotry busters."[15]

Artistic expression with this purpose may also be a mode of survival: the creation itself comprises resistance to hegemonic forces. Hip hop has taken numerous subaltern communities by storm, giving vital voice to young people who have been marginalized by their religious, racial, ethnic, geopolitical, or class identities – and there are profound spiritual threads through the music.[16] Women in Mexico's Zapatista movement offer another example, fighting for women's and Indigenous rights together. They retrieved the subjugated knowledge of their Mayan culture and blended it with

---

[15] Jessica Baldanzi and Hussein Rashid, eds., *Ms. Marvel's America: No Normal* (Jackson: University Press of Mississippi, 2020), viii.

[16] See Alejandro Nava, *Street Scriptures: Between God and Hip-Hop* (Chicago: University of Chicago Press, 2022); Su'ad Abdul Khabeer, *Muslim Cool: Race, Religion, and Hip Hop in the United States* (New York: New York University Press, 2016).

their Catholic identities to establish a place for themselves in the world. As one woman describes the life-saving value of their artistic work, "We drew, sculpted, and sang our way into empowerment."[17]

13.4 CHALLENGES

It is important to be aware of challenges in deploying the arts for interreligious engagement. Many parallel the issues we find in other interreligious modalities. For example, questions of power intrude: the power of curation and definition determine who is represented and what messages are likely conveyed. Western academic paradigms in art history may limit the way we conceive of programs, as does the understanding of religion itself. Human and financial resources in struggling communities can be limiting in another way; artistic projects are labor intensive and sometimes require substantial materials. How can we make the work sustainable?

The emotional power of the arts catalyzes special concerns as well. There is the potential to retraumatize when grappling with difficult material. Or the process itself might accidentally reinforce stereotypes or reproduce structural inequity, doubly problematic because participants have been asked to make themselves vulnerable. In planning and facilitation, attention to these dynamics can cultivate and maintain trust.

We should recognize that the arts, like other powerful tools of expression, can be used to divide as much as bridge. In establishing particularity, this capacity is not problematic. Yet art has also been used for polemical religious purposes. In Claudio Coello's work, "The Triumph of Saint Augustine" (1664), Augustine is raised upon a cloud and lays waste to figures of hell and Paganism below. The thirteenth-century Strasbourg Cathedral displays two beautiful but disturbing statues: the Church is represented by a noble woman, staff and chalice

---

[17] William Dyrness, "The Poetic Formation of Interfaith Identities: The Zapatista Case," in *The Arts as Witness in Multifaith Contexts*, ed. Roberta R. King and William A. Dyrness (Downers Grove: InterVarsity Press, 2019), 219.

in her hands, crown upon her head, looking boldly into the future. The Synagogue is also a woman, but she holds a broken spear, the tablets of divine instruction hanging limply at her side. She is gazing down – or she would be, except that she is blindfolded. These figures embody the Christian theological conviction that Judaism was superseded and Jews do not understand either the salvific coming of Jesus or their own scripture. Other medieval art was less subtle, showing Muslims and Jews as monstrous or damned in hell.[18] Architecture can convey similarly polemical messages. Constructed after the Rashidun Caliphate defeated the Byzantine Empire in the seventh century, "Jerusalem's Islamic monuments yield an allegory of supersession which is no less deliberate than that of St. Peter's Basilica and the other signs of Christian mastery of the once-Pagan capital of Rome."[19]

Even when not polemical, structural biases reinforce distorted images of the "other" (see Chapter 6). Yet these artistic expressions can become teachable moments. Through interpretation and critique, interreligious groups learn the contexts and impact of historical hostility, and commit to forging a different path. This kind of didactic intervention raises a question that should be considered in many artistic ventures: how much historical or cultural context is necessary to facilitate understanding, and how do we incorporate it without infringing on the affective, participant-centered dimensions of the experience?

Special cultural and religious sensitivities also present challenges. Does the presence of figural art or music automatically eliminate some groups from the interreligious table? What kinds of images might offend – and does that mean they must be avoided?

[18] See Debra Higgs Strickland, *Saracens, Demons, and Jews: Making Monsters in Medieval Art* (Princeton: Princeton University Press, 2003).
[19] Tim Winter, "The Last Trump Card: Islam and the Supersession of Other Faiths," *Studies in Interreligious Dialogue* 9, no. 2 (1992): 145–46, https://doi.org/10.2143/SID.9.2.2003988.

Our experience of art can be profoundly changed by the company with which we experience it. Andrew Smith, Director of Interfaith Relations for the Bishop of Birmingham, relates a story from the Birmingham Conversations project which uses the arts to spark interfaith conversation. Participants representing six faith traditions went together to the local museum/art gallery. Most of the art was Christian, although there is also a "Faith Gallery" with artifacts from several lifestances. Since many narratives represented in the paintings were unfamiliar to some in the group, it generated great questions – but several participants took offense at the frequent nudity. Standing alongside a Muslim woman as Smith viewed a painting of Mary breastfeeding Jesus, an image so familiar to him, they laughed together at the awkwardness it generated. But they were still able to talk about how they view Mary and Jesus in their respective faiths.[20] What kind of preparation might be helpful to navigate these sensitivities?

Since art frequently pushes against boundaries, it presses on all kinds of tender spots. Consider the art installation "The Dialogue: Iconostasis for World Peace," which can be viewed at the Pasos Peace Virtual Museum.[21] In Orthodox Christian architecture, an iconostasis is a wall of icons that separates the sanctuary from the nave. Mary Jane Miller and Valentin Gómez created an artistic model with seventeen gods from diverse traditions represented across the top, a second tier of master teachers and philosophers, and a bottom tier with forty prayer wheels in forty different languages. The adaptation of a recognizable Christian Orthodox art form, the suggestion of equivalency, and other aspects of the piece can offend – even as the intent is to recontextualize the figures to promote global unity.

---

[20] Smith, "Art and Interfaith Conversation," *The Interfaith Observer*, March 15, 2019, www.theinterfaithobserver.org/journal-articles/2019/3/12/art-and-interfaith-conversation.

[21] Pasos Peace Museum, www.pasospeacemuseum.org.

Some artwork is intended as socio-religious critique. Andres Serano's *Piss Christ*, a photograph of Jesus on the cross submerged in urine, caused an uproar when it debuted in 1987. The artist maintained that it was a statement about the cheapening of the image of Christ and hypocrisy among some of his followers. Spanish artist Abel Azcona spelled out *pederastia* and other provocative words in purloined communion wafers, intended to critique power and corruption within the Catholic Church (2015).[22]

It can be challenging to address religious or artistic critique in interreligious space since the instinct to foster appreciative understanding and amicable relationship can suppress it. Participants might be hesitant to share that they do not like something, lest it convey dislike of the religion from which it stems or otherwise offend. If they have theological objections, should they be shared? In co-creative endeavors, the dynamics of rejecting a contribution are complicated by religious difference. And, as mentioned in Chapter 9, the stories we tell often incidentally imply things about others; this holds true in multiple forms of artistic expression. The satirical musical *The Book of Mormon* focuses on The Church of Jesus Christ of Latter-Day Saints but suggests many religious stories are silly. Mel Gibson's *The Passion of the Christ* presented Jews in a terrible light. Air India set the Sikh *"Ik Onkar"* symbol on the tail of the Boeing 787 flying a new route from London to Amritsar; it means "there is only one god," a conviction that is partly responsible for Guru Nanak's break from common forms of Hindu thought. Standing at the beginning of Sikh scripture, the symbol cannot help but tell a story about the religion he left behind.

While interreligious projects do not need to take up controversial art, sometimes the issues raised confront us in the public square, as illustrated in the following case.

[22] Daniel Moulin-Stozek and Anna K. Dulska, "Interreligious Narratives and Contra-Religious Aesthetics in the Material Culture of Navarra, Northern Spain," *CrossCurrents* 68, no. 3 (September 2018): 412–13, https://doi.org/10.1111/cros.12322.

Case Summary: "Chalking Muhammad"[1]

In April 2010, Comedy Central broadcast of the 200th episode of *South Park*. To celebrate this milestone, producers Trey Parker and Matt Stone filled the episode with many of the famous people they had lampooned during the show's history, including religious figures. Aware that most contemporary Sunni authorities forbid images of the Prophet Muhammad, and mindful of the "Danish Cartoon Controversy" that led to protest and violence (2005–06), Parker and Stone disguised the prophet in a bear costume.

Protest from some quarters that this approach nonetheless disrespected the prophet included a warning on the website Revolution Muslim that the producers might be inviting violence. So, in the next episode, they covered the character with a "censored" stamp and bleeped out the prophet's name.

Unsurprisingly, this pleased no one. The press picked up the story and it set off a furious debate over free speech, respect for/criticism of Islam, and self-censorship. One cartoonist responded with a tongue-in-cheek sketch titled "Everybody Draw Muhammad Day." The idea captured many Americans' imaginations and numerous college campuses decided to act on the suggestion.

At Northwestern University, the Secular Humanists for Inquiry and Free Thought (SHIFT) opted to participate. Members of the Muslim-cultural Students Association (McSA) responded with a letter to the student newspaper stating that, while they valued free speech, they were disappointed it was done in a way disrespectful to Muslims. The conflict animated the campus for some time, with additional letters to the editor, community organizing, and meetings with student leaders and administration.

Questions for Consideration

1. Is any artistic expression beyond the pale? How do you balance the competing values of free speech and religious sensitivity?
2. Do you respond differently to the offense some Christians took at *Piss Christ* or *Pederastia*? Why or why not?

3. How might you utilize the arts differently to respond to the controversy, either before or after the chalking incident?

4. What do the following details add to your reflections? Are you inclined to read them to deepen the complexities or to support your position?

   (a) Shi'a tradition is not as restrictive as Sunni teaching about depictions of the prophet and both have multiple images, especially before 1500. Historically, the primary religious concern about imagery of Muhammad was its potential to invite idolatry.

   (b) There was a Qatar delegation on campus during the controversy, and some Muslim students worried that the chalking gave the impression they were abetting a culture hostile to Islam.

---

[1] Adapted from Karla Suomala, *Case Studies for Exploring Interfaith Cooperation: Classroom Tools* (Chicago: Interfaith Youth Core, 2013), 3–8.

14 Conflict Transformation

**Conflict is normal in human relationship. Although religious differ-
ence can be a contributing factor, religious teachings also inspire
building bridges and reaching toward reconciliation. This chapter
explores the field of conflict transformation, the role of religion in
conflict, and strategies to navigate these spaces. Focused on skill-
building rather than program design and facilitation, it introduces
intercultural intelligence, narrative mediation, interest-based bargaining, and non-violent communication. Effective leadership requires
self-awareness about our instinctive responses to conflict, so the
chapter also presents the Thomas–Kilmann paradigm to help readers
explore their reactions.**

14.1 WHAT IS CONFLICT TRANSFORMATION?

Conflict *transformation*[1] builds on the field of conflict *resolution*
with several key shifts in perspective and methodology. First, it
affirms that conflict is normal in human relationship. This is not a
sanction for violence. Some conflicts cannot be resolved, but they can
be reframed to be more generative and less destructive. Conflict
transformation also recognizes that – especially in situations of power
imbalance – "resolution" frequently covers up injustices in an eager-
ness to end strife. Conflict is sometimes the necessary motor for
change. Reverend Dr. Martin Luther King, Jr. reflects on this truth
in his "Letter from a Birmingham Jail," responding to clergy who
claimed to support civil rights but opposed his activism.

---

[1] This chapter is adapted from Rachel S. Mikva, "Training for Leadership in Multifaith
Contexts: Conflict Transformation," in *The Georgetown Companion to
Interreligious Studies*, ed. Lucinda Mosher (Washington, DC: Georgetown
University Press, 2022), 441–50, https://doi.org/10.2307/j.ctv27qzsb3.47.

"Nonviolent direct action," he writes, "seeks to create such a crisis and foster such a tension that a community which has constantly refused to negotiate is forced to confront the issue."[2]

Rather than asking, "How do we make this conflict go away?" conflict transformation teaches us to ask, "What does the conflict change, and what changes do the various stakeholders seek?" Rather than viewing the conflict itself as the problem, we seek to understand the underlying causes and the constraints on the vision of change that stakeholders desire. Changes work at personal, inter-personal, inter-group, cultural, and structural levels. They may be cognitive, emotional, perceptual, spiritual, economic, cultural, political, social, and/or systemic.

According to John Paul Lederach, the goal of conflict transformation is to "respond to the ebb and flow of social conflict as life-giving opportunities for creating constructive change." These processes seek to reduce violence and increase justice while engaging real-world problems in human relationships and social structures. In this work, we cannot view the conflict in isolation; its presenting issues are shaped by longer-term relational, institutional, structural, and cultural factors. Lederach speaks of the present epi*sode* as a window through which we can see the bigger picture – what he calls the epi*center*. With that broader lens, conflict transformation attempts to be crisis-responsive without being crisis-driven.[3] Another useful image is Máire Dugan's nested theory of conflict: we cannot get to the immediate problem without unpacking the layers of concern in which it is embedded.[4] The previous case about chalking Muhammad, for instance, is not only about free speech versus respect for religious difference on campus. There are questions of assimilation and belonging, the Muslim world's perception of American Muslims, the

---

[2] King, "Letter from a Birmingham Jail," www.africa.upenn.edu/Articles_Gen/Letter_Birmingham.html.

[3] Lederach, *The Little Book of Conflict Transformation: Clear Articulation of the Guiding Principles by a Pioneer in the Field* (New York: Good Books, 2003), 14, 23–39.

[4] Dugan, "A Nested Theory of Conflict," *A Leadership Journal: Women in Leadership – Sharing the Vision* 1 (July 1996): 9–20.

Danish cartoon controversy in the background, the context of Islamophobia in the West, and so on.

14.2 ROLE OF RELIGION IN CONFLICT AND CONFLICT TRANSFORMATION

Religions are frequently birthed through conflict: they spar with each other and with cultural practices in their efforts to shape individual souls or the character of society. At the same time, their teachings of self-transcendence and attending to the needs of others animate a capacity for conflict transformation. Several historical examples are discussed in Chapter 3; this chapter focuses on contemporary events.

Conflict is sometimes defined as a difference that matters. Leaders in multifaith contexts recognize that differences in lifestance often matter quite a bit. Adapting W. E. B. DuBois' declaration that "[t]he problem of the twentieth century is the problem of the color line," Interfaith America's Executive Director Eboo Patel asserts, "I believe that the twenty-first century will be shaped by the question of the faith line."[5] With so many issues of racial justice still unresolved, it seems unlikely that the color line will disappear any time soon. But religion has become a more visible source of conflict on the global stage than at any time since the Middle Ages. Consider the attacks on September 11, 2001, and the decades of war that followed in their wake, rising numbers of assaults on religious minorities, and the global rise of religious fundamentalisms. The catalysts are not religion alone, but it plays a significant role. The many case summaries in this volume illustrate manifold ways in which religion gets folded into conflicts large and small.

Efforts in Interreligious Studies (IRS) sometimes ignore these elements, preferring to focus on cultivating common ground and appreciative understanding. Kate McCarthy has called it "the overly

---

[5] DuBois, *The Souls of Black Folk* (Chicago: A. C. McClurg, 1904), 13; Patel, *Acts of Faith: The Story of an American Muslim, the Struggle for the Soul of a Generation* (Boston: Beacon Press, 2007), xv.

irenic impulse."[6] As we have seen, religious difference can spark multiple kinds of conflict even when everyone wants to get along. Interfaith families struggle to agree on what spiritual path to provide for their children. Schools and places of work are faced with the challenge of accommodating a range of religious practices and balancing competing needs. Organizational partners encounter tension between their commitment to constructive engagement across difference and their own convictions around gender, sexuality, and reproductive justice. Ideas about how we embody religious values in our collective public life are controversial. Relationships suffer, court cases abound, and sometimes conflicts lead to violence.

Religion can also serve as a convenient justification for ethnic, national, cultural, economic, and other hostilities. China claims that its persecution of Uighurs is necessary to root out Muslim extremism, but it stems from the Chinese Communist Party's desire to establish Han nationalism as a unifying force and to suppress any cultural/religious identities that might compete. The Bible was frequently cited in support of slavery in the United States, but the driving forces were systemic racism and economic exploitation rather than Scripture. Assigning religious significance to political, cultural, and economic claims conveys a sense of ultimacy that can "change the rules" for what might otherwise be considered acceptable.

Religion, however, is not the primary, inevitable driver of violence that reductionist readings sometimes suggest.[7] First, as noted before, it is practically impossible to isolate the role of religion. When teenage arsonists in New York burn a Sikh Temple to the ground thinking they are destroying a mosque after 9/11, or a city in Italy refers to Muslims who do not eat pork or non-halal meat as Islamic

---

[6] Email exchange with the author, June 2022.

[7] See R. Scott Appleby, *The Ambivalence of the Sacred: Religion, Violence, and Reconciliation* (Lanham: Rowman & Littlefield, 2000).

fundamentalists,[8] their conviction that these brown people in unfamiliar religious garb or with unfamiliar practices do not and cannot "belong" is based on ethnicity as well as faith. Religious difference deepens distrust of racialized others, and racism delegitimizes the ethical and theological convictions of minoritized religions.

Second, internal pluralities and historical contexts yield multiple possibilities for the role of faith. We have numerous examples of people from diverse lifestances working for positive social change – participating in productive conflict inspired by their religious convictions. Liberation theologians in Latin America stood up to oppressive regimes, advancing concern for the marginalized and a "preferential option for the poor." The Satyagraha movement in India and the fight for civil rights in the United States were both deeply grounded in religious values and communities. The Black Lives Matter movement has a more eclectic spirituality, often borrowing from traditional African practices; it too fashions ritual and sacred space to support its activists and animate its call for justice.

Religion also cultivates certain qualities that can be effective in building peace and facilitating conflict transformation. There are teachings of nonviolence and reconciliation, processes of repentance and forgiveness, notions of interdependence and transcendence, commitments to personal accountability and collective wellbeing. Religious institutions often have extensive networks for communication, with the moral authority to organize action. For example, KAICIID – an international interreligious organization – organized a high-level meeting in 2014 with policymakers and religious leaders to protect religious minorities in Iraq and Syria during the violence there (which was also religiously inspired). The US Institute of Peace and

---

[8] See Maria Chiara Giorda, "Different Illiteracies for Different Countries," in *Religious Literacy, Law and History: Perspectives on European Pluralist Societies*, ed. Alberto Melloni and Francesca Cadeddu (Abingdon: Routledge, 2019), 29.

similar organizations increasingly acknowledge the essential role of religion in their work.[9]

In Liberia, Leymah Gbowee led Christian and Muslim women to demand an end to civil war and the violence against women that inevitably accompanied it. Every day for over a year, they gathered to pray, sing, and dance for peace. They got religious leaders to join them, the public to acknowledge them, and the media to cover them – pressuring leaders to negotiate peace. Once they succeeded and talks began, they remained vigilant; after an agreement was signed, they remained active in demobilization, disarmament, reintegration, reconciliation, dialogue, and peace building.[10] Although the conflict had little to do with religion, the divide among faith communities was ever present; solidarity between women of diverse faiths provided a model for transcending discord. Religious difference became the basis for forging peace. Gbowee went on to earn an MA in Conflict Transformation from Eastern Mennonite University in 2007 and shared in the Nobel Peace Prize in 2011.

Beyond this sort of "Track Two" diplomacy, religious and inter-religious groups work to transform conflict on a variety of levels. Campus-based spiritual life centers often take the lead in creating more welcoming space for people of diverse lifestances and in facilitating dialogue when issues emerge. Faith-based organizations pursue violence prevention in urban areas plagued by gangs. They have been involved in victim–offender reconciliation programs – affirming personal responsibility, reformability of human character, and possibilities of forgiveness.

They speak up locally when conflict breaks out around the world; their voices may not impact the global scene, but they can

---

[9] See, for example, David R. Smock, ed., *Interfaith Dialogue and Peacebuilding* (Washington, DC: USIP, 2002).

[10] See George Kieh, "Ending Liberia's Second Civil War: Religious Women as Peacemakers," Berkeley Center for Religion, Peace, and World Affairs, September 25, 2013, https://berkleycenter.georgetown.edu/publications/ending-liberia-s-second-civil-war-religious-women-as-peacemakers.

strengthen relationship and highlight religious teachings that advocate a different path. Muslim and Jewish religious leaders in Chicago, for example, hammered out a joint statement in the wake of the 2008 war in Gaza. As they spoke together, they used the dialogue technique (Chapter 10) with three columns – including (a) areas of agreement and (c) convictions on which they would never agree – and they concentrated on the middle category, where careful listening to diverse perspectives slowly led them to sow common ground.

It is also worth exploring foundational values in individual lifestances that can undergird conflict transformation. In Jain, Buddhist, and Hindu traditions, for instance, the principle of *ahimsa* (alternatively *ahinsa*) is a key virtue – avoiding harm to any life form. Spiritual practices of repentance and reconciliation, like native Hawaiian *ho'oponopono* (literally "setting to right") and Judaism's *teshuvah* (literally "turning"), catalyze the work of repair.

In collaborating on *Interfaith Just Peacemaking*, Muslim, Christian, and Jewish scholars grounded the ten Just Peace practices in the teachings of their traditions. While they acknowledged that their religions had been deployed to justify war as well, they drew from scripture and centuries of religious thought/practice to illuminate how faith commitments could transcend difference to advance peace and justice. Organizations like Religions for Peace and the Parliament of the World's Religions rely on these shared traits to "cultivate harmony among the world's religious and spiritual communities and foster their engagement with the world and its guiding institutions in order to achieve a just, peaceful and sustainable world."[11]

---

[11] This was Parliament's mission statement; it has since been simplified. See "The Council for a Parliament of the World's Religions," November 13, 2011, www .theinterfaithobserver.org/journal-articles/2011/11/13/the-council-for-a- parliament-of-the-worlds-religions.html.

14.3 INTERRELIGIOUS AND INTERCULTURAL INTELLIGENCE

There is no one-size-fits-all approach to conflict transformation because culture is always a factor. Scholars and practitioners of conflict management address ways that cultural differences lead to discord or shape the way people respond to contentious situations – analyses that have implications for navigating diverse spiritual life-stances as well. Michelle LeBaron tells of hiring a young Chinese woman to conduct interviews about conflicts that different immigrant groups experience. The researcher returned from her first assignment with no data because her subject insisted that he experienced no conflict as an immigrant. LeBaron recognized that some people and some cultures are reticent to talk about conflict with strangers, and that the older Chinese gentleman who was being interviewed might have expected deference from this young woman rather than probing questions. She also realized, however, that it might be partly attributable to his Confucian education, which taught him to notice harmony rather than its absence.[12]

Cultural differences can lead to mistrust or misunderstanding. Cultures that emphasize individualism may consider more collectivist ones oppressive; in turn, collectivist cultures may interpret individualism as narcissism, with no concern for the common good. Low-context cultures rely on explicit and direct communication; they tend to focus on issues. High-context cultures communicate a great deal implicitly – through body language, status, and tone, with rules expected to be understood rather than spelled out. The emphasis is often on interpersonal relationships. It is not a simple binary, of course. The USA is a low-context culture, but events like family gatherings and religious rituals demonstrate high-context characteristics. There are also multiple sub-cultures that affect interactions.

---

[12] LeBaron, *Bridging Cultural Conflicts: A New Approach for a Changing World* (San Francisco: Jossey-Bass, 2004), 26–27.

Many cultural differences link to lifestance and get woven into the nest of conflict. Worldviews about particularism and universalism, linear and cyclical conceptions of time, fatalism and free will, world-facing and world-effacing ethics are influenced by religious teachings. They shape attitudes toward science, medicine, government, music, foods/alcohol, dress, and multiple aspects of daily life that get lodged in culture. (In turn, culture also shapes the ways people interpret their spiritual tradition. Consider, for example, how Christianity emphasizes different teachings depending on one's political party and how it looks quite different depending on where you are in the world.)

It is easy to assume that everyone sees the world the way we do or that our own cultural perspective is superior. And it is easy to see how these attitudes can impede communication, understanding, and relationship. So training in interreligious leadership begins with an embrace of multiplicity – being radically aware that all people do not see *anything* the same way. It cultivates fluency in multiple traditions and the multiple ways in which each is lived out. It facilitates visibility for frequently submerged aspects of culture by guiding people to share what is important to them and why.

We need to be aware of our own culture's ways of knowing and being, and be sensitive to the workings of culture in our interactions with others. Christine Hong advocates the pursuit of interreligious and intercultural intelligence, a quality she associates with the Korean concept of *noon-chi* (literally "eye-measure"). "Intelligence" here is not competency or mastery "but a specific posture and expectation toward listening and understanding across difference."[13] Various interreligious leadership guidelines emphasize capacities that cultivate such intelligence, including humility, compassion, creativity, hospitality, open-mindedness, patience, and self-critical awareness. These qualities help us navigate cultural conflict.

---

[13] Christine J. Hong, *Decolonial Futures: Intercultural and Interreligious Intelligence for Theological Education* (Lanham: Lexington Books, 2021), 8.

Case Summary: Religion, Culture, and the Coronavirus Vaccine[1]

By the time the World Health Organization declared COVID-19 a pandemic in March 2020, governments and pharmaceutical companies were feverishly working on vaccines. By the end of the year, they had one in hand and others were approved shortly thereafter. As always, wealthy nations had more access and means of distribution. Not everyone within these countries, however, was clamoring for doses – particularly in the USA. Some individuals and communities suspected the pandemic was a hoax, some were angry about mask mandates and restrictions on public gatherings, and some believed that the vaccine was dangerous or part of a government conspiracy. Tensions across these cultural divides were high. People spit on store clerks who reminded them to wear a mask; others wished Covid upon those who were unvaccinated.

Religious communities responded in diverse ways: most scrambled to deliver programs and worship remotely, and strived to support people in crisis – those who were ill, lost jobs, suffered domestic abuse, or struggled with mental health issues exacerbated by the pandemic. They preached about collective sacrifice and highlighted the justice issues that came to light, including disparate health outcomes based on race and class, and "essential workers" without paid sick leave or health insurance. Some congregations, however, organized large gatherings against lockdown orders, including a few that became super-spreader events. Several groups filed suit against the government, arguing that public health restrictions interfered with their freedom of religion – from limitations on assembly to work-related vaccine requirements. Although denomination after denomination issued public statements in support of vaccination, 10 percent of individuals claimed that their religion prohibited it.

Approximately one-third of Americans were vaccine-hesitant, but by the end of 2021, ~85 percent of adults were vaccinated. Some had waited to see how others fared, or their employer required it. Religious communities were reportedly effective agents in shifting behavior, encouraging those who were resistant to get vaccinated. Preaching, congregation-based vaccine clinics, and other initiatives made a difference.[2]

Questions for Consideration

1. What cultural and religious factors do you believe shaped people's responses to the vaccine and to the pandemic overall?
2. What role, if any, did your lifestance play in your own response?
3. How did you respond to people who approached the pandemic differently than you? How might intercultural, interreligious intelligence help navigate pandemic-related conflict?

[1] The Tanenbaum Center for Interreligious Understanding published a useful booklet, "Vaccines and Our Health: What Do You Need to Know? A Look at the Intersection of Religion, Law, and Vaccines" (2021).

[2] Interfaith America, "Survey: Faith-Based Approaches Supporting Vaccinations Likely to Move Vaccine-Hesitant Americans toward Acceptance," April 22, 2021, www.interfaithamerica.org/survey-faith-based-approaches-supporting-vaccinations-likely-to-move-vaccine-hesitant-americans-toward-acceptance.

14.4 NARRATIVE MEDIATION

One tool of conflict transformation that is particularly well-suited for multifaith contexts is narrative mediation. People live their lives through stories, and religious traditions have woven narrative deep into the fabric of spiritual life through sacred texts, testimony, and folklore. Even rituals, frequently designed to reexperience an event in the life of the community, are rooted in narrative. Stories are not simply tales we tell, but shapers of relationship, experience, and worldview.

The process of narrative mediation makes room for divergent stories to be told and gradually works toward a new story that the parties can compose together.[14] In the Israeli-Palestinian conflict, which is not fundamentally religious but has substantial religious dimensions, each people has a compelling story of why they belong

[14] See John Winslade and Gerald Monk, *Practicing Narrative Mediation: Loosening the Grip of Conflict* (San Francisco: Jossey-Bass, 2008).

to and in that place. Each perspective includes historical experiences of injustice that must be heard to foster reconciliation. We may disagree with one telling or another, but we cannot tell them that it is not their story. Palestinian activist Sami Awad, who has long worked to foster peace, justice, and understanding between the peoples of the land, engages with wildly diverse groups to help fashion a new narrative, one that acknowledges the mutual trauma and transforms it.

Religious traditions have long memories; the past is assumed to have relevance for the present. Many lifestances also have a future vision for a world made whole, which can help people move past historical conflict toward shared goals and dreams.

Consider this story about Nelson Mandela. In 1999, having retired as president of South Africa in keeping with his promise to serve only one term, Mandela spoke at the Parliament of the World's Religions convened in Cape Town. A man at the back stood up and began chanting a praise song for an African chief. Mandela let the song wash over him; then he pointed in the direction of his imprisonment on Robben Island and said, "I would still be there, where I spent a quarter century of my life, if it were not for the Muslims and the Christians, the Hindus and the Jews, the African traditionalists and the secular humanists, coming together to defeat Apartheid."[15] In these efforts, there were aspects of narrative mediation. The Kairos document called upon the shared sacred stories of Christians of all races to catalyze a renewed moral vision – to tell a new story together. The Truth and Reconciliation Commission, inspired by religious notions of forgiveness and Indigenous traditions of *ubuntu* and restorative justice, also emphasized the value of telling one's story.[16]

---

[15] Eboo Patel, *Interfaith Leadership: A Primer* (Boston: Beacon Press, 2016), 127.

[16] Eric Patterson, "South Africa: The Religious Foundations of the Truth and Reconciliation Commission" (Washington, DC: Berkeley Center for Religion, Peace, and World Affairs, 2013), 7.

One practice of narrative mediation is to externalize the problem to reframe the conflict. In the "Chalking Muhammad" case (see Chapter 13), the problem is not the group of students whose priority is free speech, nor is it Muslims who are deeply offended by depictions of the Prophet Muhammad. The problem is that their values collided in the wake of the *South Park* controversy. A related practice requires that we avoid essentialist understandings. Depending on your own priorities, you may feel that the free speech advocates were insensitive, acting out of anger and entitlement. Or you may think that the Muslim activists and their allies were overly sensitive, unwilling to accept a constitutional principle that is foundational in American culture. Of course, you may not think any of those things; the point is that those qualities are not part of the groups' *essence*. They were determined by the story of conflict.

Sometimes we "position" people when we frame a conflict: I tried to reason with them, but they wouldn't listen. In my telling, I acted appropriately and the fault is theirs. If they told the story, the positions would likely reverse. We are also positioned by larger cultural assumptions, like the idea that rational conversation is superior to emotional expression – diminishing the voice of those who respond emotionally. Here is an example more directly connected to religious conflict: evangelical Christians in the USA often believe their desire to argue policy positions based on their faith is marginalized by a secular public square, while other people may feel that faith gets wielded like a trump card and positions their own arguments at a disadvantage. Narrative mediation guides us to be mindful of such positioning and to unpack the stories that shape it.

Double listening is a useful practice, attending both to the story that is being told and others that are not. Sometimes a story is not told simply because there is no one present who can articulate it. As acknowledged in previous chapters, interreligious gatherings must always be concerned about voice and representation. Who is not (yet) at the table? Several years ago, I organized a panel discussion at our progressive seminary called "Women in Traditional Religion" because the stories we were telling about oppression of women – pointing to gender roles, modesty requirements, sexual mores, theology, and lack of opportunities for leadership – left another story untold. Three religiously traditional women came and spoke about their sense of agency in working for change and living in creative fidelity with more conservative religious expression.

Sometimes the untold story is another factor in the "nest" of conflict – background and context that we need to understand, for example. Intersectionality illuminates how we are always situated in multiple story lines. A report of conflict may address religious identity but ignore racial and gender identities that factor into it, or fail to recognize how it is part of broader social issues. Consider the case of a Sikh employee for an airline that refused to let him wear a turban while in a customer service position. He filed a lawsuit, but the court ruled that the airline satisfied its responsibility for "reasonable accommodation" by offering him a different job at the company. As a matter of law, the conflict is limited to interpretation of Title VII of the 1964 Civil Rights Act. Yet there are untold stories of prejudice about why a turban might affect his effectiveness at customer service, a long history of American corporations giving in to such bias, and questions of shame in not being considered fit for public view.[17]

There is potentially another story in this conflict, an unrealized story of hope about a corporate culture that truly values diversity. Remembering to name this story, too, is essential if the parties want to craft an alternative story together. Narrative mediation looks to uncover these stories – moments of remorse amidst angry exchanges, gestures of flexibility in a story of obstinacy, glimmers of cooperation in place of competition, and other exceptions to the conflict story – even if they were quickly swallowed by a sea of strife. In the case of the airline, instances of respect for employees, or values that the

---

[17] Robert W. Tuttle and Jesse Merriam, "Sikh Americans and Religious Liberty," Pew Research Center, December 3, 2009, www.pewforum.org/2009/12/03/sikh-americans-and-religious-liberty.

company wants to embody, can be lifted up – not to excuse its present behavior but as a means of "calling them in" to transform the story of conflict.

14.5   OTHER TOOLS FOR FACILITATING CONSTRUCTIVE CONFLICT

Interest-Based Bargaining. Since conflict often presents itself as a set of mutually exclusive demands, it can be helpful to move people from arguing about their positions to discussing their interests. In the process, they move from being adversaries to being problem-solvers, from a goal of victory to a goal of agreement. Interests still collide, so the problem does not go away, but participants discover a far greater range of possible actions and definitions of success.

This perspective is illustrated by an iceberg; the conflict visible on the surface is only a small part of what is afloat. Underneath, there are a variety of interests for which people are advocating – potentially including relevant shared values. Imagine that a professor on campus says or publishes something deeply offensive about people of a minoritized race or religion. The conflict takes shape with dichotomous positions: the professor must be fired vs. the professor has tenure and freedom of speech and cannot be fired for unpopular opinions. This frame will usually lead to no change, given that the latter position is technically correct. If the protesting community shifts to articulate their *interests*, however, they may be able to gain ground. Minoritized students would benefit from greater recognition of daily discrimination and the ways it undermines their success in school; they need better integration of their voice within leadership and their experience within curriculum, and campus-wide attention to how academic theories impact their real lives.

The simplest tool to facilitate this shift is to move from asking what to asking why, from what you want to why you want it. IRS, which routinely explores languages of values and incessantly asks why, can effectively utilize this tool of conflict transformation.

Nonviolent Communication. There is an enormous body of work on nonviolent communication (NVC) that can be useful in studying or engaging difference. NVC invites us to speak honestly but carefully about our own experience and to respond with empathy to the experience of others. People may not think of speech as violent; we do not wield a bat or a gun. Many religious traditions recognize, however, that words can both inflict harm and stimulate healing. Incorporating their teachings about how we speak to one another with basic insights of NVC can be advantageous for Interreligious Studies and engagement.

Asking open-ended questions is one valuable practice. "Do you believe in God?" for example, is a closed question. It asks for a yes/no answer, treats monotheistic definitions as normative, and may even suggest that there is a right answer and a wrong one. "What do you believe about divinity or transcendence?" still privileges a question that might be of greater importance to the questioner than to the respondent, but at least it is open-ended.

A standard approach to NVC focuses on four categories: observations, feelings, needs, and requests. We begin by observing what people say and do, recording them in our mind without assigning value. We say what we see but not what we think of it, and we ask what others notice. We then conduct an emotional audit of sorts, identifying what we are feeling. Sharing these feelings in nonviolent communication requires that the words describe ourselves without insinuating what another person is doing. We may be hurt, scared, or angry – but if we say we are being ignored, manipulated, pressured, or mistreated, these all suggest that someone else is doing something to us and it invites defensiveness. Choosing words of feeling rather than judgment is more difficult than it sounds; NVC guides provide lists with specific suggestions.[18] We seek to understand the experience of other parties to the conflict by inquiring about their feelings too. Then

---

[18] Marshall B. Rosenberg, *Nonviolent Communication: A Language of Life* (Encinitas: PuddleDancer Press, 2015), 41–48.

we each identify needs connected to the feelings we have named, and general or specific requests that might suggest a way forward.

Imagine a case in which a Pagan teacher resigns after parents protest her spiritual practice. How might nonviolent communication foster a different result?

Observations

- I heard that you believe in multiple gods and goddesses.
- I notice that there are many parents of my students at this school board meeting.

Feelings

- I am fearful that my child may be taught values I cannot support.
- I am fearful that I may lose my job on account of my spiritual identity.

Needs

- I need a clear idea of how Pagan concepts will and will not be addressed in class.
- I need support from the board for my free exercise of religion and trust from parents in my professionalism as a teacher.

Requests

- Would you be willing to work together to draft guidelines for how to navigate questions about your faith that may come up in class?
- Would you be willing to affirm my freedom of religion as a teacher and read this age-appropriate book about religious freedom with your child?

The steps can feel contrived, and nonviolent communication does not come naturally to many people. Like all tools, we become more adept at handling them with practice.

Even with careful utilization of conflict transformation strategies, however, efforts to get contesting parties to become problem-solvers together can be overwhelmed as events unfold.

Case Summary: "Driven by Faith"[1]

Steve Wareham, Airport Director at the Minneapolis-St. Paul International Airport (MSP), had a problem. For years, he worked with drivers, taxi companies, airport management, and other stakeholders to improve customer service. But one issue was not easily resolved. A significant percentage of taxi drivers in the area were Muslim immigrants from Somalia, many of whom believed that their faith did not allow them to transport alcohol. They refused service to passengers with duty-free bags that clearly had alcohol inside.

Passengers who were refused service were unhappy. They were often forced to wait or shuffled in and out of a taxi – or they simply felt insulted, sometimes rejected by multiple cabs in a row. Drivers were also unhappy because the taxi ordinance does not allow refusing service and they had to go to the end of the line if they did, sometimes waiting hours for another fare.

Wareham had tried to work collaboratively to remedy the problem. For a while, the taxi starter provided bags to travelers to cover up the duty-free bags, encouraging a "don't ask, don't tell" approach. Eventually, however, drivers refused service to those customers as well. One cab company suggested referring passengers with alcohol to a company with few Muslim drivers, but the loss of business for others was substantial. Customer complaints continued.

Wareham explored whether other airports in the USA had this issue, and how airports in Muslim-majority countries handled it, but the answers did not yield a clear resolution. He hoped to bring stakeholders together again through the taxi advisory council to transform this knotty conflict – forging an agreement between the drivers, owners, Metropolitan Airports Commission (MAC, also representing customer interests), and community representatives. Working together with the director of Landside, the department handling parking and commercial vehicles at the airport, they drafted an agenda for seven council meetings:

1. Background, agenda setting, Department of Human Rights representative;
2. Customer feedback: passengers, airlines, convention and visitors bureau;
3. Taxi Industry: drivers, owners, company representation;
4. Religious leaders of diverse faiths;
5. Ground transportation experts;
6. Taxi regulators;
7. Legal opinions.

Things did not go exactly as planned. The drivers asked to bring their religious leaders to the second meeting; these scholars delivered a *fatwa* (a legal decision based on Islamic jurisprudence) explaining that transportation of alcohol is not allowed for observant Muslims. Even though this preemptively cut off many potential options, at the next meeting stakeholders agreed on a decision-making process and two key goals: (1) a seamless system for the customer, (2) accommodation whenever possible for drivers who did not want to transport alcohol.

After discussing multiple approaches, the parties agreed that drivers whose religious convictions prevent them from transporting alcohol would install a "top light" on their cabs. Unless no other cab was readily available, passengers carrying alcohol would be directed to a taxi without a top light. A Memorandum of Understanding (MOU) was drafted in August 2006, scheduled to begin in November, run for six months, and then be formally evaluated.

In the interim, however, local and national media coverage intensified, some with an alarmist tone. Daniel Pipes published a piece in *The New York Post* calling the airport's proposed accommodation "Sharia in America." MAC received hundreds of angry emails, prompting the agency to withdraw from the MOU and consider harsher penalties for refusal of service. Controversy continued as a few of the Muslim cab drivers refused service around the city to gay couples, transgender individuals, and passengers with guide dogs. A group of imams were removed from a plane at MSP due to "suspicious activity" – primarily praying at the gate.

Public comments to the agency, submitted in writing from all over the USA and abroad, were overwhelmingly opposed to accommodating the drivers' concerns; some expressed frustration about cultural conflicts catalyzed by increasing Muslim presence in America. A formal hearing presented more balanced testimony illuminating the competing concerns of religious freedom and customer service.

In April 2007, MAC voted to suspend drivers for thirty days for their first refusal of service, and for two years if they did it a second time. The airport held a job fair for drivers seeking other employment. Two drivers filed suit but lost in court. Muslims in the community responded in various ways. Some were disappointed that the compromise agreement was never implemented, and others felt that religiously strict voices were given too much weight. But they all felt that the standing of the Muslim community in Minneapolis-St. Paul and beyond was damaged by the conflict.

Questions for Consideration

1. This episode of conflict sets customer service in tension with religious freedom, but the nest of conflict involves other issues as well. What are the various concerns that stakeholders bring to the table?
2. Review the various stakeholders' perspectives and recognize where your own sympathies lie and why. What would you hope to see as the outcome?
3. What aspects of conflict transformation seem embedded in Wareham's approach? Why did they not work, and what would you do in response?
4. If you were a community member or religious leader in the city, how might you engage this conflict?

[1] Adapted from Elinor Pierce, "Driven by Faith," The Pluralism Project (Harvard University, 2008), https://pluralism.org/driven-by-faith; Steve Wareham, *Taxicab Cultural Clash at the Minneapolis-St.Paul Int'l Airport: Driven by Faith or Customer Service? Muslim Taxi Drivers Refuse Passengers with Alcohol* (Saarbrücken: Lambert Academic Publishing, 2010).

14.6   UNDERSTANDING OUR OWN RESPONSE TO CONFLICT

It is important to recognize our intuitive responses to conflict to be effective facilitators of transformation. A commonly used interpretive taxonomy is the Thomas–Kilmann Instrument (TKI), which establishes quadrants based on two axes (Figure 4). The vertical axis measures assertiveness and the horizontal axis measures cooperativeness. There are various free and fee-based inventories designed to discern an

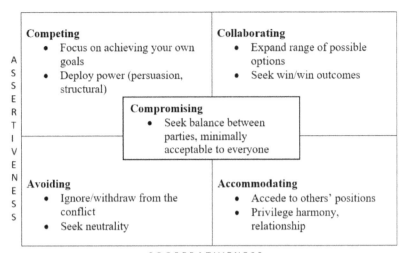

FIGURE 4 Thomas–Kilmann conflict analysis paradigm

individual's balance; it can also be illuminating to present a group with a conflict to address and then reflect together on their behaviors.[19]

Most of us have one or two dominant styles of response, but we have some experience with and capacity for all of them. We also naturally shift depending on context; our roles in family dynamics, for example, are frequently different from those at work or school and can impact our responses to conflict.

Some quadrants invite value-based judgments: competers are bossy, for example, and accommodators let people run roughshod over them. Yet each can be appropriate in particular situations, so the instrument is layered with contextual analyses. Competing might be the best choice in an emergency when decisive action must be taken, or when there is an unpopular but necessary course, or when parties to the conflict would otherwise abuse less assertive participants. Accommodating is valuable when creating good will is paramount, harmony is vital, or someone else's greater expertise is evident. Questions that guide the best approach include: How important is

[19] Kenneth W. Thomas and Ralph H. Kilmann, *Thomas–Kilmann Conflict Mode Instrument (TKI)*, APA PsycTests. 1974, https://doi.org/10.1037/t02326–000.

the issue? What is the nature of the relationship? How much time is available? What are the power dynamics of the situation? What are the goals? Awareness of our natural inclinations and contextual factors enhances our effectiveness in conflictual situations.

Consider the challenges identified in this chapter or elsewhere. How do your own reactions to conflict shape the way you think about them, and the ways you might respond? Reflexivity – your ability to examine your own feelings, motives, and reactions and to understand how they influence you – is again vital to interreligious engagement. As James Baldwin notes regarding racial difference:

> The questions which one asks oneself begin, at last, to illuminate the world, and become one's key to the experience of others. One can only face in others what one can face in oneself. On this confrontation depends the measure of our wisdom and compassion. This energy is all that one finds in the rubble of vanished civilizations, and the only hope for ours.[20]

Given that conflict is a natural part of life, it is part of the encounter with religious difference. Even with the plethora of challenges detailed throughout this book, however, there is much more beauty, wisdom, collaborative spirit, and growth in the space of meeting. This volume of introduction is also an invitation to discover those possibilities. So we conclude with the definition that launched us on this study:

> The field of Interreligious Studies (IRS) entails critical analysis of the dynamic encounters – historical and contemporary, intentional and unintentional, embodied and imagined, congenial and conflictual – of individuals and communities who orient around religion differently. It investigates the complex of personal, interpersonal, institutional, and societal implications.

---

[20] Baldwin, *Nobody Knows My Name: More Notes of a Native Son* (New York: First Vintage international ed., 1993), xiii–xiv.

Bibliography

Albright, Madelaine. *The Mighty and the Almighty*. New York: HarperCollins, 2006.

Alsultany, Evelyn. *Arabs and Muslims in the Media: Race and Representation after 9/11*. New York: New York University Press, 2012.

Amaladoss, Michael. *Interreligious Encounters: Opportunities and Challenges*. Ed. Jonathan Y. Tan. Maryknoll: Orbis Books, 2017.

"Americans Deeply Divided by Party on Ideals of Religious and Ethnic Pluralism." *PR Newswire*, February 21, 2019. www.prnewswire.com/news-releases/new-prrithe-atlantic-survey-americans-deeply-divided-by-party-on-ideals-of-reli gious-and-ethnic-pluralism-300799351.html

Amir-Moazami, Schirin. "Dialogue as a Governmental Technique: Managing Gendered Islam in Germany." *Feminist Review* 98, no. 1 (2011): 9–27.

Amoah, Elizabeth. "Indigenous African Religions and Inter-Religious Relationship." International Interfaith Centre. October 22, 1998. http://iicao.org/iic-resources/lectures/african-indigenous-religions-and-inter-religious-relationship

Appleby, R. Scott. *The Ambivalence of the Sacred: Religion, Violence, and Reconciliation*. Lanham: Rowman & Littlefield, 2000.

Audi, Robert, and Nicholas Wolterstorff. *Religion in the Public Square: The Place of Religious Convictions in Political Debate*. Lanham: Rowman & Littlefield, 1997.

Austin, William G., and Stephen Worchel, eds. *The Social Psychology of Intergroup Relations*. Monterey: Brooks/Cole, 1979.

Baer, Drake. "18 Companies that Are Extremely Religious." *Business Insider*. December 11, 2014. www.businessinsider.com/companies-that-are-extremely-religious-2014-12

Baha, Abdul. *Abdul Baha on Divine Philosophy*. Ed. Isabel Fraser Chamberlain. Boston: Tudor Press, 1918.

Bailey, Jennifer. *To My Beloveds: Letters on Faith, Race, Loss, and Radical Hope*. St. Louis: Chalice Press, 2021.

Bailey, Julius H. *Down in the Valley: An Introduction to African American Religious History*. Minneapolis: Fortress Press, 2016.

Baldanzi, Jessica, and Hussein Rashid, eds. *Ms. Marvel's America: No Normal*. Jackson: University Press of Mississippi, 2020.

Baldwin, James. *Nobody Knows My Name: More Notes of a Native Son*. New York: Vintage, 1993.

Barbato, Melanie. "Interreligious Art in Light of Hindu and Buddhist Thought." *CrossCurrents* 68, no. 3 (September 2018): 336–51. https://doi.org/10.1111/cros.12316

Barbato, Melanie. "'Dear Hindu Friends': Official Diwali Greetings as a Medium for Diplomatic Dialogue." *Religion* 50, no. 3 (2020): 353–71. https://doi.org/10.1080/0048721X.2020.1754599

Barnes, Michael. *Interreligious Learning: Dialogue, Spirituality, and the Christian Imagination*. Cambridge: Cambridge University Press, 2011. https://doi.org/10.1017/CBO9781139003285

Barrows, John Henry. "Review and Summary." In *The World's Parliament of Religions*, ed. John Henry Barrows, 2:1557–82. Chicago: Parliament Publishing, 1893.

Barton, John. *Better Religion: A Primer for Interreligious Peacebuilding*. Waco: Baylor University Press, 2022.

Bayoumi, Moustafa. "Racing Religion." *CR: The New Centennial Review* 6, no. 2 (2006): 267–93.

Beachem, Lateshia. "Two Workers Fired for Not Attending Company's Prayers, Lawsuit Says." *Washington Post*. June 29, 2022. www.washingtonpost.com/nation/2022/06/29/north-carolina-prayer-lawsuit

Bellah, Robert. "Civil Religion in America." *Dædalus, Journal of the American Academy of Arts and Sciences* 96, no. 1 (1967): 1–22.

Bender, Courtney, and Pamela E. Klassen, eds. *After Pluralism: Reimagining Religious Engagement*. New York: Columbia University Press, 2010.

Benedict, Jeff. *The Mormon Way of Doing Business: Leadership and Success through Faith and Family*. New York: Warner Business Books, 2007.

Benedikter, Roland. *Religion in the Age of Re-globalization: A Brief Introduction*. Cham: Palgrave Macmillan, 2022. https://doi.org/10.1007/978-3-030-80857-0

Berling, Judith A. *The Syncretic Religion of Lin Chao-En*. New York: Columbia University Press, 1980. https://doi.org/10.7312/berl94240

Berling, Judith A. *Understanding Other Religious Worlds: A Guide for Interreligious Education*. Maryknoll: Orbis Books, 2004.

Beydoun, Khaled A. *American Islamophobia: Understanding the Roots and Rise of Fear*. Berkeley: University of California Press, 2018.

Bidwell, Duane R. *When One Religion Isn't Enough: The Lives of Spiritually Fluid People*. Boston: Beacon Press, 2018.

Biechler, James, and H. Lawrence Bond, eds. and trans. *Nicholas of Cusa on Interreligious Harmony: Text, Concordance and Translation of De Pace Fidei*. Lewiston: Edward Mellen, 1991.

Blakemore, Scott. "Faith-Based Diplomacy and Interfaith Dialogue." *Brill Research Perspectives in Diplomacy and Foreign Policy* 3, no. 2 (2019): 1–124. https://doi.org/10.1163/24056006-12340010

Bleich, Eric, and A. Maurits Van der Veen. "Media Portrayals of Muslims: A Comparative Sentiment Analysis of American Newspapers, 1996–2015." *Politics, Groups, and Identities* 9, no. 1 (2018): 20–39. https://doi.org/10.1080/21565503.2018.1531770

Boase, Roger, ed. *Islam and Global Dialogue: Religious Pluralism and the Pursuit of Peace.* London: Routledge, 2005. https://doi.org/10.4324/9781315589909

Bock, Jan-Jonathan, John Fahy, and Samuel Everett, eds. *Emergent Religious Pluralisms.* Cham: Palgrave MacMillan, 2019.

Bordas, Juana. *Salsa, Soul, and Spirit: Leadership for a Multicultural Age.* Oakland: Berrett-Koehler, 2012.

Bourdieu, Pierre. *The Logic of Practice.* Trans. Richard Nice. Stanford: Stanford University Press, 1990.

Boys, Mary E., and Sara S. Lee. *Christians and Jews in Dialogue: Learning in the Presence of the Other.* Woodstock: Skylight Paths, 2008.

Brailovskaya, Tatiana, ed. *Faith for the Earth: A Call to Action.* Nairobi: United Nations Environment Programme, 2020.

Brannon, Valerie C. "No More Lemon Law? Supreme Court Rethinks Religious Establishment Analysis." *Congressional Research Service.* June 21, 2019. https://sgp.fas.org/crs/misc/LSB10315.pdf

Braunstein, Ruth, ed. *Religion, Humility, and Democracy in a Divided America.* Bingley: Emerald Publishing, 2019.

Brecht, Mara, and Reed Locklin, eds. *Comparative Theology in the Millennial Classroom: Hybrid Identities, Negotiated Boundaries.* New York: Routledge, 2015. https://doi.org/10.4324/9781315718279

Brown, Daniel S., Jr., ed. *A Communication Perspective on Interfaith Dialogue: Living within the Abrahamic Traditions.* Lanham: Lexington Books, 2013.

Buber, Martin. *I and Thou.* Trans. Walter Kaufmann. Edinburgh: T. & T. Clark, 1970.

Bucar, Liz. *Stealing My Religion: Not Just Any Cultural Appropriation.* Boston: Harvard University Press, 2022. https://doi.org/10.4159/9780674279995

Buswell, Robert Evans, Jr. "Buddhism in Korea." In *The Religious Traditions of Asia: Religion, History, and Culture,* ed. Joseph M. Kitagawa, 347–54. Abingdon: Routledge, 2002. https://doi.org/10.4324/9781315029641

Cadge, Wendy, and Emily Sigalow. "Negotiating Religious Differences: The Strategies of Interfaith Chaplains in Healthcare." *Journal for the Scientific Study of Religion* 52, no. 1 (2013): 146–58. https://doi.org/10.1111/jssr.12008.

Cadge, Wendy, and Shelly Rambo, eds. *Chaplaincy and Spiritual Care in the 21st Century*. Chaplaincy Innovation Lab. Chapel Hill: University of North Carolina Press, 2022.

Cannon, Katie. *Black Womanist Ethics*. Eugene: Wipf and Stock, 2006.

Carpenter, Steven P. *Mennonites and the Media: Mentioned in It, Maligned by It, and Makers of It*. Eugene: Wipf and Stock, 2014.

Carter, Stephen L. *The Culture of Disbelief: How American Law and Politics Trivialize Religious Devotion*. New York: Anchor Books, 1994.

Center for Global Education. "Belief Systems along the Silk Road." Asia Society. https://asiasociety.org/education/belief-systems-along-silk-road

Chancey, Mark A. "A Textbook Example of the Christian Right: The National Council on Bible Curriculum in Public Schools." *Journal of the American Academy of Religion* 75, no. 3 (September 2007): 554–81. https://doi.org/10.1093/jaarel/lfm036.

Chandhoke, Neera. *Rethinking Pluralism, Secularism and Tolerance: Anxieties of Coexistence*. New Delhi: Sage, 2019.

Chazan, Robert. *Barcelona and Beyond: The Disputation of 1263 and Its Aftermath*. Berkeley: University of California Press, 1992.

Chazan, Robert. *The Jews of Medieval Western Christendom 1000–1500*. Cambridge: Cambridge University Press, 2006. https://doi.org/10.1017/CBO9780511818325

Cheetham, David, Douglas Pratt, and David Thomas, eds. *Understanding Interreligious Relations*. Oxford: Oxford University Press, 2013.

Chemen, Silvina, and Francisco Canzani. *A Dialogue of Life: Toward the Encounter of Jews and Christians*. New York: New City Press, 2015.

Chireau, Yvonne. *Black Magic: Religion and the African American Conjuring Tradition*. Berkeley: University of California Press, 2003.

Chittick, William. *Imaginal Worlds: Ibn al-'Arabi and the Problem of Religious Diversity*. Albany: State University of New York Press, 1994.

Christensen Center for Teaching and Learning at Harvard Business School. "Case Method in Practice." www.hbs.edu/teaching/case-method/Pages/default.aspx

Christensen, Linda. *Reading, Writing, and Rising Up: Teaching about Social Justice and the Power of the Written Word*. Milwaukee: Rethinking Schools, 2000.

Chua, Amy. *Day of Empire: How Hyperpowers Rise to Global Dominance – And how They Fall*. New York: Doubleday, 2007.

Clooney, Francis X. *Comparative Theology: Deep Learning across Religious Borders*. Hoboken: Wiley, 2010.

Clooney, Francis X. *Learning Interreligiously: In the Text, In the World.* Minneapolis: Augsburg Fortress, 2018.

Cobb, John B., Jr. *Beyond Dialogue: Toward a Mutual Transformation of Christianity and Buddhism.* Eugene: Wipf and Stock, 1998.

Cohen, Cynthia E., Roberto Gutiérrez Varea, and Polly O. Walker, eds. *Acting Together: Performance and the Creative Transformation of Conflict*, 2 vols. Oakland: New Village Press, 2011.

Cohen, Mark R., Sydney H. Griffith, Hava Lazarus-Yafeh, and Sasson Somekh, eds. *The Majlis: Interreligious Encounters in Medieval Islam.* Weisbaden: Harrassowitz, 1999.

Cohen, Naomi W. *Jews in Christian America: The Pursuit of Religious Equality.* New York: Oxford University Press, 1992.

Cohn-Sherbok, Dan. *Messianic Judaism: A Critical Anthology.* London: Bloomsbury, 2000.

Collins, Drew. *The Unique and Universal Christ: Refiguring the Theology of Religions.* Waco: Baylor University Press, 2021.

Conteh, Prince Sorie. *Traditionalists, Muslims, and Christians in Africa: Interreligious Encounters and Dialogue.* Amherst: Cambria, 2009.

Cornille, Catherine. *The Im-Possibility of Interreligious Dialogue.* New York: Crossroad, 2008.

Cornille, Catherine, and Christopher Conway, eds. *Interreligious Hermeneutics.* Eugene: Cascade, 2010.

Cornille, Catherine, ed. *The Wiley-Blackwell Companion to Inter-Religious Dialogue.* Chichester: John Wiley & Sons, 2013. https://doi.org/10.1002/9781118529911

Cox, Harvey. *Common Prayers: Faith, Family, and a Christian's Journey through the Jewish Year.* Boston: Houghton Mifflin Harcourt, 2001.

Coyle, Marcia. "The Supreme Court's Religion Conundrum." Interactive Constitution. February 8, 2021. https://constitutioncenter.org/interactive-constitution/blog/the-supreme-courts-religion-conundrum

Cragg, Kenneth. "Constance E. Padwick, 1886–1968." *The Muslim World* 59, no. 1 (January 1969): 29–39, https://doi.org/10.1111/j.1478-1913.1969.tb00471.x

Crenshaw, Kimberlé. "Mapping the Margins: Intersectionality, Identity Politics, and Violence against Women of Color." *Stanford Law Review* 43, no. 6 (July 1991): 1241–99. https://doi.org/10.2307/1229039

Cullen, Seamus. "Shinto in Japan." Columban Interreligious Dialogue. https://columbanird.org/shinto-in-japan

Cunningham, David S., ed. *Hearing Vocation Differently: Meaning, Purpose, and Identity in the Multi-Faith Academy.* Oxford: Oxford University Press, 2018.

D'Costa, Gavin. *Vatican II: Catholic Doctrines on Jews and Muslims*. New York: Oxford University Press, 2014. https://doi.org/10.1093/acprof:oso/9780199659272.001.0001

Dalai Lama. *Towards True Kinship of Faiths: How the World's Religions can Come Together*. New York: Three Rivers, 2010.

Dallal, Ahmad S. *Islam without Europe: Traditions of Reform in Eighteenth-Century Islamic Thought*. Chapel Hill: University of North Carolina, 2018.

Davis, Adam, ed. *Hearing the Call across Traditions: Readings on Faith and Service*. Woodstock: Skylight Paths, 2011.

Delgadillo, Teresa. *Spiritual Mestizaje: Religion, Gender, Race, and Nation in Contemporary Chicana Narrative*. Durham: Duke University Press, 2011.

Demarest, Leila, Amélie Godefroidt, and Arnim Langer. "Understanding News Coverage of Religious-Based Violence: Empirical and Theoretical Insights from Media Representations of Boko Haram in Nigeria." *Journal of Communication* 70, no. 4 (2020): 548–73. https://doi.org/10.1093/joc/jqaa011

Department for Communities and Local Government. *Face to Face and Side by Side: A Framework for Partnership in Our Multifaith Society*. Wetherby: Communities and Local Government Publications, 2008.

Depoortere, Frederiek, and Magdalen Lambkin, eds. *The Question of Theological Truth: Philosophical and Interreligious Perspectives*. Amsterdam: Rodopi, 2012.

Díez-Bosch, Míriam, Josep Lluís Micó Sanz, and Alba Sabaté Gauxachs. "Typing My Religion: Digital Use of Religious Webs and Apps by Adolescents and Youth for Religious and Interreligious Dialogue." *Church, Communication and Culture* 2, no. 2 (2017): 121–43. https://doi.org/10.1080/23753234.2017.1347800

Dinnerstein, Leonard. *Antisemitism in America*. New York: Oxford University Press, 1994.

Doroshenko, Larisa. "Far-Right Parties in the European Union and Media Populism: A Comparative Analysis of 10 Countries during European Parliament Elections." *International Journal of Communication* 12 (2018): 3186–206.

Doss, Erika. "Public Art Controversy: Cultural Expression and Civic Debate." *Monograph* (October 2006).

Dubler, Joshua, and Isaac Weiner, eds. *Religion, Law, USA*. New York: New York University Press, 2019.

Dugan, Máire. "A Nested Theory of Conflict." *A Leadership Journal: Women in Leadership – Sharing the Vision* 1 (July 1996): 9–20.

Duss, Matthew, et al. "Fear Inc. 2.0: The Islamophobia Network's Efforts to Manufacture Hate in America." Center for American Progress. February 11, 2015. www.americanprogress.org/article/fear-inc-2-0

Eck, Diana L. *A New Religious America: How a "Christian Country" Became the World's Most Religiously Diverse Nation*. New York: HarperCollins, 2002.

Eck, Diana L. *Encountering God: A Spiritual Journey from Bozeman to Banaras*. Boston: Beacon Press, 2003.

Eck, Diana L. "Prospects for Pluralism: Voice and Vision in the Study of Religion." *Journal of the American Academy of Religion* 75, no. 4 (2007): 743–76. https://doi.org/10.1093/jaarel/lfm061

Elahi, Farah, and Omar Khan, eds. *Islamophobia: Still a Challenge for Us All*. London: Runnymede Trust, 2017. www.runnymedetrust.org/projects-and-publications/equality-and-integration/islamophobia.html

Elijah Interfaith Institute. "The Elijah Educational Network and Bibliodrama." https://elijah-interfaith.org/bibliodrama

Elsheikh, Elsadig, Basima Sisemore, and Natalia Ramirez Lee. "Legalizing Othering: The United States of Islamophobia." Haas Institute for a Fair and Inclusive Society. September 2017. https://belonging.berkeley.edu/sites/default/files/haas_institute_legalizing_othering_the_united_states_of_islamophobia.pdf

Engebretson, Kath, Marian de Souza, Gloria Durka, and Liam Gearon, eds. *International Handbook of Inter-religious Education*. Dordrecht: Springer, 2010.

Ennis, Ariel. *Teaching Religious Literacy: A Guide to Religious and Spiritual Diversity in Higher Education*. Abingdon: Routledge, 2017. https://doi.org/10.4324/9781315206356

Eric J. Ziolkowski, ed. *A Museum of Faiths: Histories and Legacies of the 1893 World's Parliament of Religions*. New York: Oxford University Press, 1993.

Esack, Farid. *Quran, Liberation and Pluralism: An Islamic Perspective of Interreligious Solidarity against Oppression*. London: Oneworld, 1996.

Esposito, John, ed. *The Oxford History of Islam*. Oxford: Oxford University Press, 1999. https://doi.org/10.1093/acref/9780195107999.001.0001

Esposito, John, and Ibrahim Kalin, eds. *Islamophobia: The Challenge of Pluralism in the 21st Century*. Oxford: Oxford University Press, 2011.

Essa, Ahmed. *Studies in Islamic Civilization: The Muslim Contribution to the Renaissance*. Herndon: International Institute of Islamic Thought, 2012.

Etherington, Norman, ed. *Missions and Empire*. Oxford: Oxford University Press, 2005.

Farisi, Muhammad Imam. "*Bhinneka Tunggal Ika* [Unity in Diversity]: From Dynastic Policy to Classroom Practice." *Journal of Social Science Education* 13, no. 1 (Spring 2014): 46–61. https://doi.org/10.4119/jsse-687

Faulk, Kent. "Roy Moore Timeline: Ten Commandments to Gay Marriage Stance." May 7, 2016. www.al.com/news/birmingham/index.ssf/2016/05/roy_moore_timeline_ten_command.html

Fernandez, Eleazar S., ed. *Teaching for a Multifaith World*. Eugene: Wipf and Stock, 2017.

Fernández-Morera, Darío. *The Myth of the Andalusian Paradise: Muslims, Christians and Jews under Islamic Rule in Medieval Spain*. Wilmington: Intercollegiate Studies Institute, 2016.

"Fighting Over Darwin, State by State." Pew Research Center. February 3, 2014. www.pewforum.org/2009/02/04/fighting-over-darwin-state-by-state

Fletcher, Jeannine Hill. *Monopoly on Salvation? A Feminist Approach to Religious Pluralism*. New York: Continuum, 2005. https://doi.org/10.5040/9781472549938

Fletcher, Jeannine Hill. *Motherhood as Metaphor: Engendering Interreligious Dialogue*. New York: Fordham University Press, 2013. https://doi.org/10.5422/fordham/9780823251179.001.0001

Foltz, Richard. *Religions of the Silk Road: Premodern Patterns of Globalization*. 2nd ed. New York: Palgrave Macmillan, 2010.

Forbes, Bruce David, and Jeffrey H. Mahan, eds. *Religion and Popular Culture in America*. 3rd ed. Berkeley: University of California Press, 2017.

Ford, David. "Flamenco, Tai-Chi and Six-Text Scriptural Reasoning: Report on a Visit to China." *Cambridge Inter-Faith Programme*. October 2012. www.interfaith.cam.ac.uk/resources/lecturespapersandspeeches/chinavisit

Foucault, Michel. *Power/Knowledge: Selected Interview and Other Writings, 1972–1977*. New York: Pantheon Books, 1980.

Fraser, James. *Between Church and State: Religion and Public Education in a Multicultural America*. 2nd ed. Baltimore: Johns Hopkins University Press, 2016.

Fredrickson, George. *Racism: A Short History*. Princeton: Princeton University Press, 2002.

Freire, Paulo. *Education for Critical Consciousness*. New York: Seabury Press, 1973.

Freire, Paulo. *Pedagogy of the Oppressed*. Trans. Myra Bergman Ramos. New York: Bloomsbury, 2014.

Galchinsky, Michael. *Jews and Human Rights: Dancing at Three Weddings*. New York: Rowman & Littlefield, 2007.

Ghumman, Sonia, Ann Marie Ryan, Lizabeth A. Barclay, and Karen S. Markel. "Religious Discrimination in the Workplace: A Review and Examination of Current and Future Trends." *Journal of Business and Psychology* 28, no. 4 (2013): 439–54. https://doi.org/10.1007/s10869-013-9290-0

Gieser, Thorsten. "Experiencing the Lifeworld of Druids: A Cultural Phenomenology of Perception." PhD diss., University of Aberdeen, 2008.

Gilbert, Martin. *The Holocaust: A History of the Jews of Europe during the Second World War*. New York: Henry Holt, 1985.

Gimaret, Daniel, and Guy Monnot, trans. *Livre des Religions et des Sectes*. Leuven: Peeters/Unesco, 1986.

Giordan, Guiseppe, and Andrew Lynch, eds. *Interreligious Dialogue: From Religion to Geopolitics*. Leiden: Brill, 2019. https://doi.org/10.1163/9789004401266

Gobo, Prisca Abiye. "Nollywood, Religion, and Development in Nigeria." *Semantic Scholar*. June 30, 2020. https://doi.org/10.37284/eajis.2.1.177

Goddard, Hugh. *A History of Christian–Muslim Relations*. Chicago: New Amsterdam Books, 2000.

Goldschmidt, Henry. "Being There: What Do Students Learn by Visiting Houses of Worship?" *CrossCurrents* 68, no. 3 (September 2018): 1–18.

Goodman, Kathleen M., Mary Ellen Giess, and Eboo Patel, eds. *Educating about Religious Diversity and Interfaith Engagement: A Handbook for Student Affairs*. Sterling: Stylus, 2019.

Goshen-Gottstein, Alon, ed. *Sharing Wisdom: The Benefits and Boundaries of Interreligious Learning*. Eugene: Wipf and Stock, 2018.

Goshen-Gottstein, Alon, ed. *The Religious Other: Hostility, Hospitality, and the Hope of Human Flourishing*. Eugene: Wipf and Stock, 2018.

Goshen-Gottstein, Alon, ed. *Religious Truth: Towards a Jewish Theology of Religions*. Littman Library of Jewish Civilization. London: Liverpool University Press, 2020.

Graef, Dana. "Learning the Language of Interfaith Dialogue: The Religious Life Council at Princeton University." *CrossCurrents* 55, no. 1 (Spring 2005): 106–20.

Graham, Daniel W. "Heraclitus (fl. c. 500 B.C.E.)." *Internet Encyclopedia of Philosophy*. https://iep.utm.edu/heraclit

Green, Todd H. *Fear of Islam: An Introduction to Islamophobia in the West*. 2nd ed. Minneapolis: Fortress Press, 2019.

Green, William Scott. "Otherness within: Towards a Theory of Difference in Rabbinic Judaism." In *To See Ourselves as Others See Us: Christians, Jews, "Others" in Late Antiquity*, ed. Jacob Neusner, and Ernest S. Frerichs, 49–69. Chico: Scholar Press, 1985.

Grefe, Dagmar. *Encounters for Change: Interreligious Cooperation in the Care of Individuals and Communities*. Eugene: Wipf and Stock, 2011.

Gregory, Raymond L. *Encountering Religion in the Workplace: The Legal Rights and Responsibilities of Workers and Employers*. Ithaca: Cornell University Press, 2011.

Griera, Mar, and Alexander K. Nagel. "Interreligious Relations and Governance of Religion in Europe: Introduction." *Social Compass* 65, no. 3 (2018). https://doi .org/10.1177/0037768618788274

Griffin, David Ray, ed. *Deep Religious Pluralism*. Louisville: Westminster John Knox, 2005.

Grim, Melisa, and Brian Grim. "Religious Freedom and Business Case Studies." 2016. https://religiousfreedomandbusiness.org/business-case-studies-temple ton-religion-trust

Gross, Rita. *Religious Diversity: What's the Problem? Buddhist Advice for Flourishing with Religious Diversity*. Eugene: Cascade, 2014.

Grundmann, Christoffer H., ed. *Interreligious Dialogue: An Anthology of Voices Bridging Cultural and Religious Divides*. Winona: Anselm Academic, 2015.

Grung, Anne Hege. "Interreligious Dialogue: Moving between Compartmentalization and Complexity." *Approaching Religion* 1, no. 1 (May 2011): 31. https://doi.org/10.30664/ar.67467

Gurin, Patricia, et al. "Diversity and Higher Education: Theory and Impact on Educational Outcomes." *Harvard Educational Review* 72 (2002): 330–67. https://doi.org/10.17763/haer.72.3.01151786u134n051

Gustafson, Hans. *Learning from Other Religious Traditions: Leaving Room for Holy Envy*. Pathways for Ecumenical and Interreligious Dialogue. New York: Palgrave Macmillan, 2018.

Gustafson, Hans, ed. *Interreligious Studies: Dispatches from an Emerging Field*. Waco: Baylor University Press, 2020.

Hall, David, ed. *Lived Religion in America*. Princeton: Princeton University Press, 1997.

Halsall, Paul. "Urban II (1088–1099): Speech at Council of Clermont, 1095, Five Versions of the Speech." *Internet Medieval Sourcebook*. December 2017. https://sourcebooks.fordham.edu/source/urban2-5vers.asp#robert

Halstead, John. "Why Did Over a Dozen Bloggers Leave Patheos?" *Huffpost*. February 6, 2017. www.huffpost.com/entry/why-did-over-a-dozen-writers_b_ 14603506

Hamilton, Clive. "What History Can Teach Us about Climate Change Denial." In *Engaging with Climate Change*, ed. Sally Weintrobe, 16–32. Abingdon: Routledge, 2013. https://doi.org/10.4324/9780203094402

Hanson, Judith, and Ike K. Lasater. *What We Say Matters: Practicing Non-Violent Communication*. Boulder: Shambhala, 2016.

Harris, Elizabeth, Paul Hedges, and Shanthikumar Hettiarachchi, eds. *Twenty-First Century Theologies of Religion: Retrospection and Future Prospects*. Leiden: Brill, 2016. https://doi.org/10.1163/9789004324077

Haynes, Charles, and Oliver Thomas. *Finding Common Ground: A First Amendment Guide to Religion and Public Schools*. Nashville: First Amendment Center, 2007.

Heckman, Bud, with Rori Picker Neiss, eds. *InterActive Faith: The Essential Interreligious Community-Building Handbook*. Woodstock: Skylight Paths, 2008.

Heclo, Hugh, and Wilfred McClay, eds. *Religion Returns to the Public Square: Faith and Policy in America*. Baltimore: Johns Hopkins University Press, 2003.

Hedges, Paul. "Interreligious Studies." In *Encyclopedia of Sciences and Religion*, ed. A. Runehov and L. Ovideo, 1076–80. New York: Springer, 2013.

Hedges, Paul. *Controversies in Contemporary Religion*. 3 vols. Westport: Praeger, 2014.

Hedges, Paul, ed. *Contemporary Muslim–Christian Encounters: Developments, Diversity and Dialogues*. London: Bloomsbury Academic, 2015. https://doi.org/10.5040/9781474220293

Hedges, Paul. "The Secular Realm as Interfaith Space: Discourse and Practice in Contemporary Multicultural Nation-States." *Religions* 10, no. 9 (August 2019), doi.org/10.3390/rel10090498

Hedges, Paul. *Religious Hatred: Prejudice, Islamophobia and Antisemitism in Global Context*. London: Bloomsbury Academic, 2021.

Hedges, Paul. *Understanding Religions: Theories and Methods for Studying Religiously Diverse Societies*. Berkeley: University of California Press, 2021.

Heft, James L., Reuven Firestone, and Omid Safi, eds. *Learned Ignorance: Intellectual Humility among Jews, Christians, and Muslims*. Oxford: Oxford University Press, 2011. https://doi.org/10.1093/acprof:osobl/9780199769308.001.0001

Hegel, Georg. *Encyclopaedia of the Philosophical Sciences*. Trans. and ed. Klaus Brinkmann and Daniel Dahlstrom. Cambridge: Cambridge University Press, 2010.

Heim, S. Mark. *Salvations: Truth and Difference in Religion*. Maryknoll: Orbis Books, 1995.

Heim, S. Mark. "Dreams Fulfilled: The Pluralism of Religious Ends." *Christian Century* 118, no. 2 (January 17, 2001): 14–19.

Heschel, Abraham Joshua. "No Religion Is an Island." *Union Seminary Quarterly Review* 21, no. 2 (1966): 117–34.

Hick, John. *An Interpretation of Religion: Human Responses to the Transcendent.* 2nd ed. New Haven: Yale University Press, 2005.

Hick, John, and Paul Knitter, eds. *The Myth of Christian Uniqueness: Toward a Pluralistic Theology of Religions.* Eugene: Wipf and Stock, 2005.

Hicks, Douglas. *Religion and the Workplace: Pluralism, Spirituality, Leadership.* Cambridge: Cambridge University Press, 2003.

Holman, Peggy, Tom Devane, and Steven Cady, eds. *The Change Handbook.* San Francisco: Berrett-Koehler Publishers, 2007.

Hong, Christine J. *Decolonial Futures: Intercultural and Interreligious Intelligence for Theological Education.* Lanham: Lexington Books, 2021.

Horaczek, Nina. "Propaganda War in Europe: The Far-Right Media." *Falter.* 2019. www.europeanpressprize.com/article/propaganda-war-europe-far-right-media

Hornung, Maria. *Encountering Other Faiths.* Mahwah: Paulist Press, 2007.

Howard, Thomas Albert. *The Faiths of Others: A History of Interreligious Dialogue.* New Haven: Yale University Press, 2021.

Hustwit, J. R. *Interreligious Hermeneutics and the Pursuit of Truth.* Lanham: Lexington Books, 2014.

Huxley, Aldous. *The Perennial Philosophy: An Interpretation of the Great Mystics, East and West.* New York: Harper & Bros, 1945.

Ibn al-'Arabī. *The Tarjuman al-Ashwaq.* Trans. Reynold Nicholson. London: Royal Asiatic Society, 1911.

Igoe, Molly. "Corporate America Leads in Exposing Americans to Diversity." *Public Religion Research Institute.* July 29, 2019. www.prri.org/spotlight/corporate-america-leads-inexposing-americans-to-diversity

Illman, Ruth. *Art and Belief: Artists Engaged in Interreligious Dialogue.* London: Routledge, 2012. https://doi.org/10.4324/9781315728728

Interfaith America. "Survey: Faith-Based Approaches Supporting Vaccinations Likely to Move Vaccine-Hesitant Americans Toward Acceptance." April 22, 2021. www.interfaithamerica.org/survey-faith-based-approaches-supporting-vaccinations-likely-to-move-vaccine-hesitant-americans-toward-acceptance

Interfaith Youth Core and CCCU. "Evangelicals and Interfaith Engagement: Assessing Evangelical Resources, Motivations, Hesitancies, and Hopes." February 21, 2021. www.interfaithamerica.org/evangelical-christians-want-to-get-to-know-their-neighbors-heres-why

Interfaith Youth Core and Dominican University, "Interfaith Leadership in Action." www.ifyc.org/interfaithleadership/lesson8

Ipgrave, Julia, Thorsten Knauth, Anna Körs, Dörte Vieregge, and Marie von der Lippe, eds. *Religion and Dialogue in the City: Case Studies on Interreligious Encounter in Urban Community and Education.* Münster: Waxmann, 2018.

Irwin, Lauren, and Zak Foste. "Service-Learning and Racial Capitalism: On the Commodification of People of Color for White Advancement." *Review of Higher Education* 44, no. 4 (Summer 2021): 419–46.

Jacobsen, Rhonda Hustedt, and Douglas Jacobsen. *No Longer Invisible: Religion in University Education*. Oxford: Oxford University Press, 2012. https://doi.org/10.1093/acprof:oso/9780199844739.001.0001

Jamil, Uzma. "Can Muslims Fly? The No Fly List as a Tool of the 'War on Terror'" *Islamophobia Studies Journal* 20, no. 10 (2017): 72–86. https://doi.org/10.13169/islastudj.4.1.0072

Janmohamed, Shelina. *Generation M: Young Muslims Changing the World*. London: I. B. Tauris, 2016.

Jewish Community Relations Council of New York. "Spiritual Deception Matters." www.jcrcny.org/wp-content/uploads/2013/07/H-CFAQs.pdf

Johnston, Douglas, and Cynthia Sampson. *Religion: The Missing Dimension of Statecraft*. Oxford: Oxford University Press, 1994.

Jones, Robert P. *The End of White, Christian America*. New York: Simon & Schuster, 2016.

Jones, Sarah E. "A Catholic City?" *Church and State* 68, no. 1 (January 2013): 12–13.

Joshi, Khyati Y. "The Racialization of Hinduism, Islam, and Sikhism in the United States." *Equity and Excellence in Education* 39, no. 3 (November 2006): 211–26. https://doi.org/10.1080/10665680600790327

Kandiyoti, Dalia. *The Converso's Return: Conversion and Sephardi History in Contemporary Literature and Culture*. Stanford: Stanford University Press, 2020.

Kant, Immanuel. *Religion within the Boundaries of Mere Reason and Other Writings*. Trans. Allen Wood and George di Giovanni. Cambridge: Cambridge University Press, 1998. https://doi.org/10.1017/CBO9780511809637

Kaplan, Jane. *Interfaith Families: Personal Stories of Jewish-Christian Intermarriage*. Westport: Praeger, 2004.

Karabell, Zachary. *Peace Be Upon You: Fourteen Centuries of Muslim, Christian, and Jewish Conflict and Cooperation*. New York: Vintage, 2008.

Kaveny, Cathleen. *Prophecy without Contempt: Religious Discourse in the Public Square*. Cambridge, MA: Harvard University Press, 2016.

Kaye, Miriam Feldmann. "Scriptural Reasoning with Israelis and Palestinians." Cambridge Inter-Faith Programme. www.interfaith.cam.ac.uk/resources/scripturalreasoningresources/srwithisraelisandpalestinians

Kazanjian Jr., Victor H., and Peter L. Laurence, eds. *Education as Transformation: Religious Pluralism, Spirituality, and a New Vision for Higher Education in America*. 3rd ed. New York: Peter Lang, 2000.

Kearney, Richard, and Eileen Rizo-Patron, eds. *Traversing the Heart: Journeys of the Interreligious Imagination*. Leiden: Brill, 2011.

Kearns, Erin M., Allison E. Betus, and Anthony F. Lemieux. "Why Do Some Terrorist Attacks Receive More Media Attention than Others?" *Justice Quarterly* 36, no. 6 (2019): 985–1022. https://doi.org/10.1080/07418825.2018.1524507

Kessler, Gary. *Studying Religion: An Introduction through Cases*. 3rd ed. Boston: McGraw Hill, 2007.

Khabeer, Su'ad Abdul. *Muslim Cool: Race, Religion, and Hip Hop in the United States*. New York: New York University Press, 2016.

Khabeer, Su'ad Abdul, et al., eds. "Islamophobia Is Racism." 2022. https://islamophobiaisracism.wordpress.com

Khalil, Mohammad Hassan, ed. *Between Heaven and Hell: Islam, Salvation, and the Fate of Others*. Oxford: Oxford University Press, 2013. https://doi.org/10.1093/acprof:oso/9780199945399.001.0001

Kieh, George. "Ending Liberia's Second Civil War: Religious Women as Peacemakers." Berkeley Center for Religion, Peace, and World Affairs. September 25, 2013. https://berkleycenter.georgetown.edu/publications/ending-liberia-s-second-civil-war-religious-women-as-peacemakers

Kilp, Alar. "Religion in the Construction of the Cultural 'Self' and 'Other.'" *ENDC Proceedings* 14, no. 2 (2011): 197–222.

Kim, Jinwung. *A History of Korea: From "Land of the Morning Calm" to States in Conflict*. Bloomington: Indiana University Press, 2012.

King, Martin Luther, Jr. *Stride Toward Freedom: The Montgomery Story*. New York: Harper, 1958.

King, Martin Luther, Jr. "Letter from a Birmingham Jail." www.africa.upenn.edu/Articles_Gen/Letter_Birmingham.html, 1963.

King, Richard. *Orientalism and Religion: Postcolonial Theory, India, and "The Mystic East."* London: Routledge, 1999.

King, Roberta Rose, and Sooi Ling Tan, eds. *(un)Common Sounds: Songs of Peace and Reconciliation among Muslims and Christians*. Eugene: Cascade, 2014.

King, Roberta Rose, and William A. Dyrness, eds. *The Arts as Witness in Multifaith Contexts*. Downers Grove: InterVarsity Press, 2019.

Kitagawa, Joseph M., ed. *The Religious Traditions of Asia: Religion, History, and Culture*. Abingdon: Routledge, 2002. https://doi.org/10.4324/9781315029641

Knitter, Paul F. *One Earth, Many Religions: Multifaith Dialogue and Global Responsibility*. Maryknoll: Orbis Books, 1995.

Knitter, Paul F. *Introducing Theologies of Religions*. Maryknoll: Orbis Books, 2012.

Knitter, Paul F. ed. *The Myth of Religious Superiority: A Multifaith Exploration.* Maryknoll: Orbis Books, 2005.

Kosmin, Barry A., and Seymour P. Lachman. *One Nation Under God: Religion in Contemporary American Society.* New York: Harmony Books, 1993.

Kujawa-Holbrook, Sheryl A. *God beyond Borders: Interreligious Learning among Faith Communities.* Eugene: Pickwick Publications, 2014.

Kurdek, Lawrence. "Perspective Taking as the Cognitive Basis of Children's Moral Development: A Review of the Literature." *Merrill-Palmer Quarterly of Behavior and Development* 24, no. 1 (January 1978): 3–28.

Kwok Pui-lan. *Globalization, Gender, and Peacebuilding: The Future of Interfaith Dialogue.* New York: Paulist Press, 2012.

Lamptey (now Rhodes), Jerusha. *Never Wholly Other: A Muslima Theology of Religious Pluralism.* Oxford: Oxford University Press, 2014. https://doi.org/10.1093/acprof:oso/9780199362783.001.0001.

Lange, Armin et al., eds. *An End to Antisemitism!* – A five-volume open-access scholarly work. DeGruyter, 2019–2021. www.degruyter.com/serial/aeas-b/html.

Langer, Ruth, and Stephanie VanSlyke. "Interreligious Prayer: An Introduction." *Liturgy* 26, no. 3 (2011): 1–10. https://doi.org/10.1080/0458063X.2011.562448.

Largen, Kristin Johnston. *Interreligious Learning and Teaching: A Christian Rationale for a Transformative Praxis.* Minneapolis: Fortress Press, 2014.

Law, Ian, Amina Easat-Daas, and S. Sayyid. "Counter-Islamophobia Kit." Center for Ethnicity and Racism Studies. University of Leeds. 2017.

LeBaron, Michelle. *Bridging Cultural Conflicts: A New Approach for a Changing World.* San Francisco: Jossey-Bass, 2004.

Lederach, John Paul. *The Little Book of Conflict Transformation: Clear Articulation of the Guiding Principles by a Pioneer in the Field.* New York: Good Books, 2003.

Lederach, John Paul. *The Moral Imagination: The Art and Soul of Building Peace.* Oxford: Oxford University Press, 2005. https://doi.org/10.1093/0195174542.001.0001.

Lee, Der Huey. "Xuanzang (Hsüan-tsang) (602–664)." *Internet Encyclopedia of Philosophy.* www.iep.utm.edu/xuanzang/.

Lehmann, Karsten, ed. *Talking Dialogue: Eleven Episodes in the History of the Modern Interreligious Dialogue Movement.* Berlin: De Gruyter, 2021. https://doi.org/10.1515/9783110529173.

Leirvik, Oddbjørn. *Interreligious Studies: A Relational Approach to Religious Activism and the Study of Religion.* New York: Bloomsbury, 2014. https://doi.org/10.5040/9781472594655.

Leopold, Anita Marie, and Jeppe Sinding Jensen, eds. *Syncretism in Religion: A Reader*. New York: Routledge, 2014. https://doi.org/10.4324/9781315538228.

Leukel-Schmidt, Perry. *Religious Pluralism and Interreligious Theology*. Maryknoll: Orbis Books, 2017.

Levinas, Emmanuel. *Totality and Infinity: An Essay on Exteriority*. Trans. Alphonso Lingis. Dordrecht: Kluwer Academic Publishers, 1961.

Levine, Sheen S., and David Stark. "Diversity Makes You Brighter." *New York Times*, December 9, 2015. www.nytimes.com/2015/12/09/opinion/diversity-makes-you-brighter.html

Lewis, Bernard. *Islam in History: Ideas, People, and Events in the Middle East*. New York: Open Court, 2013.

Li, Chenyang. "Bring Back Harmony in Philosophical Discourse: A Confucian Perspective." *Journal of Dharma Studies* 2 (2020): 163–73. https://doi.org/10.1007/s42240–019-00047-w

Lim, Francis Khek Gee, ed. *Mediating Piety: Technology and Religion in Contemporary Asia*. Leiden: Brill, 2009. https://doi.org/10.1163/ej.9789004178397.i-240

Lim, Francis K. G., and Bee Bee Sng. "Social Media, Religion, and Shifting Boundaries in Globalizing China." *Global Media and China* 5, no. 3 (July 15, 2020): 261–74. https://doi.org/10.1177/2059436420923169

Lipstadt, Deborah E. *Antisemitism Here and Now*. New York: Schocken Books, 2019.

Lockman, Zachary. *Contending Visions of the Middle East: The History and Politics of Orientalism*. Cambridge: Cambridge University Press, 2010. https://doi.org/10.1017/CBO9780511804342

Longhurst, Christopher. *Pictorial Art for Interreligious Dialogue*. KAICIID Dialogue Centre, Vivid Publishing, October 2021. www.vividpublishing.com.au/pictorialart

Lorber, Ben. "Taking Aim at Multiracial Democracy: Antisemitism, White Nationalism, and Anti-Immigrant Racism in the Era of Trump." Political Research Associates. October 22, 2019. https://politicalresearch.org/2019/10/22/taking-aim-multiracial-democracy

Loskota, Brie. "Understanding Religious Literacy Content Creators and Providers in Education, Journalism, and New Media: A Report for the Arthur Vining Davis Foundations." Center for Religion and Civic Culture. August 31, 2021. https://crcc.usc.edu/understanding-religious-literacy-content-creators-and-providers-in-education-journalism-and-new-media

Lubet, Steven. "Witch Hunt in a Public School." *SFGate*. April 16, 2000. www.sfgate.com/opinion/openforum/article/Witch-Hunt-in-a-Public-School-2764193.php

Lunby, Knut, ed. *Contesting Religion: The Media Dynamics of Cultural Conflicts in Scandinavia*. Berlin: DeGruyter, 2018. https://doi.org/10.1515/9783110502060

Lupu, Ira C., David Masci, and Robert W. Tuttle. "Religion in the Public Schools." Pew Research Center. October 19, 2019. www.pewforum.org/2019/10/03/religion-in-the-public-schools–2019-update

Maccoby, Hyam, ed. and trans. *Judaism on Trial: Jewish-Christian Disputations in the Middle Ages*. Plainsboro: Associated University Presses, 1982. https://doi.org/10.2307/j.ctv1rmjqp

Mahan, Jeffrey. *Media, Religion and Culture: An Introduction*. London: Routledge, 2014. https://doi.org/10.4324/9781315777061

Marsden, Lee, and Heather Savigny, eds. *Media, Religion, and Conflict*. London: Routledge, 2010. https://doi.org/10.4324/9781315594552

Marshall, George. "Communicating with Religious Communities on Climate Change." *Journal of Interreligious Studies* 19 (Summer 2016): 24–34.

Marshall, Paul. "Can For-Profit Corporations Be Religious?" Religious Freedom Institute. July 25, 2020. www.religiousfreedominstitute.org/cornerstone/can-for-profit-corporations-be-religious

Marshall, Paul, Lela Gilbert, and Roberta Green Ahmanson, eds. *Blind Spot: When Journalists Don't Get Religion*. Oxford: Oxford University Press, 2009. https://doi.org/10.1093/acprof:oso/9780195374360.001.0001

Masuzawa, Tomoko. *The Invention of World Religions: Or, How European Universalism Was Preserved in the Language of Pluralism*. Chicago: University of Chicago Press, 2005.

Mayall, James, and Sara Silvestri. *The Role of Religion in Conflict and Peacebuilding*. London: British Academy, 2015.

Mays, Rebecca Kratz, ed. *Interfaith Dialogue at the Grass Roots*. Geneva: Ecumenical Press, 2009.

Mazumdar, Sanjoy, and Shampa Mazumdar. "Planning, Design, and Religion: American's Changing Urban Landscape." *Journal of Architectural and Planning Research* 30, no. 3 (Autumn 2013): 221–43.

McCarthy, Kate. *Interfaith Encounters in America*. New Brunswick: Rutgers University Press, 2007.

McGraw, Barbara, and Jo Renee Formicola, eds. *Taking Religious Pluralism Seriously: Spiritual Politics on America's Sacred Ground*. Waco: Baylor University Press, 2007.

McKim, Robert. *On Religious Diversity*. Oxford: Oxford University Press, 2012.

McKim, Robert, ed. *Religious Perspectives on Religious Diversity*. Leiden: Brill, 2016. https://doi.org/10.1163/9789004330436

McLaren, Brian. *Why Did Jesus, Moses, the Buddha and Mohammed Cross the Road?* Nashville: Jericho Books, 2012.

Meddeb, Abdelwahab, and Benjamin Stora, eds. *A History of Jewish-Muslim Relations: From the Origins to the Present Day*. Trans. Jane Marie Todd and Michael B. Smith. Princeton: Princeton University Press, 2013.

Meer, Nasar. "Racialization and Religion: Race, Culture and Difference in the Study of Antisemitism and Islamophobia." *Ethnic and Racial Studies* 36, no. 3 (2013): 385–98. https://doi.org/10.1080/01419870.2013.734392

Meir, Ephraim. *Interreligious Theology: Its Value and Mooring in Modern Jewish Philosophy*. Berlin: de Gruyter, 2015. https://doi.org/10.1515/9783110430455

Meister, Chad, ed. *The Oxford Handbook of Religious Diversity*. Oxford: Oxford University Press, 2010. https://doi.org/10.1093/oxfordhb/9780195340136.001.0001

Melloni, Alberto, and Francesca Cadeddu, eds. *Religious Literacy, Law and History: Perspectives on European Pluralist Societies*. Abingdon: Routledge, 2019.

Mendelssohn, Moses. "Letter to Johann Casper Lavater." In *Disputation and Dialogue: Readings in the Jewish-Christian Encounter*, ed. Frank Ephraim Talmage, 265–72. New York: KTAV Publishing House, 1975.

Menocal, María Rosa. *The Ornament of the World: How Muslims, Jews and Christians Created a Culture of Tolerance in Medieval Spain*. New York: Back Bay Books, 2002.

"Message from the Pontifical Council for Interreligious Dialogue to Hindus for the Feast of Deepavali, 21.10.2019," https://press.vatican.va/content/salastampa/en/bollettino/pubblico/2019/10/21/191021a.html

Merrigan, Terrence, and John Friday, eds. *The Past, Present, and Future of Theologies of Interreligious Dialogue*. London: Oxford University Press, 2017. https://doi.org/10.1093/acprof:oso/9780198792345.001.0001

"Michigan School Change Policy on Honor Student Witch." *ACLU*. March 25, 1999. www.aclu.org/press-releases/michigan-school-changes-policy-honor-student-witch

Mikva, Rachel S. "Reflections in the Waves: What Interreligious Studies Can Learn from the Evolutions of Women's Movements in the United States." *Journal of Ecumenical Studies* 53, no. 4 (Fall 2018): 461–82. http://doi.org/10.1163/9789004420045_009

Mikva, Rachel S. *Dangerous Religious Ideas: The Deep Roots of Self-Critical Faith in Judaism, Christianity, and Islam.* Boston: Beacon Press, 2020.

Mikva, Rachel S. "With No One to Make Them Afraid: A Jewish Perspective on Safeguarding Religious Freedom." *Cultural Encounters* 16, no. 1 (2021): 19–26.

Mikva, Rachel S. "Readings for Resilience: Reflections on the COVID-19 Pandemic and beyond." In *Doing Theology in Pandemics: Viruses, Violence, and Vitriol,* ed. Zachary Moon, 143–62. Eugene: Wipf and Stock, 2022.

Mikva, Rachel S. "An Acorn Is Not a Tree." In *With the Best of Intentions: Interrogating Interreligious Mistakes,* ed. Lucinda Mosher, Elinor Pierce, and Or N. Rose. Maryknoll: Orbis Books, forthcoming 2023.

Miller, Jerry L., ed. "Topical Issue: Is Transreligious Theology Possible?" *Open Theology* 2, no. 1 [2016]: 261–302.

Mitchell, Jacob. *Interfaith Cooperation and American Higher Education: Recommendations, Best Practices and Case Studies.* Chicago: Interfaith Youth Core, 2017.

Moerdler, Zahava. "Racializing Antisemitism: The Development of Racist Antisemitism and Its Current Manifestations." *Fordham International Law Journal* 40, no. 4 (2017): 1281–325.

Molendijk, Arie L. *Friedrich Max Müller and the Sacred Books of the East.* Oxford: Oxford University Press, 2016. https://doi.org/10.1093/acprof:oso/9780198784234.001.0001

Molokotos-Liederman, Lina. "The Role of Popular Culture in the Interfaith Encounter: A Soft Power?" Woolf Institute. June 15, 2020. www.woolf.cam.ac.uk/blog/the-role-of-popular-culture-in-the-interfaith-encounter-a-soft-power

Monforte, Olivia. "After Receiving Backlash for Her Religion, One Student Reclaims Her Identity as a Witch." *Mustang News.* February 3, 2020. https://mustangnews.net/after-receiving-backlash-for-her-religion-one-student-reclaims-her-identity-as-a-witch

Monroe, James T., ed. and trans. *Hispano-Arabic Poetry.* Berkeley: University of California Press, 1974.

Moore, Diane. *Overcoming Religious Illiteracy: A Cultural Studies Approach to the Study of Religion in Secondary Education.* London: Palgrave Macmillan, 2007. https://doi.org/10.1057/9780230607002

Mosher, Lucinda, Axel Marc Oaks Takacs, Or N. Rose, and Mary Elizabeth Moore, eds. *Deep Understanding for Divisive Times: Essays Marking a Decade of the Journal of Interreligious Studies.* Newton Centre: Interreligious Studies Press, 2020.

Mosher, Lucinda, ed. *The Georgetown Companion to Interreligious Studies.* Washington, DC: Georgetown University Press, 2022. https://doi.org/10.2307/j.ctv27qzsb3

Moulin-Stozek, Daniel, and Anna K. Dulska. "Interreligious Narratives and Contra-Religious Aesthetics in the Material Culture of Navarra, Northern Spain." *CrossCurrents* 68, no. 3 (September 2018): 412–26. https://doi.org/10.1111/cros.12322

Moyaert, Marianne. *Fragile Identities: Towards a Theology of Interreligious Hospitality.* Amsterdam: Rodopi, 2011.

Moyaert, Marianne. "Inappropriate Behavior? On the Ritual Core of Religion and Its Challenges to Interreligious Hospitality." *Journal for the Academic Study of Religion* 27, no. 2 (2014): 222–42. https://doi.org/10.1558/jasr.v27i2.222

Moyaert, Marianne, and Joris Geldhof. *Ritual Participation in Interreligious Dialogue: Boundaries, Transgressions, and Innovations.* London: Bloomsbury, 2015. https://doi.org/10.5040/9781474242165

Msila, Vuyisile Theophilus. *Ubuntu: Shaping the Current Workplace with (African) Wisdom.* Randburg: Knowres, 2015.

Muller, A. Charles. "The Buddhist-Confucian Conflict in the Early Chosŏn and Kihwa's Syncretic Response: The Hyŏn chŏng non." Presented at the Annual Meeting of the American Academy of Religion, Chicago, November 20, 1994.

Murell, Nathaniel Samuel, William David Spencer, and Adrian Anthony McFarlane, eds. *Chanting Down Babylon: The Rastafari Reader.* Philadelphia: Temple University Press, 1998.

Naranja, Daniel Njoroge. *Beyond Mediation: Exploring Indigenous Models, Narratives and Contextualization.* London: Rowman & Littlefield, 2020.

Nash, Robert. *Religious Pluralism in the Academy: Opening the Dialogue.* New York: Peter Lang, 2001.

Nava, Alejandro. *Street Scriptures: Between God and Hip-Hop.* Chicago: University of Chicago Press, 2022.

Ndekha, Lewis. "Ambivalence in Interreligious Relations in Malawi: Is an African Model of Interreligious Relations Possible?" www.academia.edu/10682091

Neiwert, David. "Far Right Extremists Have Hatched Far More Terror Plots than Anyone Else in Recent Years." *Reveal.* June 22, 2017. https://revealnews.org/article/home-is-where-the-hate-is

Neuhaus, John. *The Naked Public Square: Religion and Democracy in America.* Kentwood: W. B. Eerdmans, 1984.

Nhat Hanh, Thich. *Love in Action: Writings on Nonviolent Social Change.* Berkeley: Parallax Press, 1993.

Nhat Hanh, Thich. *The Heart of the Buddha's Teaching*. New York: Harmony Books, 2015.

Nhat Hanh, Thich. *Interbeing: The Fourteen Mindfulness Trainings of Engaged Buddhism*. 4th ed. Berkeley: Parallax Press, 2020.

Niebuhr, Gustav. *Beyond Tolerance: Searching for Interfaith Understanding in America*. New York: Viking, 2008.

Nirenberg, David. "Slay Them Not: A Review of Paula Fredriksen's *Augustine and the Jews*." *The New Republic* 240, no. 4 (March 18, 2009): 42–7. https://newrepublic.com/article/64630/slay-them-not

Nirenberg, David. *Anti-Judaism: The Western Tradition*. New York: W. W. Norton, 2013.

"No Handshake Exemption for Muslim Students, Swiss Canton Rules." *Middle East Eye*, May 25, 2016. www.middleeasteye.net/news/no-handshake-exemption-muslim-students-swiss-canton-rules

Nortey, Justin. "Republicans More Likely than Democrats to Believe in Heaven." Pew Research Center. November 21, 2021. www.pewresearch.org/fact-tank/2021/11/23/republicans-more-likely-than-democrats-to-believe-in-heaven-say-only-their-faith-leads-there

Nostra aetate. www.vatican.va/archive/hist_councils/ii_vatican_council/documents/vat-ii_decl_19651028_nostra-aetate_en.html

Nussbaum, Martha C. *Liberty of Conscience: In Defense of America's Tradition of Religious Equality*. New York: Basic Books, 2008.

Nweke, Kizito Chinedu. "Multiple Religious Belonging (MRB): Addressing the Tension between African Spiritualities and Christianity." *Theology Today* 77, no.1 (April 2020): 76–88. https://doi.org/10.1177/0040573620902412

Obama, Barack. "Call to Renewal." *New York Times*, June 28, 2006. www.nytimes.com/2006/06/28/us/politics/2006obamaspeech.html

Ogude, James. *Ubuntu and the Reconstitution of Community*. Bloomington: Indiana University Press, 2019.

Okechukwu, Daniel. "Old Nollywood Demonised Traditional Religions: New Cinema Says 'No More.'" *African Arguments*, January 28, 2020. https://africanarguments.org/2020/01/old-nollywood-demonised-traditional-religions-new-cinema-says-no-more

Omer, Atalia, R. Scott Appleby, and David Little, eds. *Oxford Handbook of Religion, Conflict, and Peacebuilding*. Oxford: Oxford University Press, 2015. https://doi.org/10.1093/oxfordhb/9780199731640.001.0001

Pace, Enzo. "Religious Minorities in Europe: A Memory Mutates." *Religions* 12, no. 11 (2021): 918. https://doi.org/10.3390/rel12110918

Panikkar, Raimon. *A Dwelling Place for Wisdom*. Louisville: Westminster John Knox, 1993.

Patel, Eboo. *Acts of Faith: The Story of an American Muslim, the Struggle for the Soul of a Generation*. Boston: Beacon Press, 2007.

Patel, Eboo. "Toward a Field of Interfaith Studies." *Liberal Education* 99, no. 4 (Fall 2013): 38–43.

Patel, Eboo. *Interfaith Leadership: A Primer*. Boston: Beacon Press, 2016.

Patel, Eboo. *Out of Many Faiths: Religious Diversity and the American Promise*. Princeton: Princeton University Press, 2018.

Patel, Eboo, Jennifer Howe Peace, and Noah Silverman, eds. *Interreligious/Interfaith Studies: Defining a New Field*. Boston: Beacon Press, 2018.

Patterson, Eric. *South Africa: The Religious Foundations of the Truth and Reconciliation Commission*. Washington, DC: Berkeley Center for Religion, Peace, and World Affairs, 2013.

Patton, Laurie L. "Toward a Pragmatic Pluralism." *Emory Magazine* (Autumn 2006). www.emory.edu/emory_magazine/autumn2006/essay_pluralism.htm

Paustian, Karin (Karima). "Interfaith Families: A Muslim Perspective, Part 1." *European Judaism* 53, no. 1 (March 2020): 93–97. https://doi.org/10.3167/ej.2020.530112

P'bitek, Okot. *Decolonizing African Religion: A Short History of African Religions in Western Scholarship*. New York: Diasporic Africa Press, 2011.

Peace, Jennifer Howe. "Coformation through Interreligious Learning." *Colloquy* 20, no. 1 (Fall 2011): 24–26.

Peace, Jennifer Howe, Or N. Rose, and Gregory Mobley, eds. *My Neighbor's Faith: Stories of Interreligious Encounter, Growth, and Transformation*. Maryknoll: Orbis Books, 2012.

Pennington, Rosemary, and Hilary E. Kahn, eds. *On Islam: Muslims and the Media*. Bloomington: Indiana University Press, 2018.

Pew Research Center. "Table: Religious Diversity Index Score by Country." April 4, 2014. www.pewresearch.org/fact-tank/2014/04/04/u-s-doesnt-rank-high-in-religious-diversity

Phan, Peter C. *Understanding Religious Pluralism: Perspectives from Religious Studies and Theology*. Eugene: Pickwick Publications, 2014.

Phillips, Katharine W. "How Diversity Makes Us Smarter." *Scientific American* (October 1, 2014). www.scientificamerican.com/article/how-diversity-makes-us-smarter

Piaget, Jean. *The Moral Judgment of the Child*. New York: Simon & Schuster, 1965.

Pierce, Elinor J. *Pluralism in Practice*. Maryknoll: Orbis, forthcoming 2023.

Pinn, Anthony. *Varieties of African American Religious Experience: Toward a Comparative Black Theology*. Minneapolis: Fortress Press, 2017.

Pitzele, Peter. *Scripture Windows: Toward a Practice of Bibliodrama*. Los Angeles: Torah Aura Productions, 1998.

Pluralism Project, The. Harvard University. https://pluralism.org

"Politician Quits after Refusing to Shake Women's Hands." *The Local*, April 20, 2016. www.thelocal.se/20160420/swedish-politician-quits-after-refusing-to-shake-womens-hands

Polyakov, Emma O'Donnell. *Antisemitism, Islamophobia, and Interreligious Hermeneutics: Ways of Seeing the Religious Other*. Leiden: Brill, 2019.

Poorthuis, Marcus. *Rituals in Interreligious Dialogue: Bridge or Barrier?* Newcastle-upon-Tyne: Cambridge University Scholars, 2020.

Pratt, Douglas, and Angela Berlis, eds. "Themed Issue: Belief Diversity and the Lived Experience of Religion." *Studies in Interreligious Dialogue* 27, no. 2 (2017), 1–169.

Prothero, Stephen. *God Is Not One: The Eight Rival Religions That Run the World – And Why Their Differences Matter*. New York: HarperOne, 2010.

Pugliese, Marc A., and Alexander Y. Hwang, eds. *Teaching Interreligious Encounters*. New York: Oxford University Press, 2017. https://doi.org/10.1093/oso/9780190677565.001.0001

Pulcini, Theodore. *Exegesis as Polemical Discourse: Ibn Ḥazm on Jewish and Christian Scriptures*. Atlanta: Scholars Press, 1998.

Putnam, Robert D., and David E. Campbell. *American Grace: How Religion Divides and Unites Us*. New York: Simon & Schuster, 2010.

Rajesh, Noel. "Monks Battle to Save Forest." *Down to Earth*. September 15, 1992. www.downtoearth.org.in/news/monks-battle-to-save-forest–30134

Rappeport, Alan. "Hobby Lobby Made Fight a Matter of Christian Principle." *New York Times*, June 30, 2014. www.nytimes.com/2014/07/01/us/hobby-lobby-made-fight-a-matter-of-christian-principle.html

Rawls, John. *Political Liberalism*. New York: Columbia University Press, 1993.

Richardson, E. Allen. *Strangers in This Land: Religion, Pluralism, and the American Dream*. Jefferson: McFarland & Co., 2010.

Rockenbach, Alyssa N., et al. *IDEALS: Bridging Religious Divides through Higher Education*. Chicago: Interfaith Youth Core, 2020.

Rodriguez-Plate, S. Brent. "Seeing the Other in Cinema: Interreligious Connection through the Senses." *Journal of Beliefs and Values* 38, no. 3 (May 2017): 1–9. https://doi.org/10.1080/13617672.2017.1317528

Rose, Or, Homayra Ziad, and Soren M. Hessler, eds. *Words to Live By: Sacred Sources for Interreligious Engagement*. Maryknoll: Orbis Books, 2018.

Rosenberg, Marshall B. *Nonviolent Communication: A Language of Life*. Encinitas: PuddleDancer Press, 2015.

Rumi, Jalal al-Din Muhammad. *The Quatrains of Rumi*. Trans. Ibrahim Gamard and Rawan Farhadi. New York: Sufi Dari Books, 2008.

Rushdie, Salman. *Satanic Verses*. New York: Random House, 1997.

Sacks, Jonathan. *The Dignity of Difference: How to Avoid the Clash of Civilizations*. London: Continuum, 2002.

Salem, Feryal. "The Challenges and Opportunities in Training Muslim Chaplaincy Students for a Burgeoning New Field." *Journal of Pastoral Theology* 32, no. 1 (January 2022): 47–54.

Salvatierra, Alexia, and Peter Heltzel. *Faith-Rooted Organizing: Mobilizing the Church in Service to the World*. Downers Grove: IVP Books, 2013.

Saunders, Martin. "Bryan Stevenson: Four Steps to Really Change the World." *Christianity Today*, July 16, 2015. www.christiantoday.com/article/bryan-ste venson-four-steps-to-really-change-the-world/59211.htm

Sawyer, Toby. "Does Smudging Belong in the Workplace?" Native Case Studies. https://nativecases.evergreen.edu/collection/cases/does-smudging-belong-in-the-workplace

Scheitle, Christopher P., and Elaine Howard Ecklund. "Examining the Effects of Exposure to Religion in the Workplace on Perceptions of Religious Discrimination." *Review of Religious Research* 59 (2017): 1–20. https://doi .org/10.1007/s13644-016-0278-x

Schenck, Rob. "What's Gone Wrong with Evangelicals #7: Abortion and Its Politicization." September 9, 2020. www.revrobschenck.com/blog/2020/9/ 7/whats-gone-wrong-with-evangelicals-7-abortion-and-its-politicization

Schliesser, Christine, S. Ayse Kadayifci-Orellana, and Pauline Kolontai. *On the Significance of Religion in Conflict and Conflict Resolution*. London: Routledge, 2021. https://doi.org/10.4324/9781003002888

Schlosser, Lewis Z. "Christian Privilege: Breaking a Sacred Taboo." *Journal of Multicultural Counseling and Development* 31 (January 2003): 44–51. https:// doi.org/10.1002/j.2161-1912.2003.tb00530.x

Schmidt-Leukel, Perry. *Religious Pluralism and Interreligious Theology*. Maryknoll: Orbis Books, 2017.

Segal, Neha, et al. "Diversity and Pluralism." Pew Research Center. June 29, 2021. www.pewforum.org/2021/06/29/diversity-and-pluralism

Seitz, David K. "'It's Not about You': Disappointment as Queer Pedagogy in Community-Engaged Service-Learning." *Journal of Homosexuality* (October 2018): 305–14. https://doi.org/10.1080/00918369.2018.1528078

Seligman, Adam B. *Living with Difference: How to Build Community in a Divided World*. Berkeley: University of California Press, 2015.

Shafiq, Muhammad, and Mohammed Abu-Nimer. *Interfaith Dialogue: A Guide for Muslims*. London: International Institute for Islamic Thought, 2011.

Shah-Kazemi, Reza. *The Spirit of Tolerance in Islam*. London: I. B. Tauris, 2012.

Shainkman, Mikael, ed. *Antisemitism Today and Tomorrow: Global Perspectives on the Many Faces of Contemporary Antisemitism*. Brighton: Academic Studies Press, 2018.

Shimron, Yonat. "What Happened to the Nonbelief Channel at Patheos?" *Religion News Service*, January 4, 2022. https://religionnews.com/2022/01/04/what-happened-to-the-nonbelief-channel-at-patheos

Shoemaker, Terry, and James Edmonds. "The Limits of Interfaith? Interfaith Identities, Emerging Potentialities, and Exclusivity." *Culture and Religion* 17, no. 2 (May 2016): 200–12. https://doi.org/10.1080/14755610.2016.1183688

Singh, Simran Jeet. *The Light We Give: How Sikh Wisdom Can Transform Your Life*. New York: Riverhead Books, 2022.

Slessarev-Jamir, Helene. *Prophetic Activism: Progressive Religious Justice Movements in Contemporary America*. New York: New York University Press, 2011.

Small, Christopher. *Musicking: The Meanings of Performing and Listening*. Hanover: University Press of New England, 1998.

Smart, Ninian. *The Religious Experience of Mankind*. Upper Saddle River: Prentice Hall, 1969.

Smelt, Walter. "Promoting Religious Literacy in a Digital Age." *Harvard Divinity Bulletin*, August 18, 2016. https://news-archive.hds.harvard.edu/news/2018/08/18/promoting-religious-literacy-digital-age

Smith, Andrew. "Art and Interfaith Conversation." *The Interfaith Observer*, March 15, 2019. www.theinterfaithobserver.org/journal-articles/2019/3/12/art-and-interfaith-conversation

Smith, Christopher. "Anti-Islamic Sentiment and Media Framing during the 9/11 Decade." *Journal of Religion and Society* 15 (2013): 1–15.

Smith, Linda Tuhiwai. *Decolonizing Methodologies: Research and Indigenous Peoples*. New York: Zed Books, 2012.

Smock, David R., ed. *Interfaith Dialogue and Peacebuilding*. Washington, DC: USIP, 2002.

Soper, J. Christopher, Kevin R. den Dulk, and Stephen V. Monsma. *The Challenge of Pluralism: Church and State in Six Democracies*, 3rd ed. Lanham: Rowman & Littlefield, 2017.

Spivak, Gayatri Chakravorty. *Critique of Postcolonial Reason: Toward a History of the Vanishing Present*. Cambridge, MA: Harvard University Press, 1999. https://doi.org/10.2307/j.ctvjsf541

Spivak, Gayatri Chakravorty. "Can the Subaltern Speak?" In *Can the Subaltern Speak? Reflections on the History of an Idea*, ed. Rosalind Morris, 21–78. New York: Columbia University Press, 2010.

Steenland, Sally, ed. *Debating the Divine: Religion in 21st Century American Democracy*. Washington, DC: Center for American Progress, 2008.

Stendahl, Krister. "From God's Perspective We Are All Minorities." *Journal of Religious Pluralism* 2 (1993). www.jcrelations.net/articles/article/from-gods-perspective-we-are-all-minorities.html

Stewart, Dafina Lazarus, Michael M. Kocet, and Sharon Lobdell. "The Multifaith Campus: Transforming Colleges and Universities for Spiritual Engagement." *About Campus* (March–April 2011):10–18. https://doi.org/10.1002/abc.20049

Stone, Bryan. "Interfaith Encounters in Popular Culture." *The Journal of Religion and Popular Culture* 25, no. 3 (2013): 403–15. https://doi.org/10.3138/jrpc.25.3.403

Stopes-Roe, Harry. "Humanism as a Life Stance." *New Humanist* 103, no. 2 (October 1988): 19–21.

Stratford, Walter Blair. *The Art of Interfaith Spiritual Care: Integration of Spirituality in Health Care Regardless of Religion or Beliefs*. Eugene: Wipf and Stock, 2016.

Strickland, Debra Higgs. *Saracens, Demons, and Jews: Making Monsters in Medieval Art*. Princeton: Princeton University Press, 2003.

Stroop, Chrissy. "Secularism in the U.S. Is Larger, More Diverse and More Dynamic Than Ever, but You Wouldn't Know It from the Media." *Religion Dispatches*, February 4, 2022. https://religiondispatches.org/secularism-in-the-us-is-larger-more-diverse-and-more-dynamic-than-ever-but-you-wouldnt-know-it-from-the-media

Suchocki, Marjorie Hewitt. *Divinity and Diversity: A Christian Affirmation of Religious Pluralism*. Nashville: Abingdon Press, 2003.

Sullivan, Winnifred Fallers. *The Impossibility of Religious Freedom*. Princeton: Princeton University Press, 2005.

Suomala, Karla. *Case Studies for Exploring Interfaith Cooperation: Classroom Tools*. Chicago: Interfaith Youth Core, 2013.

Swidler, Leonard, Khalid Duran, and Reuven Firestone. *Trialogue: Jews, Christians, and Muslims in Dialogue*. New London: Twenty-Third Publications, 2007.

Swidler, Leonard, and Marc H. Tanenbaum. *Jewish-Christian Dialogues*. American Jewish Committee, January 1, 1966. www.bjpa.org/Publications/details.cfm?PublicationID=14018

Syeed, Najeeba, and Heidi Hadsell, eds. *Critical Perspectives on Interreligious Education: Experiments in Empathy*. Leiden: Brill, 2020. https://doi.org/10.1163/9789004420045

Tanenbaum Center for Interreligious Understanding, "Vaccines and Our Health: What Do You Need to Know? A Look at the Intersection of Religion, Law, and Vaccines," 2021. https://tanenbaum.org/wp-content/uploads/2021/10/Vaccine-Paper-2021-Final.pdf

Tanenbaum Center for Interreligious Understanding, "Religious Diversity Checklist." https://tanenbaum.org/about-us/what-we-do/workplace/workplace-resources/religious-diversity-checklist

Taylor, Barbara Brown. "My Holy Envy of Other Faith Traditions." *Christian Century*, March 13, 2019. www.christiancentury.org/article/critical-essay/my-holy-envy-other-faith-traditions.

Thistlethwaite, Susan Brooks, ed. *Interfaith Just Peacemaking: Jewish, Christian, and Muslim Perspectives on the New Paradigm of Peace and War*. New York: Palgrave Macmillan, 2012.

Thomas, Kenneth W., and Ralph H. Kilmann. *Thomas–Kilmann Conflict Mode Instrument (TKI)*. APA PsycTests, 1974. https://doi.org/10.1037/t02326–000

Tinker, George E. *Spirit and Resistance: Political Theology and American Indian Liberation*. Minneapolis: Fortress Press, 2004.

Topor, Lev. *ISGAP Report: Antisemitic Influence Campaigns: Project Nemesis*. Institute for the Study of Global Antisemitism and Policy. June 26, 2022. https://isgap.org/wp-content/uploads/2022/06/Project-Nemesis-Report-Lev-Topor-1-1.pdf

Townes, Emilie. *In a Blaze of Glory: Womanist Spirituality as Social Witness*. Nashville: Abingdon Press, 1995.

Treat, James, ed. *Native and Christian: Indigenous Voices on Religious Identity in the United States and Canada*. New York: Routledge, 1996.

Trulear, Howard Dean. "Theological Education and Social Justice as Vocation." Presentation at *Current and Future Trends in Theological Education*, June 2018.

Tsuria, Ruth. "The Space between Us: Considering Online Media for Interreligious Dialogue." *Religion* 50, no. 3 (2020): 437–54. https://doi.org/10.1080/0048721X .2020.1754598

Tuttle, Robert W., and Jesse Merriam. "Sikh Americans and Religious Liberty." Pew Research Center. December 3, 2009. www.pewforum.org/2009/12/03/sikh-americans-and-religious-liberty

Upadhyaya, Nidhi. "Atheists Find Community on YouTube – And in Person." *Religion News Service*, December 3, 2021. https://religionnews.com/2021/12/ 03/atheists-find-community-on-youtube-and-in-person

Upton, Charles. *The Way Forward for Perennialism: After the Antinomianism of Frithjof Schuon.* Hillsdale: Sophia Perennis, 2022.

Varshney, Ashutosh. *Ethnic Conflict and Civic Life: Hindus and Muslims in India.* New Haven: Yale University Press, 2003.

Vellenga, Sipco. "Anti-Semitism and Islamophobia in the Netherlands: Concepts, Developments, and Backdrops." *Journal of Contemporary Religion* 33, no. 2 (May 2018): 1750–92. https://doi.org/10.1080/13537903.2018.1469257

Vivekananda. "Vivekānanda (1863–1902)." In *A Source-Book of Modern Hinduism*, ed. Glyn Richards, 77–90. London: RoutledgeCurzon, 1996. https://doi.org/10 .4324/9780203990612

Wald, Kenneth, and Allison Calhoun-Brown. *Religion and Politics in the United States.* 8th ed. Lanham: Rowman & Littlefield, 2018.

Walker, Alice. *Anything We Love Can Be Saved: A Writer's Activism.* New York: Ballantine, 1998.

Wang, Robin R. "Yinyang (Yin-Yang)." *Internet Encyclopedia of Philosophy.* https://iep.utm.edu/heraclit

Washington, George. "George Washington's Letter to the Hebrew Congregation of Newport." https://tourosynagogue.org/history/george-washington-letter/wash ington-seixas-letters

Wasserstrom, Steven. "Islamicate History of Religions?" *History of Religions* 27, no. 4 (1988): 405–11. https://doi.org/10.1086/463130

Weiss, Helmut, Karl H. Federschmidt, Daniël Louw, and Linda Sauer Bredvik, eds. *Care, Healing, and Human Well-Being in Interreligious Discourse.* Stellenbosch: African Sun Media, 2021.

Weisse, Wolfram, Katajun Amirpur, Anna Körs, and Dörthe Vieregge, eds. *Religions and Dialogue: International Approaches.* New York: Waxmann, 2014.

Wenger, Tisa. *Religious Freedom: The Contested History of an American Ideal.* Chapel Hill: University of North Carolina Press, 2017.

Wertheimer, Linda K. *Faith Ed: Teaching about Religion in an Age of Intolerance.* Boston: Beacon Press, 2015.

Wheatley, Margaret. *Turning to One Another: Simple Conversations to Restore Hope to the Future*. San Francisco: Berrett-Koehler, 2002.

Whitaker, Roy. "Religious Dialogue across Lines of Difference: Mormons, Evangelicals, and Others Agreeing to Disagree." *Mormon Studies Review* 2 (2015): 105–15.

Wilkinson, Dan. "Patheos Removes Blog of Christian Whistleblower." *Unfundamentalist*. May 28, 2018. http://unfundamentalists.com/2018/05/patheos-removes-blog-of-christian-whistleblower

williams, angel Kyodo, Rod Owens, and Jasmine Syedullah. *Radical Dharma: Talking Race, Love, and Liberation*. Berkeley: North Atlantic Books, 2016.

Williams, Patrick, and Laura Chrisman, eds. *Colonial Discourse and Post-Colonial Theory*. New York: Columbia University Press, 1994.

Wilson, Tom, and Riaz Ravat. *Learning to Live Well Together: Case Studies in Interfaith Diversity*. London: Jessica Kingsley, 2017.

Winslade, John, and Gerald Monk. *Practicing Narrative Mediation: Loosening the Grip of Conflict*. San Francisco: Jossey-Bass, 2008.

Winston, Diane, ed. *Small Screen, Big Picture: Television and Lived Religion*. Waco: Baylor University Press, 2009.

Winston, Diane, *The Oxford Handbook of Religion and the American News Media*. Oxford: Oxford University Press, 2012. https://doi.org/10.1093/oxfordhb/9780195395068.001.0001

Winter, Tim. "The Last Trump Card: Islam and the Supersession of Other Faiths." *Studies in Interreligious Dialogue* 9, no. 2 (1992): 133–55. https://doi.org/10.2143/SID.9.2.2003988

Wolf, Arnold Jacob. "The State of Jewish Belief." *Commentary* (August 1966). www.commentary.org/articles/jacob-agus-2/the-state-of-jewish-belief

World Council of Churches. "Greetings from the WCC General Secretary on the Occasion of Diwali." October 25, 2019. www.oikoumene.org/resources/documents/greetings-from-the-wcc-general-secretary-on-the-occasion-of-diwali

Wuthnow, Robert. *America and the Challenges of Religious Diversity*. Princeton: Princeton University Press, 2005.

Yarbrough, Denise. "Mapping the Discourse: A Case Study in Creating 'Interfaith Community' on a 'Multi-Faith' Campus." *Journal of Interreligious Studies* 13, no. 13 (2014): 50–66.

Younes, Ali. "Saudi TV Network Accused of 'Promoting Normalisation' with Israel." *Al Jazeera*, May 7, 2020. www.aljazeera.com/features/2020/5/7/saudi-tv-network-accused-of-promoting-normalisation-with-israel

Zine, Jasmine, ed. *Islam in the Hinterlands: Exploring Muslim Cultural Politics in Canada*. Vancouver: UBC Press, 2012.

Ziolkowski, Eric J., ed. *A Museum of Faiths: Histories and Legacies of the 1893 World's Parliament of Religions*. New York: Oxford University Press, 1993.

Zwartz, Barney. "Religion in the Media: How Has It Changed, Where Is It Going, Why Does It Matter?" *ABC News*, August 24, 2016. www.abc.net.au/religion/religion-in-the-media-how-has-it-changed-where-is-it-going-why-d/10096622

Index

Milton Keynes UK
Ingram Content Group UK Ltd.
UKHW010808020923
427944UK00014B/90

9 781108 826600